40

Human Communication and Its Disorders

Daniel R. Boone

University of Arizona

PRENTICE-HALL, INC., Englewood Cliffs, N.J. 07632

Library of Congress Cataloging-in-Publication Data

Boone, Daniel R.
  Human communication and its disorders.

  Includes bibliographies and index.
  1. Communicative disorders.   2. Communicative
disorders in children.   3. Speech therapy.
4. Audiology.   I. Title.
RC423.B655   1987   616.85'5   86-25159
ISBN 0-13-444720-4

to the loved ones of my life

Editorial/production supervision: Virginia L. McCarthy
Interior design: Janet Schmid
Cover design: Janet Schmid
Cover photo: used with permission of
   Good Samaritan Medical Center, Phoenix, Arizona
Manufacturing buyer: Harry P. Baisley

Printed in the United States of America

10 9 8 7 6 5 4 3 2

ISBN 0-13-444720-4   01

Prentice-Hall International (UK) Limited, *London*
Prentice-Hall of Australia Pty. Limited, *Sydney*
Prentice-Hall Canada Inc., *Toronto*
Prentice-Hall Hispanoamericana, S.A., *Mexico*
Prentice-Hall of India Private Limited, *New Delhi*
Prentice-Hall of Japan, Inc., *Tokyo*
Prentice-Hall of Southeast Asia Pte. Ltd., *Singapore*
Editora Prentice-Hall do Brasil, Ltda., *Rio de Janeiro*

Contents in Brief

Contents

5 | Disorders of Communication in Children   95

6 | Disorders of Communication in Adults   129

7 | Disorders of Hearing 157

8 | Disorders of Language in Children 189

9   Disorders of Language in Adults   221

Preface

This book offers the reader a first look at human communication and its disorders. While the book in its early chapters takes a look at some of the normal processes of communication, its excitement and focus can be found in the clinical chapters. For it is in the clinical chapters that we see the people, children and adults, with various kinds of communicative disorders. The people we talk about and the people in the occasional photographs in the book are actual people who have struggled or continue to struggle to communicate. The text, it is hoped, represents the profession of audiology and speech-language pathology in its current literature and state of knowledge as completely as an introductory text by one author can elect to do.

The book was written with an appreciation of the reader who is perhaps a sophomore in college still looking for a professional career or a student who is beginning a major in audiology and speech-language pathology. Or the reader may be a student or a professional in another discipline, such as teaching, special education, psychology, social work, linguistics, nursing, dentistry, or medicine, who is interested in communication disorders. Or the reader may be a professional peer of the author. I have attempted to "turn on" the reader of this book with the same excitement in looking at and treating clinical disorders of hearing-language-speech that I have experienced in a lifetime of clinical experience.

A topic as diverse and large as human communication and its disorders is difficult to house in the pages of one book. For this reason, the reader will find several themes in *Human Communication and its Disorders (An Introduction)* that may aid one in organizing some of the information presented into some kind of useful meaning. In the early chapters dealing with normal communication, our first theme develops as we focus on the sounds that babies hear and make, finding that these sounds eventually emerge as aural-oral language, the most powerful communicative tool that human beings acquire. A second theme is that human beings seem to have a biologic propensity for developing language and speech; however, the complexity of the listening and talking task is so great that one must wonder why only about 10 percent of the total population has a communication disorder. We might expect the incidence of such communication disorders to be much higher. Another theme of the book is that we can best understand communication disorders if we discuss the various processes that may be involved (such as hearing, language, articulation, voice, and fluency) rather than providing a focus on causation and management of various etiologic disorders (such as cerebral palsy or cleft palate). Therefore, for any one disorder, such as cerebral palsy, we consider how the parameters of hearing, language, articulation, voice, and fluency could be involved.

Our subsequent treatment focuses on the processes that are involved rather than on the disorder per se.

Most people with communication disorders can be helped to communicate more effectively. It is my hope that this clinical optimism will show in these pages. Working with persons with communication disorders is an exciting endeavor. I hope, also, that this book will portray for you that excitement.

Daniel R. Boone, Ph.D.
University of Arizona
Tucson, Arizona

1

One of the marvels of human communication is that so many of us are able to use it so well. The modalities of human communication include our ability to touch, to voice, to gesture, to see, to hear, to listen, to speak, to read, and to write. Only on occasion does the normal communicator have a lapse in communicative effectiveness, such as not understanding what someone says or having trouble saying something. People with communication disorders, however, may experience problems communicating in many situations. In this book, we will look at aspects of normal communication only as a prelude to our focus on communication disorders and the people who have them.

An Introduction to Human Communication and its Disorders

Human **communication** takes many forms. In this chapter of *Human Communication and its Disorders,* we will first look at examples of normal communication, including everything from signs of comfort between a mother and a child to captive students listening to the narrative lecture by a professor. Some verbal fragments from actual cases of people with communication disorders will then be presented in a beginning attempt to help us appreciate the limitation to normal living that communication disorders impose on an individual. Most of the chapter will be spent in looking at various systems (biologic, social-linguistic) that together make up perhaps the most complex of all human behaviors, communication.

While many forms of animal life give evidence of communication, what sets the human being clearly apart from all other species is the human potential for an eventually acquired system of language. Language and communication are not the same thing. Language as a part of communication is a coded system of words and rules that make it the most organized mode for communicating. Language is the highest form of communication.

SOME FORMS OF HUMAN COMMUNICATION

Real-life examples of different transcripts of human communication illustrate the many forms that communication can take between human beings:

A fifty-three-year-old farmer from mid-state Illinois was going to take his first commercial flight from the O'Hare field in Chicago. While waiting in line with his luggage at the check-in counter, he began talking with a friendly businessman who was waiting to check in for the same flight. Whatever they said to each other, the other understood well, until the businessman arrived at the counter and said, without being asked anything by the clerk, "I'll have a smoking window." It was several flights later before the farmer knew what the other man had meant.

Here we see a unique use of words that have meaning to the listener (the clerk) who has the same symbol code as the speaker; for the other listener (the farmer), the literal meaning of the words made no sense.

A mother held her crying fifteen-month-old baby in her arms and applied a hot-water bottle to the baby's left ear. As she did so, she placed her face on the baby's cheek and whispered, "La, na, na, na, na, na. Now it won't hurt anymore." The mother began to hum softly at about the time that the baby stopped crying. The baby nestled against his mother's face as she continued to hum her melody of comfort.

> Emotions such as concern and love can be communicated to another person by holding and touching. Often, we add words that have a common meaning and ordering between speaker and listener. Or we can make up sounds, or hum, or sing, varying our mode of communication to meet the needs of self and the perceived needs of the other person.

Twenty-seven students sat in a lecture room, one without any windows, listening to their professor. The professor, who had taught the course nine times before, was lecturing: "One might question, uh, the relational meanings that best describe, uh, the language of young children. Remember, that Bloom said (as well as Sinclair or, uh, and Bowerman) that it is possible to put in a logical order the kind of language experiences that occur in a typical order of, uh, let us say, emergence."

> Some of the poorest communication may exist in the lecture. This lecturer's poor word order and interruptions related to word-retrieval pauses competed against effective communication. The meaning of the material can be difficult for the student without the teacher's problems in sentence formulation. The listeners may not be listening for many reasons, such as the instructor's poor narrative, fatigue from a previous activity, lack of ventilation in the closed room, and other real-world or imagined concerns.

An old woman revealed her worry about her husband's health when she told him, "You've never had a sick day in your life, Ralph, and Dr. Countryman knows that. That's why he'll be concerned when you tell him about this new lump." The husband answered, "If I went in there worrying about a lump, he'd run me out and tell me to 'peddle my onions somewhere else.'"

> The wife attempted to mask her worry about the newly discovered lump by convincing her husband that he has always been well and that the doctor (instead of her) will be concerned when he learns about the lump. The husband wants to be sure. His use of the idiomatic phrase had no literal meaning and was spoken to elicit further assur-

ance from his spouse. The pragmatics (use) of language is interesting here, in that much more is communicated than the words that were said.

We begin to learn as infants the language or languages that have been spoken around us. Before we ever go to school, we learn the vocabulary and the rules for language usage. The meanings and multiple meanings of words we learn over a lifetime. The actual use of the language, which is so dependent on life experience and the present situation in which we find ourselves, varies according to the needs of both the speaker and the listener. As we shall see later in this chapter, the complexity of various speech and language systems required for normal communication prevents simple understanding. We must have not only the words available to represent our thoughts when communicating, but also the intent to communicate. Then we must have the biologic and physical equipment to express the thoughts in speech. We must add the listeners to the communicative act—how they look, how they hear, how they understand, how they react. Human communication requires an interaction between two or more people, with the dimension and shape of the interaction determined by one another's reactions. The complexity of communication is so great that it is no wonder that over 10 percent of the speaking population in the United States demonstrate some disorder of communication. The real wonder may well be that some 90 percent of the population communicate well enough to avoid being classified as having a communication handicap.

Later in Chapters 5 through 13, we will consider separately various developmental and acquired communication disorders in both children and adults. At this point in our study, however, there may be no better way for us to appreciate the enormity of a communication disorder than to review the cases of a few people who have serious problems in understanding or speaking. Each of the people reported here is a real person who in the last few years has been struggling to communicate with less handicap by receiving the professional services of an audiologist or speech-language pathologist (the official designation of the professional persons providing services in hearing or speech and language, as described by the American Speech-Language-Hearing Association*).

As far as his mother knew, John was born with a severe hearing loss, perhaps related to her having had rubella (German measles) during pregnancy. Now, at age three, he wears a hearing aid in each ear to compensate partially for his severe hearing loss, which has left him with basically no hearing beyond 1,000 Hz (mid- to high-frequency loss), with a moderate loss for the lower frequencies. John attends well to other people, and his best mode of communication is visual, using facial expressions and gestures effectively for most of his wants. Despite wearing hearing aids since he was six months old and despite a year and a half of speech training in a hard-of-hearing

---

*The American Speech-Language-Hearing Association and its certification program for audiologists and speech-language pathologists will be discussed in Chapter 13.

nursery, he has a spoken vocabulary of only about 20 words. His mother's primary concern is that John be able to enter a normal kindergarten in a few years, in spite of counseling efforts by the audiologist, who suggests that the boy continue to be placed in a special program for the hearing-impaired.

Beth is a twenty-three-year-old student teacher who developed bilateral vocal nodules, or bumps on both vocal folds. Before noon every day, she loses her voice completely, making it impossible to control the 26 children in her fourth-grade class. She has been warned by her master teacher that she will lose her student-teacher status if she does not improve her voice. Seeking help in a voice clinic at a university hospital, Beth was told that she speaks at the very bottom of her pitch range, clears her throat constantly, speaks in a loud voice with pronounced hard glottal attack, with a vocal focus that is "in the bottom of her throat." She has consulted two ear-nose-throat physicians (otorhinolaryngologists), who have each told her separately that she has two small nodules, one on each vocal fold, which are not big enough to explain the severe voice symptoms she is experiencing. Both recommended that she receive voice therapy. Subsequent voice-therapy attempts have been thwarted by school and teaching activities that give her neither time for practice nor time for therapy. Recent counseling efforts with Beth were successful in making the point that her kind of voice problem (hoarseness and loss of voice related to vocal nodules) could probably be well resolved with voice therapy. She has not yet, however, made her first therapy appointment.

Carl, age fifty-seven, was a captain with a major airline until he developed a severe sensorineural hearing loss when he was fifty-five. Unable to pass the hearing-examination phase of his flight physical, he was forced to take early retirement from the airline. Later, in consultation with an audiologist, he revealed that he had flown Air Force propeller-driven fighter bombers during the Korean War, exposing his ears to loud engine noises. His hearing loss, thought to have originated from this loud-noise exposure, continues to progress. He has subsequently been fitted with two in-the-ear hearing aids and is able to understand almost everything that is said to him. He has enrolled in a speech reading course and has improved his skills in watching faces and lips and in guessing at speaking cues as his customers (he now sells real estate) speak to him.

Bruce, age sixty-nine, is a retired executive, who suffered a stroke while sleeping, awakening with a right-sided paralysis (hemiplegia) and aphasia (loss of language and speech). His sudden symptoms transformed him from a golf-playing, fun-loving retiree in Arizona to a man unable to speak any words (he has a nonfluent aphasia) except occasional profanity and unable to move his right arm and leg. The patient and his wife reacted initially to the severe disability with disbelief and denial, hoping that, with proper medical attention within the first few days of onset, his symptoms would go away. After several weeks of continued disability, Bruce and his wife sought rehabilitation, which included speech-language pathology services. Bruce began receiving twice-weekly group therapy and daily individual speech therapy (plus physical and occupational therapies). His wife attended a weekly spouse group and received individual counseling with a social worker in the rehabilitation center. As his speech improved (he now can repeat six-word sentences after someone else and generate two-word phrases on his own), his profanity lessened and his overall spirits improved dramatically. He is now about 18 months post onset from the stroke, and both Bruce and his wife seem to accept the relative permanence of his disability.

Karen, a thirty-three-year-old attorney, had stuttered badly all her life. She would repeat words over and over, and sometimes she would fix her mouth in a tight, twisted manner and be unable to say anything. Although she received trial speech therapy for her stuttering while in high school, she felt that it did not help her. While attending a university, Karen was the victim of a savage beating and sex crime. Her attacker was arrested and subsequently tried for his crime. Unfortunately, he was acquitted, in part because of Karen's inability to speak during her attempts to testify against him during the trial. During counseling sessions with a psychologist, she was advised to receive speech therapy for her stuttering. She began receiving individual therapy twice weekly and participated in a young-adult stuttering group at the university speech clinic. She began to realize in therapy that most of her life had been spent trying not to stutter, and she found that she was beginning to do a lot of things to keep from speaking (such as fixing her mouth so tightly that no words would come out). The therapy basically taught Karen how to speak easily, prolonging the vowels in her speech. As the result of her difficulties in court, she had become fascinated with law and the criminal system, which was so designed that it permitted a criminal (she knew that the man had attacked her) to get off without being sentenced. Upon graduation from the university, she went to law school and became an attorney. She continues in speech therapy, but her speech now permits her to function as an assistant district attorney prosecuting criminal cases in California.

We have taken a brief look at five people who have communication disorders, most of whom will learn to adjust to the disorders for the balance of their lives. John, the three-year-old hard-of-hearing boy, will always be dependent on the amplification provided by hearing aids; eventually, he may develop relatively normal language and speech. After voice therapy, Beth, with bilateral vocal nodules, could in time develop a normal voice; she would, however, have to watch vocal excesses and practice a close self-monitoring of her voice usage for her whole life. The ex-airline captain, Carl, will always need to wear hearing aids and employ speech reading in order to compensate for his hearing loss (which is probably progressive). Bruce will spend his last years with right hemiplegia and a nonfluent aphasia, communicating as much by gesture and facial expression as by using actual words. Karen, the young attorney who stuttered, profited greatly from both individual speech therapy and a weekly stuttering group; her speech improved so much that she was able to prosecute cases in court.

There are many forms of communication disorders, ranging from babies who never learn to talk, to the occasional older person who loses effective language skills as part of a deteriorating senile dementia. Communication disorders may affect our ability to hear, to listen, and to understand what others say; they may affect the voice we use when we speak; or they might impair our articulation of the speech sounds, the fluency of speech, or the language symbols and code we use when we communicate to others. Some children never learn to communicate by using the graphic skills of reading and writing, and because of this disability they may be classified as having a "learning disability"; also, most people who acquire aphasia not only lose the ability to speak but may be impaired in their ability to read and to write.

As a prelude to our appreciation of the complexity of communication and the way that humans communicate, let us first discuss the fascinating biologic readiness we have for communication. We will then consider how the emotional aspects of communication are often replaced in part with a more efficient tool for communication, language. In Chapters 2 through 4, we will discuss in greater detail normal hearing and listening, normal voice, language, and speech.

BIOLOGIC READINESS FOR COMMUNICATION

Much of the human being's propensity for **aural** (understanding the spoken word) and **oral** (speaking) **language** is related to biological systems that not only permit but are facilitative for such behavior. While it is fascinating to observe the listening and speaking abilities of other forms of life, the most advanced linguistic task performed by an animal is often a primitive linguistic task in a mature man or woman. For example, Lilly (1961), in his descriptions of training the dolphin, presents fascinating data about the dolphin's ability to listen to English and "say back" to the investigators a string of primitive utterances through his blowhole. The dolphin has demonstrated through many experiments incredible auditory performance, including remarkable auditory memory span for repeating monosyllabic words; Lilly reports that dolphins can say back ten discrete words to the experimenter in the same sequence in which they were presented. On the expressive side, it is always fascinating to hear the speech patterns of the parrot or crow (whose tongue has been clipped) that speaks a series of words that have been repeated previously in the bird's presence. A hypothetical but dramatic comparison between the parrot's "I want a

FIGURE 1-1 The utterance of a parrot compared to the utterances of a toddler.

cracker'' and the three-year-old toddler's infinite use of the same kind of utterance is seen in Figure 1-1.

The toddler can add many new words to the ''I want'' utterance and generate many new ideas through new and novel sentences. There is no question that when the toddler was an infant (let us say, eleven months old) and the parrot was the same age, the parrot's utterances might have far exceeded the precision and intelligibility of the toddler's attempts at speech. The toddler would soon catch up and pass the bird in number of utterances. Although humans begin their speaking tasks far more slowly than other animal forms that can make speech sounds, young children eventually experience an accelerated acquisition of language that will permit them to utter an infinite number of word combinations.

It was Lenneberg's thesis in his *Biological Foundations of Language* (1967) that language behavior in humans is a species-specific behavior that is a natural consequence occurring in young humans who hear and observe the language of other humans. As biologic systems mature, the language consequences of such maturity become apparent. When the neural and physical systems are biologically ready to perform (through a natural process of growth and maturity), it is then possible for various linguistic behaviors to occur. The acquisition of a language for the human, then, is as species-specific as it is for a dog learning to bark at a stranger or for a cat learning to hiss at a perceived enemy.

The normal human being has the physical equipment required for the acquisition and development of aural-oral language, requiring only exposure to other people communicating in a particular language. Few of us require any formal instruction to learn the particular language known as our native language. We learn to understand what others say, and we learn to talk by being around other human beings who use spoken language to talk to one another and to us. Obviously, if infants or young toddlers were never around other people who spoke, they would not be able to learn aural-oral language. We shall see in later chapters that some children experience great difficulties in learning to speak because of hearing loss or deafness or being deprived of a normal exposure to other people in their environment.

Let us consider some of the biologic components that are essential for the reception and expression of normal human communication, reserving more specific detail for ensuing chapters.

The Biologic Mechanisms of Listening

As we shall discuss in Chapters 2 and 3, the human auditory system has many structures, each contributing to hearing, perception, and listening. The simplified drawing of the ear (Figure 1–2) shows a human hearing mechanism that does not differ significantly from the ears of other primates. The human ear at the time of birth

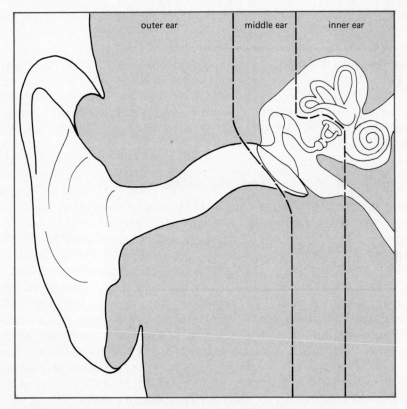

FIGURE 1-2   A schematic drawing of the outer, middle, and inner ear.

is ready to function and does not require a growth period before hearing begins. As seen in Figure 1–2, the ear can be divided for study purposes into three parts: the outer ear, the middle ear, and the inner ear. The sounds in the environment travel as sound waves through the outer ear canal toward the eardrum (tympanic membrane), which sits at the end of the canal. The eardrum is then set into vibration, with these vibrations corresponding to the energy that was transmitted by the sound wave. Through its vibrations, the tympanic membrane (which is the outer wall of the middle ear) causes the three tiny bones within the middle ear to vibrate. This middle-ear bone vibration in effect causes the fluid within the inner ear to move in direct response to the external vibrations that came into the external ear as sound waves, as will be explained in Chapter 3. As the fluid in the inner ear moves, it in turn moves tiny hair cells. The movement of these hair cells is converted into electrical energy, which is then transmitted via the eighth cranial nerve to the brainstem. From the brainstem, the auditory pathways carry the neural impulses (which at this point represent external sound) up to the brain.

The hearing mechanism is ready to function at birth. Many newborn babies, particularly those who are judged "high risk," are tested to determine the presence or absence of normal hearing (Northern and Downs, 1974). Most developmental scales of infant growth and development describe normal infants responding early to environmental noises, and particularly to the human voice. Babies will often prefer to turn to find the source of a human voice rather than search for some kind of environmental sound, such as a ringing bell. We shall study in greater detail in Chapters 2 and 3 the mechanisms of hearing and how the hearing system works, with some emphasis given to the orderly acquisition of auditory verbal skills through infancy and early childhood. It would appear that the auditory system is well designed in the typical normal person to serve a primary role in human communication.

The Biologic Mechanisms of Speech

Although the complexities of human speech require biologic mechanisms not found in any other species, some mammals demonstrate respiratory skills superior to ours. The sperm whale can dive under water and hold its breath for 90 minutes; the beaver in the pond can be observed to hold its breath for 15 minutes; a few humans who are underwater swimmers can hold their breath for two and a half minutes (Prosser and Brown, 1961). The ability to take a quick respiratory inspiration (take in breath) and parcel out its expiration (let breath out) to activate the laryngeal mechanism of voice can also be found in many animal forms. For example, the cow takes a quick inspiration and follows it with a prolonged expiration, activating the larynx and producing the voicing pattern (phonation) that we perceive as "moo." The "moo" is produced by the cow's phonating while the mouth is closed and the tongue is in a particular neutral position, with the phonation resonating in the nasal cavities. The human, unlike any other animal, can prolong an expiration and voice and unvoice the outgoing airstream to match the voicing characteristics required for particular sounds. It is the actual production of the barrage of sounds (consonants and vowels) that humans can produce in running speech that completely separates us from other mammals.

In human respiration, our everyday biologic breathing at rest is much like that of other primates; we take in a breath in about the same time unit as we expire one. However, when we go to speak or sing, we take in a quick breath followed by a prolonged expiration. During speech, we use fewer breaths and the inspiration-expiration length varies continually, according to what we want to say. Hixon and Abbs (1980) have written that "the typical speaker draws in about twice as deep a breath when refilling his bellows during ongoing conversational speech as he does during resting breathing" (p. 60). What is amazing during speech and singing is the quickness of the refill of air. We take quick inspirations followed by an expiration long enough to hold all of the units of the desired verbal message.

The vocal folds during quiet breathing remain in an open position. All air coming into the lungs likewise passes between the open vocal folds, and all outgoing air from the lungs passes between the folds. The human voice requires the vocal folds to come together across the airway with the outgoing, passing airstream setting them into vibration. The small intrinsic muscles of the larynx that bring together and separate the vocal folds are among the fastest-moving muscles of the human body (as discussed in Chapter 3).

The loudness and pitch of the voice is constantly changing in speech. The individual word is often referred to as the **segment** of the utterance. The melody and intonation of the whole utterance including and beyond the word are known as the *suprasegmentals*. We shall consider melody flow and suprasegmentals in much greater detail in Chapters 2 and 4. It does appear that most speech is said as part of a voicing melody, with the sound of the voice carrying part of the communicative message. The old adage, "It isn't what you say but how you say it," may well be related to the melodic flow of voice, with intonation patterns and *stress* (changes in pitch, loudness, and duration) carrying meaning to the listener.

The outgoing airflow sets up vibrations of the vocal folds, which produce sound waves that are perceived by listeners as voice. These sound waves originate at the base of the vocal tract, which, as we see in Figure 1–3, begins with the vocal folds. Above the folds is the tubular vocal tract, which is composed of the pharynx, with two lateral extensions, the oral and nasal cavities. As we see in Figure 1–3, the overall vocal tract in the human being resembles the letter *F*. Somewhat peculiar to the human species is a very sensitive soft palate (**velum**), which rapidly opens or separates the oral cavity and nasal cavity by its movement. This mobile soft palate (which is composed of muscle and membranous tissue) drops during quiet breathing, coupling the oral and nasal cavities. During speech (when no nasal consonants are spoken), the palate makes firm contact with the lateral and posterior walls of the pharynx, in effect preventing the nasalization of vowels. Whenever the speaker produces in English the three nasal consonants (*m, n, ing*), the soft palate drops, allowing the sound wave and airflow to continue from the oropharynx into the nasal passages, permitting nasalization of the nasal consonants. In running speech, the velum "keeps busy" elevating for oral productions and dropping for the nasal consonants. Any deviation in this rapid velar valving is perceived by listeners as a prob-

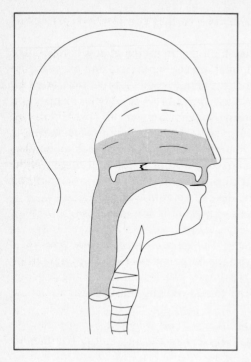

FIGURE 1-3   The tubular vocal tract looks like a capital *F.*

lem in nasal resonance. In some languages of the world, such as Chinese and French, there is increased nasalization of vowels; the velum makes less complete contact with the pharyngeal walls, permitting the right degree of nasalization for the particular language spoken.

One of the miracles of speech is the rapid production of speech sounds within the mouth. The human, as compared with other primates, has a relatively small mouth shaped by small, powerful lips; the intricate muscular anatomy of the human lips permits a vast array of fine and subtle movements (Lenneberg, 1967). The lower jaw (mandible) has fine muscular controls that permit small adjustments in its opening and closing.

By viewing lateral X-ray films of someone speaking, one can appreciate the remarkable synchrony between lip, jaw, tongue, and velum movements that typify normal speech. The degree of oral opening (as produced by both jaw and tongue movements) determines the particular vowel (as explained in Chapters 2 and 3); vowels are produced by the overall shape of the vocal tract, primarily within the oral cavity. The human tongue is particularly endowed with neuromuscular controls, which enable it to produce the rapid series of sounds and their combinations (syllables and words) that we hear in speech. It has been established that the typical adult speaker can produce about five syllables per second (Fletcher, 1978), obviously requiring extremely rapid movements of the tongue. The rapid sequential array of sounds in the production of a single word (let alone a phrase or a sentence) requires that the production gestures of lips, jaw, tongue, and velum "will overlap and intermingle" (Hixon and Abbs, 1980, p. 83).

The mechanisms for both the reception and the production of speech are difficult to understand. For our own convenience we assign alphabet letters for most sounds (but not all), but we both read and listen to the production of these sounds in a *gestalt;* that is, we see or hear the whole word. The human being has the capability of analyzing an utterance into its sound components, and if we desire to do so, we can produce a particular sound in isolation. Normally, however, in aural-oral language, we neither hear sounds as separate entities nor produce them as discrete units. Even words are not read or heard as separate units by the typical reader or listener. For example, when we listen to someone speaking rapidly a foreign language in which we have only limited ability, we experience the feeling that the speaker is speaking too fast. The words seem to run together, and we experience difficulty extracting the meaning of the total utterance.

In both reading and listening, we group words into phrases and sentences, with comprehension actually facilitated by such grouping. Our ability to understand communication appears to require a combination of visual or hearing sensitivity, with perception of these sensations organized into some kind of meaning. Once we begin to talk about language and meaning, we move into cerebral function and the ever-elusive topic of language and thought. In Chapters 2 and 4 we will look at normal language, and we will look at disorders of language in children and adults in Chapters 8 and 9.

EMOTIONAL AND LINGUISTIC ASPECTS OF COMMUNICATION

Although defects in the biologic systems may certainly cause or contribute to communication disorders, often the causes are more subtle, more difficult to identify. For example, sometimes our emotions and feelings prevent effective communication. There is less exactness in our interpretation of the emotions of others than there is in interpretation of their words, since the word system requires a common code between speakers. It is easy to misunderstand another's emotional expressions. We will see in Chapters 2 and 4 that there is much emotion communicated by our facial expressions, our gestures, and particularly by our voices.

Emotional Expression

Vocalization in early infancy expresses the infant's various biologic need states and soon becomes the primary mode of communication for the baby's affective mood states. The earliest **vocalizations** in the first few months of life appear to be crying related to the baby's various biologic discomforts (pain, hunger); Wasz-Hockert and others (1968) have written that the baby's primary caregivers seem to be able to differentiate its cries and know by the cry whether the baby has a gas pain, a full diaper, or a hungry stomach. Around the third month, the young infant begins to vocalize various sounds of contentment, mostly with a cooing sound that seems to be made up primarily of prolonged vowel sounds. By six months of age, the baby has been using laughter as an interaction response for several months. Sroufe (1979) has written that babies six to seven months old seem to enjoy their interactions with others and use pitch and loudness changes in their babbling to represent their affective moods. By nine to twelve months of age, babies enjoy enough motor control over their speech mechanisms to be able to portray with voice their various affective moods. These emotional vocalizations are usually accompanied by appropriate facial expressions and body gestures.

Vocalization as an expression of emotion increases in frequency in the youngster's life from twelve to eighteen months. Emotional expression by voice is spontaneous and unplanned. As youngsters begin to acquire words, they use the voice's emotional coloring when speaking. Many of these early vocal patterns of emotionality are used for a lifetime. Although emotional expression is uncoded and spontaneous (by definition, emotion does not have intent), it can always influence the verbal message. Its influence, however, is always changing because there is no coding or vocal rule to follow in the production of spontaneous emotional vocalization.

Language usage is much more rule-bound. Our use of language becomes our primary mode of communication, and to be effective communicators, we must master the various systems of language. Up to the age of about twenty-one months, when toddlers begin to replace the use of jargon and nonverbal voicing patterns with occasional words, they enjoy relative voicing freedom in expressing their emotional selves and need states to others. When language begins to be used as the primary mode of communication, they must follow the rules of a particular language. To be understood by others, any language must be rule-governed. Random vocalizations and made-up words (neologisms) are no longer tolerated.

The study of language structure today generally recognizes four components, three of which have rather specific rules for usage. These components are phonology, semantics, syntax, and pragmatics. Let us look at each briefly at this point, studying them in greater detail in ensuing chapters.

Phonology

When a word is spoken, there are specific rules to follow in saying the sounds. **Phonology** is the study of the rules for the sounds or phonemes of a language as observed in spoken syllables and words. An example of a phonological rule in English would be that following a voiced consonant, such as /d/, the plural /s/ is actually said with the voiced opposite (**cognate**) /z/. For example, for the word *bed,* its singular form would be written phonetically as *bed* and the plural form would be *bedz.*

Phonologic rules also govern the stress (loudness, pitch, duration) given to words, which may affect their meaning. In the ambiguous sentences that follow, the same words when said with different stress have two different meanings: "John painted the white hóuse" (the stress is put on *house,* which makes it like a lot of other white houses) or we could say "John painted the Whíte House" (by putting the stress on *White,* we know John painted the great mansion on Pennsylvania Avenue in Washington, D.C.).

Semantics

The second component of language is **semantics,** the study of words and their meanings. The semantic component has its own rules for the meanings of words and word combinations. Each word may have a single referent (it always means one thing), or the same word may have different meanings, depending on the context in which it is used. For example, in these ambiguous sentences the same words have two meanings:

"The shooting of the police was awful." (What poor shots they were.)

"The shooting of the police was awful." (It was a sad day when policemen and policewomen were shot.)

Developmentally, we go from the first word at about age one year to tens of thousands of words by age forty-one (or thirty-one or sixty-one), and this total vocabulary is known as our **lexicon.**

Syntax

The third language component, **syntax,** provides the rules for how words can be combined into phrases and sentences of various types. Often the most efficient communicator is one who has mastered the syntactic rules, presenting words in an absolute word order that facilitates comprehension. Once again by looking at ambiguous sentences, we can illustrate how slight changes in syntax can produce two different meanings. For example, "I saw the wild native dance" can have two meanings; by altering the words a bit, the two meanings more clearly emerge, and "I saw the dance of the wild native" is quite distinctly different from the original "I saw a wild native dance."

Pragmatics

Pragmatics is the study of language in context. It looks at the verbal interaction between speaker(s) and listener(s) and the outcomes of such interactions. Bate (1982) has written, "The pragmatics of language is language in use—what people do with words and how they adapt what they say to the needs of differing listeners and situations" (p. 17).

It is only in recent years that we have looked beyond the linguistic focus on phonology and syntax; in the past there had been more interest in structure than use. Through the work of Rees (1980), Prutting (1979) and Bloom and Lahey (1978), the field of speech-language pathology has taken a much more active role than previously in looking at language effects. Phonology, semantics, syntax, and pragmatics (or form, content, and use) are now looked at closely in the child with a language disorder.

By the time children attend kindergarten, they have developed and acquired the phonologic, semantic, and syntactic skills that will be used for a lifetime of verbal communication. It would appear that pragmatic skills develop a bit more slowly. We learn to use language effectively (some of us never seem to learn this) in relation to our overall cognitive development and social experience. In time, we seem to learn what to say and when to say it. Verbal skills, particularly vocabulary related to cognitive experience, apparently reaches its most mature state at about the age of sixty.

Most children learn aural-oral language without formal training. Their experience with the multiple interactions between care-givers and others in the first five years of life is usually sufficient to enable them to understand the speech of others and to speak. It would appear that there is a biologic readiness that enables the infant and young child to acquire aural-oral language with amazing speed, somewhat independent of any formal need for training. The communicative skills of reading and writing, however, are obviously skills that they must acquire in a more formal learning situation.

As mentioned in the opening of this chapter, about 10 percent of the population has some problem in aural-oral communication. Some people have difficulties hearing; or if they hear, they do not understand. Others have problems in producing speech sounds correctly, while others may have problems in using their voices. Many children and adults have problems understanding or formulating language. Let us conclude this introductory chapter with a brief overview of some of the communicative disorders we will consider in much greater detail in later chapters of this book.

COMMUNICATION DISORDERS

The biologic and social-linguistic systems that are part of normal communication are sometimes faulty, sometimes resulting in a communication disorder. There are over 22 million people of all ages with aural-oral communication handicaps in the United States. Although many people with hearing and talking problems receive adequate treatment of their communicative handicap, many others do not.

Audiology and speech-language pathology is the profession (see Chapter 13) that plays the primary habilitative and training role for children and adults with communicative disorders (ASHA, 1975). Audiologists focus on problems of hearing, both diagnostic and habilitative, working closely with physicians (otolaryngologists, pediatricians, neurologists), dentists, classroom teachers and special-education specialists, psychologists, and hearing-aid dealers. Speech-language pathologists play a primary habilitative role, dealing with such problems as articulation disorders, voice problems, language disorders, and stuttering; they also work closely with psychologists, physicians (pediatricians, neurologists, neurosurgeons, psychiatrists, otolaryngologists, physiatrists), teachers, special educators, and social workers. We will define and look at the role of these other specialists in Chapter 13.

There are different ways to classify communication disorders. One way is to designate whether a disorder is *functional* or *organic* in cause or origin. A child who stutters or an eight-year-old child who still says "wabbit" for "rabbit" are examples of functional disorders (perhaps free of organic causation). A child who is deaf or a man who has lost his speech and language (aphasia) from a stroke are examples of organic disorders.

Although such a classification system may provide some guide to causation of the disorder, it offers little direction specific to management or treatment of the disorder. When the disorder began provides some knowledge specific to the *developmental* effects (beginning at birth or in infancy or early childhood) of such a disorder on one's communication. In general, the earlier one acquires a disorder (such as being born with a cleft lip and palate), the more severe the effects on communication. In Chapter 5 we discuss disorders of communication in children that are primarily developmental in type, and in Chapter 6 we look at various kinds of communication problems in adults, most of which are acquired.

Acquired disorders imply that prior to the acquisition of the problem, communication development and performance were perhaps normal. Children can acquire communicative disorders. Vocal nodules in a nine-year-old hyperactive boy would be an example of an acquired problem that is not very serious, as opposed to meningitis in a girl of the same age, who then, as a result of brain changes, loses her hearing and some of her speech/language capabilities.

The majority of adult communication problems are acquired, with the individual enjoying normal communication up to the time of onset of the communication disorder (which may be the result of an accident or some disease). Whereas the developmental-acquired dichotomy perhaps helps us to appreciate developmental effects of particular communication disorders, focusing on time of onset does not particularly facilitate treatment.

The classification system we use in this text is related to the process of communication that is involved. Any communication disorder can involve one or more processes: hearing, language, articulation, voice, and fluency. These five areas constitute the model that the American Speech-Language-Hearing Association (ASHA) requires training programs to follow in the practicum training of graduate students who are studying to be speech-language pathologists or audiologists.

In Table 1–1, Clinical Areas of Practicum, we see a summary of clinical experiences classified in the left-hand column by age group: preschool, school-age, and adult. The five clinical processes (or parameters) are listed across the top of the table. The hearing experience is classified by ASHA as diagnostic or habilitative-rehabilitative audiology. The graduate student in clinical training must have some supervised clinical experience, when possible, in each of the 15 cells (three age groups times five parameters). Any child or adult with a communicative disorder can fit into at least one of the five clinical parameter columns.

TABLE 1–1
Clinical Areas of Practicum

Age	Clinical Parameter				
	Hearing	Articulation	Voice	Language	Fluency
Preschool					
School-Age					
Adult					

Let us now present five people, each with a different communication problem. As you read each case history, first determine the patient's age group, and then identify the clinical parameters that may be involved. We will summarize the age-parameter data in Table 1–2 by inserting the name of the patient (Rudolpho, Danny, Bonnie, Gordon, or Abner) in the clinical cell that applies. Note that Danny's problem (stuttering) involves only fluency, while Bonnie's problem (deafness) affects all five clinical areas: hearing, language, articulation, voice, and fluency.

Rudolpho, age thirteen months, was evaluated by team members of a university orofacial-disorders clinic. He was born in Mexico with a bilateral cleft lip and palate. While his lip was grossly repaired surgically within a few weeks of his birth, he still has a poor lip (with the anterior roof of his mouth, the premaxilla, attached to it) and a virtually open hard and soft palate. All of his voicing attempts at speech (or when crying) appear to come out of his nose, since there is open coupling between his oral and nasal cavities. He was examined by the plastic surgeon, who recommended immediate surgery to attempt to get the premaxilla back into the anterior opening of his hard palate. Both the audiologist and otolaryngologist found that the boy had a moderate middle-ear infection, which was producing a moderate hearing loss. The speech-language pathologist felt that Rudolpho exhibited normal language (Spanish) comprehension but urged early surgical intervention in an attempt to minimize his severe hypernasality. The boy and his mother were going to live temporarily with his uncle in Tucson, so the first stage of surgery could be started. The social worker on the team met with the speech-language pathologist, the plastic surgeon, and the boy's mother in an attempt to arrange the temporary move from Mexico to Tucson.

Danny, age four, was brought to a speech-language clinic by his parents because "he stutters." His history shows that he experienced normal early physical and speech-language development. He has an older sister, age nine, who has normal speech. At about 36 months, he began to repeat whole words, particularly when he was formulating sentences. The word repeti-

TABLE 1–2
Clinical Areas of Practicum

Age	Clinical Parameter				
	Hearing	Articulation	Voice	Language	Fluency
Preschool	Rudolpho	Rudolpho	Rudolpho		
					Danny
School-Age	Bonnie	Bonnie	Bonnie	Bonnie	Bonnie
Adult		Gordon	Gordon		Gordon
	Abner			Abner	

Rudolpho, thirteen months, cleft lip and palate
Danny, four years, stuttering
Bonnie, eight years, deafness
Gordon, fifty-two years, amyotrophic lateral sclerosis
Abner, eighty-one years, hearing loss and dementia

tions in recent months began to be replaced with syllable repetitions. His mother read a pamphlet in the pediatrician's office at about that time that explained some of the warning signs that might signal the development of stuttering. Having a maternal uncle who has been a severe stutterer all of his life, Danny's family voiced concern that Danny's repetitions might be early stuttering. As part of his speech evaluation, Danny was placed in a normal preschool program for observation. His repetitions appeared to be disfluent responses that looked to be wholly free of tension. Danny was not making any deliberate efforts to end his repetitions, seeming in fact unaware of them. In addition to the preschool speech nursery, in which Danny experienced success, his parents attended several counseling sessions on normal dysfluency and were given direct suggestions for creating an atmosphere in which Danny could be more verbally spontaneous. A follow-up contact with the family two years after he was first seen revealed a six-year-old boy with normal speech fluency.

Each of the preschool children described had different clinical problems. Rudolpho may well have had a hearing loss plus a probable articulation problem related to his cleft palate, with malalignment of anterior structures in his mouth, as well as a severe problem of hypernasality (a voice-resonance problem). Fortunately, Danny's speech dysfluency was accompanied by very little tension; with placement in a normal preschool nursery school and with parent counseling, the disfluency seemed to go away.

As an example of a clinical disorder in the school-age child, let us select a little girl who illustrates multiple clinical problems that are typical of a youngster who is deaf.

Bonnie, age eight, was born deaf, probably related to her mother's having had a series of undiagnosed infections (with high fever) early in her pregnancy. At age eighteen months, her deafness was diagnosed. The finding was that Bonnie had a bilateral sensorineural hearing loss including the speech range thresholds (500 Hz, 1K, 2K) at 90 decibels. She had some usable hearing at the bottom of her frequency range and was subsequently fitted with binaural hearing aids. Bonnie was placed in a preschool for the deaf that included total communication (amplification, speech and lip reading, finger spelling, and manual signs). When she began first grade, her aural-oral language was judged to be three years behind, and her articulation was grossly unintelligible. She has since shown remarkable growth in overall language, which seemed to be helped when she was introduced to reading and writing in school. Her speech is still difficult to understand, as she makes many articulation errors (vowels and consonants that are not visible); her voice has a ''back in the throat'' quality and sounds hypernasal, with many pitch changes; and the overall speed of her talking appears markedly slower than that of many of the other children in classrooms for the deaf. Bonnie is now receiving academic training and speech-voice therapy in a state school for the deaf. While her reading, writing, and arithmetic skills are third-grade level, her spoken language lags far behind her ability to sign and communicate with others who know manual communication (signing).

Because of her deafness, Bonnie has involvement in all of the clinical areas in which graduate students in training must have some supervised experience while working with clients.

Let us now look at two adult clients who show a mixture of clinical involvements. For each of the cases presented, the reader might see if the clinical areas that are involved can be identified.

Gordon, age fifty-two, was a railroad engineer for 29 years before experiencing some problems speaking and moving his left leg. For three months his symptoms worsened. He continued to work on the railroad (driving freight and passenger trains for Amtrak), feeling that his increased symptoms were related to fatigue. He was subsequently evaluated by a neurologist at a university hospital, who diagnosed his problem as ''lower motor neuron disease.'' About five months after the beginning of symptoms, he was evaluated by the speech-language pathologist, who found him to have a moderately severe dysarthria characterized ''by slurred consonants, shortness of breath, with hypernasality.'' The speech evaluation found the patient to have a marked reduction in oral speed related to an inability to move his tongue quickly for normal speech production, a problem swallowing coarse foods, a marked reduction in respiratory control for expiration, and a paralyzed soft palate. Speech therapy was initiated, which gave him an immediate improvement in intelligibility, including some counseling to speak with less volume; using less effort to speak, he sounded clearer. Gordon has now had the disease (diagnosed as amyotrophic lateral sclerosis) for two years, is wheelchair-bound, and can only swallow small sips of liquids.

Gordon exhibits problems in articulation related to his poor tongue functioning, his voice is markedly hypernasal because of his paralyzed velum, and he is forced to speak slowly (a fluency problem) because he cannot move his articulators fast enough to permit a normal rate of speech. His respiratory problems and severe feeding problems are now considered life-threatening, unresponsive to any kind of medical or physical management.

Abner, an eighty-one-year-old retired insurance broker, has had hearing loss for the past 20 years. Because of his increased difficulties understanding what others were saying, he returned to a university hospital for an audiological evaluation. During the history taking, it was noticed (and confirmed by his housekeeper) that Abner was showing evidence of confusion about time and place. Audiological testing revealed that his hearing acuity was not too different from what it was when tested five years previously. The audiologist was more concerned about his confused state than his hearing loss per se. She subsequently referred him to a neurologist and the hospital speech-language pathologist. Abner was diagnosed as having Alzheimer's disease, which was responsible for the cognitive deficits he was showing. Intellectual and language testing confirmed considerable deficits in cognitive-related language function (such as using multiple meanings of words, ambiguities, and the like). He was encouraged to continue to wear his hearing aid; the housekeeper and the patient's son received counseling from the speech-language pathologist on keeping the home environment as structured as possible and working out rigid scheduling for Abner to follow. Abner continues to live at home with the considerable and patient help of his housekeeper.

This tragic case of an older man illustrates a breakdown in communication from two causes: first, a hearing loss that had been well compensated-for over the years by wearing hearing aids; second, a progressive senile dementia that is causing much language confusion in attempts to relate to other people. The brief history suggests that both the hearing loss and the dementia could not be lessened with any kind of direct therapeutic intervention. Family and home counseling to help them all cope with a deteriorating condition was about all the audiologist and speech-language pathologist could offer the patient.

REVIEW QUESTIONS

Before we go on to subsequent chapters and look at various aspects of human commu- nication and its disorders, let us ask some study questions:

1. Give examples of nonverbal and verbal communication.

2. What evidence is there that the human being has a biologic propensity for language and speech?

3. Is a person's affect or emotionality expressed best by the use of language? Explain.

4. Define these parts of language: phonology, syntax, semantics, pragmatics.

5. What are the five clinical parameters designated by ASHA for clinical practicum? Give examples of clinical disorders for each parameter.

6. Is it surprising to you that there are so many communication disorders? Discuss.

hearing   voice
language   fluency
articulation

REFERENCES

ASHA 1973–1974 Committee on Language (1975). Meeting the needs of adults and children with disorders of language: the role of the speech pathologist and audiologist. *ASHA, 17:* 273–278.

Bate, C. P. (1982). The pragmatics of language. *Communicative Disorders, 2:* 17–30.

Bloom, L., and Lahey, M. (1978). *Language Development and Language Disorders.* New York: Wiley.

Fletcher, S. G. (1978). *Diagnosing Speech Disorders from Cleft Palate.* New York: Grune and Stratton.

Hixon, T. J., and Abbs, J. H. (1980). Normal speech production, in *Introduction to Communication Disorders,* ed. T. J. Hixon, L. D. Shriberg, and J. H. Saxman. Englewood Cliffs, N.J.: Prentice-Hall.

Lenneberg, E. H. (1967). *Biological Foundations of Language.* New York: Wiley.

Lilly, J. C. (1961). *Man and Dolphin.* Garden City, N.Y.: Doubleday.

Northern, J. L., and Downs, M. P. (1974). *Hearing in Children.* Baltimore: Williams and Wilkins.

Prosser, C. L., and Brown, F. A. (1961). *Comparative Animal Physiology* (2nd ed.). Philadelphia: Saunders.

Prutting, C. A. (1979). Process: the action of moving forward progressively from one point to another on the way to completion. *Journal of Speech and Hearing Disorders, 44:* 3–30.

Rees, N. S. (1980). Learning to talk and understand, in *Introduction to Communication Disorders,* ed. T. J. Hixon, L. D. Shriberg, and J. H. Saxman. Englewood Cliffs, N.J.: Prentice-Hall.

Sroufe, A. (1979). Socioemotional development, in *Handbook of Infant Development,* ed. J. Ofosky. New York: Wiley.

Wasz-Hockert, J., Lind, J., Vourenkoski, V., Partanen, T., and Valonne, E., (1968). *The Infant Cry: a Spectrographic and Auditory Analysis.* London: Heinemann Medical Books.

2

We are born with an auditory system ready to function. Beginning with an early startle reaction in the very young infant, we will see a developing auditory system reacting to an ever-increasing array of auditory stimuli. The infant is particularly alert in response to the sounds of the human voice. We will see how the biologic noises that babies make at around three months of age are substituted by vocalizations that seem to represent infants' emotions. The affective mood is heard in the sound of the voice, particularly in changes in pitch, stress, and rhythm. Toddlers communicate by listening to and understanding much of what is said and by expressing emotions with their voices to supplement the few words they are first able to say. Much of the random vocalization of affective communication is gradually replaced by specific production of words (some dimensions of emotionality may always remain in the voice). To be intelligible, words require speech motor productions that must be relatively free of error. We will end the chapter by looking at recognized speech sounds, *phonemes,* that are used in spoken English.

The Sounds of Communication

While the first few weeks of an infant's life are primarily filled with the biologic events of feeding, elimination, and sleeping, it is not long before the parents or caregivers begin to experience a two-way communication with the infant. It is a thrilling moment in a young household when a mother can exclaim about her baby, "He's looking at me and starting to smile." What has been a one-way communication, the giving and caring by the parent, begins to be modified when the infant gives back some kind of response. Since communication generally involves two or more people, the one-way giving by the parent is not true communication. The communication message between infant and others around the baby consists of the nonverbal messages of the child and the nonverbal and verbal messages of the doting (it is hoped) parents or caregivers. The early actions of the infant are related to biologic and emotional states and, therefore, are more reflexive in nature. The parents and caregivers often interpret these early reflexive responses as intended messages that the baby is attempting to communicate.

While the baby is born with an auditory system ready to function, most communication by parents with the newborn is by nonverbal voicing and hugging and touching. We do not typically talk much to the newborn, apparently with the realization that the new baby "wouldn't understand us." The typical parent in the first few months of the infant's life will supplement changes in voice (the typical adult speaks with a baby voice to the new infant) with exaggerated facial expressions and head postures. Holding and touching the baby, coupled with vocalization, are often the primary modes of nonverbal communication. As we shall see in this chapter, the primary communicative channel in the languages of the world becomes increasingly auditory as the infant matures. We shall use the terms *aural* and *oral* throughout this text to designate respectively the listening to and speaking of spoken language. From the beginning of life, there is a highly developed auditory system that permits the early acquisition of aural language skills.

ACOUSTIC ASPECTS OF SOUNDS

Our understanding of the reaction of babies to sound and of the various kinds of sounds they generate will be helped by a brief look at two acoustical aspects of sound, **intensity** and **frequency.** What we perceive as the loudness of a sound can be given a relative measurement of intensity using the **decibel** scale. The faintest sound that most humans can detect has been established as a sound pressure of .0002 dynes/cm^2; this level is used as the reference point for the decibel scale. Zemlin (1981) has defined the decibel (dB) as a "quantitative unit of relative sound intensity or sound pressure, based on the logarithmic relationship of amplitudes or pressures of two sounds, one of which serves as the reference" (p. 641). Any sound for which we want to determine its intensity is compared to the .0002 dynes/cm^2 reference level. The decibel scale employs a logarithmic scale, which gives us a relative sound intensity level (relative to the normal reference level) for any particular sound. A 10 dB sound, for example, like a whisper from someone standing about ten feet away from us, would be hardly audible. Standing beside a runway when a large commercial jet plane takes off might produce intensity levels that one would hear in excess of 120 dB. Some possible intensity levels of common sounds (borrowed in part from the work of Northern and Downs, 1978) are seen in Table 2–1. Of some interest to us at this point is the relative lack of loudness of the human voice as compared to many of the environmental sounds around us. Yet, we will see that the developing infant seems to give priority to finding the human voice, seeking it out from a background of varied intensities and frequencies (pitch levels).

Frequency is the measurement of the pitch of a sound. Most sounds that we hear in the environment are a combination of several pitches. A musical note, however, such as middle C (or C_4) on the musical scale, is more likely to represent a pure or single frequency; on some kind of frequency analyzing equipment the musical note of C_4 produced by a piano would yield a frequency value of approximately 256 cycles per second. This means that the piano string (C_4) when struck by the piano hammer would vibrate 256 times in one second. The vibrating movements of the piano string would alternately increase and decrease the density of the

TABLE 2–1
Possible Intensity Levels of Common Sounds

Decibel (dB) Level	Common Sounds
10–20	Whispering, over five feet away
30	A ticking watch
40	Birds chirping out the window
50–70	Conversational voice
70	Babies crying over ten feet away
80	Inside a '76 Ford Falcon parked by highway
80	Dog barking in same room
90	Telephone ringing on work desk
90	Yelling at the umpire at a ball game
100	Outboard motor
110	An evening in a disco
120	Playing lead guitar in a rock band

air molecules surrounding it, setting up a sound wave. Our ears perceive the sound wave as a pitch at middle C; our measuring devices give us the value of 256 cycles per second. The number of complete cycles representing frequency is expressed in Hertz (Hz); the middle C value would be expressed as 256 Hz. For those of us who sing or play musical instruments and produce unknowingly a flat tone (lower than the target model), our Hz value would be less than 256 Hz (in some church choirs considerably less). Or the soprano that we hear singing most of her notes sharp (she is unaware of it, of course) could be producing C_4 at values near 270 Hz or higher.

We might better understand the concepts of intensity and frequency if we take a brief look at how we measure the intensity-frequency responses of the human ear. By testing a person in a quiet room, as we will discuss in greater detail in Chapter 7, we are able to plot how well the person hears each frequency tested and at what intensity level. An electronic instrument, an **audiometer,** is used, which generates the frequencies (known as pure tones) with increasing or decreasing levels of intensity. The person's responses are plotted on an **audiogram.** A sample audiogram of a person with normal hearing can be seen in Figure 2–1. It shows the frequencies listed in the horizontal row at the top of the audiogram, with the lowest pure tone representing 250 cycles per second or Hz and the highest at 8,000 Hz. Intensity, the measured loudness, is represented in decibels (dB), listed in the column on the left margin. A typical normal threshold is at 0, and the most intense signal that can be plotted on most audiograms is 110 dB. The typical audiometric examination uses an airborne signal, with the person listening to the signal through earphones. The

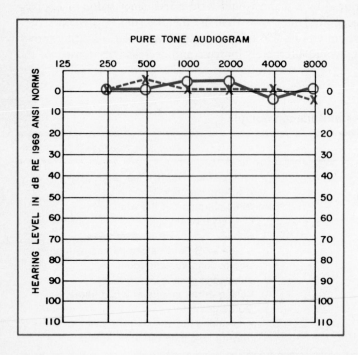

FIGURE 2–1 A normal audiogram with intensity thresholds near 0 across the frequency range (250–8,000 Hz).

right-ear response is plotted with a red circle, and the left-ear response is plotted with a blue X. If a hearing loss is found, the examiner may test also by bone conduction, obtained by putting a sound vibrator on the mastoid bone area behind the ear. Bone-conduction symbols are plotted by using a > for the right ear and a blue < for the left ear. In this sample audiogram, only air-conduction thresholds were plotted, as the person demonstrated normal hearing (some fluctuation of threshold is expected in any normal audiogram).

Human beings with normal hearing can detect frequencies from about 20 to 20,000 Hz. What we perceive as the human voice is heard at the lower end of the frequency range, as shown in summary form in Table 2–2. The infant voice, produced by small, thin vocal folds, is the highest of human voices, roughly near 350 Hz; at age nine, before the onset of puberty, boys and girls produce a voice pitch (known as fundamental frequency or F_o) roughly near middle C, or 260 Hz; the adult female voice conversationally is often near 210 Hz; the thicker, heavier vocal folds of the adult male vibrate more slowly, producing a fundamental frequency near 125 Hz. Consonant sounds, particularly fricatives, which are produced by impeding the airflow within the mouth, are usually higher in frequency, especially the six speech sounds listed in Table 2–2. It should be noted that the whole vocal tract participates in resonance of voice and speech sounds; the consonant-frequency values listed in Table 2–2 represent the peak frequency display for the particular sound. The frequency of the vocalization of a cat and a dog (listed for comparison purposes) were recorded by the author and analyzed on a frequency analyzer. The normal ear of the infant is able to hear the lowest to the loudest of intensities and throughout the human-frequency range.

TABLE 2–2
The Fundamental Frequency of Human Voice and Other Animal Sounds

Frequency level of voice in Hz.	Source
380	Infants cooing in the crib
260	Boys and girls at age nine talking
210	An adult woman saying "hat"
125	An adult man saying "bat"
375	An adult cat meowing
260	A mature Labrador barking
Between 4,000 and 8,000	Articulation of consonant /s/ or /z/
Between 6,000 and 7,000	Articulation of consonant /f/ or /v/
Between 7,000 and 8,000	Articulation of the "th" sound (unvoiced or voiced)

Hz values are derived in part from Minifie, F. D. (1973), Speech acoustics, in *Normal Aspects of Speech, Hearing, and Language*, ed. F. D. Minifie, T. J. Hixon, and F. Williams. Englewood Cliffs, N.J.: Prentice-Hall.

THE DEVELOPMENT OF AUDITORY SKILLS

For many years, expectant mothers have reported to their obstetricians that they experienced fetal kicking in what seemed to be direct response to some kind of loud environmental sound. This could well be true. It has been shown that the human **cochlea** (the organ of hearing) is fully formed and functional by the twentieth week of gestation (Marlowe, 1982). It has further been established by Bench (1968) that infants in utero are surrounded by an internal sound in the womb that has been measured at 72 decibels in intensity (a moderately loud sound). Testing of fetal auditory responses is now available in most hospitals, primarily when there is some suspicion of fetal trauma from disease or accident. At the time of a normal birth, we have a hearing system that has been active for at least the last third of the pregnancy. For newborn infants considered to be at risk, it is possible to test their hearing mechanisms to determine the presence or absence of normal hearing (Northern and Downs, 1978). The overwhelming number of newborn babies (**neonates**) demonstrate perfectly normal hearing.

Perhaps the most remarkable research findings (De Casper and Fifer, 1980; Eilers and Gavin, 1980; Marlowe, 1982) about the neonate's hearing function is the rapid emergence of the neonate's ability to discriminate the mother's voice from other female voices (as measured by changes in sucking rate). The newborn likewise demonstrates some awareness of the rhythm and loudness of the caregiver's voicing patterns by moving "precisely and synchronously in response to the prosodic markers in speech" (Marlowe, 1982, p. 30). It would appear that newborns are listening to the sounds of their environment during most of the waking hours.

Much of the observations that have been made and knowledge we have of the auditory function in the first few months of life are based on studies that measure changes in the baby's sucking patterns or heart rate. A sound or speaking pattern is introduced, and any change in sucking performance or heart rate is measured. This provides some indication that the baby has perceived the tested stimulus. A consistent finding is that babies seem to seek out the human voice (particularly that of the mother) very early, often even when there is fairly loud background noise in the home or nursery. The normal infant learns early (by two months) to couple the auditory modality with the visual, demonstrating both learning and memory. For example, as babies hear their caregivers approaching the crib, they will become quiet. If the caregiver is holding a bottle or the mother is exhibiting a breast, a baby will begin sucking motions. Developmentally, the baby becomes selective in paying attention to sight and to sound.

By three months of age, the baby will cease an activity upon hearing a sound, particularly a spoken sound. The normal hearing baby at this age will react to a sound with eye-widening or eye-blinking, or will be aroused from sleep, and will begin to turn the head slightly in an attempt to identify the source of the sound. In their research, Northern and Downs (1978) have documented the maturation of head-turning postures in developing normal babies. By four months, the babies can turn the head laterally; by seven months, the head can be lowered in the search to identify a sound; by thirteen months, babies can localize sound from the side, from below, and from above; beyond sixteen months, the head posturing develops further, making possible sound localization in any spatial plane. These kind of head posturings are recognized in auditory testing of infants using a number of kinds of noisemakers; the infant is placed centrally in a testing room and various noisemaker sounds are presented at different positions around the baby. The same procedure is used by introducing sounds through speakers set at a variety of positions within the sound room; the baby's head turn toward the speaker from which the sound comes is considered a correct response (Nozza and Wilson, 1984). The localization of the sound is plotted according to how loud the stimuli had to be to provoke the head turn (or eye movement) of the baby, providing in effect a hearing-sensitivity test of the baby both for frequency (pitch) and intensity (loudness).

How babies react to sound has become a part of most communication and language evaluation testing batteries. A typical format might include this kind of information, as seen in Table 2–3. Such behavioral information specific to how babies respond to sound has been developed from numerous sources. The presence or absence of these kinds of auditory behaviors is often evaluated by audiologists, child psychologists, pediatricians, and speech-language pathologists as part of a developmental assessment or a hearing-language-speech evaluation of a particular child.

The baby's social development is closely tied with aural language inputs. During the first several months, the baby pays increasing attention to other people, displaying an amazing ability to identify the voices of the people nearby. The baby can not only turn to the voice of a person nearby, but will often reward the speaker with a smile, particularly if the person is familiar. The wonderful cooing with smiling or laughing behavior at three to four months of age makes the baby a pleasure to be with for the parents or caregivers. If the caregiver's voice is angry or unpleasant, the baby seems to respond appropriately. Similar reactions are seen in

TABLE 2–3
Infant Reactions to Sound

Three months	Ceases activity with sudden noises
	Heeds spoken voices
Six months	Hears noisemakers
	Localizes sounds by head turning
	Selects human voice from background
Nine months	Understands "no" when spoken
	Understands and responds to own name
	Listens to and imitates sounds
Twelve months	Follows one-level spoken commands
	Obeys command, "Give it to me"

puppies and other responsive pets, with the sound of one's voice often shaping the animal's response; for example, a loud negative yell at a puppy will result in a sudden cowering (ears down, tail down) of the frightened animal. Babies respond appropriately to much more subtle vocalizations. The mother soon feels a closer bond to the baby as the baby responds with its own vocalization to the mother's varying vocal emotions. In about the eighth month, there is a marked maturing of the auditory verbal behaviors of the baby. Rediehs (1982) has written about babies at this age:

> Having just learned to recognize and respond to his name, the baby now begins to understand a few words and starts to become compliant to very simple commands. In the eyes of many adults, these are the first signs of becoming a "real person" and that makes the child worth being around (p. 8).

It is also at about this age that babies begin using voicing sounds similar to the language they have been hearing. While the baby is still speaking in what sounds like a jargon with no recognizable words, the overall sound of the utterances begins to sound like the languages that have been spoken around the infant. We hear in the normal nine-month-old the **prosody** of the parent language. By prosody, we mean that the voicing patterns of the utterance have a distinctive rate, inflection, and rhythm. For example, in their jargon speech, Chinese babies at this age begin to include the tonality (the up-and-down singsong) of the Chinese language. Little Mexican babies the same age begin to show the rhythm patterns of spoken Spanish. The distinctiveness of these prosodic patterns begins to provide evidence that babies have been actively hearing the spoken patterns of the people around them. Up until eight or nine months, the voiced babble-jargon of the infant is somewhat universal in sound; babies the world over sound the same way at the same age. This is not so in the normal baby after nine months. Now the baby begins to add intention to communication, using voice in a way to cause some kind of action. Babies are now able to set their own goals in advance and use previously learned behaviors such as expression and gesture, coupling them with voicing patterns that further demonstrate what is intended.

Normal babies eleven months of age and older also demonstrate evidence of past listening (they have learned the meaning of words) when presented with a simple spoken instruction, such as, "Give me the ball." After this request, a baby will reach for a ball nearby and give it to the other person. Such infants have learned the meaning of many spoken words even though they cannot say them.

There is some evidence that infants would understand more if speech sounds and words were not presented in such rapid succession. As we shall see in future chapters, language is spoken exceedingly fast, with little or no break in vocalization between a series of spoken words. From the listener's point of view, the words seem to run together (which is similar to what we experience when we hear someone speak rapidly in a foreign language that we are learning and have yet to master). The infant must hear our running speech as a similar auditory "whole." The eleven-month-old infant recognizes what is said when the referent is actually in view. If we say, "Give me the ball," and the ball is not in the foreground, the infant may not respond correctly to the command. If, however, the ball is among several objects in front of the baby, the infant may make the correct selection. Comprehension of the spoken word for a single command (a verb and a noun, such as "get ball") is present in the infant ten months old.

Although ten-month-old babies use expressions and gestures to match their language-sounding vocalizations, it is difficult for others around them to know exactly what they are communicating. The lack of words (words are coded and have more exact meaning to the listener) is supplemented by rather complicated voicing patterns, patterns that not only sound remarkably like the parent language but carry some meaning in their stress and intonations. The listener seems to know what the baby is "saying" despite the lack of words. Babies at ten months show a marked increase in intentional communicative behaviors; they seek out a communication, knowing perhaps for the first time in their lives that they can initiate an action on their own. They begin to differentiate between their own actions and those of someone else, facilitated by their newly developed ability to understand the simple verbal statements of others. After someone else speaks, infants seem to know that it is their turn to respond, by jargon or some kind of motor action. Previous responses, such as crying, begin to be replaced by pointing or reaching, often supplemented with prosodic vocalizations that seem to resemble the parent language.

Babies nine to ten months old show another auditory behavior, the ability to retain what someone else has said in the way of a vocalization game, such as "ba-ba-ba-ba-ba," hold it in memory for eight to ten seconds, and then repeat it. Most listeners do not wait long enough (the eight-to-ten-second input-output loop seems to be required) after they give the baby a spoken stimulus for the baby to repeat after them. Babies at ten months love to sit unassisted (a recently acquired motor skill) and play these auditory, echolalic (repeating back) games with the parent or caregiver. It has been this writer's experience with babies this age that they are willing to play the echolalia game on and on, long after the initiator of the play has tired of the activity. In this kind of vocal play with the baby, we see the beginning of intentional verbal acts, with the receiving of a vocal-play stimulus followed by the repetition of the same stimulus. The articulation of the consonants may not be the same, but the baby will usually preserve the vowels and the prosody rhythm of the original stimulus.

In the socialized babbling and vocal play of the eleven-to-twelve-month-old baby, we begin to see that the child's utterance is often in direct response to the spoken utterance of someone else. The baby shows a clear intent to communicate. Babies this age are still unable to say intelligible words. A pure **linguist** (one who is not clinically involved) might say such a child is still at the prelinguistic stage of development, reserving the linguistic stage for that time when the first spoken words begin to emerge. While it is true that twelve-month-old infants may be considered prelinguistic in that they may not yet have said their first words, normal infants this age demonstrate a remarkable understanding of the spoken word. They can follow single spoken commands correctly, many times in the absence of an actual object

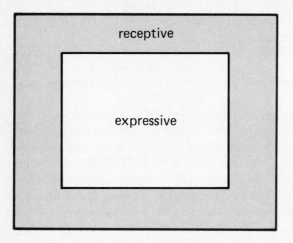

FIGURE 2-2 Receptive language skills exceed expressive language skills. We often understand more words than we are able to express in sentences.

that may be the referent (the object the word stands for) of the word. Babies now know the meaning of a word symbol representing an object that is or is not immediately present.

The developing auditory language system has served babies well in the first year of life. Their linguistic comprehension of what is said far exceeds the ability to formulate a linguistic expression, such as a word, or a phrase, or a sentence. For a lifetime of language function, it is important to remember that comprehension and our cognitive knowledge base will far exceed our ability to express that knowledge verbally (see Figure 2-2). This figure is included only to help us remember that receptive language (the ability to understand what we hear and read) far exceeds our **expressive language** (the ability to speak or write). We may be accused of "talking over our heads" when our knowledge base does not exceed our expressive-word capacity.

THE EMOTIONAL SOUNDS OF COMMUNICATION

The first three months of life are primarily biologic in focus, with infant survival depending on feeding, eliminating, and sleeping. At about three months of age, we begin to see the emergence of the normal infant's emotional self. The affective or emotional aspects of the individual appear to play primary roles in shaping the early sounds produced by the infant. How one feels affectively may be heard in the sound of the voice, in the prosodic rhythm patterns of vocalization, not only in infancy but for a lifetime. We have all been involved in a situation in which the listener interprets something quite differently than the speaker intended. Sometimes this difference in interpretation is related to the emotional coloring of the speaker's message; the voice, the body posture, or the facial expression may communicate one thing, while the person's words may say something else. Or the breakdown in the communication may be related to the listener's emotional state being at great variance with that of the speaker. Or we may have experienced making an innocent remark to someone who has had or is having a very difficult time emotionally. Our remark, in effect, becomes the "last straw," and the listener overreacts.

Much of the affective state of communication may have its origin in infancy. Let us look at how the infant communicates emotion by the sound of the voice and the changing vocal patterns of loudness, pitch, and duration. As we have seen in this chapter, the auditory system of the newborn is usually intact, with the neonate reacting to various environmental sounds, particularly startle-type noises. Most of the baby's vocalizations involve crying behaviors related to hunger and pain, according to Wasz-Hockert and others (1968); these early vocalizations of discomfort can be differentiated (pain from hunger) by care-givers. These early vocalizations probably are more related to varying physiologic states than to actual changes in emotion.

In summarizing the work of many writers, Blount (1982) concluded that babies first begin to show real emotion by facial expression (particularly smiling) and voicing patterns in about the third month of life. Smiling appears to be a particularly powerful mechanism that elicits a favorable response from the caregiver. During the second and third months, voicing patterns seem to emerge when the baby is happy; vocalizing also seems to increase when someone familiar is with the baby (Buhr, 1980; Eimas, 1974). It would appear that at three months, babies the world over, regardless of the languages spoken around them, use the same voicing patterns, the cooing response (heavily laden with vowels) that accompanies self-contentment. When babies this age are aroused and cry, caregivers of the world seem to be able to differentiate between anger, hunger, and pain. Babies three months old communicate by using vocal changes, primarily in the dimensions of pitch and duration (Stark, 1980; Wasz-Hockert and others, 1968).

In about the fifth or sixth month of infancy, babies begin the vocal self-play of babble, chaining consonant and vowel sounds together on one continuous expiration. Parents may hear the baby in the adjoining room make a continuous series of babble sounds, seemingly for his or her own enjoyment. When someone disturbs the baby during such play, the babbling will usually cease (Mowrer, 1950). Babble sounds in various language cultures seem to sound the same; that is, these language-sounding vocalizations do not yet take on the melody and rhythm (prosody) of the languages the baby has been hearing. At six to seven months, babies respond to pleasure with smiling and laughter; at this age, they seem to enjoy interaction with others and show happiness at being an "initiator" of behavior (Sroufe, 1979). Babies will seek out interactions with their caregiver and demonstrate many emotions by facial expressions and low- or high-pitched and soft or loud vocalizations that seem to represent their affective mood.

Babies nine to twelve months of age experience remarkable affective changes. As we have seen in our discussion of auditory function, babies this age seek out social contact with familiar people. Sroufe (1979) describes this period of infant emotionality as a time when active attachment to others takes place, with babies demonstrating affective emotion (caring, love) toward their parents and other caregivers. While babies this age generally show their emotions clearly and begin to demonstrate "awareness and cognitive anticipation" (Blount, 1982, p. 157), they also begin to use highly differential prosodic voicing patterns. With improved motor control over the voicing mechanisms, babies are now capable of controlling their voices to match their affective states. In addition, we see appropriate changes in facial expression, body posture, and gesture. At nine to twelve months, babies' emotions show. Despite the baby's emergency skills of intention to communicate, the ability to hide an emotion has not developed yet. The sound of the voice and the look on the face are open and unmasked.

While most linguistic research has focused on the word and its referential meaning and the early emergence of grammar, which we will discuss in some detail in Chapter 4, some linguists, such as Crystal (1973), place greater importance on the emotionally laden jargon vocalization heard toward the end of the first year. Crystal feels that the emergence of different sounds all articulated on a continuous outgoing airstream serve as the precursors of true language (using words). The inflection of the baby's jargon at nine to twelve months seems to carry meaning to listeners. Such voicing patterns after the arrival and use of the first spoken words are known as *suprasegmentals* (the prosodic voicing patterns beyond the *segment,* or the word). Not only do the suprasegmentals (loudness changes, pitch variability, duration changes) carry meaning, but the voicing melody itself may well serve as the structure to which words will be added as they are acquired. Blount (1982) writes that the "prosodic, paralinguistic, and intonational features, in fact, carry the expressive function of speech in adult interaction, even to the extent of overriding, in given instances, the referential function of speech" (p. 156). Or sometimes the voice carries the affective aspects of the message more than the words do.

At about twelve to thirteen months of age, babies seem to know that the sound of language and language itself are used to announce the relationships and the roles of the people around them. Crystal (1973) gives examples of how twelve-month-olds have been observed to use many different voices in their play, with each voice representing a different toy animal. It has also been observed (Rees, 1980) that the youngster this age develops "call sounds," patterns of sounds that represent particular desires; for example, when a baby boy wants to be picked up by his father, he reaches toward his father and makes a series of patterned vocalizations that seem to "say" that he wants to be picked up. A similar vocalization pattern (without words) is uttered each time the boy makes the "pick me up" gesture. Rees (1980), when commenting on these early infant vocalizations, writes that the "beginnings of communication are at the beginnings of infancy. Surely the child has developed considerable knowledge of and control over communication variables well before he has uttered his first intelligible 'word'" (p. 11).

At twelve to eighteen months, the first recognizable words often emerge, and they are frequently said in the "right" places in the continuous voicing pattern. The emergence of the first word signals the beginning of the linguistic period. The segment or the word takes on a more exact meaning than the affective jargon vocalization. The utterance is no longer wholly dependent on the expression of emotion and want by vocal inflection and stress. However, twelve- to eighteen-month-olds seem to rely little on their few acquired words, and continue to use jargonized vocal behaviors as the primary mode of communication. With their voices, toddlers are able to communicate such emotions as love, happiness, surprise, shame, fear, and anger (Blount, 1982). As we will see in Chapter 4, even in the dramatic period of *lexicon* (vocabulary) and *syntax* (relationship of word to word) acquisition, affective voicing continues to be part of the linguistic message. Actually, for a lifetime, the sound of our voices reveals our affective selves.

THE SPOKEN SOUNDS OF COMMUNICATION

We have seen that in the first twelve months of life, babies experience a developing perception of the sounds (spoken and otherwise) around them and begin to parrot some of these sounds, for either their own benefit or that of a listener. More often, the baby listens and makes no direct vocal response, frequently matching environmental sounds with visual happenings, developing a cognitive base of recognition between auditory and visual stimuli. Babies have learned about their world through visual perceptions and the sounds, touches, and smells about them. Much of this sensory learning has not required any kind of immediate response. Also, babies begin to use a variety of vocalizations, many of which seem to portray their inner emotional state. There is also developing simultaneously a *phonologic* (the rules for combining sound segments into larger linguistic units) system that combines the perceptual-emotional-cognitive systems, first in the development of prelinguistic sounds and eventually in the production of the sounds of speech.

   The study of the developing phonologic system in the young child has, over the years, raised many issues about emerging language. Schwartz (1984) feels that these "issues fall into four major areas: the nature of production; the nature of perception; the relationship between production and perception; and the relationships among phonologic acquisition, cognitive development, and other aspects of language acquisition" (p. 32). Having looked, earlier in this chapter, at perceptual and emotional influences on sounds that babies produce, let us look at speech-sound production in this prelinguistic period (birth to twelve months) for the balance of the chapter, reserving our remarks on cognition and language acquisition for Chapter 4. Let us begin by tracing the early nonlanguage vocalizations of infants and see how they modify in time, eventually becoming the sounds of language. Borrowing from the work of Oller (1980), Schwartz (1984), and Stark (1980), there appear to be roughly five stages in the development of speech production prior to the emergence of the first words, at about twelve to thirteen months; they are listed in Table 2–4.

TABLE 2-4
Five Stages of Speech Production Development

Stage	Approximate Age	Description of Stage
I	Birth to six weeks	Reflexive, vegetative sounds
II	Six weeks to four months	The "goo" stage, cooing and laughter
III	Four to seven months	Vocal play and expansion
IV	Seven to ten months	Reduplicated and repetitive babbling
V	Eleven to thirteen months	Unreduplicated babble; jargon

Let us look at each stage separately, primarily from the perspective of the production of the sound. We will also comment on what appear to be deviations from normal sound development, which may have clinical implications later as the child is expected to talk.

Stage I: Four to Six Weeks

There is ample evidence that the first six weeks of vocalization are reflexive in nature, primarily related to the infant's various experiences of comfort and discomfort. However, although there are some parental reports that a caring mother can differentiate the cries of an infant this age, knowing, for example, that the cry about a full diaper sounds quite different from the cry over a gas pain or the cry of hunger. A strict behaviorist might say that the young infant four to six weeks of age learns that crying can bring relief from hunger or pain and that the infant uses the behavior to meet the needs of whatever its physiologic state may be. This may be giving more cognitive credit to the new infant than his or her basic intelligence warrants at this age. These reflexive sounds seem to have more vowel-type vocalizations, often sounding like the high front vowels within the oral cavity, such as "eeh." Any difference in vowel sound is produced by changes in the opening of the mouth and the position of the tongue. Some of the vegetative vocalizations sound almost like consonants, with the tongue moving in such a way that the vowel sounds seem to be impeded within the mouth, sounding nearly like the back consonants, /k/ and /g/ (Winitz, 1969, reporting on the work of O. Irwin and his associates). Oller (1980) reports that many of the vocalizations of the normal baby from birth to six weeks sound as if they are nasal in resonance, indicating some coupling between the oral and nasal cavities.

The normal infant this age is quite active in making these vegetative, reflexive vocalizations. A baby with a questionable central nervous system perhaps resulting in severe muscular-motor problems (which eventually might be diagnosed as "cerebral palsy") might show some decrement in overall vocalization or produce vocalizations of a different type. A baby born with a severe cleft palate might show excessive nasalization of all sounds.

Stage II: Six Weeks to Four Months

The typical baby six to eight weeks old begins to make vocalizations beyond the primitive biologic sounds that characterize Stage I. Early voicing attempts (Stage I) were primarily used to portray various biologic-distress states. Now the baby begins to show pleasure sounds, such as cooing and laughter (laughter emerges in about the third or fourth month). Schwartz (1984) calls these vocalizations the "goo" sounds, an indication that the infant this age now has better motor control, allowing the use of the pulmonary-vocal systems with some volition. In a happy, contented state, the baby seems to feel like cooing or laughing. The early cooing attempts appear to be undifferentiated, composed usually of a repetitive consonant (C) followed by the same repetitive vowel (V); the typical repetitive chain might include a series of CVCVCVCV, such as "ma-ma-ma-ma" or "ba-ba-ba-ba." In about the third month, the infant seems to have developed sufficient control of tongue, lips, and palate to enjoy using bilabial nasal sounds (such as the "ma") as part of prolonged vocal play. Much of this early vocal play seems to be generated by the baby for his or her own amusement, and usually ceases when there is a noise in the room, particularly when a person approaches the baby's crib.

At about three months of age, babies seem to use vocalization in an interactive way (Bloom, 1979). When someone is with them and makes various sounds (changing the inflection and stress of one's voice), babies will have qualitative vocal reactions. In effect, from a behavioral point of view, babies react in a contingent way; their vocal reactions are contingent on the preceding vocal behaviors of the caregiver or mother. While babies may not increase their number of vocalizations in response to another person's vocalizing, there appear to be qualitative differences in their vocalizations: differences in pause time before vocalizing and changes in the vocal pattern (Bloom and Esposito, 1975). At four months of age, there is far more laughter, either self-generated or reactive to the caregiver's interaction. Caregivers who make funny faces and funny noises will often evoke similar facial reactions and laughter in the four-month-old baby. At this age, babies now produce self-generated babble sounds for their own enjoyment that appear more differentiated (still using the CVCVCVCV chain) but change the consonant, sounding more like "ma-ma-pa-ma" or "ta-ma-ta-ma."

Significant departures in vocalization development in infants this age may or may not have clinical implications for future speech and language development. Van Riper and Emerick (1984) have written, "Over and over again in taking the case histories of children with very severe articulation disorders or speech delay we have found parents telling us that these children cried much more than their other babies" (p. 88). This writer has observed that, in some children with severe language delay, the parents reported more crying than happy sounds of cooing and laughter at three to four months of age. The absence of differentiated babble and laughter may give some indication that the baby lacks the neuromuscular control to use the oral muscles in such a finely tuned manner. The young child who is tested eventually and found to be mentally retarded may have shown, at three or four months of age, clear evidence of a delay in establishing differential babbling and appropriate laughter. It is doubtful, however, that such disorders as autism (see Chapter 5) and severe hearing loss (Chapter 7) could be detected as early as the third or fourth month by the baby's inability to show appropriate cooing and laughing.

Stage III: Four to Seven Months

Normal babies four to seven months old demonstrate good control of the respiratory and oral mechanisms and are able to produce a large variety of speech-sounding utterances. Many months before babies are able to say words, they can produce a variety of *phones,* or speech sounds. Such sounds are not true *phonemes* (smallest unit of sound in a language that can be distinguished), because true expressive language does not "officially" arrive until the production of the first words. The normal baby spends many hours making these highly differentiated sounds. At six months of age, for example, the baby typically makes sounds of four or five syllables with and without voicing on the same outgoing pulmonary expiration, such as "ma-ti-na-ta-da," complete with varying inflections. The differentiated babbling of all babies at five to six months basically sounds alike. Their vocalizations do not yet take on the prosodic and suprasegmental characteristics of the languages around them.

Schwartz (1984) has written that characteristic of the Stage III period are exploratory phonetic behavior, vocal play, and expansion. Babies are continually experimenting with their vocalization repertoire. They make sounds on inspiration as well as expiration. They make high-pitched shrieks and low-pitched growls. Vocalizations for their own enjoyment are different from those they use in interactions. The babble self-play appears to be more for their own consumption than for anyone else; if a caregiver enters the room, the babbling may stop. When being held and interacting with others, babies will demonstrate an expansion of an utterance; that is, they will change the series of sounds in a sequence and may alter the length of the pause between the individual syllabic productions and the length of time between the strings of differentiated syllables. For the reader who wants to know more about this fascinating vocalization period, the work of Bloom (1979); Bloom and Esposito (1975); Ferguson (1983); Oller (1980); Schwartz (1984); and Stark (1980) is useful.

The vocalization of babies six and seven months old is now used with obvious intent. They apparently realize the effects of their vocalizations on the environment around them. Cole (1982) has written, "They begin to repeat actions in an effort to recreate results, and they learn to differentiate between themselves and others and between an object and its movement or location" (p. 13). They make vocalizations with inflections in an obvious response to their perceptions, probably for some desired effect. Parents report that they react to the baby's vocalizations at six to seven months as if the baby vocalized with some intention and expectation of outcome. The typical baby this age vocalizes and looks toward an object, and the parents in turn reach for the object and hand it to the baby. Vocalizations with others at this age rarely occur as isolated acts (Stern, 1977) and are often part of an action scheme that incorporates other behaviors (turning, smiling) used by the baby for some kind of effect. These first intentional acts using vocalization in interaction are quite probably true precursors of more complex language behaviors yet to come.

One of the prominent characteristics toward the end of the four-to-seven-month period is babies' apparent fascination with their own babbling. At this age, they often appear to listen carefully to their own babble and then repeat it with a slight change in the overall pattern. This is where deaf and very-hard-of-hearing babies do not appear like their normal hearing counterparts; at about six months of age, deaf babies appear to cease self-vocal play. Preferred contacts with the environment may appear more visual than auditory. Babies who appear like younger ones, without highly differentiated babbling and the obvious vocalizing self-play, may be giving early indications that they are slower in overall development, which may be part of a more general mental retardation. It would be difficult clinically, however, to make predictions of future articulatory and language competency based on the observed performance differences of most babies this age. A baby with gross neuromuscular problems might be spotted, not only by obvious problems in crawling or in sitting balance, but by a lack of neuromuscular control of oral structures sufficient to permit differentiated babbling.

Stage IV: Seven to Ten Months

It is during this stage that babies' sounds begin to resemble the languages they have been hearing. Up until this time, differentiated babbling and vocal play are observed in babies the same age in most language cultures. At about eight months of age, we begin to hear the prosodic melody patterns (as carried by voicing) that characterize the parent language. As vocal inflections develop, we begin to hear the voice asking questions, showing surprise, or making what sound like commands. Babies this age develop a repertoire of voicing sounds, such as using different voices when playing with toy animals or using inflectional voicing patterns with caregivers that carry a vocal message (Crystal, 1973). Some of the patterns of linguistic stress (Fry, 1978), such as changes in duration (time), intensity (loudness), and frequency (pitch), that typify any one particular language can be heard in the early babbling jargon of many Stage IV babies. Such stress and prosody in the jargon flow predate the child's first words by several months.

A chain of syllables with correct inflectional patterns can often be heard, such as "ba to na pu?" Such an utterance is directed toward a listener, with the baby often searching to make eye contact with the listener, causing the listener to feel almost obligated to answer the jargon question with a "yes" or "no." Or the baby may appear to demand an object from the listener, then give it back, and demand it again. The baby begins to experience role changes, first as the asker, then as the giver, and then again as the asker. The sound of the voice carries as much of the message as the reaching gestures or looking at the object. Such interactions provide babies with experience in the change of action, agent, and object roles (Bruner, 1978), which are all communication roles they will soon be playing with greater effectiveness when they add words to their jargon vocalizations.

Their jargon displays many combinations of consonants and vowels, and there does not appear to be a one-to-one representation for a particular object or desire. That is, the baby is not using the same combination of sounds to represent particular words. While many of the consonant-vowel combinations are repeated, many others are unique. The intention of the utterance is more to be heard in the inflection and prosody than in the consonant-vowel combination. Of some interest here is the pioneer work of Orvis Irwin (reported by Winitz, 1969), who looked at the developing sound changes in infant vocalization. Irwin reported that the baby nine months of age is able (motorically) to produce back-sounding vowels (see the vowel chart in Chapter 3, Table 3–2) with much greater frequency. We now hear front, middle, and back vowels sandwiched between many different consonants. Babies create stress and inflection in their sounds by lengthening or shortening the vowels or changing their intensity or frequency level. The jargon is now more varied, with a host of consonantlike sounds often representing sounds not just limited to those of the parent language, such as English. Many of the consonants will drop out of babies' speaking repertoire as they get older and attempt to say words (which require exact specificity of production in order to be understood by others as true words). With the jargon flow at nine to ten months, there is no demand for specificity, and the voicing appears to flow easily, with no demand that babies produce any specific sounds (such as phonemes). As they use their intended vocalized jargons as an intended communication, however, babies begin to use the inflectional patterns that represent particular need and want states that have been heard in the parent language.

Parents of babies ten months old "swear" that their babies are actually talking. This is particularly true of parents of the first-born child, who are much more likely to react to each of the baby's speechlike utterances than parents who are already beleaguered (sometimes they feel this way) with many previous children. Babies in Stage IV are fun to play with. They enjoy playing sound games, often reacting to the parent's model with exact or altered vocalization patterns of their own; or babies may amaze their parents with novel, innovative jargon not previously heard. As mentioned previously in this chapter, the consonant-vowel vocal interaction may be enhanced if the adult model is followed by sufficient silence (perhaps eight to ten seconds) to permit the baby the time to make the vocal imitation.

How well the babies this age interact with others and the quality of their vocalizations may each have clinical implication for future communicative competence. Normal babies nine to ten months of age enjoy vocal play with others and seem to enjoy the human interaction both in play and during various care-giving tasks (feeding, bathing, diapering). The absence of such enjoyment in babies this age may be symptomatic of future communicative interaction problems. Such interactional comfort cannot help but provide the baby with an atmosphere that promotes the secure experience of taking turns voicing and communicating with a sympathetic and cooperative listener. Such comfort and success in communication may go a long way in giving the baby the confidence needed for future attempts at communication. As Van Riper and Emerick (1984) have written, " . . . in this socialized babbling or vocal play of the baby we find the basic pattern of communication, of sending and receiving, although it is only sounds, not meaningful messages, that are batted back and forth'' (p. 93). Perhaps the baby whose play attempts and reaching out toward others go unheeded is not experiencing the give-and-take of **dyadic** (two-people) **communication** required for successful communication-skills development. Some future language problems may have their genesis in the first year if babies receive little satisfaction or reinforcement from their early attempts to communicate. As speech scientists such as Kent (1981) and Netsell (1981) measure and describe the various physical characteristics of infant vocalization specific to respiration, duration, pitch, quality, and resonance, we will know better what constitutes normal vocalization behavior. Then we might be in a better position to evaluate the appropriateness of such vocalization in any one baby. If greater normative data were available on the physical characteristics of normal babbling and jargon, babies with vocal-production problems (from many causes) could be identified early, with possible corrective clinical procedures then appropriately initiated.

Stage V: Eleven to Thirteen Months

In Stage V, we begin to see the infant crawl or turn toward, or by some physical action seek contact with, another person, vocalizing freely, with prosodic inflections that are sometimes accompanied by pauses. This period is characterized by ''non-reduplicated or variegated babbling'' (Schwartz, 1984), which means that the jargon sounds are individualized and not very often repeated. The infant is beginning to show real control over the stress and intonation of vocalization, with the jargon pattern closely resembling the language the baby has been hearing. Ingram (1976) presented a number of diary studies that described particular babies at eleven to twelve months who were beginning to use the same vocalization pattern for the same repeated context. There was still enough phonetic variability (changes in the production of the sounds) to prevent the utterances from being classified as true words. Most of the vocalization utterances at this age often sound more like phrases; they are longer than what would be perceived as single words.

The baby this age is producing the immediate precursor to true words, in what Schwartz (1984) describes as vocalizations that are characterized by phonetically consistent forms known as **protowords** (primitive, early forms of an actual word). The jargon vocalization appears more related to the affective, emotional state of the infant, and is, therefore, rather free-flowing and without tight structure. The protowords have much greater specificity and appear to be more object- or action-specific. Sometimes, in our observation of babies this age, we hear a protoword embedded in the free prosodic jargon. At other times, we observe a combination of prosodic jargon, then a slight pause, followed by the production of a protoword. It would seem that the first true words that often appear at twelve to thirteen months do not come suddenly, but have developed gradually, from babble to jargon to protowords, and then finally to a true word with relative phonetic stability.

Despite the arrival of the first few words, typical one-year-olds seem to attempt most of their communication by continuing differentiated jargon. The first words are not said very often. The jargon pattern becomes longer, sounding more like real language and occasionally containing a real word. In fact, the actual words are rarely said in isolation at this age, but rather are contained in the regular jargon flow, sounding almost as if they were produced in the correct syntactic (word-order) form. Much of the intended message is understood by the listener, however, not by the occasional word but by the general intonational pattern of the utterance. Despite the baby's achievement in producing the first several words that are understood clearly by others and in many cases receiving much positive reinforcement, the typical baby does not acquire many more actual words at twelve or thirteen months. In the six months that follow the first word, the baby acquires very few other words, with a vocabulary of perhaps no more than 50 words by age eighteen months. The ages twelve to eighteen months are often described in the literature as the period of "the first 50 words" (Nelson, 1973).

As the baby attempts to speak, a selective process for saying only certain words can be observed (Ferguson, 1978). In the continuing imitative games that the Stage V baby likes to play, there is some selectivity regarding the kinds of sounds chosen for play. Babies imitate the sounds they can physiologically produce; if the sounds within the sound-game are too complex to make, the babies will usually simplify the utterance, perhaps changing the consonant to one they can produce, and preserving the vowel that was in the model. As the first words arrive, we see some phonologic selectivity; the first words are those that are relatively less motorically complex to say. Many of the first words may involve the same consonant, often sounds such as /m/ and /b/; in most languages, babies' first words appear to be phonetically simple, often including the /m/ and /b/ sounds that we use in English. Leonard and others (1978) have pointed out that children this age may well comprehend the meaning of words that are beyond their phonologic capability to produce. It would appear that the selectivity process for production is basically related to the child's ability to produce the sounds of a particular word.

Our interest up to this point has primarily been in the sounds of language, describing in some detail the vocalization development that characterizes the prelinguistic phonological development of babies. In Chapter 4, we will take a closer look at the overall language development of children, starting at about twelve months of age (where this chapter ends). We will see that the jargon voicing continues, with its appropriate inflection, but begins in future months to be replaced by coded (words become references for things) and rule-bound language. Affective voicing begins to be supplemented by the gradual acquisition of actual-word language.

The baby this age who shows serious limitation in spontaneous jargon and vocal play may be failing to use skills that are necessary prerequisites for language learning. Some such children appear to be more fascinated by their own body movements and internal feelings than aware of the external stimuli around them. Instead of vocal playing and making intentional efforts to communicate, they may withdraw within themselves. Children twelve to thirteen months of age who are so withdrawn may show a marked reduction in responsiveness to the people around them, preferring to engage in activities that only seem to involve the self. Such youngsters may be showing symptoms of mental retardation, or central-nervous-system pathology, or some kind of psychiatric-adjustment problem. Children who are responding differently from their normal peers need a thorough medical-psychological evaluation, perhaps supplemented by hearing-language-speech testing, to determine if some kind of remediation program (such as a medication regimen) can improve communicative responsiveness.

It would appear that normal language development is facilitated by infant experiences with vocal play and communication dialogues that include the baby's jargon and the listener's appropriate and reactive responses. Some remediation programs for certain children with language disorders may need to promote a more playful, spontaneous communication situation (promoting vocal play, jargon vocalization, vocal interactions between child and listener), rather than working on language learning per se (Cole, 1982; Ling, 1976). There is perhaps no better way to build the needed foundations for interactive communication than by the infant's vocal games and spontaneous jargon vocalization.

THE SPEECH SOUNDS OF LANGUAGE

Up to this point in this text, whenever we wished to illustrate a spoken utterance, we used the alphabet of the English language. When we described the differentiated jargon of a baby as "ba-to-na-pu," we used the alphabet sounds that nearest represented the sounds we heard. The ordinary alphabet letter may look the same in different words, but it often does not sound the same. For example, the letter *a* in English may have many different sounds, depending on where the speaker lives and the usage of the *a* in the particular word. A ready example could be seen in the following sentence, designed to show the multiple pronunciations of the letter *a:* "Jane's cat ran to Father's aching arms." Reading this sentence aloud serves to illustrate well the different possible pronunciations of the vowel *a*. Speech-language pathologists transcribe clinical utterances using the symbols of the International Phonetic Alphabet (IPA); each symbol in the IPA represents a specific *phoneme,* or the smallest sound unit of speech. Each speech sound, correct or incorrect, can be transcribed using the IPA symbols exactly as the speech was heard. For the balance of this text, our clinical transcriptions of someone's isolated speech attempts will employ the IPA symbols. In Chapter 3, we will present a description of the physiology of the production of each phoneme.

Table 2–5 lists 52 phonemes included in the International Phonetic Alphabet. The first sounds listed are consonants that are produced by some kind of constriction of airflow and sound wave by movements and placement of the tongue, lips, teeth, and palate. The many different forms of vowels are then grouped together; vowels are generally produced by a relatively open vocal tract that is continually changing shape (such as high or low tongue carriage) for each vowel. The diphthongs are actually blends of two vowels together and are produced by delicate adjustments of vocal-tract configuration. We will look more thoroughly at the physiology of individual sound production in Chapter 3.

TABLE 2-5
The International Phonetic Alphabet (IPA)

Phonetic Symbol	Word Examples	Phonetic Symbol	Word Examples
		Consonants	
m	mama, come	r	rain, arrow
p	papa, cop	l	lamp, pillow
b	baby, bob	ʃ	she, fish
t	total, tot	tʃ	chip, pitch
d	daddy, bad	dʒ	jet, fudge
k	cake, book	θ	thin, with
g	gog, tag	ð	those, bathe
n	none, bun	w	won, swim
f	fife, wife	ʍ	when, white
v	vote, love	j	yes, yuppie
ŋ	wing, bring	ʒ	treasure, version
s	sin, bliss	ɔ	oh, oh
z	zoo, booze	h	ham, behind
		Vowels	
i	each, see	ɒ	paw, song
ɛ	head, bet	ɜ	bird, curls
ɪ	itch, bit	ɚ	percent, soldier
æ	sack, bad	u	you, booboo
e	bake, aching	ʊ	cooker, book
ɑ	bother, mockery	ʌ	money, hug
a	class, banned	ə	upon, surrender
o	phone, comb	ɔ	ball, fog
		Diphthongs	
ai	bye, sigh	ur	sure, lure
au	bow, wow	ɔr	bore, Capricorn
ɔi	boy, boil	ɪr	fear, beard
ɛr	bear, fair	aɪr	sire, tired
ɑr	yarn, car	aʊr	our, bower

REVIEW QUESTIONS

Let us consider the following study questions:

1. What evidence do we have that babies hear in the first three months of life?

2. What are the differences between the biologic-vegetative noises and the affective-emotional sounds that babies make?

3. What are the vocalization behaviors in Stage III and Stage IV babies? How do they differ?

4. How does the differentiated jargon at 11 months differ from the baby's use of the first words at 13 months?

5. Are vocal play and interactive jargon necessary prerequisites for future normal communication? Comment.

6. Listen to babies at about one year of age. Can you hear inflectional patterns that appear consistent? Do you hear protowords or actual words?

REFERENCES

Bench, J. (1968). Sound transmission to the human fetus through the maternal abdominal wall. *Journal of Genetic Psychology, 113:* 85–87.

Bloom, K. (1979). Evaluation of infant conditioning. *Journal of Experimental Child Psychology, 27:* 60–70.

Bloom, K., and Esposito, A. (1975). Social conditioning and its proper control procedures. *Journal of Experimental Child Psychology, 19:* 209–222.

Blount, B. (1982). Emotional expression, in *Language Development.* Vol. 2: *Language, Thought and Culture,* Ed. S. Kuczaj II. Hillsdale, N.J.: Lawrence Erlbaum.

Bruner, J. (1978). From communication to language: a psychological perspective, in *The Social Context of Language,* ed. I. Markova, pp. 17–48. New York: Wiley.

Buhr, R. (1980). Emergence of vowels in an infant. *Journal of Speech and Hearing Research, 23:* 73–94.

Cole, P. (1982). *Language Disorders in Preschool Children.* Englewood Cliffs, N.J.: Prentice-Hall.

Crystal, D. (1973). Linguistic mythology and the first year of life. *British Journal of Disorders of Communication, 8:* 29–36.

Crystal, D. (1975). *The English Tone of Voice.* London: Edward Arnold.

DeCasper, A., and Fifer, W. (1980). Of human bonding: newborns prefer their mother's voices. *Science, 208:* 1,174–1,176.

Eilers, R., and Gavin, W. (1980). Theories and techniques of infant speech perception research, in *The Communication Game.* Chicago: Johnson and Johnson Round Table Series, pp. 25–30.

Eimas, P. (1974). Linguistic processing of speech by young infants, in *Language Perspectives: Acquisition, Retardation, and Intervention,* ed. L. Lloyd, and R. Schiefelbusch. Baltimore: University Park Press.

Ferguson, C. (1978). Learning to pronounce: the earliest stages of phonological development in the child, in *Communicative and Cognitive Abilities—Early Behavioral Assessment,* ed. F. Minifie and L. Lloyd. Baltimore: University Park Press.

Ferguson, C. (1983). Reduplication in child phonology. *Journal of Child Language, 10:* 239–244.

Fry, D. B. (1978). The role and primacy of the auditory channel in speech and language development, in *Auditory Management of Hearing-Impaired Children,* ed. M. Ross and T. G. Giolas. Baltimore: University Park Press.

Ingram, D. (1976). *Phonological Disability in Children.* New York: Elsevier North Holland.

Kent, R. (1981). Articulatory-acoustic perspectives on speech development, in *Language Behavior in Infancy and Early Childhood,* ed. R. Stark. New York: Elsevier North Holland.

Leonard, L., Schwartz, R., Folger, M., and Wilcox, M. (1978). Some aspects of child phonology in imitative and spontaneous speech. *Journal of Child Language, 5:* 403–416.

Ling, D. (1976). *Speech and the Hearing-Impaired Child: Theory and Practice.* Washington, D.C.: A. G. Bell Association for the Deaf.

Marlowe, J. (1982). Hearing in infancy: the development of auditory skills and the audiological evaluation. *Seminars in Speech, Language, and Hearing,* ed. J. Marlowe, *3:* 28–44.

Mowrer, O. (1950). On the psychology of talking birds—a contribution to language and personality theory, in *Learning Theory and Personality Dynamics,* ed. O. Mowrer. New York: Ronald Press.

Nelson, K. (1973). Structure and strategy in learning how to talk. *Monographs of the Society for Research in Child Development, 38:* 1–2.

Netsell, R. (1981). The acquisition of speech motor control: a perspective with directions for research, in *Language Behavior in Infancy and Early Childhood,* ed. R. Stark. New York: Elsevier North Holland.

Northern, J., and Downs, M. (1978). *Hearing in Children* (2nd ed.). Baltimore: Williams and Wilkins.

Nozza, R., and Wilson, W. (1984). Masked and unmasked pure-tone thresholds of infants and adults: development of auditory frequency selectivity and sensitivity. *Journal of Speech and Hearing Research, 27:* 613–622.

Oller, D. (1980). The emergence of speech sounds in infancy. *Child Phonology.* Vol. 1: *Production,* ed. G. Yeni-Kamshian, J. Kavanaugh, and C. Ferguson. New York: Academic Press.

Rediehs, G. (1982). Social and cognitive development: the first three years. *Seminars in Speech, Language, and Hearing,* ed. J. Marlowe, *3:* 1–13.

Rees, N. (1980). Learning to talk and understand, in *Introduction to Communication Disorders,* ed. T. Hixon, L. Shriberg, and J. Saxman. Englewood Cliffs, N.J.: Prentice-Hall.

Schwartz, R. (1984). The phonologic system: normal acquisition, in *Speech Disorders in Children,* ed. J. Costello. San Diego: College-Hill Press.

Sroufe, A. (1979). Socioemotional development, in *Handbook of Infant Development,* ed. J. Ofosky. New York: Wiley.

Stark, R. (1980). Stages of speech development in the first year of life, in *Child Phonology.* Vol. 1: *Production,* ed. G. Yeni-Kamshian, J. Kavanaugh, and C. Ferguson. New York: Academic Press.

Stern, D. (1977). *The First Relationship: Infant and Mother.* Cambridge, Mass.: Harvard University Press.

Van Riper, C., and Emerick, L. (1984). *Speech Correction: An Introduction to Speech Pathology and Audiology* (7th ed.). Englewood Cliffs, N.J.: Prentice-Hall.

Wasz-Hockert, J., Lind, J., Vourenkoski, V., Partanen, T., and Valonne, E. (1968). *The Infant Cry: A Spectrographic and Auditory Analysis.* London: Heinemann Medical Books.

Winitz, H. (1969). *Articulatory Acquisition and Behavior.* New York: Appleton-Century-Crofts.

Zemlin, W. (1981). *Speech and Hearing Science Anatomy and Physiology* (2nd ed.). Englewood Cliffs, N.J.: Prentice-Hall.

3

The Physical Mechanisms of Communication

As we have seen in the first two chapters, the baby possesses a central nervous system that enables the hearing mechanism and the speech-voicing systems to participate in human communication. Primitive hearing and voicing responses become more complex as the infant matures. In this chapter, we will look briefly at the basic physical mechanisms that are used in aural-oral communication. We will then examine the function or physiology of the various sites. Let us begin with an overview of the human nervous system, which will lead us to an understanding of the anatomy and physiology of the ear and the hearing system. Finally, we will study the structures and function of the speech and voicing mechanisms, primarily the respiratory system, the larynx, and the resonating-articulating structures of the throat, mouth, and nose.

It is important for the reader to realize while studying this chapter that the physical mechanisms described do not function independently of one another during communication. Sometimes a discussion of a particular anatomic site and its function can so capture our attention that we forget that the structures and systems being studied do not in actuality operate independently from other such parts and systems. In this chapter, we will look briefly at the anatomy and physiology of those anatomic sites that play a primary role in aural-oral communication (the understanding and expression of spoken sounds and words). Before we can appreciate the magnitude and effects of communication handicaps, we need to have some appreciation of normal structure and function. It must also be remembered that the various anatomical sites we discuss not only play a primary role in communication, but have other functions; for example, although the oral cavity plays a primary role in speech, it is vital in breathing, feeding, and other biologic functions as well. For the student requiring greater in-depth understanding of human anatomy and physiology related to communication, we will cite for further study the work of particular authors who present much more extensive descriptions than will be found here.

THE NERVOUS SYSTEM

The remarkable ability of the human being to communicate so efficiently is related primarily to a most complex nervous system that permits (and even facilitates) communication between a person and his or her environment, other creatures, and other people. While other animal nervous systems may have particular features that permit them to perform a particular behavior "better" than human beings (for example, predator birds have more acute eyesight than humans, while the porpoise may have a more advanced auditory system), it is the complex human brain that allows the human being to understand and use so well the various subtleties of human language. The nervous system can be grossly divided into two parts, the **central nervous system** (CNS) and the **peripheral nervous system** (PNS). We will consider each separately.

Central Nervous System

While both the brain and the spinal column are considered the two primary structures of the CNS, it is the highly intricate brain that enables the human to engage in high-level functions, such as reading a book and remembering for future reference particular parts of that book. For many years, the localizationists mapped particular areas of the surface of the brain, the **cortex,** designating a specific area of the brain as having a specific function; for example, in 1882, Wernicke felt that a particular posterior area of the temporal lobe had much to do with the understanding of spoken language (Brodmann Area 42 of the temporal lobe is still known today as Wernicke's area). Today, there is greater appreciation of the nonlocalization view, which feels that, while discrete areas of the brain may indeed have some specificity of function, the various areas of the brain function holistically together.

The major portion of the brain is composed of the left and right *cerebral hemispheres.* Each of these two hemispheres is a grossly symmetrical, near-mirror image of the other, although in recent years subtle anatomical, structural differences between the two hemispheres have been found.

There are four major lobes in each hemisphere. The **frontal lobe** (anterior to the fissure of Rolando) contains the primary motor cortex and apparently those cortical areas that have much to do with intellect and wisdom. The **parietal lobe** (which begins immediately posterior to the fissure of Rolando) contains the primary body-sensory cortex and is believed vital for overall sensorimotor functioning. Among the functions of the **occipital lobe** appear to be visual perception and recognition; this area is thought to be a vital cortical one for the ability to read. The **temporal lobe,** located below the Sylvius fissure, contains primary auditory cortex and is thought to contribute to overall listening and the ability to understand what others are saying. For a more complete description of both classical localization and nonlocalization specific to the functions of the four lobes in each hemisphere, the reader might wish to read the summary presentation of Kertesz (1979).

One only has to look at the coronal section of a hemisphere (Figure 3-1) to appreciate the nonlocalization argument. That is, much of the localization argument deals with the function of the cortex. However, as we see in the coronal view, only a relatively small part of the brain is composed of cerebral cortex; most of the brain area is composed of subcortical structures. For a detailed look at neuroanatomy, with much focus given to the cerebral hemispheres, the reader should become familiar with the classic new edition of Netter's *Nervous System* (1986). (Netter, a physician-artist, has created many anatomical plates, each with detailed narrative descriptions of the anatomy and physiology of the particular site.) The outer layer of the hemisphere contains the *cerebral cortex,* which is approximately a quarter of an inch thick. At the time of birth, the cortex contains millions of *neurons* (although we lose cortical neurons throughout our life-span, we never have more than we started with as a newborn). The neurons are neatly arranged in six layers within the cortex; each layer contains neurons with a similar function, such as the motor neurons in layer five or the sensory neurons in layer four. The neuron

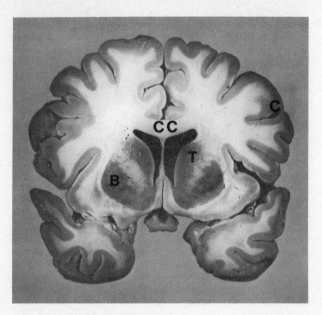

FIGURE 3-1   A photograph of a coronal section of the brain. *B* is placed on the basal ganglia; *T* is on the thalamus; *CC* is the corpus callosum (the bundle of nerve fibers that connect the two hemispheres); *C* is placed on a section of the cerebral cortex. Used with permission of University of Arizona, Tucson.

is the smallest functional unit of the nervous system; each neuron is composed of a **nucleus** in a cell body. Extending from the neuronal body is one long fiber called the **axon;** the axon conducts the nervous impulse away from the neuron. Picking up impulses and transmitting them to the neuron are the **dendrites,** tiny receptive fibers. Below the cortex, we see the white matter of the hemisphere, which is composed of millions of axons compressed together, appearing as one white field. These nerve fibers are either ascending to the brain, descending from it, or crossing over (transverse fibers). More centrally in the coronal section, we see the **thalamus (a** gray body of neurons), which has much to do with the organization of sensory impulses. More laterally and deep within the hemisphere, we see the gray bodies of several neuronal nuclei, the *basal ganglia,* which have much to do with the organization and control of motor impulses.

The *cerebellum* is central and lies below the cerebral hemispheres, and plays an important coordinating role in the central nervous system. Many sensory impulses from various peripheral sites (such as many fibers from the auditory system) pass into the cerebellum; many motor fibers exit from it. This sensorimotor mixing enables the cerebellum to coordinate motor behavior, such as rate, force, and direction of motor movements. The **brainstem** is the bridging structure between the two hemispheres and the spinal cord below. Many of the nerve fibers originating in the cortex, basal ganglia, and thalamus descend into the brainstem. The **cranial nerves** (part of the peripheral nervous system) originate in the brainstem. From peripheral sensory stations, such as the ears, the eyes, and the muscles of the limbs, come sensory impulses into the brainstem. It would appear, then, that much of the brainstem serves as a conduit for the motor nerves descending from above and for the sensory nerves ascending from below and from their peripheral sites. The brainstem leads into the **spinal cord** or *column* (the upper end of which is known as the **medulla**). The spinal column consists of millions of axons traveling in numerous nerve tracts, ending at various gray neuronal nuclei, all stationed in sequence throughout the length of the spinal cord. There are 31 pairs of spinal nuclei, each with their own spinal nerves that carry either motor or sensory impulses out to or away from the muscles and glands located in the neck, trunk, and four extremities.

The central nervous system is so organized that the right side of the body receives its innervations from the left cerebral hemisphere; left-sided body functions are directed by the right cerebral hemisphere. Massive bundles of motor nerve fibers are organized into two tracts, the **pyramidal** and **extrapyramidal tracts.** The pyramidal tract is most developed among mammals in the human, originating as axons leaving the motor cortex and descending without interruption to the medulla, at the top of the spinal cord, where the fibers cross over to the opposite side, continuing down to and terminating at the appropriate spinal nucleus. While extrapyramidal fibers originate in the cortex, they descend to a number of gray nuclei in the thalamus and basal ganglia areas, where it is speculated that some sensorimotor "neural mixing" takes place. The pyramidal tract functions like a "neural turnpike," with impulses traveling straight through on axons without stopping; the extrapyramidal fibers could be likened to a "neural country road," stopping and cross-checking as they descend to lower levels. This illustration may demonstrate the difference in functional capability between the two tracts:

A woman is carrying a paper cup full of coffee across her mother-in-law's newly carpeted living room. The cup is much too full, and the coffee is splashing up, burning her fingers. Her first impulse is to drop the cup and save her fingers (an extrapyramidal-tract reaction). Her wisdom and experience tell her that to drop the coffee cup will result in a big mess on the floor and the wrath of her mother-in-law. Using pyramidal-tract function, she continues to grip the coffee cup and search for a nearby piece of furniture to set it on. The pyramidal tract can occasionally override more primitive sensorimotor reactions and then make possible a planned, deliberate motor response. Pyramidal tract functioning allows us to do something volitionally, making motor choices among several motor options (such as whether to drop or hold the cup).

Among the higher cerebral functions made possible by the complex human central nervous system is the ability to understand and express language. There is overwhelming evidence that language functions appear to lateralize to the left cerebral hemisphere as the infant-child matures. As we discuss normal language in the next chapter, we will review some of the evidence that supports language lateralization. The clinical disorder **aphasia,** particularly as described in adults in Chapter 10, is usually the result of the patient's acquiring a left-hemisphere lesion from a stroke or an accident. Although language functions appear to be lateralized in the brain, the normal functions of motor speech (voicing, articulation, prosody, resonance) appear to require intact bilateral cerebral participation (as discussed in Chapter 5).

Peripheral Nervous System

The nerves that bring sensory information into the CNS and deliver motor impulses to peripheral glands and muscles are collectively known as the *peripheral nervous system*. Those 12 paired nerves that make their entry into or exit from the cranial space that houses the central nervous system are known as the *cranial nerves*. The 31 paired nerves that make their entry into or exit from the nuclei of the spinal column are known as the *spinal nerves*.

All of the 12 cranial nerves have some function specific to communication. They are listed serially (I through XII) in the descending anatomic order in which they are found in the brainstem and medulla:

    I. Olfactory (located under the anterior base of each hemisphere), serves the sense of smell

    II. Optic (originates in retina), serves vision

    III. Oculomotor (upper pons), eye movements

    IV. Trochlear (lateral, upper pons), eye movements

    V. Trigeminal (mid-pons), motor: jaw movements; sensory: face

    VI. Abducens (lower pons), eye movements

    VII. Facial (base of pons, upper medulla), motor: facial muscles; sensory: anterior two-thirds of tongue, soft palate

    VIII. Auditory (base of pons, upper medulla), sensory for hearing and vestibular system

    IX. Glossopharyngeal (upper medulla), motor: pharynx; sensory: posterior one-third of tongue, pharynx

    X. Vagus (mid-medulla), motor: larynx, pharynx, soft palate, diaphragm, heart, abdominal viscera; sensory: heart, lungs, larynx, throat, GI tract, external ear

    XI. Accessory (lower medulla), motor: large muscles of head, neck, shoulders

    XII. Hypoglossal (lower medulla), motor: many muscles of tongue, supralaryngeal muscles

The *spinal column* is grossly divided so that the center of the column is composed of ascending or descending nerve tracts. At 31 levels of the spinal column, there are anterior and posterior nuclei. From the anterior nuclei, the 31 paired motor nerves exit that innervate (depending on their level and site) the muscles of the chest, the abdomen, the anal-genital area, and the four extremities. The posterior nuclei or ganglia in the spinal cord have sensory functions. Sensory nerves come into the posterior spinal nuclei from various peripheral sites, such as glands, tissues, joints, and muscles. Much of the peripheral sensory information is "handled" reflexively at the spinal level, where various sensorimotor reflexes may occur. Or the sensory information may be passed up into the central nervous system through the medulla into the cerebellum, where sensorimotor adjustments may be made. Or the sensory information may travel to the thalamus, where it may be collated and processed. Some sensory impulses from the spinal ganglia probably arrive directly (with little filtering or adjustment along the way) to the sensory cortex.

THE HEARING SYSTEM

Basic to human communication is hearing. We will look at how the ear miraculously converts physical sound waves into neural impulses by a process known as **transduction.** Our understanding of hearing will be facilitated by a separate look at the structure and function of the outer ear, the middle ear, the inner ear, and the central auditory system.

The Outer Ear

In some animals, the **auricle,** what we see as the outer ear, is very large and movable (horse, rabbit), enabling the animal to locate a sound without any movement of the head. The human external ear is smaller, and fixed on the sides of our heads. The many shapes and sizes of ears we see in the people around us seem to have no particular relevance to an individual's hearing sensitivity. The rounded auricle collects those sound waves coming to it and funnels them into the **ear canal** or *auditory meatus* (see Figure 3–2). The ear canal originates in the auricle and extends about 2.5 cm (in the adult), terminating at the *eardrum,* or *tympanic membrane.* The walls of the canal, or meatus, contain many hair follicles and cells that secrete *cerumen,* a waxlike substance that apparently protects the outer ear from foreign objects and insects. For a detailed look at the auditory mechanism and its function, there are a number of basic texts that provide detailed pictures and sketches of the various sites within the auditory system, including Daniloff, Schuckers, and Feth (1980), Giolas (1982), and Zemlin (1981).

The Middle Ear

The sound waves that travel through the ear canal eventually hit the tympanic membrane, setting it in vibration. In effect, the tympanic membrane separates the outer ear from the **middle ear.** The tympanic membrane is the outer, lateral wall of the small middle ear, which is "about the size of a garden pea with a ceiling, a floor and walls" (Van Riper and Emerick, 1984, p. 405). There are three tiny bones (the smallest in the body), known as the **ossicles,** that articulate with one another and make up the structures within the middle ear; they are the *malleus,* the *incus,* and *stapes.* The malleus (a hammer-shaped bone) is attached to the inner side of the

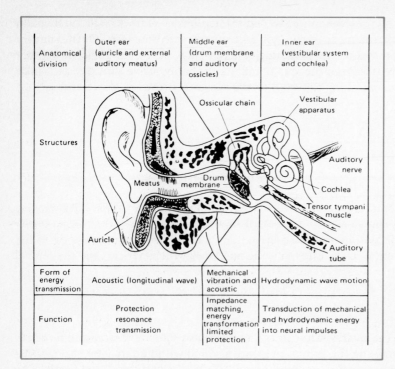

Anatomical division	Outer ear (auricle and external auditory meatus)	Middle ear (drum membrane and auditory ossicles)	Inner ear (vestibular system and cochlea)
Structures			
Form of energy transmission	Acoustic (longitudinal wave)	Mechanical vibration and acoustic	Hydrodynamic wave motion
Function	Protection resonance transmission	Impedance matching, energy transformation limited protection	Transduction of mechanical and hydrodynamic energy into neural impulses

FIGURE 3-2 A schematic drawing of the anatomical divisions of the hearing mechanisms and their functional roles. Used with permission of Zemlin, W. R. (1981), from *Speech and Hearing Science* (2nd ed.). Englewood Cliffs, N.J.: Prentice-Hall.

tympanic membrane; when the tympanic membrane vibrates, it sets the malleus into vibration. Because the malleus is attached to the incus, it makes the incus vibrate. The incus in turn causes the stapes, to which it is attached, to vibrate.

The middle-ear cavity is ventilated by the **eustachian tube,** which originates in the nasopharynx and terminates lateral to the tympanic membrane. Middle-ear ventilation is essential for maintaining a cavity atmosphere, which permits free vibration of the ossicles by keeping fluids out of the middle ear and maintaining the same air pressure within the middle ear and outside in outer ear. Fluid in the middle ear (such as might be experienced when one has a cold) and negative pressure (such as one might feel when the eustachian tube remains closed when changing altitudes while flying) can produce temporary conductive hearing impairment.

The transduction process (changing energy from one form to another) begins in the middle ear. The displacements of the tympanic membrane in response to the sound-wave variations produces a mechanical motion. This motion in turn sets up vibratory patterns in the ossicular chain. The vibrations move across the ossicular chain, thanks to the tensions provided by the small muscles in the middle ear (the *stapedius* and the *tensor tympani*) and their supporting ligaments and tendons. Finally, the vibrating stapes is attached to a tiny footplate that fits on the *oval window* of the inner ear. The footplate of the stapes has a much smaller area than the inner surface of the tympanic membrane. This reduction in size from one end of the ossicular chain to the other reduces the amount of energy allowed to pass through the ossicles into the inner ear, which has the effect of increasing the pressure or force on the fluid within the inner ear. As the footplate vibration moves the fluid in the inner ear, we now have hydraulic movement as our energy source. For the beginning student, McClelland (1985) gives an excellent description of the transduction process and overall function of the middle ear in far greater detail than we have presented in this chapter.

The Inner Ear

The eighth cranial nerve, the auditory nerve, originates in the two principle structures of the inner ear. The three *semicircular canals* form the vestibular portion of the inner ear, which plays a primary role in helping us maintain balance. The second major structure of the inner ear is the snail-shell-shaped *cochlea,* which transforms the vibratory-hydraulic displacement energy within it into neural impulses and sends them to the brain. Similar to the retina, which translates visual physical energy into neural impulses, the cochlea converts acoustic energy into neural impulses, which are then interpreted as hearing by central structures within the central nervous system.

The footplate of the stapes is attached directly to the **oval window;** stapedial movements cause the oval window to displace inward, moving the fluids within the cochlea. The vestibule or basilar end of the cochlea begins at the oval window. The cochlea, which coils upward, making about two and a half full turns, is divided down the middle by the *basilar membrane* for most of its entire length up into the apex of the cochlear shell. If we were to remove the cochlea and straighten it out, we would see that the chamber above the basilar membrane has its origins at the oval window; the fluid within the upper chamber continues into the lower chamber at the end of the basilar membrane. The lower chamber ends at the **round window.** Each time the oval window is displaced inward, the displaced fluid within the cochlea bulges the round window outward into the middle ear. This fluid movement produces a corresponding movement of the basilar membrane.

Situated on the basilar membrane is a third duct, the *cochlear duct,* in which is found the *organ of Corti,* which contains many fine hair cells. These tiny hair cells, when displaced by the traveling wave of cochlear fluid, generate "an alternative current whose waveform closely approximates the original acoustic pressure wave at the tympanic membrane" (McClelland, 1985, p. 156). These neural impulses spread out of the cochlea and become part of the auditory portion of the eighth nerve. Of some interest is that the fifteen thousand or more hair cells within the organ of Corti are all laid out with some frequency specificity; that is, at the basilar end of the cochlea are those hair cells that seem to represent high-frequency hearing, while at the apical end of the cochlea are housed those hair cells that, when stimulated, seem to "report" the lower frequencies. This same frequency-specific layout can be found within the central nerve itself and within the *cochlear nucleus* (the termination of cranial nerve number eight and the beginning of the auditory pathways) in the medulla.

The Central Auditory System

A brief look at the central auditory system finds cranial nerve number eight conducting the impulses from the cochlea to the first synaptic station within the cochlear nucleus in the medulla. From the cochlear nucleus originate the auditory pathways; some go to the cerebellum; others go to the inferior colliculi in the brainstem. Most auditory fibers (if not all) end up for a final synaptic mixing in the posterior part of the thalamus, in the **medial geniculate** bodies. From the geniculates, the pathways go directly to the primary auditory cortex (Brodmann area 41). It has also been reported by Penfield and Roberts (1959) and Minckler (1972) that massive bundles of auditory fibers leave the posterior-lateral walls of the thalamus (the pulvinar bodies) and go directly to posterior-temporal-lobe–inferior-parietal-lobe cortex. These thalmocortical fibers may well play an essential role in the understanding of the spoken word.

THE VOCAL MECHANISMS

As we saw in the first two chapters, the vocal mechanisms at birth and early infancy begin producing vegetative sounds that seem to accompany and signal various biologic and emotional need states. As infants mature, their vocalizations become more complex. As babies use the voice in communication, they begin to change their vocal stress patterns and to take turns with the listener. The linguistic utterance requires a quick respiratory inspiration followed by a prolonged expiration, which activates the laryngeal vocal folds, producing the voice. As we look at the structure and function of our vocal mechanisms, we will first consider the vocal activating system, respiration; secondly, we will review the laryngeal vibrating system, which produces phonation (voice); finally, we will examine the pharyngeal, oral, and nasal cavities as components of the resonance system specific to their contribution to vocal resonance.

The Respiratory System

The primary function of the respiratory system is to sustain life through the continuous exchange of gases; that is, primarily the exchange of carbon dioxide for oxygen. Since the body cannot store oxygen, it requires a continuous renewal of its oxygen supply, usually from 12 to 18 inspirations-expirations (breath cycles) per minute. For the majority of persons without some kind of respiratory disease, the breath cycle continues for each of us almost unnoticed and without difficulty.

       The human as a species demonstrates far more control of the breathing mechanism than any other mammal. When singing or talking, we have the capability of taking in a quick inhalation followed by a prolonged expiration, which activates the phonation for singing or talking. The musculoskeletal thorax, as seen as part of the drawing in Figure 3–3, can expand its size by active muscle contraction. On inspiration, for example, when the **diaphragm** (a composite of many muscle fibers and tendons) contracts, it descends, increasing the vertical dimension of the chest; lifting the shoulders also increases the vertical dimension of the chest, but not as efficiently as diaphragmatic movement. The horizontal dimension of the chest can be increased by action of the **intercostals** and other chest muscles. The outside of the lung adheres to the inside of the chest wall. Therefore, when the chest expands by active muscular contraction, the lungs within the chest are stretched, increasing their size, resulting in a decrease in density of the air within the lungs (intrapulmonary air). With the reduction of pulmonary air density, the outside atmospheric air comes rushing in. On expiration, the chest wall becomes smaller (both by muscle contraction and by relaxation of several inspiratory muscles). The abdominal muscles can also contract, assisting in expiration, applying some force from below on

FIGURE 3–3   The musculoskeletal thorax, identifying four structures: neck accessory muscles, ribs, sternum, and large chest muscle (*pectoralis major*).

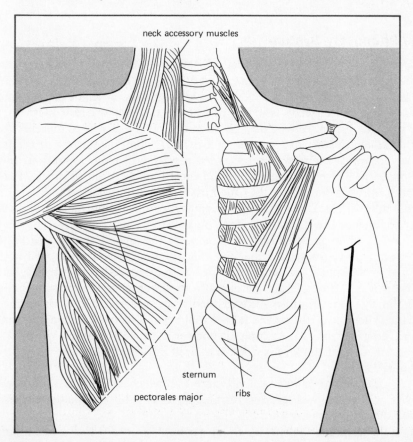

the ascending (relaxed) diaphragm. The lungs become smaller. Normal lung tissue is highly elastic, and recoils back to a smaller size when no longer stretched. As the lungs collapse, the air within them develops a greater density than atmospheric air, and the pulmonary air rushes out of them until intrapulmonary and atmospheric pressures are the same. At this point, the inspiration phase begins again. In summary, inspiration is related to thoracic expansion (greater lung area produces lower intrapulmonary pressures), while expiration is related to a decrease in thoracic size (less lung area produces denser air). The movement of air in and out of the lungs is achieved, then, by differential air pressures created by the active muscular contraction (and relaxation) of thoracic and abdominal muscles.

The inherent forces, active muscular contraction and the natural elasticity of the lungs, work, for example, during sleep in a natural, synergic way. Our "in" breath is about as long as our "out" breath. When we sing or talk, however, volitional forces are able to change the normal in-and-out pattern, enabling us to take a quick inspiration and follow it with a prolonged expiration, which we use for phonation. For a clear and detailed understanding of the mechanisms of breathing, the reader might wish to examine two references: Hixon and Abbs (1980) and Zemlin (1981).

The Phonatory System

Phonation, or voice, is produced in the larynx by vibration of the vocal folds. While phonation is a vital part of communication, the primary function of the larynx is to guard the airway against aspiration, the inhalation of fluids or other matter into the airway. The larynx sits at the top of the trachea, where it plays its primitive valving role. When we swallow, the larynx elevates and several muscle valves in the larynx come together in a valving shut-off; this combined lifting of the larynx and valve closure of the airway protects the airway well from aspiration. In some individuals with structural damage to the vocal folds (a result of cancer, for instance) or with muscular impairment of the larynx (perhaps as part of a degenerative neuromuscular disease), the valving mechanism can be compromised and the patient may experience life-threatening choking spells.

The human voice represents perhaps the highest function of the larynx in the mammal. To appreciate the view that the human voice may well not be some kind of evolutionary accident, one only has to listen to the sheer beauty and control of the voice as heard in an operatic aria or the singing of a popular ballad or the vocal interpretations of an accomplished actor or actress. The communicative and artistic functions of the larynx take it well beyond its basic valving responsibilities. The average person, for example, is unaware of the valving role of the larynx, and when asked what the larynx does, may well answer, "We make our voices in our throats."

The larynx can be seen in Figure 3-4, which shows a left-lateral view of the larynx, with the **cricoid cartilage** forming the base of the larynx; the **thyroid cartilage** articulates above the cricoid. In this photograph of the larynx, we see the right **arytenoid cartilage** (the left arytenoid has been removed) sitting on top of the pos-

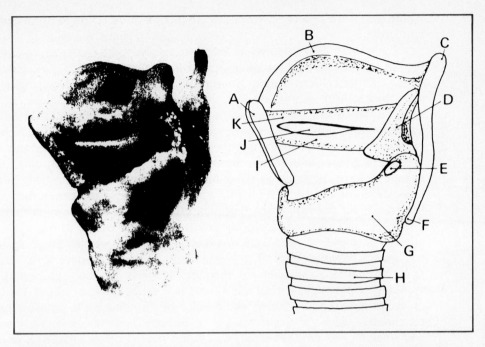

FIGURE 3–4 A lateral left view of the larynx is shown with the left thyroid cartilage removed. The untouched photograph is remarkable in its view of the ventricle opening between the true folds and the false folds. Structures may be identified by viewing the line drawing letter identifications: (*A*) cut edge at lamina of thyroid cartilage; (*B*) arch of the thyroid cartilage; (*C*) superior horn of the thyroid cartilage; (*D*) arytenoid cartilage, right; (*E*) articular facet of the cricoid and arytenoid cartilage; (*F*) inferior horn of the thyroid cartilage; (*G*) cricoid cartilage; (*H*) tracheal ring; (*I*) vocal fold, right; (*J*) ventricle; (*K*) ventricular fold, or false fold.

terior cricoid signet. The thyroid cartilage (half of which has been removed) is shield-shaped, and forms the prominent anterior wall of the larynx; in many young men, we can see the prominent thyroid cartilage (Adam's apple). The vocal folds originate just below the thyroid notch (the notch one can feel with the fingertips just above the middle of the thyroid cartilage). From the thyroid cartilage, the vocal folds extend posteriorly to the anterior base of the arytenoid cartilage. The two pyramid-shaped arytenoids move and rotate on their mounts on the cricoid cartilage by action of several intrinsic muscles in the larynx. For example, when the posterior cricoarytenoid muscles contract, they move the arytenoid cartilages in such a way as to pull the vocal folds apart; the posterior cricoarytenoid muscles, therefore, are known as laryngeal abductors (they separate the vocal folds). The lateral cricoarytenoids (laryngeal adductors) rotate the arytenoids together in such a way that they adduct the folds together. This intrinsic muscle action is extremely rapid, permitting the speaker, while voicing a word, to produce in milliseconds the voiceless consonants within that word by a rapid vocal-fold abduction often followed by an equally rapid adduction.

Another intrinsic muscle function is to lengthen (stretching and tensing) or to shorten (relaxing and thickening) the folds; either action has some effect on pitch level. Thinner folds vibrate more quickly, producing higher frequencies (pitches), with thicker folds vibrating more slowly, producing lower frequencies. The area between the vocal folds is known as the **glottis.** When the vocal folds are brought together (adduction), they are in the phonation position. The outgoing airflow builds up below the glottis, causing increased subglottal air pressure. When this subglottal pressure is greater than the air pressure above the approximated folds, the airflow pushes between the folds, in effect blowing them apart. The elasticity and mass of the vocal folds and the effect of a vacuum that builds up between them caused by the passing air (known as the Bernoulli effect) brings the separated folds back together again. This opening-closing produces what is known as one cycle of phonation. The speed of the vibratory cycle is dependent on the mass, elasticity, and tension of the vocal folds. Tiny vocal folds in babies produce high voices. Nine-year-old children, regardless of their sex (puberty has not yet begun), produce speaking voices very near middle C on the musical scale, or about 260 vibrations or cycles per second. The speaking voice of an adult male, whose larynx is approximately twice the size it was before puberty, is about an octave lower than it was when he was nine years old. Its pitch is near C below middle C, or about 125 cycles per second. The adult female, whose larynx is usually half again as big as it was when she was nine, typically speaks near G below middle C, which is close to 200 cycles per second. The normal pitch of the speaking voice is primarily determined by the size and mass of the vocal folds.

Frequency changes (which can be measured on frequency-analyzing equipment) or pitch changes (the perceptual change in pitch) are produced by the action of several of the intrinsic muscles of the larynx. When the **cricothyroid muscles** at the anterior-lateral borders of the larynx contract, they produce an elongation of the vocal folds, which has the effect of tensing the folds. The thinner, tenser folds produce higher frequency vocalization (higher pitch). A lowering of pitch is produced by the relaxation of the cricothyroid muscles and the shortening of the **thyroarytenoid** muscles (vocal folds). When the vocal folds themselves contract by action of their thyroarytenoids, they in effect become thicker, producing a slower rate of vibratory cycle. For a much more detailed and graphic look at laryngeal functions of phonation, including frequency and intensity, the reader may wish to consult Broad (1973) and Zemlin (1981).

Remembering that voice is basically the product of an aerodynamic event—that is outgoing airflow causes the vocal folds to vibrate—changes in intensity or loudness of the voice are produced by changes in **subglottal pressure.** A larger expiratory air volume meets the resistance of a closed glottis, resulting in an increase in subglottal pressure. With increased subglottal pressure, when the airflow finally breaks through and flows between the approximated folds, the folds are blown apart with greater force. The greater velocity, which produces in turn a greater displacement of vocal fold, results in an increase in intensity of the phonation without necessarily any change in frequency of pitch. Many times, however, when speaking in a louder voice, people also elevate the pitch (a trained singer or speaker can learn to increase intensity without variation in frequency). It does appear that an increase in vocal intensity is basically produced by increasing the expiratory volume of air used to produce the vocal utterance.

The Resonance System

When we say that the larynx is at the base of the vocal tract, we are basically saying that the sound waves created by vibrations in the larynx travel up through the other structures of the airway, primarily the hypopharynx, the oropharynx, the oral cavity, the nasopharynx, and the nasal cavities. The source of the voice is the larynx. The eventual outflow of sound waves that are recognized as the human voice is the result of the filtering of that sound by the resonance system. The first structure of the vocal tract through which the sound waves travel is immediately adjacent to and above the larynx, the *hypopharynx* (H) (see Figure 3–5). After studying the hypopharynx by videoendoscopy (putting an illuminated lens behind the velum, looking down at the pharynx and the larynx, and viewing the picture on a television monitor), we find that the hypopharynx and the *oropharynx* (O) (the throat area at the level of the oral cavity) are constantly changing shape as resonating cavities. In a fascinating videoendoscopic tape distributed by the Voice Foundation (1985) of two famous impersonators, Rich Little and Mel Blanc, we can see that much of the muscle action used to produce many different voice impersonations takes place in the pharyngeal cavities. The height of the pharynx changes as the larynx rises (shortens the pharynx) or lowers (lengthens the pharynx). The overall shape and width of the pharynx changes as the tongue comes back and the posterior and lateral pharyngeal walls change shape. Although the pharynx plays an important role in shaping vocal resonance, it obviously plays two other vital roles, as a conduit for both the airway and the passage of nutrients from the oral cavity to the esophagus.

The oral cavity is constantly changing. We see in Figure 3–5 that it is formed anteriorly by the lips and the front teeth with the tongue, which is constantly changing positions as we speak, forming the oral cavity floor. The overall opening of the mouth and openness within the oral cavity have primary influences on oral resonance.

Anyone who has been in a choir or taken a singing lesson remembers the teacher's reminder, ''Open your mouth.'' An open mouth will often facilitate vocal resonance. Laver (1980) describes as ''settings'' the overall configurations that an individual uses for resonance, such as the amount of lip action, the opening of the jaw, the height of the tongue, and so forth. We all have our own setting of the vocal tract, which contributes to each person's unique sound. The pitch and resonance of our voices are what contribute to each one's unique sound, so individualized that a few words on a telephone will usually allow the listener to recognize a familiar voice.

The roof of the oral cavity is formed anteriorly by the bony hard palate and posteriorly by the soft palate (also known as *velum*). Where the velum meets

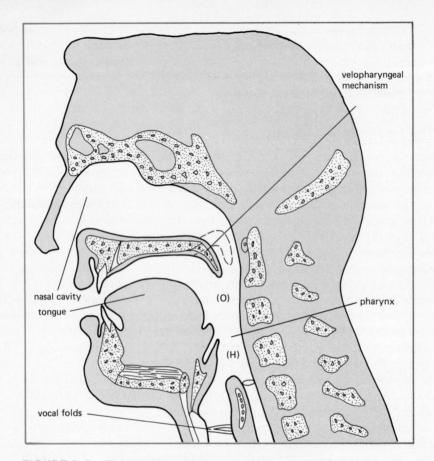

FIGURE 3–5 The vocal tract, depicting the shape of the oral and nasal cavities.

the pharynx is the beginning of the nasopharynx, which leads into the nasal cavity. This site, known as the **velopharyngeal port,** is the anatomic site where sound waves and airflow can be diverted out of the oral cavity or allowed to pass through into the nasopharynx and nasal cavity. The velum is a muscular, moving structure. It hangs down during normal breathing, which in effect connects the nasal cavity with the oral cavity. This nasal-oral coupling is the normal respiration configuration and the position required for the nasal resonance of the three nasal consonants in English: /m/, /n/, and /ŋ/. When the velum lifts itself by muscular action (sometimes assisted by the posterior pharyngeal wall moving in anteriorly a bit), the velopharyngeal port is closed. This closed position is required for the oral resonance of all the vowels and consonants in the English language except the three nasal sounds. If we were to say *banana,* for example, the initial /ba/ would require a raised velum, producing a closed port, the /n/ would require a rapid velar drop, with the next vowel /æ/ requiring closure again, only to be followed by another rapid drop for the next /n/, ending with an elevated velum again for the vowel /ɔ/. Failure to move the velum rapidly enough to match the phonemic demands of the utterance can result in a listener's perceiving the utterance as excessively nasal. Many problems of excessive nasal resonance, **hypernasality,** are related to faulty velopharyngeal closure, which could be related to a number of factors, such as cleft palate, a short velum, an injured palate, paralysis or weakness of the velopharyngeal muscles (such disorders are discussed in several subsequent chapters). A less common resonance disorder is **denasality,** insufficient nasal resonance, often related, in effect, to excessive velopharyngeal closure. The *nasopharynx,* the pharynx above the velar closure site, may become blocked with swollen tissues (perhaps because of allergies and colds) that will block the passage of sound waves and airflow through the nasal cavities. Excessive tonsil and adenoid tissue in the nasopharynx and nasal cavities will sometimes create enough obstruction to give the voice a denasal vocal quality.

THE MECHANISMS OF SPEECH

While the tongue is the most important structure for articulate speech, we will look also at other structures used in speech articulation, such as the lips, the teeth, the mandible, and the palate; then we will consider how these structures modify the outgoing airstream and sound waves by their movements and adjustments, shaping the consonants, vowels, and diphthongs of our spoken language.

The Tongue

Looking again at Figure 3–5, we can see that the tongue occupies most of the space of the oral cavity. The tongue body is a composite of intrinsic muscles, or muscles within it, that enable it to change its shape easily (curled, pointed, and so on). The extrinsic tongue muscles come from various sites, such as the hyoid bone, and insert into the tongue; the extrinsic muscles allow the tongue to be elevated, lowered, protruded, and retracted. How our tongue is postured, which Laver (1980, p. 43) calls "lingual settings," influences the overall sound and resonance of the voice. The production of vowels and diphthongs is primarily caused by the overall lingual setting and shape produced by these continuous movements of muscles that shape the oral cavity. Most consonants are produced by vocal-tract constriction, resulting in airflow restriction produced by precise movements of the tongue.

The Lips

The lips represent the end (or the beginning) of the oral vocal tract and play some role in overall vocal resonance. The labial role in speech, however, is primarily in articulation of some consonants, such as /m/ or /b/. The lips are composed of facial muscles (primarily the circular **orbicularis oris**) that enable the lips to pucker, to spread, to make a circle. The lips, as the entryway to the oral cavity and the most visible structure of the mouth, play a vital role in sucking, chewing, kissing, smiling (and other nonverbal affective behaviors).

The Teeth

The hard palate is circled on three sides by the *alveolar process,* or bony ridges that house the teeth sockets on the **maxilla** (or upper jaw). Occluding with the maxillary teeth are the **mandible** (lower jaw) teeth below, playing their vital role, the mastication of food. Our teeth primarily play this masticatory role, with their contribution to speech articulation somewhat secondary. However, a few English sounds, such as /f/ and /v/, are made by labial-dental contact, with the lower lip being tucked under the upper central incisors. The alveolar ridge behind the base of the maxillary teeth is an important contact point for the tongue tip for the production of such sounds as /n/, /s/, /z/, /t/, /d/.

The Mandible

The movement of the mandible plays a primary part in the quick opening or closing of the oral cavity. Some mandibular movement contributes to changes in the shape and size of the oral cavity needed for the production of different vowels. The normal speaker moves the mandible in quick synergic movements with the lips and tongue during normal speech. If, however, a speaker were to talk with a pipe in his mouth, the mandible would stay closed to trap the pipestem, which would require an immediate compensatory adjustment of the tongue and lips to maintain speech articulation. Optimal speech production and vocal resonance require continuous mandibular movement. Occasionally, we see patients with voice problems who speak with a clenched jaw most of the time, requiring the tongue to make all the muscle movements needed for vowel differentiation. Speaking this way, with the attendant lip and teeth closure, is inefficient, and often results in a muffled voice and sloppy articulation.

The Palate

The bony hard palate and the muscular soft palate make up the structure called the **palate,** the roof of the mouth. The hard palate begins at the alveolar ridge and tooth sockets of the maxillary dentition. It is an arched body with a vaulted ceiling that contributes greatly to oral resonance. The tongue moves freely, making its various articulatory movements within the vault of the palatal arch. Attached posteriorly to the hard palate just beyond the last molar tooth is the muscular soft palate. The soft palate is composed of four extrinsic muscles (paired) attached to the skull and the pharynx that lift the palate for voicing and lower it for breathing and for the voicing of nasal consonants. Usually, the entire soft palate, including the four paired muscles and the dangling appendage below, the *uvula,* is called the *velum.* We discussed previously, in the section "The Resonance System," the importance of the velum in its contact with the pharynx (at the site of the velopharyngeal port) in separating the oral cavity from the nasal cavity for oral vocal resonance.

The Function of Speech

While the mouth plays an important biologic role specific to digestion and respiration, one of its most complex functions physiologically is speaking. One has only to view an X-ray film, such as in cinefluorography, to appreciate the fantastic adjustments of the mouth required in normal speech. In connected speech, we see a series of overlapping, synergic movements characterized by movements of the jaw, the lips, changes in position and contour of the tongue, and continuous velopharyngeal adjustments. One might quickly conclude that articulation timed precisely with voicing or unvoicing along with required changes in resonance is just too complicated to be possible. How anyone is able to say 150 words or the equivalent of over 600 phonemes per minute defies a clear understanding. Also, as we discussed in Chapter 2, all of our articulated speech is added on to a prosodic pattern that is related to continuously changing respiratory and laryngeal adjustments. It becomes obvious that we speak in a "muscular synergic whole," very much as we use the clutch and gearshift in a car or serve a ball in tennis. For gear-shifting, or serving, or speaking, a particular muscle movement does not exist in isolation but is part of a collection of movements, many of them overlapping and many in rapid sequence.

The flow of articulatory movements used for the series of phones produced in running speech is continuous and constantly changing. Any one sound in isolation has a specific series of requirements or "targets, ideal places of contact, forces of contact, particular shapes, particular airflows, and particular patterns of movement necessary for a given speech sound" (Daniloff, 1973, p. 198). Speech articulation is a motor behavior that requires muscular specificity (one has to be on target, or listeners will hear another phone) with a continuously variable rate and rhythm. The sounds that precede or follow a particular sound will influence the production of that sound, a process often called sound **assimilation.** For example, if we said, "Tea, too," the production of the /t/ phone in each word will be slightly different; the high vowel /i/ in *tea* will bring the tongue tip slightly more forward than for the production of /t/ followed by /u/. Assimilation provides some evidence that speech production is organized by the nervous system in larger units than the single phone. Production of a phone in running speech is often simultaneous with the production of an adjacent phone preceding or following the target phone, a process known as **coarticulation.** If we said the word *tram,* the production of the phonemes /t/ and /r/ would be said sequentially, with the vowel /æ/ influencing their production and coarticulated (said at the same time) with the production of the final consonant /m/.

There are approximately (the number varies according to the classifier) 44 phonemes in the English language. These sounds of spoken English can be broadly classified into two categories, consonants and vowels. Within each category, they can be further classified as to the site of their production within the vocal tract and how they are produced (in effect, their physiology or method of production).

Consonants. During the production of consonants, the vocal tract is completely or nearly constricted or obstructed (vowels are made with a relatively open tract). In Table 3–1, the consonants in English are listed with examples of how each phoneme sounds, citing their place and manner of production separately. If the consonant is voiced, an asterisk is placed above it. We see the manner of production in the left-hand margin. There are seven consonants (/p/, /b/, /t/, /d/, /k/, /g/, /ʔ/) that are classified as *stops* or **plosives,** produced by a brief cessation of airflow, followed by a sudden release of the sound. It should be noted that some of the paired consonants are *cognates,* sounds that have a similar manner and place of production, differing only on the dimension of voice or no voice, such as /b/ and /p/. The **fricative** consonants (/f/, /v/, /θ/, /ð/, /s/, /z/, /ʃ/, /ʒ/, and /h/) are created by having an articulator form a tight constriction that produces some audible noise of airflow (voiced or unvoiced). All of the nine fricatives are also **continuants,** as they can be continued as long as the airflow is present. The **affricate** consonants (/tʃ/, /dʒ/) are combinations of a stop and a fricative. Only three consonants in the English language (/m/, /n/, and /ŋ/) are produced with the nasal port open, allowing their production to be nasalized. There are two commonly recognized liquid, or lateral, consonants: first, the lateral (/l/), produced by the tongue tip coming down from the central alveolar ridge with openings on the side of the tongue from which the airflow and sound wave escape; the second liquid is the consonant /r/ that is produced by two points of lingual constriction on the anterior hard palate (just posterior to the alveolar ridge) and on the anterior velum. The last consonant grouping in Table 3–1 is the glide sounds (/w/, /ʍ/, /j/), which are often classified as semivowels that become consonants because of added constriction. The anatomical sites of production, or the "Place of Production" in Table 3–1, basically work from front (bilabial) to back (glottal), involving the various structures of articulation: lips, teeth, sites on the tongue, hard palate, velum, and laryngeal glottis.

Through the processes of assimilation and coarticulation, the production of consonants is continually influenced by their adjacent vowels; that is, high front vowels, such as /i/, will often pull the point of articulation slightly forward, while back vowels, such as /u/, may bring lingual contact points slightly posterior.

Vowels. The production of vowels and **diphthongs** (a combination of two vowels) is produced by differential shaping of the vocal tract, primarily by movements of the mandible, lips, and tongue. For each of these phones there is a distinctive shaping of the vocal tract. For example, in the production of the /i/ vowel, the vocal tract is shaped by the tongue as high and forward as possible, with the jaws relatively approximated and the lips slightly withdrawn. We see in the vowel chart of Table 3–2 that the /i/ vowel is produced not only anteriorly but higher than any other vowel. Conversely, we see that the /ɑ/ vowel is produced lowest in the oral cavity, with the mandible dropped and the back of the tongue held low. None of the 15 vowels we have listed requires any kind of vocal-tract constriction (phones with

TABLE 3-1
The Consonants in English

Manner of Articulation	Place of Production						
	Bilabial	Labio-dental	Inter-dental	Alveolar	Palatal	Velar	Glottal
Stop or plosive	p (pa)			t (toe)		k (kick)	ʔ (bot̪le)
	b̊ (bat)			d̊ (doe)		g̊ (gap)	
Fricative		f (fat)	θ (thin)	s (sip)	ʃ (shoe)		h (hip)
		v̊ (vat)	ð̊ (that)	z̊ (zip)	ʒ̊)(azure)		
Affricate				tʃ (chop)			
				dʒ̊ (job)			
Nasal	m̊ (mom)			n̊ (nun)		ŋ̊ (sing)	
Lateral				l̊ (lap)			
				r̊ (rare)			
Glide	ẘ (wall)				j (yes)		
	ʍ (when)						

*Consonant is voiced.

constriction were classified as consonants). Diphthongs, such as /ai/ or /ɔi/, are assimilated blends of two separate vowels, producing a two-vowel glide. Production of a diphthong requires a quick sequence of vocal-tract adjustments, usually involving rapid movements of the tongue from low to high (or vice versa) and back to front or front to back.

The vowel chart basically follows the superior contour of the tongue at the particular front-central-back sites where each vowel is produced. Anteriorly, the tongue tip is highest and most forward for /i/. It is slightly lower and back for /I/. The mid-anterior position is seen for /e/ and slightly lower and back for /ɛ/. Both /æ/ and /a/ require the lowest anterior positioning. The /r/ consonant basically exists only in the initial or medial positions in words. Although we write the orthograph r in words like *bird* or *water,* we represent these sounds with the phonemes /ɝ/ and /ɚ/. In speech, /ɝ/ and /ɚ/ are actually vowels produced with the tongue in a high, central position, as shown in Table 3–2. The unstressed vowel at the end of a word like *polka* is represented by the phoneme /ə/, produced with the tongue with a medium height and a central anterior-posterior positioning. The /ʌ/ vowel has the same central positioning, slightly lower in height than /ə/. There are five back vowels with the tongue withdrawn posteriorly; each vowel is differentiated by a change in the vertical height of the tongue. In order from high to low are /ũ/ ʊ/, /o/, /ɔ/, /a/.

As discussed in Chapter 2, it is the vowels of speech that allow us to hear the voice of the speaker. The sound of one's voice, such as whether it is hoarse or

TABLE 3-2
A Vowel Chart Showing the Primary Production Site Within the Oral Cavity of Each English Vowel

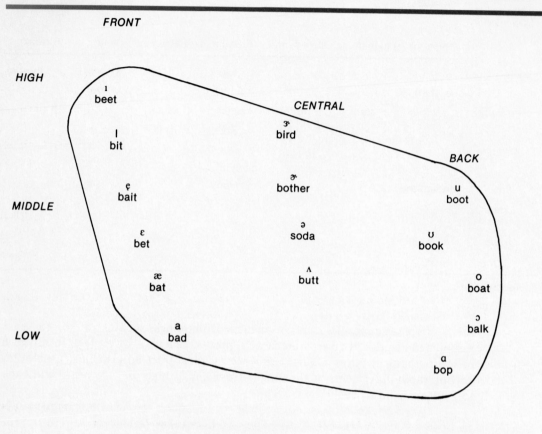

hypernasal, is determined by listening to vowel production. Each vowel of a particular language has its own distinctive production characteristics. While consonants play a primary role in speech intelligibility, the vowels we utter also contribute to how well someone else can understand us. For example, listening to an Australian speaker and an American speaker, one will perceive the same English with the same consonants imbedded in markedly different vowels and diphthongs. The consonants will sound similar to the two speakers, but they will experience real difficulties understanding each other's different vowels.

For the reader who desires a more thorough understanding of the structures and function of speech, these references are helpful: Daniloff (1984); Daniloff, Schuckers, and Feth (1980); Ferguson (1978); and Zemlin (1981, Chapter Four).

REVIEW QUESTIONS

It would appear that as the complex human central nervous system matures, it plays an increasingly more complicated role in communication. Feeding into the nervous system is the continuous bombardment of environmental sounds and speech signals of spoken language. Our review of hearing function in Chapter 2 and our look at the auditory system in this chapter have given us a glimpse of the intricacies of our ability to hear. Equally impressive are the expressive modalities (speech and voice) of language, seen in our ability to control an outgoing breath stream sufficiently to produce voice in the larynx, only to have these primitive laryngeal phonations shaped by a supraglottal resonance system. Then, as the airstream and sound waves reach the oral cavity (and to a lesser extent the nasal cavity), they are shaped by constrictions and openings within that cavity, producing what we perceive as consonants and vowels. In Chapter 4, we will look more closely at the development of language and speech in the young child. Let us first consider the following questions:

1. What evidence is there that language in communication between human beings is a species-specific ability?

2. Explain how external sound vibrations are converted by the ear and brain to neural impulses that are perceived as sound.

3. Is laryngeal voice possible without activation by the respiratory system? Explain.

4. What is meant by denasality? Hypernasality?

5. What is meant by articulatory assimilation and coarticulation?

6. In general, how does the production of consonants differ from the production of vowels?

REFERENCES

Broad, D. J. (1973). Phonation, in *Normal Aspects of Speech, Hearing, and Language,* ed. F. D. Minifie, T. J. Hixon, and F. Williams. Englewood Cliffs, N.J.: Prentice-Hall.

Daniloff, R. G. (1973). Normal articulation processes. In *Normal Aspects of Speech, Hearing, and Language,* ed. F. D. Minifie, T. J. Hixon, and F. Williams. Englewood Cliffs, N.J.: Prentice-Hall.

Daniloff, R., ed. (1984). *Speech Science.* San Diego: College-Hill Press.

Daniloff, R., Schuckers, G., and Feth, L. (1980). *The Physiology of Speech and Hearing.* Englewood Cliffs, N.J.: Prentice-Hall.

Ferguson, C. (1978). Learning to pronounce: the earliest stages of phonological development in the child, in *Communicative and Cognitive Abilities—Early Behavioral Assessment,* ed. F. Minifie and M. L. Lloyd. Baltimore: University Park Press.

Giolas, T. (1982). *Hearing Handicapped Adults.* Englewood Cliffs, N.J.: Prentice-Hall.

Hixon, T. J. and Abbs, J. H. (1980). Normal speech production, in *Introduction to Communication Disorders,* ed. T. J. Hixon, L. D. Shriberg, J. H. Saxman. Englewood Cliffs, N.J.: Prentice-Hall.

Kertesz, A. (1979). *Aphasia and Associated Dis-*

orders: Taxonomy, Localization, and Recovery. New York: Grune and Stratton.

Laver, J. (1980). *The Phonetic Description of Vocal Quality.* London: Cambridge University Press.

McClelland, K. D. (1985). Hearing mechanism, in *Speech, Language, and Hearing: Normal Processes and Disorders* (2nd ed.), ed. P. Skinner and R. Shelton. New York: Wiley.

Minckler, J. (1972). Functional organization and maintenance, in *Introduction to Neuroscience,* ed. J. Minckler. St. Louis: C. V. Mosby.

Netter, F. H. (1986). *CIBA Collection of Medical Illustrations, Vol. I, Nervous System.* West Caldwell, N.J.: CIBA Pharmaceutical Co.

Penfield, W. and Roberts, L. (1959). *Speech and Brain Mechanisms.* Princeton, N.J.: Princeton University Press.

Van Riper, C. and Emerick, L. (1984). *Speech Correction: An Introduction to Speech Pathology and Audiology* (7th ed.). Englewood Cliffs, N.J.: Prentice-Hall.

Voice Foundation (1985). *The Voice of the Impersonator* (videotape cassette developed by R. Feder). New York: The Voice Foundation.

Zemlin, W. R. (1981). *Speech and Hearing Science Anatomy and Physiology* (2nd ed.). Englewood Cliffs, N.J.: Prentice-Hall.

4

The Language of Communication

While many animals, birds, and reptiles show signs of communication with one another, only the human being can use an intricate and organized language system as part of communication. Much of human communication is nonverbal, employing various vocal noises, gestures, and postures to communicate feelings and wants to others. Such nonverbal communication is often spontaneous and frequently without intent, lacking the specificity and power of language. Language offers an organized way of communicating. Through the use of word symbols and a system of rules for the usage of the words, language offers the very young child an efficient way for communicating with others in the culture. We will look in this chapter at the various components of language and how they are used in communication. We will then consider the question of whether language is innate or learned as revealed by some of the theories of language acquisition. Finally, we will examine language as it develops from sounds to sentences in the first few years of life.

Human communication is an exchange of feelings, knowledge, and wants between two or more people. As we have seen in Chapters 1 and 2, such communication is both nonverbal and verbal. We have seen that in the first year of life, the baby communicates primarily by voicing changes accompanied by facial expression and gestures. These nonverbal vocalizations in the early part of life are primarily expressions of internal biologic states the baby is experiencing. We discussed in Chapter 2 that these nonverbal vocalizations become affective in nature, interpreted by those around the baby as communicating emotion. The vocalizations begin to develop prosodic patterns like the speech melody patterns that the child has been hearing. When we left our discussion of infant vocalization in Chapter 2, twelve- to thirteen-month-olds were just beginning to say their first words. The child's knowledge of the language (language *competence*) begins to show by the actual use of the language (language *performance*). While there are many who would argue that the child has already been showing both language competence and performance (such as following spoken directions) for many months before the arrival of the first words, the saying of the first words is usually heralded by **linguists** (scientists who study language) as the true beginning of the linguistic period of development.

THE COMPONENTS OF LANGUAGE

Linguistics is the scientific study of language, the structure of its sound systems, words, phrases, sentences, and meanings. We will now look closely at some of the components of language structure. Rather than define terms per se, we will discuss each of the components as part of overall linguistic structure.

Phonology

Phonology is the study of the sounds of speech. Since the beginning of the study of linguistics in the early 1900s, phonology has been a primary area of study, with linguists looking at children's developing sound patterns (Ingram, 1981). Much of current phonologic investigation focuses on uncovering the rules required for the use of speech sounds or phonemes as used in combination in syllables and words. In reading the phonological literature, there are four terms (*phone, allophone, pho-*

neme, and *phonetic*) that are often confusing; let us define each and distinguish them from one another. A **phone** is the actual speech sound produced by a speaker, whether accurate or not. **Allophones** are groups of phones that are variations of a speech sound but to the listener may be heard as a single phoneme. A **phoneme** is the smallest speech sound that can be identified by a listener and makes a semantic difference when combined with other phonemes. For example, with the word *hat,* written phonetically as *hæt,* by changing one phoneme, the vowel /æ/ to /I/, we change the word to *hit.* In this text, we indicate phonemes (speech sounds) when we place slash marks around the sounds, such as /a/ or /k/. In Chapter 2, we presented 52 individual phonemes listed as part of the International Phonetic Alphabet. **Phonetics** is the study of the physiology or motor production of speech sounds and their acoustic output.

Much of phonology is related to the application of specific rules of production. Vowels are produced with the voice. Consonants may be either voiced or unvoiced. There are specific rules for voicing or unvoicing in pluralization. If we were to pluralize the words *hat* and *hit,* we would add the unvoiced consonant /s/. Pluralization of a noun ending in a voiced consonant requires the use of the voiced cognate of /s/, the phoneme /z/. For example, if we were to pluralize the word *bed,* we would add the /z/ phoneme, writing the word in phonetics as *bɛdz.* Phonologic rules are not confined to the sounds within the word or the *segment,* but also to the sound of the voice before, during, after the segment, known as *suprasegmental* sounds. For example, questions require rising inflections, declarative statements require a downward inflection at the end, and so forth.

It would appear that children develop their phonologic skills in a systematic manner, attempting to produce the adult phonologic standard. Because of physical immaturity and relative inexperience in talking, children are basically forced to simplify the adult speech sound-production system into the sounds they can say. This simplification process will receive much focus in our discussion of the treatment of articulation disorders, in Chapter 10.

Syntax

Syntax is the study of where words and suprasegmental stress patterns fit in a particular utterance. Where the word is placed in a phrase or sentence will shape the meaning of the utterance. Similarly, where the words in the sentence receive some suprasegmental stress will contribute to meaning. The focus of most linguists in performing some kind of syntactic analysis, however, is usually on word placement rather than on voicing sound differences. According to Chomsky (1965) and his theory of transformational grammar, every sentence has both a "deep" and a "surface" structure. Deep structure is related to the semantic intent of the utterance or the meaning of the sentence. For example, the ambiguous sentence, "The kissing of the boys was terrible," might have several deep-structure meanings related to boys being kissed (by someone), or to boys kissing one another, or to the fact that the boys were very bad kissers. The surface structure corresponds to the form of the sentence; form can be altered to meet semantic intent. Altering form to meet the needs of meaning is known as a transformation. Our three meanings related to boys kissing might be said using these different forms:

> It's terrible that they kissed the boys.
> The boys' kissing was terrible.
> The boys were poor kissers.

In a situational context, the ambiguous kissing sentence could probably have even more meanings. New words and grammar forms, placed in the proper order, would be able to portray the multiple meanings of the original ambiguous sentence.

Syntax requires that words be placed in the proper order. "Dishes she for pottery the bought the kitchen" is a meaningless sentence when the words are placed in such a random order; the same words placed in correct syntactic order would say, "She bought the pottery dishes for the kitchen." We find in the English language that nouns generally precede the verbs in a sentence, articles usually precede nouns, adjectives precede nouns, and adverbs generally follow verbs. When we go to produce a sentence, we begin with some intention to make an utterance that has some meaning to the listener (or reader); this is the deep structure of the utterance. The form and the structure of the utterance are determined by our past learning and use of the rules of the language; the word selection, the word order, and the grammar all show themselves in the surface structure of the sentence.

We will talk more about syntax in the next section of this chapter, when we discuss language acquisition. Problems in syntactic usage as seen in language-impaired children and adults will be presented in Chapters 8 and 9.

Morphology

Morphology is the study of the use of **morphemes** in words, in word inflections, in various grammar tenses (such as past tense), and in plurality. A *morpheme* is the smallest unit of a language that has meaning. It can be an actual word, one of several parts of a word, the beginning of a word (prefix, such as *un-*), or a word ending (suffix, such as *ing*). The following words contain one morpheme; they cannot be divided into any smaller units and still carry meaning:

> train
> orange
> window

These words contain two morphemes (if one were removed, it would change the meaning):

> necktie
> oranges (the /s/ is a morpheme, changing the meaning)
> thunderstorm

These words contain three morphemes:

> baseballs
> uncovered (the *un* changes *cover,* and the *ed* denotes the past)
> unwinding

As we acquire our lexicon, or vocabulary, it is composed of many words that are single morphemes or combination of morphemes. The single word can often be changed in many ways by adding morphemes to the root word. For example, the root verb *cover,* by the addition of morphemes, can have many different meanings:

to cover	(place something over)
uncover	(to find what is underneath)
covered	(covered in the past)
uncovered	(uncovered in the past)
covers	(actively covering)
uncovers	(actively uncovering)
covering	(actively covering)
uncovering	(taking off covers)
discover	(find what is there)
discovered	(found what was there)
discovers	(actively finding)

One can quickly see how using a prefix or suffix can expand one's vocabulary and that some different-looking words may have similar meanings. We could also list a series of nouns related to the noun *cover* by adding morphemes before or after the word:

cover	
covers	(plural form)
covering	
discovery	
coverer	(one who covers)
coverlet	(an outer cover, such as a bedspread)
recovery	

Morphology is basically the study of the rules for producing and combining morphemes in a particular language. Morphology is closely related to phonology and semantics. The vocal inflections used to stress or unstress a particular morpheme for a particular word meaning also require some phonologic skill. Since the addition of morphemes to another morpheme alters meaning, morphologic changes of words obviously play an important role in the study of semantics.

Semantics

Semantics is the study of the rules for word meaning and word combinations. Our basic use of language as a tool for communication is to transmit meaning to someone else. Hubbell (1985) noted: "Meaning is the bridge between the thoughts and experiences of individuals and the sequences of sounds they produce to symbolize those thoughts and experiences. Words symbolize concepts, and concepts represent experiences or reality'' (p. 33).

Of interest here is how young children attach meaning to a particular phonological sequence they have been hearing, and how their meaning for a word develops into adult meaning. It would appear that as children hear words associated with particular actions and behaviors in social contexts, they begin to assign meaning to those words. Eventually, a word stands for those actions and feelings, without the need for the original context. As the child develops cognitively through various experiences, there is a greater coupling of words with meaning. The child begins to use "words to refer to or represent external objects and events" (Clark, 1979, p. 193). Two kinds of meaning seem to develop for words, *denotative* and *connotative*. *Denotative* meaning is the literal meaning of the word; for example, for the word *milk,* we can use the dictionary definition of "a whitish fluid that is secreted by the mammary glands of female mammals for the nourishment of their young" as a literal, denotative meaning (few of us have thought of this meaning very often). A connotative meaning of the word *milk* for an American might be "the refrigerated thirst-quencher that today comes in cartons instead of bottles," or for the four-year-old Arab child who is still taking the mother's breast, the word might mean, "the warm fluid that comes from Mother when she holds me on her lap." Besides the denotative, more literal meaning of a word by the society in general that speaks the language, the connotative meaning is in a sense the private meaning of the individual, perhaps developed over time through personal experience associated with the word. The speaker learns the rules of the semantic system using words appropriately specific to both their denotative and connotative meanings.

Slobin (1970) and Bloom and Lahey (1978) present a system that determines meaning from nonnouns, or *relational* words. These relational words (adjectives, verbs, adverbs) can be used with a single *substantive* word in many different combinations, producing many separate meanings. Many semantic studies focus on the relational words rather than on the substantive nouns, which are much more denotative or exact in their meaning. For example, the noun *shoe* produces in the mind of the listener a possible picture of a leather covering of the foot mounted on a thicker sole. We can use relational words with the *shoe* and produce many different meanings:

If the shoe fits, wear it.	(a nonliteral, proverbial meaning)
It fits like an old shoe.	(proverb, or, from experience, old shoes feel good on the foot)
Make a ringer with a horseshoe.	(horse morpheme changes meaning and ringer requires specialized knowledge of horseshoe game)
You can't stop with worn shoes.	(a brake shoe is ineffective when worn)

The relational words may designate the contextual meaning of the noun. In the preceding examples, we see that often the noun *shoe* (which we immediately think is the object we wear on a foot) has many other meanings that we would understand if we were present in the particular context when the utterance was made; if we were not present, the relational words could provide us the meaning cues.

Disagreements in interpreting what someone else intends to say may be sometimes related to different interpretations of word meaning. Someone says a word to a gathering of people in the hope that everyone assembled will make the same interpretation of the word; the literal meanings of the word may compete with its private meanings, often resulting in many different interpretations from that intended by the speaker. The power of the word has been studied historically outside the field of linguistics by such speech-communication experts as Baccus (1950) or Chase (1954), as well as by speech pathologists (who were also semanticists) such as Johnson (1946). Linguists in the past several decades have placed more emphasis on syntax than on semantics, although Slobin (1970), Clark (1973), and Lyons (1977), among others, have focused on the meaning, or semantic function, of the utterance. With the more recent participation by linguists in the study of cognitive science and artificial intelligence, there appears to be an upsurge of interest in the study of meaning or semantics.

Pragmatics

How we use our words and in what situations is the focus of *pragmatics,* the study of the use of language in context. After the first six months of life, spontaneous vocalization begins to be replaced with intentional vocalization accompanied by expression and gesture (Oller, 1980). From about the age of nine months, the baby enjoys interaction with the caregiver, using vocalization appropriately for such games as pat-a-cake and peek-a-boo; in such games the child is using vocalization with the physical action of the game (which Bates [1976, p. 426] calls "preverbal performatives"). Even between twelve and eighteen months, the youngster uses single-word responses (called "performative acts" by Bates) more as part of a physical action with the caregiver than as true words that represent concepts (Bates, 1976). The performative act is always done with intent, and the child's use of performative utterances is for the purpose of declaring, promising, asking questions, and so forth (Bates and others, 1977).

Hubbell (1985) presents a clear way of looking at the components necessary for successful pragmatic behavior: repertoire, context, and decision making. A *repertoire* is the number of things one is able to do in a particular activity. For example, in baseball, a successful pitcher's repertoire might include a fast ball, a slider, a sinker, and a knuckle ball. A voice impersonator's repertoire might include vocal imitations of all of the male contract players at Warner Brothers in the 1940s. The language repertoire of children might include vocabulary, phonologic skills for saying words, proper use of grammar, and knowing how to talk and when to speak to different people. The *context,* the situation in which we find ourselves, has much to do with what we say and how we say it. A young college freshman provided a vivid description of context and language pragmatics when she said, "My girl voice is still there for my folks, I just kid all the time with my roommates, I use this old-lady voice when I talk to my teachers, and with my boyfriend we hardly say any words to one another." Our situation influences how we speak, what we say, and even whether we want to speak or not. Both comprehension and expression involve *decision making*. By using our knowledge of the rules of language and our interpretations of the words we have encountered, we decide what the speaker's utterances mean. We also decide (often very quickly, if not instantly) what parts of our language repertoire we are going to use in a particular situation.

Another useful way for studying pragmatics is to employ the *speech acts* theory, developed by Searle (1969), which places its focus on the speaker's intention rather than on the words one uses. In fact, the speech acts approach can be used for analyzing pragmatic skills in prelinguistic children, who may communicate through gestures that indicate either assertion (giving) or request (asking). Assertions are almost as varied as topics of communication, while requests are usually for some kind of action or information. Searle further describes three kinds of verbal intents: asserting, requesting, and ordering. For a successful communication, the speaker must use the language that truly represents the intent. Other linguists looking at pragmatics have applied speech acts analysis for looking at verbal interactions of young children and others around them (Dore, 1976; Ervin-Tripp, 1977). Probably one of the most innovative approaches to looking at child interactions and use of language in particular social settings is the work of Prutting and others (1978), who developed a content and interaction analysis scale for looking at interactive communicative acts. Such an analytical approach enables the investigator to look at a child's utterance, the reaction of the listener to the utterance, and the child's reaction to the listener and to the continuous interaction of the communication (nonverbal and verbal). In Figure 4–1, we see two children communicating, one by listening and one by whispering.

APPROACHES TO THE STUDY OF LANGUAGE ACQUISITION

There is probably no cross-cultural human skill that develops in a more orderly fashion than spoken language. It appears that during the first year of life all over the world, infants hear the languages spoken around them and eventually organize what they hear into some kind of meaning. Toward the end of the first year, all babies are able to respond to greetings, their name, and, in response to verbal commands, make simple motor responses, using the objects in their immediate environment. Their primary expressive function toward the end of the first year is a rather complex voicing pattern that resembles in a remarkable way the spoken patterns of the languages they have been hearing. The first spoken words are followed by the orderly acquisition of one- and two-word utterances; these first words have primary value to the baby, such as *ma* and *mi(lk)*. These first words are also relatively easy to say, and phonetically not too complex. As language is acquired during

FIGURE 4-1 Two children communicating, one by listening and one by whispering. Used with permission of Good Samaritan Medical Center, Phoenix, Arizona.

the second year, children are able to produce (and understand) longer and increasingly complex language constructions. Children acquire a *grammar* (rules of structure and sequence) of the language through its everyday use. As children put two or three words together, they will employ the rules of the grammar to keep the words in the form and sequence needed to facilitate comprehension by the listener. Children soon learn that, to be understood by the listener, the verbal message must be said in a way reasonably similar to the language code of the listener.

Toddlers in the second and third year of life acquire the language of their culture with very little effort. It would seem that the human has a natural biologic propensity for acquiring a language requiring only that we live in an environment where language is spoken. The stages of language learning are so predictable cross-culturally that linguists have been able to formulate theories about language acquisition and function that seem to have application to all languages, such as English, Arabic, Korean, or Spanish (to cite four languages with remarkably different prosodic-melody patterns).

While there appears to be some uniformity across language cultures regarding the acquisition and form of language, there is a great diversity of theories of language. Over the years, many scholars from different backgrounds have studied language: the philosopher and the psychologist have looked at the relationship between language and thought; the linguist has studied the origins and forms of language; the psychologist and biologist have viewed language from its naturalistic origins; the neurologist, psychologist, and speech-language pathologist have studied the neurological foundations of both normal and disordered language; the child-development specialist, the linguist, and the psychologist have looked at cognition and language. The predictability and the exact ordering of language facilitate its study, often offering the scientist an exactness that might not exist in his or her primary discipline, such as cognitive psychology or speech-language pathology. While some of the diversity of opinion about language is related to the particular discipline studying linguistic phenomena, some of the diversity is related to the chronology or history of studying language. Over the years, there have been major shifts in focus and viewpoint on language. The historical time when language acquisition is studied (such as in 1950, as opposed to 1970) has a primary shaping role in one's approach to the topic. While it would be convenient and encouraging to identify a sequential and progressive theme in the study of language over the years, it appears that there is some randomness, and perhaps even circularity (we may now be where we were), in our study of normal language.

Primary to the study of language is some recognition of the historical *nature-versus-nurture* argument. The naturalistic point of view says that we have a natural, biologic propensity for the learning of language, which is only waiting to be stimulated by a language culture. The nurture point of view says that we learn language because of the events outside the organism and that language acquisition can best be understood from a learning perspective. Among the many theoretical approaches to the acquisition of language that are available, let us select five approaches (listed in Table 4-1), and cite a few of the primary theorists who have advocated that particular point of view:

TABLE 4-1
Five Approaches to Language Acquisition

Approach	Proponents
Naturalistic (innateness)	Chomsky, 1965; Lenneberg, 1967; McNeill, 1970
Structural (rule-governed)	Braine, 1963; Bloom, 1973; Brown, 1973
Behavioral (learning)	Skinner, 1957; Staats, 1968; Bandura, 1969
Cognitive	Whorf, 1956; Piaget, 1963; Sinclair-deZwart, 1979; Bloom, 1974
Pragmatic	Bates, 1975; Bruner, 1975; Halliday, 1975

It must be recognized that any selection or listing of theoretical approaches to language acquisition is an oversimplification. Further, there is considerable overlap of view between particular approaches, as well as single proponents advocating several theories. Cruttenden (1979) advocates a "balanced viewpoint" in consideration of various approaches to language acquisition, recognizing that there is some truth in each. In this introductory work, our intent is to present each approach briefly, with no attempt to advocate any one theory of language acquisition. We believe that all five acquisition theories are interrelated and meaningful.

The Naturalistic Approach

There is no other form of animal life that can demonstrate such a complex language (in both a spoken and written form) as is found in the human. Lenneberg (1967) writes that language is a "species-specific" behavior found only in humans and made possible by an innovative and complex central nervous system with a body structure that makes this high form of communication possible. Just as ducklings know how to swim or dogs know how to bark without training, the human baby is "imprinted" (Lorenz, 1958) with a nervous system that requires only language stimulation to begin the miraculous task of language acquisition. The **naturalistic approach,** sometimes called the maturation or innateness approach, recognizes that the infant is born with the basic physical equipment (neural, structural) required to be able to understand and express spoken language, only requiring that the infant-child be around other people who speak the language. At certain ages of overall physical and social development, the neural and physical equipment of the child likewise develop, permitting a particular language event to emerge (provided, of course, that the child has been living in a normal language environment).

There is great current interest in the neurobiologic aspects of behavior; the recent utilization of various brain-scanning devices (such as the CT-scan or regional cerebral blood flow, discussed in Chapter 9) that allow us to look at what happens in the brain when particular behaviors occur has renewed some of the credibility of the innateness approach to language acquisition and function. For example, it is well established today that the left cerebral hemisphere is the dominant one for language, regardless of the handedness of the individual. The right hemisphere seems to have much to do with rhythm, tonality, and the expression and suppression of emotions. There are some who believe (this writer is one) that the early vocalizations of babies are probably right-hemisphere-controlled, and that, as the youngster acquires the sequential ordering of words, the left cerebral hemisphere becomes dominant. The left cerebral hemisphere seems to have much to do with sequential ordering (such as language), while the right hemisphere has much to do with spontaneous, unstructured behavior (such as emotionality).

Not only is the human nervous system equipped to handle the sequentially complex aspects of language, but the listening apparatus (the external ear and the hearing system) and the expressive structures (respiration, larynx, airway, tongue, palate, dentition, lips) are all seemingly "designed" to facilitate the production of speech. As Lenneberg (1967, p. 374) has written, "There is evidence that the tissues of the brain and the rest of the body constitute an organic, interdependent unit," facilitative of the learning of aural-oral language.

Chomsky (1965), a linguist known for his generative-grammar theory, argues an innatist theory on three counts: (1) worldwide language universals, (2) the child learns language despite inconsistent and poor language models, and (3) the speed of acquisition of language. By language universals, Chomsky is referring to how language works. For example, a change in a sentence is always structure-dependent; if we wanted to transform a statement to a question (for instance, from "It is noisy in a disco" to "Is it noisy in a disco?"), we must know the structure of a sentence, changing the order of the words to reflect a change in meaning. Another type of language universal is a substantive one, referring to the category of language usage, such as a noun, an adjective, a verb, an adverb. Chomsky's theory of transformation of generative grammar further supports his innatist view of language acquisition. According to this view, any sentence has both a deep and a surface structure; deep structure is related to the semantics or meaning of the sentence, and surface structure is related to the sentence's grammar and form. The human, with species-specific "equipment" for sentence processing, learns surface structure with amazing rapidity (often despite poor modeling and inconsistencies); deep structure is tied closely to meaning and overall cognitive development. Chomsky would argue against Skinner (see "The Behavioral Approach," later in the chapter) that the rapid learning of language defies a learning model where we acquire language through positive reinforcement and generalization, but rather that our rapid acquisition of language is related to innate periods of development (as much biologic as social).

Much of what we will be discussing in the next section on structural approaches is compatible with the work of Chomsky. Both Chomsky and McNeill (1970) discussed a "Language Acquisition Device" (LAD), which provides an acquisition model consistent with the innateness theory. In the LAD model, typical young children are exposed to a corpus of language utterances in their everyday environments. Some of the utterances are incomplete, some are minimally adequate, some are normal, and some are ornate. In the LAD model (it is only a model), the utterances the children hear pass through a central mechanism that contributes to the learning of a language grammar. By continuous exposure of utterances to (and through) the LAD, children learn the grammar; developing, in effect, a grammatical competence. McNeill (1970) diagrams the LAD model simply as:

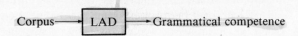

It should be remembered that competence (knowledge of the language) is not necessarily matched by performance (execution of that knowledge). From an innatist viewpoint, the LAD serves as a good model for the learning of a grammar; that is, by merely exposing the child to the utterances of others, a language knowledge will emerge. The ordering and structure of language appears to have much to do with facilitating its acquisition.

The Structural Approach

Whatever naturalistic propensities we have in acquiring our natural language(s), it is apparent that the language must be learned. From everyday exposure to other people speaking the language in the first few years of life, we acquire (or learn) the knowledge of the language, developing competence in using it in terms of both comprehension and expression. The **structural approach** to the study of language acquisition looks at the systematic way that language develops from the single-word utterance to the adult model.

Brown (1976) writes that, in the beginning, children speak telegraphically, in single words. As in a telegram, the words selected are the "contentive" ones, such as nouns, verbs, and adjectives that make specific reference to persons, objects, actions, and qualities. Omitted are the "functor" words, such as pronouns, articles, prepositions, and many auxiliary verbs. Brown and Fraser (1963) found in their longitudinal study of six children between two and three years old that the children's early utterances were primarily contentive words, with functor words added over time in an orderly manner of acquisition. They also found that inflection and prosody were often curbed to accommodate the telegraphic way of speaking. Even on imitative tasks, the functors were more often omitted than the contentive words. Sounding very much like the oral reading of the adult telegram, the young child uses telegraphic speech in beginning speech attempts. The adult model is apparently attempted from the beginning, but emerges as telegraphic and said "as grammatical sentences from which certain morphemes have been omitted" (Brown and Fraser, 1963, p. 188).

After analyzing the utterances of children over time, Brown (1973) developed five stages of sentence construction that seem to parallel (or mirror) overall language development. The five stages were developed according to the number of words a child said per utterance, known as the MLU, or mean length of utterance of morphemes:

> Stage I (1.75 morphemes) The child is starting to put noun-verb sequences together, such as "Car go."
>
> Stage II (2.25 morphemes) The child starts to change word endings to portray grammar, as in "Cars going."
>
> Stage III (2.75 morphemes) The child begins to use questions and imperatives; for instance, "That a car?"
>
> Stage IV (3.5 morphemes) The child begins to use complex sentences; for example, "Where's car going now?"
>
> Stage V (4 morphemes) The child may use connectors and more functors, as in "Mom's in the car."

While there is obvious overlap between successive stages, Brown and his colleagues conducted a number of studies over time that showed an actual progression from saying the single word, to the two-word utterance, to the telegraphic sentence, with the gradual refinement of grammar leading to complete sentences compatible with the adult model.

Braine (1963) studied the emerging language of three children (starting at age twenty months) for six months, beginning with two-word utterances. He found that there were certain *pivot* words (key words with which the child would generate many sentences, such as the verbs *put* and *go*). Often the child demonstrated some success using a verbal segment in a particular utterance and would then use the same segment in a later situation, perhaps changing a word or two at the beginning or the end. Braine labels this use of the same segments in different contexts as "contextual generalization." Contextual generalization, according to Braine, may account for the utilization of words in certain locations in the sequence of words within various sentences. There appear to be certain classes of words that often begin sentences (such as articles and pronouns) as well as particular types of words that end sentences (adjectives and adverbs).

Much of the structuralist work of the 1960s looked at length of response of the utterance, the type of word used, grammar, and the combination of words in various syntactic forms. More emphasis was given to form than to meaning. Winitz (1964) wrote that meaning as an area of linguistic study was generally held in disfavor by contemporary linguists. It was only a matter of time, however, before the meaning of words began to be studied within the structural framework of the sentence. An early study that looked at meaning was reported by Bloom (1970), who looked at grammatically correct utterances of children that could not be understood without the listener's having some awareness of the context of the utterance. The child's intended meaning was obvious only to the child. For example, if a two-year-old says, "dog house," we do not know if he means a dog house, if he wants the dog to come in the house, if the dog is in the house when she should not be, if the dog is beside the house, and so on. The situational context, such as seeing the child point to a doghouse, would provide the listener with the meaning of the utterance. Most children appear to make the best use possible with the limited language they have learned to use. As children acquire knowledge about their world and begin to use word forms that have greater specificity, the verbal ambiguities are less common. After age three, as cognition develops, more complex syntax emerges in the child's spoken language.

The Behavioral Approach

The **behavioral approach** to language acquisition stresses the influence of the environment rather than any innate abilities of the child. Verbal learning, like any other kind of learning, can be programmed and taught. The origins of behavioral therapy perhaps started with the classical conditioning study of Pavlov, who conditioned dogs to salivate (Watson, 1970). Observing that dogs salivated when looking at meat, he then presented a tuning-fork sound whenever the meat was presented. The dogs were soon conditioned to salivate whenever they heard the tuning fork (whether the meat was present or not). Like most automatic reflexes (such as salivation) that can be conditioned, so can most forms of human behavior, including language (Skinner, 1957).

According to the behavioral approach, language is a learned, conditioned behavior. For example, the nine-month-old baby learns to attend to the voice of her care-givers; when she hears these voices and looks closely at these people, she receives various forms of comfort. She repeats the pleasure-producing behavior. Or the twelve-month-old baby says, "ma," when his mother is about to feed him. His "ma" production is followed by feeding, accompanied by much animated expression of love from the mother upon hearing the child say her name. The positive response he has received makes "ma" an attractive word to say. Every time he sees his mother (if there is enough positive reinforcement), he is likely to repeat the "ma." Or he may generalize the use of "ma" for all feeding situations, regardless of who the caregiver may be. Such inappropriate stimulus generalization will eventually be extinguished through the reactions and feeding situations the baby experiences.

Skinner (1957) developed a behavioral approach to verbal learning. Speech becomes a "verbal operant." Conditioning is based on good behaviors or operants continuing (and expanding) with positive reinforcement, while bad operants are extinguished by punishment. In terms of verbal learning, correctly said words and combinations of words are rewarded by approval or sometimes by the basic pleasure of verbalization (Cruttenden, 1979). Incorrect utterances are met with no approval and are subsequently replaced by the subject with correct (good) verbalizations. The caregiver becomes the teacher, providing reinforcements for the child's utterances, in effect shaping the child's productions to approximate those of the adult language model.

A behavioral approach to language learning places much emphasis on approval by the caregiver and society. In the first two years of life, when the child is in close proximity to a caregiver, one can appreciate that the latter has a primary role regarding the reinforcement of the child's utterances. However, the caregiver role may be as much modeling and interacting as it is reinforcing per se. Once the child reaches the age of two, it is difficult to see how a hetereogeneous society can play a consistent shaping role for one's verbalizations. Young children will encounter a great variety of linguistic models (baby talk, fragmented sentences, sentences said obtusely, in a way they will not understand) and varied reactions to their utterances (anger, annoyance, laughter, ignoring, friendliness).

It should be mentioned that the behavioral approach to language acquisition was much utilized in the 1960s and 1970s as a clinical training model for children with deficient language. Operant approaches were designed and used for stimulating language acquisition in many children with language disabilities of various kinds (see Chapter 8).

The Cognitive Approach

In the **cognitive approach** to language acquisition, we find that cognitive development is a prerequisite for language development. Children must first experience percepts and concepts specific to their environment. Since the early 1920s, Piaget (1963) has been identified as one of the leading proponents of the cognitive approach to language learning. Does the structure of language originate from some kind of special linguistic propensity or from some kind of cognitive experience? McNeill (1970) wrote: "Among the early arrivals in child language are the grammatical categories of noun and verb. Where do they come from? One hypothesis would be that they are the reflection, in language, of the final step in child intelligence" (p. 152). It would appear that the nouns and verbs come directly from the child's living experience. All infants and young children exist in an environment of things and actions (nouns and verbs). Sinclair-deZwart (1979) cites the motor-sensory period of cognitive development as coming to a close at about eighteen months, which is when the child is combining, for the first time, nouns and verbs into two-word phrases and sentences. While the adjectives and adverbs of the language may come later, they are directly related to the child's experience of doing things. The Piagetian training model provides children with motor-sensory experiences (called "conservation tasks") related to color-form-shape-position; from such conservation experiences comes a natural utilization of descriptors relative to the children's use of nouns and verbs. Children, in effect, eventually develop a grammar for representing what they have already experienced (Bloom and Lahey, 1978).

The cognitive approach forces us to look critically at word meaning. While young children can "get by" using a simple word form such as *cold* to represent various temperature states of foods, objects, and the air around them, as they develop cognitively, they will need to discriminate coldness by using such words as *cool, icy, frozen, very cold, chilly, freezing*. Until they experience gradations of cold in various situations, the word *cold* serves very well. Throughout this discussion of cognitive aspects of language acquisition, we have prefaced word acquisition with previous or ongoing cognitive experience. That is, not until we have an experience is the word representing that experience likely to emerge. Whorf (1956) and his followers have taken an opposite cognitive view, believing that the existing language of the culture facilitates the cognitive experience. Using the same example of the word *cold,* Whorf would argue that children hear the word *cold* said in conjunction with (or before or after) the physical experience of cold. The culture in which children find themselves has created a language to represent the gradations of cold they may experience. The words *cool* and *cold,* for example, will help children discriminate between these two gradations. Without the words, children may not distinguish cognitively the two temperature states.

The interaction of cognitive and linguistic development can probably accommodate both the Piagetian and Whorfian views. Some independence of cognitive development from language function can be seen in the child with a profound hearing loss. The child may have good cognitive development but be unable to use spoken language either receptively or expressively; eventually, with training, the child may be able to develop reading-writing skills commensurate with overall cognitive ability. Conversely, the interdependence of cognition and language can be seen in the retarded child, whose intelligence and linguistic skills are usually found to be similar; the retarded child's linguistic abilities often seem to mirror overall cognitive functioning.

It would appear that normal language acquisition is facilitated by the child's doing things. As children experience the world around them, their aural-oral language seems to develop. The child without this normal living exposure (because of deafness, retardation, parental restriction, lack of home setting) will often show some slowness in language acquisition. As Bruner (1975) has written:

> . . . we may say that to master a language a child must acquire a complex set of broadly transferable or generative skills—perceptual,

motor, conceptual, social, *and* linguistic—which when appropriately coordinated yield linguistic performances that can be described (though only in a limited sense) by the linguist's rules of grammar (p. 64).

The Pragmatic Approach

While the innate and structural focus of language acquisition in the 1960s was followed by the study of cognitive aspects of language in the 1970s, more recent attention has been given to how children use language, which is called *pragmatics*. The **pragmatic approach** differs from the cognitive approach by focusing on how the child interacts with others in the environment. Bates (1976) and Bruner (1975) point out that the human interaction the baby experiences in the first year of life establishes various pragmatic roles (long before the baby is using actual language). The nonverbal behaviors described in Chapter 2 are basically employed to control and manipulate the environment. The youngster begins to add words to vocal chains that were previously established and used in communication. Bruner writes that the "early language for which a grammar is written is the end result of psychological processes" already established in the first 18 months of life.

Bates (1976), whose writings have had much to do with the study of language pragmatics, looks at the verbal utterance one may use in human interaction as a "performative act," or the act the speaker intends to accomplish (such as asking questions or declaring). We speak for a purpose. The pragmatic approach to language acquisition basically says that we learn early when to say what to whom. By use of the suprasegmentals (pitch, loudness, duration, pauses), described previously, we learn, also, how to say it. Halliday (1975) lists seven human needs or functions that can be served by language. The seven needs are listed here with a language illustration for each:

1. Instrumental ("I need . . . ")
2. Regulatory ("Take the . . . ")
3. Interactional ("How are you?")
4. Personal ("I'm hungry . . . ")
5. Heuristic ("Where . . . ?")
6. Imaginative ("Why don't we . . . ?")
7. Informational ("You know that . . . ")

For the young child, these functions of language serve most interactive needs. As more complex grammar forms develop and as one acquires more vocabulary, the individual can use language to express needs with greater subtlety. Sometimes, we become so indirect in what we say that our listeners may not understand the content or the meaning of what we are saying. For example:

The father who chastised his two sons for not finishing mowing the lawn said, "All right, it'll be snowing in Los Angeles before you guys will get to the beach." The boys did not understand the intent of his remark, which was: "If you don't finish the lawn soon, I won't let you go to the beach."

Since the intent of the speaker is usually to be understood, we tend to adjust the complexity of the verbal message to accommodate our listeners.

As young children grow, so does their verbal repertoire, enabling them to use language forms that meet the particular situation. Children learn to speak (verbally and nonverbally) one way to one another, another way to their parents, and another way to the teacher or the doctor. The child soon learns that the situation or context of the communication has much to do with the form of the verbal utterance. The specific decision as to what to say, how to say it, and when is shaped by the success the child experiences in the interaction. For example, we soon learn that Grandmother wants to be called "Gramma" instead of "Kate" by her reactions to our previous use of both names, and that, in sharp contrast, Grandfather wants to be called "Doctor Dan" instead of "Grandpa." And in our interactions with both, we soon understand that Grandmother likes to speak with baby talk and that Grandfather uses a very adult language form. Not so unlike the behaviorist premise about behavior, the successful language performance must be continually adjusted by the sender to the appropriateness, level, and need of the receiver. (Like speaking and listening, textbook writing and reading have the same pragmatic requirements.) If the message is not understood or received well, it is ineffective. Conversely, the successful message is probably appropriate in most communicative dimensions.

An Overview of the Approaches

The pragmatic approach to language acquisition is not at variance with any of the other approaches and in some ways summarizes them all. It would certainly recognize that there is an innate (if not biologic) need for the baby to communicate, and, further, that the human seems endowed with species-specific mechanisms that allow and facilitate such communication. There appear to be language universals in all children, who learn different languages at about the same key points in development; there are also structural universals in the grammar of every language. The sequence and the ordering of the language is seen in its grammar. It appears that through trial and error the child acquires rule-governed language as a primary mode of communication. The behavioral approach tells us that the reinforcement "payoff" comes from satisfactory verbal interactions; pleasant verbal interactions tend to be repeated and maintained, while aversive situations tend to be extinguished (not too unlike the pragmatic approach). Our vocabularies and our grammar develop out of positive experience. The experiences we have are precursors to our acquisition of verbal knowledge, according to the cognitive theorists. Thought arises out of infant sensorimotor experience. As our thought processes become more complex through experience, the structural complexity of our language forms increases, enabling us to verbalize (receptively and expressively) higher thought processes. Finally, the communication effectiveness becomes the final determinant of how we use language.

FROM SOUNDS TO SENTENCES

Now that we have familiarized ourselves with the components of language and some of the theories about language acquisition, let us look at how language develops in the young, normal child from a chronological perspective. In Chapter 2, we talked about the baby's attention to sounds and own sound-making strategies up until the age of about twelve months. At this point we will pick up where we left off in Chapter 2, beginning with the normal child at about the age of one year. Instead of talking about "the child" (he or she), let us relate our developmental information to a mythical female child, named Sheila. Remember that Sheila (although mythical for purposes of illustration) is a typically normal child, experiencing no developmental problems and doing all the things at certain ages that little girls (and boys) are supposed to do.

Twelve to Eighteen Months

Sheila shows some dramatic gains in motor development at twelve months, standing without support, taking a few steps before falling down, and able to open a small box, using both hands. She seems to understand a number of words, particularly the names of people and things that surround her daily. At twelve months, she can say three words (one of them is "mama"), and she is entering the time, age twelve to eighteen months, that Nelson (1973) described as the period of "the first 50 words." She likes to imitate various sound games and occasional words, but does not use the imitated patterns spontaneously (Rees, 1980). In fact, between twelve and fifteen months, Sheila speaks very few words, communicating most of the time in a complex jargon that the neighbors swear is "either a foreign language or she's speaking in tongues."

At eighteen months, she walks unassisted, feeds herself with a spoon, and can play catch (poorly) with her grandfather. Her parents and grandparents speak to Sheila in shorter and simpler sentences than they use in talking to her older brother and to themselves, an observation reported by Nelson (1973) and discussed by Rees (1980). The simplified utterances that people make to Sheila probably facilitate her comprehension of the language. She can now point to a particular object when asked to do so and go look for the object in the room if it is not immediately visible. Her comprehension of spoken language at this age far exceeds her spoken vocabulary, which may number about 50 words (Leonard, 1982). What she says is primarily limited to single words, said either alone or in combination with her prosodic jargon. At this age, she is just beginning to say two words together, usually noun-verb phrases. Her interactive pragmatics are so effective, relating easily to people with her few words, vocalizations, and gestures, that her father says, "She'll never learn to talk. She won't need to. She can just laugh or cry or look cute and get anything she wants without saying a word."

Eighteen to Twenty-four Months

Now that Sheila is able to walk without falling, she spends much of her time exploring the rooms and the yard of her home. Like others her age, she places almost more priority on exploration and playing than she does on communicating with the people around her. There is far less jargon and prosodic flow to her communicative intents, replacing the jargon with actual words. When she does speak, she begins to combine two words. At twenty to twenty-one months, she is acquiring many new words and is using them in two-word utterances that are more often characterized by a noun-verb or adjective-noun word order, such as "Tiwa (her name) go" or "big ball." Most of what she says is related to actual objects and happenings, and if her family has difficulty understanding her two-word combinations, she stresses the key word to facilitate their comprehension.

By twenty-four months, Sheila is able to point to the correct pictures when asked to point to such things as a hat, a dog, a car. She follows spoken directions far better than she can speak. However, she now has a spoken vocabulary of about 300 words, combining them in two-word utterances, with an occasional three-word sentence. She uses primarily nouns, verbs, adjectives, and pronouns, omitting articles, prepositions, the "be" copular and auxiliary verbs, speaking in the telegraphic style described by Brown (1976). Her play now includes re-creating home and nursery-room scenes with her dolls and toy furniture, and giving directions and asking questions that seem to represent what she has been experiencing in both the home and day-care environments.

Twenty-four to Thirty-six Months

Sheila can now make a tower of four blocks and match objects to pictures. She likes to look at books, turning pages and pointing to objects (Anderson, Miles, and Matheny, 1963). Her cognitive development is now sufficient to permit her to think out solutions to problems before attempting to act on the solutions (Piaget, 1963). Before doing a three- or four-piece puzzle, she looks at the pieces and makes decisions about where to place them. Sheila is now starting to match her telegraphic narrations ("arm go baby") with the cognitive decisions she has made, acting out her solutions both by movements and by words. Her statements begin to reveal that she appreciates the necessity of correct word order to express her intended meaning. For example, if she were to see a boy pushing the girl down, she would probably say, "boy push girl," not "girl push boy" (Sinclair-de Zwart, 1979). Her grammar begins to reveal what she had observed (past tense) and is experiencing (present tense). At about twenty-eight months, we observe the beginning of *wh-* questions, usually related to an event involving Sheila.

At about 30 months, there is a noticeable change in the prosody of her speech, with the melody flow of her voice approximating, at times, the adult model. She is beginning to show phonologic stress to enhance meaning at the proper place in the utterance. We begin to hear functor words—*in, on, by, to, the*—which contribute greatly to the prosodic melody of her speech. Sheila enjoys the verbal interactions she has with her parents, her brother, the day-care children and teachers. At this stage of her emerging grammar, her mother and father in particular alter their language styles (simplification, greater phonologic stress, shorter sentences), which they feel necessary to maintain Sheila's interest in what they say (Bruner, 1975). She is often heard to produce an unsolicited imitation of an adult utterance that she has heard; some of these imitations are immediate, but more of them are delayed (Schwartz and Leonard, 1985).

Thirty-six to Forty-eight Months

In her third year, Sheila is beginning to show some handedness preference, can build a tower of nine or ten blocks, can copy drawings of a circle and a cross, and carries on imaginative play by herself or with others. Her phonologic skills have developed to the point at which she can produce about 50 to 70 percent of her consonants correctly (according to the adult model) and her voicing patterns add to the meaning of the words she is saying. There is never a day that goes by that Sheila does not cry, usually reacting to not getting her way about something; she cries more at home than she does in the day-care setting (where crying is a relatively rare event).

In the third year, most normal children like Sheila have a spoken vocabulary of 500 to 1,000 words (Anderson and others, 1963). Her receptive language functions have developed to the degree that, when asked to point to objects in a picture, she can point to most of them correctly; she can also repeat two or three nonsense syllables and two or three digits (which may be nonsense syllables to some children). The biggest change we observe in Sheila's use of language is that she has learned how to understand and produce sentences in social interactions. She knows how to say certain things in particular situations. Her utterances begin to serve a variety of functions; "in addition to serving declaring, requesting, and questioning functions, these children's utterances may serve functions of protesting, agreeing, joking, or qualifying" (Leonard, 1982, p. 228). She is beginning to use language comfortably in everyday life situations, adjusting what she says to fit her own needs as well as the demands of the situation.

The Fourth Year

By age four, Sheila is showing consistent preference for using one hand over the other, she can draw a figure of a person, and she can complete an eight-piece puzzle with relative ease. She can now follow a two-level command correctly, such as "Go get your white shoes and put them in Mom's shoeshine box" or "Go get Toby [dog] a treat and show Aunt Barbara how he sits." Both of these requests require that the child have a cognitive understanding of the situation as well as of word meaning and grammar. Sheila, like most four-year-olds, can follow these relatively complex two-level commands. If she is asked to repeat a sentence nine to ten words long, she can do it provided that the syntax of the utterance is not too complex; normal children's repetitions are less confounded by number of words than they are by variations in syntax (Menyuk, 1964).

Sheila now has a spoken vocabulary of over 1,500 words. In her sentence formulations we now hear the auxiliary verbs (such as *can* and *did*), proper use of negatives, and compound sentences connected by a variety of conjunctions. By forty-eight months, she has mastered over 90 percent of her consonant speech sounds, regardless of the position of the sound within the word. Her prosodic patterns continue to approximate that of the adult models around her. Her pragmatic use of language has shown a marked change; she will now change her suprasegmental voicing patterns to accommodate her listeners. She speaks more telegraphically to younger children, omitting some of her function words; she speaks quietly when Grandpa is taking his nap; she speaks more loudly to Grandpa to compensate for what she has perceived as a hearing loss. Her knowledge about the world around her and her continuing growth in understanding and producing more complex grammatical utterances has spawned an appreciation of humor; she can tell when people are kidding her and she can make some truth distortions herself to produce a "joke" on someone else.

As Sheila enters her fifth year, her language competence continues to grow with amazing facility. Before she enters kindergarten, she will have mastered much of her native language. With normal aural-oral language skills, she will now be ready to learn a different language form, reading and writing.

REVIEW QUESTIONS

The great majority of children acquire their native language with no difficulty. The amazing speed of language acquisition in normal children provides a fascinating area of study. For further study, the reader may wish to examine some of the references cited in the chapter, as well to do some additional reading in linguistics. Now let us consider a few questions based on what we have discussed.

1. How are phonology, morphology, and syntax related?

2. How are semantics and pragmatics related?

3. Comment on the statement: "Language acquisition closely parallels overall development of the child."

4. What is the *nature-nurture* argument as related to language acquisition?

5. How are the behavioral and cognitive approaches to language acquisition similar? How do they differ?

6. Write an overview of approaches to language acquisition that differs from the summary in the text.

7. When does the one-word utterance usually get replaced by the two-word utterance? How do sentences seem to develop from this point on?

REFERENCES

Anderson, R. M., Miles, M., and Matheny, P. A. (1963). *Communicative Evaluation Chart from Infancy to Five Years.* Cambridge, Mass: Educators Publishing Service.

Baccus, J. (1950). *The Total Speech Situation.* Redlands, Calif.: University of Redlands.

Bandura, A. (1969). *Principles of Behavioral Modification.* New York: Holt, Rinehart, and Winston.

Bates, E. (1975). *Language and Context: The Acquisition of Pragmatics.* New York: Academic Press.

Bates, E. (1976). Pragmatics and sociolinguistics in child language, in *Normal and Deficient Child Language,* ed. D. Morehead and A. Morehead. Baltimore: University Park Press.

Bates, E., Benigni, L., Bretherton, I., Camaioni, L., and Volterra, V. (1977). From gesture to the first word: on cognitive and social prerequisites, in *Interaction, Conversation, and the Development of Language,* ed. M. Lewis and L. Rosenblum. New York: Wiley.

Bloom, L. (1970). *Language Development: Form and Function in Emerging Grammars.* Cambridge, Mass.: MIT Press.

Bloom, L. (1973). *One Word at a Time: The Use of Single-Word Utterances.* The Hague: Moulton.

Bloom, L., and Lahey, M. (1978). *Language Development and Language Disorders.* New York: Wiley.

Braine, M. D. (1963). On learning the grammatical order of words. *Psychological Review, 70:* 323–348.

Brown, R. (1973). *A First Language: The Early Stages.* Cambridge, Mass.: Harvard University Press.

Brown, R. (1976). *A First Language.* New York: Penguin.

Brown, R., and Fraser, C. (1963). The acquisition of syntax. *Monographs of the Society for Research in Child Development, 29:* 43–79.

Bruner, J. S. (1975). The ontogenesis of speech acts. *Journal of Child Language, 2:* 1–19.

Chase, S. (1954). *The Power of Words.* New York: Harcourt Brace Jovanovich.

Chomsky, N. (1965). *Aspects of the Theory of Syntax.* Cambridge, Mass.: MIT Press.

Clark, E. (1979). What's in a word? On the child's acquisition of semantics in his first language, in *Language Development,* ed. V. Lee. New York: Wiley.

Cruttenden, A. (1979). *Language in Infancy and Childhood.* New York: St. Martin's.

Dore, J. (1976). Children's illocutionary acts, in *Discourse Relations: Comprehension and Production.* Hillsdale, N.J.: Lawrence Erlbaum.

Ervin-Tripp, S. (1977). Wait for me, roller skate, in *Child Discourse,* ed. C. Mitchell-Kernan and S. Ervin-Tripp. New York: Academic Press.

Halliday, M. (1975). *Learning How to Mean: Explorations in the Development of Language.* London: Edward Arnold.

Hubbell, R. (1985). Language and linguistics, in *Speech, Language, and Hearing* (2nd ed.), ed. P. Skinner and R. Shelton. New York: Wiley.

Ingram, D. (1981). Transivity in child language. *Language, 47:* 888–910.

Johnson, W. (1946). *People in Quandaries.* New York: Harper and Row.

Lenneberg, E. (1967). *Biological Foundations of Language.* New York: Wiley.

Leonard, L. B. (1982). Early language development and language disorders, in *Human Communication Disorders: An Introduction,* ed. G. H. Shames and E. H. Wiig. Columbus: Charles E. Merrill.

Lorenz, K. Z. (1958). The evolution of behavior. *Scientific American, 119:* 67–78.

Lyons, J. (1977). *Semantics.* Cambridge, England: Cambridge University Press.

McNeill, D. (1970). *The Acquisition of Language.* New York: Harper and Row.

Menyuk, P. (1964). Comparison of grammar of children with functionally deviant and normal speech, *Journal of Speech and Hearing Research, 7:* 109–121.

Nelson, K. (1973). Structure and strategy in learning how to talk. *Monographs of the Society for Research in Child Development, 38:* 1–2.

Oller, D. (1980). The emergence of speech sounds in infancy, in *Child Phonology.* Vol. 1. *Production,* ed. G. Yeni-Komshian, J. Kavanaugh, and C. Ferguson. New York: Academic Press.

Piaget, J. (1963). *The Origins of Intelligence in Children.* New York: Norton.

Prutting, C., Bagshaw, N., Goldstein, H., Juskowitz, S., and Umen, I. (1978). Clinician-child discourse: some preliminary questions. *Journal of Speech and Hearing Disorders, 43:* 123–139.

Rees, N. (1980). Learning to talk and understand, in *Introduction to Communication Disorders,* ed. T. Hixon, L. Shriberg, and J. Saxman. Englewood Cliffs, N.J.: Prentice-Hall.

Schwartz, R., and Leonard, L. (1985). Lexical imitation and acquisition in language-impaired children. *Journal of Speech and Hearing Disorders, 50:* 141–149.

Searle, J. (1969). *Speech Acts.* London: Cambridge University Press.

Sinclair-de Zwart, H. (1979). Language acquisition and cognitive development, in *Language Development,* ed. V. Lee. New York: Wiley.

Skinner, B. F. (1957). *Verbal Behavior.* New York: Appleton-Century-Crofts.

Slobin, D. I. (1970). Universals of grammatical development in children, in *Advances in Psycholinguistics,* ed. G. Flores d' Arcais and W. Levelt. New York: American Elsevier.

Staats, A. (1968). *Learning, Language, and Cognition.* New York: Holt, Rinehart, and Winston.

Watson, J. B. (1970). *Behaviorism.* New York: Norton.

Whorf, B. L. (1956). *Language, Thought, and Reality.* Cambridge, Mass.: Technology Press of MIT.

Winitz, H. (1964). The development of speech and language in the normal child, in *Progress in Speech Pathology,* ed. R. Rieber and R. Brubaker. Amsterdam: North Holland Publishing Co.

5

Disorders of Communication in Children

The vast majority of children develop communication skills without difficulty. They hear and understand what is said to them with no problem, they relate easily to the people and situations around them, and they speak well, with good articulation, voice, and fluency. They use the adult forms of communication with relative ease. We will consider these fortunate children in this chapter only from the perspective of their normal development. We need this perspective when we consider that some 10 percent of the children in our society struggle to gain the communication competencies so taken for granted by our normal hearing and speaking population. We will first consider those children who neither hear well nor are able to understand what they hear. We will then look at children who demonstrate problems in language (who do not acquire the miracle of language as described in the last chapter) or who struggle with problems in articulation, voice, or fluency. We will see that some children are born with a communication handicap, while others acquire their problem as they develop. Efforts must be made to identify communication problems during the preschool years or when they may first emerge, during the school years. Once a problem is identified, early intervention with remediation approaches is often effective in helping a youngster eventually achieve normal communication.

A communication disorder can be very handicapping to a child, affecting early family interactions, negatively influencing performance in school, and possibly interfering seriously with overall cognitive and social development. There are proportionately more communication handicaps among children than there are among adults, primarily because many communication disorders in children are developmental in nature. That is, as the child's communicative systems mature (and perhaps with some training to facilitate this maturity), the communication handicap is no longer present. However, if we were to use the national-incidence study data (Hull and others, 1976) as a guide to a prevalence prediction, we might conclude conservatively that about 10 percent of children under the age of eighteen demonstrate a communication disorder. At certain ages, there may be a preponderance of problems, such as middle-ear infections during the preschool years; or there may be very few at other developmental stages, such as the relative absence of articulation problems in the high-school population.

We will consider communication disorders in children from the same process approach we have developed in earlier chapters: hearing, language, articulation, voice, and fluency. This broad overview of communication disorders in children will be followed in Chapter 6 by a similar look at such disorders in adults. Subsequent chapters will examine separately various clinical disorders from the perspective of the process that is involved rather than the age of the person with the problem.

HEARING DISORDERS IN CHILDREN

Aural-oral language appears to be the primary mode of human communication. Consequently, any kind of hearing loss can compromise one's ability to use language. Hearing loss is perhaps the most common communication disorder. As we have seen in earlier chapters, hearing environmental noises and sounds such as the human voice appears to be an important requisite for both cognitive-social development and acquisition and growth of aural-oral language. Hearing a language (particularly an aural-oral one) is a primary prerequisite for learning a language. In the case of the young child, hearing impairment can seriously stunt overall development, with an obvious impact on a developing language system. Hearing disorders in children seem to exist in two ways, either as a failure of the peripheral hearing system to function adequately or as a breakdown in the central auditory system.

Conductive Hearing Loss

The most commonly occurring communication problem in young children is peripheral hearing loss related to middle-ear infection (**otitis media**). This kind of infection is often the result of a cold or allergy, which results in a buildup of fluid within the middle-ear cavity; because of eustachian-tube blockage, the fluid cannot escape. Although such infections come and go in a child with surprising frequency, they are often undetected by unsuspecting parents. The child may one day demonstrate difficulty following simple spoken instructions, and at about the time when the parents become concerned, appear to hear normally again. The hearing loss in otitis media continually fluctuates. When present, however, the loss may range from 15 to 55 dB. At the upper levels, this is severe enough to interfere with the hearing of normal conversation (see Chapter 7). Otitis media has been found to have deleterious effects on the development of speech and language (Friel-Patti and others, 1982; Ventry, 1980) in the young child. Swisher (1985), after reviewing a number of studies on the effects of otitis media, found that a number of children demonstrated "a general developmental delay rather than a specific learning disability . . . associated with a history of multiple episodes of otitis media" (p. 65). Such conductive hearing losses may take their toll on the developing child, and must be medically/surgically treated. Fortunately, otitis media, once identified, is a highly treatable disease and constitutes a major, successful portion of the practice of pediatric otolaryngology.

Conductive hearing impairment in children occasionally may be caused by various malformations of the outer or middle ear; *atresia* (closure of the external ear canal) is perhaps the most common of such congenital malformations. Depending on the degree of external ear closure, the conductive hearing loss can be mild to moderate. Atresia can usually be corrected successfully with surgery. Another conductive impairment is **otosclerosis** (a soft, bony growth around the bones of the middle ear), which, when it occurs in children, does not appear until about the late teen years. We will discuss the treatment of otosclerosis in greater detail in Chapter 7. Most conductive hearing impairment in children is related to physical conditions that are treatable, either medically or surgically. Since the preschool years in particular are important ones for the development of language, every effort should be made to provide the young child with adequate hearing.

The audiogram of a five-year-old boy with otitis media (see Figure 5–1) is typical of most conductive losses. Generally, the conductive loss has a depressed air-conduction threshold across the frequency range, producing the flat curve we see in the audiogram. Note that the boy demonstrates normal bone conduction, which indicates that his inner ear and auditory nerve appear to be functioning normally. While the priority treatment for conductive hearing loss is medical-surgical in an attempt to correct the cause of the hearing loss, children with flat, conductive losses usually profit greatly from hearing aids, even if only worn temporarily. Once

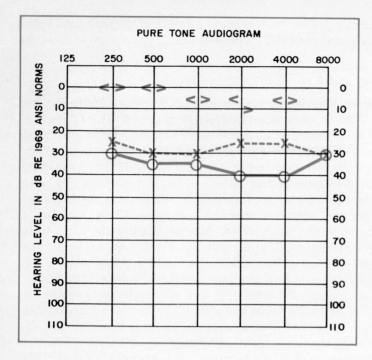

FIGURE 5-1 A typical conductive loss showing normal bone-conduction thresholds and depressed air-conduction thresholds. Tom, age five.

youngsters are fitted with an aid, they can often profit from intensive aural habilitation, learning to use the aid and respond appropriately to sound (both verbal and environmental).

Sensorineural Hearing Loss

A sensorineural (an inner-ear or auditory-nerve) hearing loss in children usually has greater impact on communication than a conductive hearing loss. Sensorineural losses (mild to severe) may be more severe than conductive losses, and most cannot be treated as successfully medically or surgically. Many such losses are *congenital,* present at the time of birth. Such losses may or may not be the result of hereditary factors. More often, the congenital sensorineural problem was acquired during the mother's pregnancy, perhaps as the result of an infectious disease such as rubella or mumps. Other examples of congenital hearing loss can be related to toxicity or trauma during the pregnancy or as the result of prolonged *anoxia* (lack of oxygen) at the time of birth. Heredity as a cause of hearing loss is occasionally a factor in the infant who is born to parents with a history of genetic hearing loss, and heredity may contribute to Rh incompatibility, which sometimes results in a hearing loss in the newborn. Other sensorineural hearing losses may be *acquired* sometime in childhood, perhaps after several years of normal language and speech development. Some viral diseases, such as measles, mumps, chicken pox, or influenza, have been known to cause serious sensorineural losses, as well as such bacterial infections (often associated with high fevers) as meningitis or diphtheria, which may cause severe hearing loss or deafness.

A sensorineural hearing loss early in a child's life can have a tremendous effect on developing language and speech. A profound loss in infancy will have greater impact on linguistic development than during the school years. The severe hearing loss depicted in the audiogram of a seven-year-old child (see Figure 5-2) shows a marked reduction in hearing beyond 2 K, with a moderate loss at lower frequencies. The boy had normal hearing until age four, when he had a severe, prolonged illness diagnosed as influenza. What he demonstrates is somewhat similar to the typical sensorineural hearing loss in children, characterized by a severe loss of hearing in the higher frequencies, with a more moderate loss in the lower end of the frequency range. Such a loss is going to interfere seriously with the auditory reception of language, requiring a massive special-education program to assure that the child experiences maximum cognitive-language development.

Profound hearing loss in the infant will seriously interfere with overall development. The listening to sounds and the production of early vowels and consonants described in Chapter 2 will be compromised. Maskarinec and others (1981), in studying the vocalization patterns of infants, found that a deaf baby showed characteristically different vocalization patterns as early as six weeks of age. The biologic and emotional vocalizations of the infant apparently require some auditory self-monitoring to be produced and continued like that of the normal-hearing infant. Therefore, the infant with a profound hearing loss requires amplification as

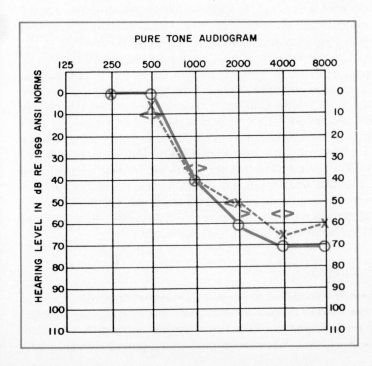

FIGURE 5-2 A severe sensorineural hearing loss acquired by a child after an illness at age four. Gaston, age seven.

soon as possible. Using some of the play audiometry and evoked response techniques described in Chapter 7, babies are testable and can be fitted with hearing aids. Alpiner and others (1977) reported that infants can be satisfactorily fitted with hearing aids as early as eight weeks of age.

Severely-hard-of-hearing and deaf children require specialized training to expose them to the everyday environmental sounds that are part of normal-hearing children's living experience. Such children need help (amplification) to hear their own vocalizations and the speech patterns of the people around them. They will need help in developing the normal rhythm (prosodic patterns) of language, practice in saying the vowels, and therapy for the production of consonants. Language itself must be taught, rather than naturally experienced, as it is by the hearing child. Language training is often facilitated by exposing the infant to a sign language, such as American Sign Language (ASL). Through signing, the child learns language. Swisher (1985) reports that, just as normal hearing children often say their first words between ten and thirteen months of age, infants who have been exposed to signing will often "produce their first signs around this age." It would appear that social-cognitive development and the acquisition of language are both facilitated by exposing such a youngster to a dual-language system (signing and aural-oral language), known as a "total" communication system (Alpiner and others, 1977).

The child who acquires a moderate-to-severe sensorineural hearing loss during the late preschool or the school-age years will be able to retain effective aural-oral communication. The boy whose audiogram depicted sensorineural loss (Figure 5–2) continues to understand the speech of others, and his own speech remains intelligible. However, despite his wearing a hearing aid for the past three years (since his hearing loss), his speech articulation has begun to show some articulatory distortions, particularly high-frequency sounds such as /s/, /z/, /ʃ/, and /tʃ/ in the final position in words. His loss is severe enough to require the special services of a school speech-language pathologist, who works with the boy to retain normal voice and prosody in his speech and provides him with auditory training focusing on the production of final consonants. Children with severe acquired hearing losses may in time begin to show some of the vocal characteristics of deaf children, such as vowel prolongation, cul-de-sac resonance, pitch variability, and hypernasality (Boone, 1983). If such children receive proper amplification and intensive auditory training, coupled with other special-education programs within their schools, they can usually remain in a regular school, integrated with normal-hearing children in as many school programs as possible. In contrast, the child who was born severely hard-of-hearing or deaf usually must attend a school for the deaf, where the total program is designed to the accommodation of that handicap.

Central Hearing Problems

Some children have serious difficulties understanding what other people say even though they demonstrate normal hearing sensitivity on audiometric examination. They are said to be experiencing an *auditory verbal agnosia* (an inability to comprehend spoken language). Other children may demonstrate a **central auditory prob-**

lem (difficulty in processing and understanding both nonverbal and verbal auditory stimuli). Such children differ from retarded or autistic children (whom we will soon discuss) in that they show marked discrepancy in their poor auditory comprehension, with normal or superior performance in reacting to visual stimuli and to the people and events in their environment. They differ from deaf children because they demonstrate normal auditory sensitivity to pure tone testing. These central auditory problems are believed to be the result of auditory stimuli reaching the brain (the problem is not a peripheral one) with inadequate processing of the perceived stimuli; the child's responses to other sensory stimuli are quite adequate.

Many children with a central auditory problem demonstrate normal responses to auditory stimuli in the first year or so of life. Rapin and Allen (1983) reported that some children with an auditory verbal agnosia experience early, normal developmental milestones in all areas, only to demonstrate a regression of verbal skills as they get older. It would appear that as aural-oral language gets more complex, children demonstrate increasing difficulties in auditory comprehension. Early identification of such an auditory verbal agnosia is essential if the child is to develop overall language and cognitive abilities, so that maximum exposure can be given to other, visual language modalities, such as signing and reading. By utilizing the intact modalities of vision and touch, the educational specialist is often able to design education programs that enable the child to learn language. The auditory deficits are often best treated by focusing on "can do" or intact skills such as touching, smelling, and looking; the intact sensory impression is then coupled with the spoken word, using the "can do" modality as the "bridge" to the deficit area.

LANGUAGE DISORDERS IN CHILDREN

Some children exhibit real difficulties acquiring and using the language code of their particular language culture, as we will develop in some detail in Chapter 8. The majority of language disorders in children occur in the preschool years. Some of these disorders persist into the school-age years (and some on into adulthood), causing learning disabilities, particularly in reading and writing. A few school-age children acquire a language disorder after they have already acquired their basic language competencies, usually as the result of some kind of disease process or injury to the brain.

Preschool Language Problems

A language disorder in a young child is basically determined by comparing the child's language function with that of normal children the same age. The early work of Chomsky (1957) seemed to initiate looking closely at the emerging syntax in the youngster's early language. Before the impact of Chomsky and his detailed analysis of syntax, particularly in comparing the emerging syntax of the youngster with that employed by normal adult speakers, much of the focus in language evaluation by the speech-language pathologist and audiologist was on attempting to find out the "cause" and the "why" of the child's language disorder. Our clinical focus in language disorders in preschool children before the early 1960s was on the identification of the *etiology* (cause) of the disorder. At this time, the audiologist and speech-language pathologist have various testing tools available to them that permit the language evaluation of the preschooler, assessing such aspects of language as syntax, semantics, and pragmatics. For each of these language parameters, clinical judgments can be made about whether a particular youngster, when compared with normal speaking children, has a language disorder. Examples of children with language disorders and some details of our language testing will be found in Chapter 8.

As discussed earlier in this chapter, hearing loss can have devastating effects on the learning of aural-oral language. Children who do not hear noises in the environment and the words of the language spoken around them will not be able to learn language without some kind of special intervention (hearing aid, language therapy, signing). Also, the vocalizations of emotion and the prosodic vocal patterns that sound like the parent language may be seriously lacking in the youngster with a severe hearing loss. The earlier a hearing loss can be detected, followed by some compensatory management, the less effect it will probably have on developing language. Like other children with language disorders caused by different etiologic problems, preschool children with moderate-to-profound hearing loss "constitute a high-risk group for subsequent academic difficulties" (Swisher, 1985).

Perhaps the most common developmental delay in preschool children is the result of **mental retardation.** Grossman (1977) defines mental retardation as a significant impairment in adaptive behavior as measured by standardized intelligence tests; retardation is characterized by intelligence quotient (IQ) scores at least two standard deviations below the average for a particular age group. For example, if the mean score on an intelligence test is 100 (with a standard deviation of 15 points above or below the mean), a youngster who scores below 70 would be considered retarded. Such a child usually performs lower in all phases of development, such as sitting independently, taking the first steps, saying the first words, putting two words together, and overall pragmatic use of language. Some children who come into a speech-language clinic demonstrating some degree of language delay are often first believed to be retarded. Subsequent observation and cognitive-language testing will usually be able to confirm or negate such suspicions.

Moderate-to-severe retardation is found generally in children who have experienced some kind of organic disorder that affected the nervous system, during either fetal development or the first few years of life. For example, most of those with intelligence quotients below 50 are children who acquired mental retardation. The profoundly retarded, with an IQ below 20, are often institutionalized in a total-care setting; language function as a goal is not possible. The second type (a much larger group) represent those whose retardation may well be related to some kind of genetic problem or who are classified as functionally retarded (Ingalls, 1978); this group generally represents the mildly retarded, with IQs ranging from 50 to 70.

It includes the children who often profit from some kind of language-intervention program. Training is given in vocabulary acquisition, morphology, syntax, and in using language functionally. Rote training in specific language tasks will often provide mildly retarded children with a language system that they can apply in everyday situations. Instead of waiting for language to develop naturally, the language-training program can facilitate the acquisition of some functional language at an earlier time in the mildly retarded child's life than would otherwise occur.

Some preschool children who demonstrate normal response to sound (normal sensitivity) and normal cognitive development display significant language impairment, with problems understanding and using spoken language. While some of these children may show the specific central auditory problem described earlier, others may demonstrate a focal language problem such as *aphasia* (impairment in the use of language as a result of brain injury). It is difficult to separate preschool children with specific aural-oral language difficulties into one of two diagnostic types: those with central auditory impairment and those with developmental aphasia. The disorders may well be the same, each with a different name. Eisenson (1971) described some children who appear to have developmental aphasia; since infancy, they have been observed to have problems understanding what is said and problems in talking, despite demonstrating normal sensory systems (normal hearing, normal vision), normal intelligence on nonverbal-performance intelligence tests, and good emotional adjustment. Acquired aphasia in children is much easier to recognize, because the child has demonstrated normal development and language until the time of the cerebral insult. Unlike the adult, who may acquire a lasting aphasia from a unilateral (usually left-hemisphere) cerebral lesion, the preschool child with a unilateral cerebral lesion will usually make a relatively rapid recovery from aphasia. The young child's brain has such *plasticity* (cerebral functions are not highly localized) that unilateral lesions can soon be compensated for by what appears to be a genuine migration of function. That is, the function of a damaged part of the brain can quickly be taken over by an undamaged part. As children get older, and certainly at the adult level, the brain demonstrates less plasticity, and recovery of lost language function is less likely to occur. Permanent and severe aphasia in young children, therefore, appears to require bilateral cerebral lesions (Mantovani and Landau, 1980).

As we will see in Chapters 8 and 9, where we will look separately at language disorders in children and adults, aphasia in children differs markedly from aphasia in adults. The earlier the onset of aphasia in a child, the less overall cognitive development the child has experienced. The aphasic adult has a lifetime of experiences to draw on in his or her attempt to compensate for the language loss. The young child may suffer a severe interruption of cognitive development because of the lack of available language. While the adult aphasic population can be divided into fluent and nonfluent types, children with aphasia generally demonstrate the nonfluent type. Such children struggle to say their words, and their syntax is severely interrupted; their speaking patterns lack the prosodic flow of melody that characterizes the fluent adult aphasic. The aphasic child is telegraphic, often with each word said separately and with some struggling. Such a child requires intensive language-speech training, with emphasis given to improving language listening skills, developing a lexicon, developing prosody, and practice given in word-phrase-sentence formulation.

In addition to aphasia, children may also occasionally experience a developmental **apraxia of speech,** an impairment in the ability "to program, combine, and sequence the elements of speech" (Jaffee, 1984, p. 166). Aphasia and oral verbal apraxia often can be found together. A child with a pure apraxia of speech would demonstrate relatively normal (sometimes superior) comprehension of the spoken word of others, but be unable to imitate a simple spoken word, such as *ball,* despite having no muscular weakness or paralysis. A brief case presentation of a nine-year-old girl with apraxia of speech illustrates the problem best:

> Cora moved to a new city at age nine. She was basically mute, unable to speak or imitate words. Her auditory comprehension and performance on nonverbal intelligence tests were normal. In a different city, she had been diagnosed as aphasic. She was subsequently enrolled in a language program that focused on auditory-cognitive activities in which she excelled. Difficulties in all oral imitative tasks prevented her from saying her first word. Cora was able to produce a few vowels correctly after several months of speech-production training.
>
> At her first evaluation session, she was tested on vowel imitation, starting by chance with the first few vowels she had learned in her old home. She produced them correctly and with relative ease. She was then given some vowel models (and monosyllabic words) to repeat; she postured her mouth and struggled to imitate them, with no success. Her mother then said, "Cora could talk if she wanted to badly enough." Immediately, the child grabbed the examiner's coat and gestured in no uncertain terms that she wanted to talk but could not. Her problem was identified as apraxia of speech. She was eventually put in a training program that encouraged her to make any kind of sounds she wished. Instead of focusing on repetition after a model, any sound she made was recorded. She was encouraged to make sounds as fast as she could. One day, as she was quickly making random sounds, she said a true word. A few other words were said over time by this random vocalization method. Today, at age fourteen, she still cannot imitate a word orally. She continues in a speech program, showing very little improvement; her ability to read and to write has progressed very well.

In oral verbal apraxia, the individual can often functionally use a word without much problem once it has become automatic. Apraxia of speech is obviously more of a phonologic than an overall language problem. However, the presence of apraxia creates a marked discrepancy between receptive language and the ability to express one's language by speech, forcing the individual to struggle at a single-word level, often lacking normal prosody for each intended utterance. Preschool children with verbal apraxia require intensive individual therapy as well as some kind of language-therapy group, where efforts are made to encourage children to say the words they are able to say to other children and the group leaders. Figure 5-3 shows two children in language therapy, one of whom has apraxia. Therapy provides a structured play setting in which concepts, meaning and vocabulary, and syntax are built into the play activities. If a boy with apraxia could say *up,* for example, some kind of spatial play would be included that would allow him to say *up* as toys were placed in various positions.

Some children have language problems that do not appear related to hearing loss, mental retardation, aphasia, or apraxia; these are sometimes categorized as **specific language impairment** (Swisher, 1985). On nonverbal tasks, the children perform very well, but language usage is impaired. Most such children speak telegraphically, demonstrating real problems in syntax (Ludlow, 1980). Motorically, they may appear somewhat clumsy, suggesting the problem has its origin in the central nervous system. While such children can often be identified in the preschool years, when some kind of intervention program should be initiated, it is during the school years that their language impairment becomes more striking, frequently presenting severe learning disabilities (Stark and Tallal, 1981).

As was discussed in earlier chapters, much of the infant's early communication involves vocalizing various emotional states. Feelings of well-being are often translated into continuous vocalization patterns that resemble, as the baby gets older, the prosodic voicing patterns of the parent language. Displeasure is usually ex-

FIGURE 5-3   Two children receiving language therapy. Used with permission of Good Samaritan Medical Center, Phoenix, Arizona.

pressed by crying. The emotional status of the youngster is well conveyed in the communication, whether it be nonverbal or in the verbal patterns that eventually develop. Youngsters who are emotionally fragile, because of either problems from within or an unfriendly environment, often demonstrate difficulties acquiring and using language. Emotional disturbances, such as autism or childhood schizophrenia, may include serious language problems as part of the total affective disorder, as we will discuss in some detail in Chapter 8. Such children require psychiatric care and close supervision, often in an institutional environment and sometimes at home.

More often, the emotional influences that may interfere with the development of normal language in the young child do not reach the dimensions of such psychoses as autism or schizophrenia. Instead, the living environment may have been less than ideal for the child. Severe tensions within the home related to such problems as divorce, a broken home, parental and sibling quarreling, physical and mental abuse, lack of adequate food and care, and abandonment are all conditions that we have identified in particular children over the years as possibly contributing to language delay. In some cases, children appear unusually frightened and uncomfortable, and restrict their interactions with others. The typical give-and-take of normal communication, for whatever reason, has been lacking. Close family members and caregivers are often unaware of any situations that could be having a negative impact on developing language and other behaviors. Fortunately, the typical child with some emotional problems can often be managed behaviorally; that is, the difficulty may be best managed by a therapy program designed to give the child success, fun, and love, with an improved environment (family counseling, foster-home placement) that offers affection and comfort with predictable stability. A child with some language delay who can become comfortable and happy will often make dramatic gains in language usage as the result of participation in a language-stimulation group (as described in Chapter 8).

Finally, there are some preschool children with what must be classified as an *idiopathic* (cause unknown) language delay. While no known cause can be identified, the children's language usage (both receptively and expressively) is below that of their age peers. Their language performance can be evaluated specifically as to how it relates to cognition, language form, and communicative effectiveness. As Hubbell (1985) has written about management, "depending on the nature and severity of the impairment and the home situation, the clinician may recommend speech and language training, placement in a nursery school or special class, referral to a psychologist or physician, or other forms of treatment" (p. 342).

Some preschool children are brought to speech-language clinics for language difficulties that are directly related to bilingualism. They may have had primary exposure to one language within the home, then have been put in a new environment where a second language is spoken, and demonstrate the obvious language problems related to such a situation. The majority of preschool children exposed to such a situation can acquire the second language without difficulty. Bilingualism, knowing two languages and using them separately as needed, is a topic that has generated much interest recently, with teaching strategies developed that can facilitate the use of two or more languages (Baker and deKanter, 1983). Some children who speak dialectal English are viewed (often incorrectly) as having a language problem. Naremore (1980) has described a "black English vernacular" in which the black child living in, say, a large city in the United States speaks a form of English that differs from the standard adult form. Such vernacular English is as rule-governed and grammatic as standard English. Instead of viewing black vernacular English as a problem, it might be better to encourage children to develop a bilingual approach to English, learning to use both vernacular and standard forms. This is often helpful as children become older and are exposed to the written form of English in school; they can use the vernacular form with family and friends or use standard English when desirable or required (such as in reading or writing).

School-age Language Problems

We have seen in earlier chapters that before normal children ever go to school, they have already acquired an aural-oral language. After several years of communicating by voicing patterns that portrayed various affective states, children have developed a lexicon with a phonologic competence that has enabled others to understand what was being said. The grammar and word order have emerged with amazing accuracy, following the adult morphologic-syntactic rules. Through trial and error, the use of language has developed, in which children basically have learned to say things in one way in a particular setting and in another way in a different setting. Such pragmatic competence demonstrates cognitive selectivity and social sensitivity, two skills often needed if children are to satisfactorily adjust to school. Before starting kindergarten, children typically demonstrate a basic mastery of aural-oral language.

Much of the focus in the beginning primary-school curriculum is on preparing children to acquire and develop a new language system, the visual-graphic one. Aural-oral language skills are important prerequisites for learning to read and write. In fact, any of the problems interfering with language in the preschool years, such as hearing loss, mental retardation, cerebral dysfunction or injury, and excessive emotionality will often carry over and interfere with learning in the school years. The majority of language problems uncovered in the school years have their genesis in the preschool years, as Swisher (1985) has written:

> In general, results demonstrate that children with a preschool language disorder constitute a high-risk group for subsequent academic difficulties. Most academic subjects are based on language concepts and the child with a preschool language disorder appears to be at risk for experiencing later language-learning problems (p. 43).

Many children mask their marginal language abilities until they go to school, when difficulty learning to read and write unmasks them (Wood, 1982). In the preschool years, their problems in aural listening, following directions, and formulating spoken responses are often attributed to general immaturity. Further, the preschool child's communicative competence is often facilitated by well-developed nonverbal behaviors that cover up the verbal deficits. When possible, normal aural-oral language skills should be established before introducing the child to a second (but highly related) language system, reading and writing. We must remember, however, that some children, such as those who are profoundly hard-of-hearing, acquire certain aural-oral skills only after being introduced to reading-writing tasks. Also, early exposure to signing for the profoundly-hard-of-hearing child is initiated to help the child acquire language, with manual signs replacing the usual spoken word symbols.

Perhaps the most common school-age language problem is **dyslexia,** defined by Kirk (1981) as a disorder "manifested by difficulty learning to read despite conventional instruction, adequate intelligence, and sociocultural opportunity." Kirk writes that the term *dyslexia* has little educational meaning and is a label that is often used too freely in place of more thorough diagnostic testing. The child who demonstrates difficulty reading may, before starting school, have been exposed to any of the conditions we have previously discussed that seem to interfere with developing normal language. The difficulty in reading (and writing) is but a further extension of the basic language problem the child has been experiencing. Sometimes the reading problem is related to an inadequate teaching situation, which may include too big a class, poor classroom conditions, and, once in a while, poor teaching (there are poor teachers!). Or the child may come from a socioeconomically disadvantaged background, or be bilingual, or speak a vernacular form of English. A small percentage of these nonreaders may show subtle signs of an overall neurological deficit that is believed to be the cause of their dyslexia (Mattis, French, and Rapin, 1975). The great majority of children classified as dyslexic appear to have difficulty learning to read because they did not master their basic aural-oral language skills before going to school.

Most school districts in the United States have well-developed adaptive-education programs that accommodate the needs of language-impaired children. Certainly, schools for the deaf and special programs for the hearing-impaired child focus on developing skills in listening, speaking, signing, reading, writing. There are language programs for the mentally retarded child, including programs in institutions for the severely retarded and special classes within school districts for children with mild to moderate retardation. Adaptive-education programs are also available for the child who is emotionally disturbed. Programs for the aphasic child and the child with profound language impairment are now available; special classrooms for the language-impaired child often include the teaching combination of a classroom teacher and a speech-language pathologist. When possible, children with a language disorder frequently spend some time in the normal classroom (known as "mainstreaming"), where they engage with normal children in as many developmental-educational activities as possible; they may then go to a special class or group for part of the day, where attention is given to a particular deficit.

There appear to be two primary approaches today to providing programs for the language-impaired child: the specific and the developmental (Perkins, 1984). In the specific approach, the etiology of the disorder (hearing loss, emotionality, and so on) provides the primary reference. Current theory in learning and cognitive psychology seems to favor the developmental approach to the remediation of language (and other areas of handicapping). Each child is assessed in terms of his or her stage of language development. The natural conditions that characterize that particular stage of development are then stressed in the training program; the child experiences these natural conditions, with some additional focus given to language models (Snyder-McLean, 1984; Swisher and Matkin, 1984). There is less direct solicitation today for immediate response by the child, which characterized our operant approaches to teaching language in the 1960s and 1970s. We find out where children are developmentally, and decide on communication strategies for the child to use when ready. Although language models are provided, coupled with cognitive experience, children are encouraged to use any response form that they feel is appropriate, such as a smile, a gesture, a sign, a word, a phrase; it is hoped that the language models that are presented in therapy will appear eventually in the children's repertoire of natural responses.

ARTICULATION DISORDERS IN CHILDREN

It is often said that the babbling and jargon heard in the baby's utterances during the first nineteen months may well contain the speech sounds of languages the world over. Sounds at this prelinguistic stage are fleeting and without coded meaning. It is not until the emergence of the first words that the speech sounds must take on some of the phonemic specificity that characterizes a particular word. That is, the baby must utter the word with enough correct phonemes to be recognized as the target word by the listener; otherwise, the utterance sounds like more jargon. As new words emerge, the toddler usually says the vowels of these words correctly. The consonants that appear easiest to produce physiologically (as discussed in Chapters 2 and 3) are usually said first. In the first three years of life, parental concern focuses on the emergence of language, new words, and new combinations of words, rather than on the precision of articulation. If the child's speech up until age three can be understood, there is usually little concern about articulation.

As the child gets older, the adult model of articulation prevails as the standard. Children must use the adult consonant form or their speech can be judged defective. Prather and her colleagues (1975) studied the emergence of the correct production of consonants in children aged two to four years, providing some norms specific to consonant acquisition. For example, at particular age levels, they found that 90 percent of the children at that age demonstrated normal production (producing the adult standard form) of certain consonants in all positions within a word. The 90 percent mastery data were:

thirty-two months:	n, m, p, h, t, k, j
thirty-six months:	f, w, ŋ, b, g, d
forty-eight months:	s
older than forty-eight months:	l, r, ʃ, tʃ, dʒ, v, z, ʒ, ð, θ

We see that, at forty-eight months, the typical youngster is able to produce 14 consonants correctly, at the beginning of a word, in the middle, and in the final position. The more complex phonemes are not produced correctly until after forty-eight months or much later. Sander (1972) summarized the articulation-acquisition data of several investigators and concluded that there were average age estimates when sounds were acquired and a much later age when 90 percent of the age population had mastered those sounds. He reported that the phonemes /s, z, v, ð/ are mastered by 90 percent of the children at age eight; the /ʒ/ appears to be the latest sound mastered by American children, with 90 percent mastery occurring at eight and a half years. We present more demographic data about sound acquisition in Chapter 10.

We will also find (and this is presented more fully in Chapter 10) that articulation defects in children can be grossly divided into two primary etiologic categories, those related to faulty phonologic processes and those related to faulty structural systems that prevent normal phonetic production. As we view separately each of these broad causes of articulation defects in children, let us remember that this separation is an artificial one, which we are making for purposes of taking a closer look at the problem. For whatever reasons, the child does not produce speech sounds with the precision required for the production of the adult articulation model (the standard to which a judgment is made specific to articulatory correctness).

Articulation Problems Related to Faulty Phonologic Processes

As children acquire new speech sounds, they tend to simplify the adult *phonologic process* (the rules that govern speech production). The three-year-old child who views and smells his mother's fresh cupcakes coming out of the oven may say with great fervor, "I dan a tutay." Perhaps in more benign circumstances he can produce the adult target speech sounds with greater accuracy; in the mouth-watering situation in which he finds himself, however, he uses a simplified version of "I want a cupcake." Many articulation errors in children are of this type, with the child at certain developmental stages employing a natural process of simplification. Ingram (1976) has discussed three such natural processes: syllable simplification (such as deleting a final consonant or unstressed syllable); assimilation (repeating sounds that are correct in front or back of the target sound); and substitution (sounds are replaced by those easier to produce). Using the cupcake example, let us look at Table 5–1, which illustrates two of the three simplifying processes.

TABLE 5–1

An Example of Natural Process Simplification

Target statement:	I want a cupcake.	
Child's statement:	I dan a tutay.	
Deletions*:	dan*	tu*tay*.
Assimilation:	—	
Substitution:	d/w	t/k t/k

The phonologic approach to articulation disorders recognizes that the child has some difficulty mastering the adult phonology of the language. In his or her attempts to use the language, the child in effect makes systematic simplifications of the phonology.

From the point of view of a phonologic process, children with an articulation problem often use simplification processes beyond the time when their age peers use them. The diagnostic evaluation of such a child's speech is basically focused on identifying the child's language usage and the particular phonologic processes used. Some typical phonologic-process examinations are presented in the Evaluation section of Chapter 10. Articulation therapy from a natural-process perspective is less phoneme-oriented and more language-rule-oriented than traditional articulation therapy. For example, rather than working on an omitted /s/ and /z/ in the final position of words with a production (practice producing the absent sound) focus, emphasis in therapy would be on teaching the rule of pluralization. Or perhaps the process analysis revealed that the child was omitting many final consonants; rather than working on specific sound deletions, the approach in therapy would be to recognize that all words have final sounds. Awareness of the final consonant requirement would play a more prominent part of therapy than working on specific production of a particular omitted sound.

Probably the majority of young children with developmental articulation problems, those whose sounds have not reached the adult production standard at a particular age, can profit from a phonologic-process approach in therapy. There are some children, however, who continue with an isolated articulation problem, such as a frontal lisp, who seem to know the phonologic rules of production but continue to make a distorted /s/. There may be no physical problem causing the /s/ distortion, but the children have learned a faulty muscular pattern for the /s/ production. Children with such focal phonetic errors profit from individual therapy, with focus on production skills. There are other children who experience a structural or physical problem that affects their acquisition of speech sounds at the time of their age peers. While such children may also have a simplification-of-process problem, they too may profit from direct work on the motor production of the incorrect sound.

Articulation Problems Related to Faulty Motor Production

Beyond the phonetic error of faulty motor placement (the children just articulate that way, with no cause identified), there are many physical problems that can contribute to faulty articulation in children. The earlier a child experiences such a problem, the greater impact it will have on developing articulation. For example, an injury to the mouth, such as a severe intraoral burn, could have devastating effects on early speech attempts by an infant, but a teenager who acquires such an injury would probably be able to compensate for the articulation skills so well that speech intelligibility could be maintained. Let us look separately at some of the physical problems in children that could contribute to articulation defects, such as hearing loss, tongue thrust, facial-oral abnormalities, cleft palate, and cerebral palsy.

Hearing Loss. Hearing loss, either conductive or sensorineural, can contribute to problems in articulation. As we have discussed earlier (and will consider later as well), hearing plays a primary role in normal language acquisition and language performance. The phonologic rules that govern one's language and the eventual production of the sounds of the language require one to be able to hear the language. The natural acquisition of aural-oral language requires both the aural stimulation and the oral practice in production. The normal-hearing child acquires the phonemes of the parent language in a predictable developmental order; the hearing-impaired or deaf child acquires these articulation skills through amplification and special teaching of oral skills.

Tongue Thrust. There are several generations of Americans who have been treated for tongue thrust as part of an overall *orthodontic* (dental specialty concerned with tooth alignment and occlusion) management program. Such people have been identified by orthodontists as placing an unusual amount of tongue pressure on anterior dentition (particularly the upper incisors), perhaps contributing to malocclusion. Many orthodontists (but not all!) feel that tongue thrust, if it exists, must be eliminated before the child can profit from wearing braces and from other orthodontic procedures. Such lingual pressures occur primarily during the initial act of swallowing (sometimes tongue thrust is called "reverse swallowing") where the tongue pushes against the upper central incisors or pushes between the upper-lower incisors as part of the beginning movement of the swallow (Mason and Proffit, 1974). Some children with identified tongue thrust also exhibit an articulation disorder thought to be associated with tongue thrust, often mispronouncing anterior sibilants, particularly /s/ and /z/. The treatment of tongue thrust has been developed as a subspecialty in the profession of speech-language pathology, with specific corrective procedures known as **myofunctional therapy,** the development of optimal intraoral lingual postures (Barrett and Hanson, 1978). While it appears today that tongue thrust is rarely the cause of articulation problems, there may well be increasing evidence that it can indeed contribute to dental malocclusion (Barrett and Hanson, 1978). The treatment of tongue thrust, with or without an accompanying speech problem, by the speech-language pathologist continues to be a controversial issue within the profession.

Oral-facial Abnormalities. There are various acquired or genetic abnormalities of the facial skeleton that can cause severe articulation problems. Many of these facial abnormalities are but part of a pattern of oral-facial anomalies that are known as a *syndrome;* that is, a certain number of predicted abnormalities occur that have been identified as a syndrome, usually named after the physician(s) who first grouped the symptoms together as a syndrome. For example, a child may be classified as having the Berry-Treacher Collins syndrome, characterized by a lack of mandible-facial growth, a downward slanting of the eyes, a notching of the lower eyelid, and *microtia* (a lack of external ear development); this syndrome is genetic in origin and may often be observed in several members of the same family. Extensive and repeated plastic surgery is usually successful in minimizing the oral-facial abnormalities that characterize Berry-Treacher Collins syndrome. Besides oral-facial abnormalities of several other syndromes, problems in communication may be part of the symptom complex including hearing loss, language delay, mental retardation, or problems in speech articulation.

Sometimes we see children in speech-language clinics who were born with facial or tongue muscles that lack neural innervation. One girl, age eight, was unable to smile, because the muscles that extended her mouth had no innervation; by extensive neuro- and plastic surgery, some of the nerve fibers used in opening the jaw were transplanted to innervate the muscle fibers used in smiling. The operation was successful, giving her not only a smile but enough functional control of her lips to improve her faulty articulation.

Occasionally, tongue problems may contribute to an articulation difficulty. A tight lingual *frenum* (tongue tie) is perhaps the most common; the small band of tissue under the tongue that contributes to anchoring the tongue is too tight, restricting both elevation and protrusion of the tongue. On protrusion, the tongue will often appear heart-shaped, indented at the tip. When such a condition can be clearly demonstrated to restrict tongue movements for some front-of-the-mouth sounds, the lingual frenum is often clipped by a surgeon, with very good results. Another structural problem of the tongue may be related to the tongue's being too large (*macroglossia*) or too small (*microglossia*), although the tongue in children seems to have a remarkable ability to accommodate to the oral cavity in which it resides. Tongue incoordinations we observe will be discussed as part of the physiological problems observed in dysarthria.

Dental abnormalities are often blamed as the cause of articulation problems. Shelton and others (1975) looked closely at the influence of various dental abnormalities on improvement in articulation therapy, concluding that even children with severe malocclusion could learn to articulate normally. Severe malocclusions, as seen in underbite or overbite, may or may not have an effect on articulation. Sometimes the orthodontic correction of malocclusion, the wearing of braces or bands, will interfere some with tongue precision, creating a possible articulation problem. Such a problem is usually temporary, with the child able to develop some excellent tongue compensations that make normal speech possible again. Absent teeth or the wearing of a dental appliance in some children may cause some articulatory distortions; such distortions are often eliminated by speech practice directed by the speech-language pathologist.

Many of these oral-facial abnormalities do contribute to phonetic errors, problems in the physiological production of the sound. Cleft lip and cleft palate are oral-facial abnormalities that typically have severe impact on developing normal articulatory skills.

Cleft Lip and Palate. About 25 percent of children with labial-palatal clefts have unilateral or bilateral clefts of the lip only; about 50 percent of the "cleft population" have unilateral or bilateral clefts of both the lip and the palate; the remaining 25 percent have only clefts of the palate (Fogh-Anderson, 1942). In summarizing clinical demographic data over time specific to lip and palate involvement, the 1942 Fogh-Andersen data seem to hold well. Specific to the incidence of lip-palate clefts, McWilliams, Morris, and Shelton (1984) wrote, "A safe, conservative estimate appears to be approximately one in every 750 live births" (p. 11). A cleft of the lip may be unilateral or bilateral. Clefts of the lip may extend only through the soft tissue of the upper lip, or they may also involve the alveolus or dental arch. Palatal clefts anteriorly may be either unilateral or bilateral (the clefting occurs on either side of the premaxilla, often trapping it forward outside the mouth and attached to the lip or tip of the nose). A large unrepaired cleft palate, with the premaxilla attached to the tip of the nose, may be seen in Figure 5–4. The surgical correction of such a defect would probably be in successive stages, closing the lip and repositioning the premaxilla back into its palatal position; closure of the probable accompanying hard- and soft-palate clefts would occur later.

Most cleft lips can be well repaired today through plastic surgery. It is rare for a cleft lip to have a lasting, permanent effect on articulation. Rather, the high success of plastic surgery pretty well assures that the baby born with a unilateral or bilateral cleft lip will eventually develop a functional lip, normal in appearance, with good mobility and quite capable of normal articulatory function. Cleft palate, while usually managed successfully, often continues to present problems in velopharyngeal closure, permitting excessive airflow and sound waves to flow through

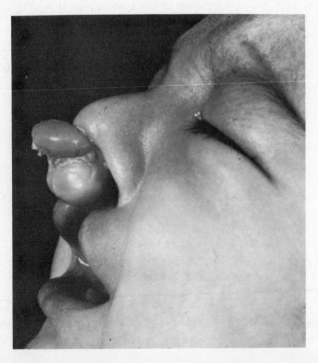

FIGURE 5-4 A newborn with a complete palatal cleft, with the upper lip and premaxilla attached to the nose. Such a defect is closed surgically in the first few weeks of life. Used with permission of University of Arizona Medical Center.

the nasal cavities, creating persistent problems of hypernasality and distortion of some phonemes, such as /s/ and /z/. Successful management of cleft palate usually requires the combined efforts of several specialists (the roles of specialists who work to alleviate various communicative disorders are described in Chapter 13), including the plastic surgeon, otolaryngologist, orthodontist, prosthodontist, audiologist, speech-language pathologist, and social worker. In most major population areas, these specialists meet regularly together as cleft-palate teams (sometimes called orofacial-disorder teams) who discuss and plan the overall management strategies required for a particular child with these lip-palate problems.

The team works closely with both the child and the family, planning the sequence of treatment steps. In the case of the cleft lip, focus is given to both cosmetic improvement and adequacy of function. Repaired lips rarely contribute to any residual articulation problem. Functional adequacy is the primary consideration for palatal clefts. Often a combination of surgery (perhaps first closing the soft palate cleft) is followed by the fitting of a prosthodontic appliance, or an **obturator.** An obturator is an acrylic plate, resembling a dental retainer that a child might wear after completing orthodontia; the obturator may be fitted over a hard-palate cleft until the child experiences more growth. Surgical closure of the hard-palate defect is usually one of the later surgical procedures. Figure 5–5 shows two approaches to minimizing the problems created by a short velum. Sometimes, after soft-palate surgery or in some children with short palates, we see inadequate velopharyngeal closure related to there being too large a gap between the velum and posterior pharyngeal wall. In sketch A of Figure 5–5, the velopharyngeal gap is closed with a bulb attached to an obturator; in sketch B, the velopharyngeal opening has been closed surgically by an inferiorly based pharyngeal flap. The primary function problem in cleft palate is *velopharyngeal insufficiency* (complete oral and nasal cavity separation is not possible), which permits excessive airflow to escape through the nose, contributing to distortion of high intraoral consonants, such as stops, fricatives, and affricates, and to excessive nasal resonance. Velopharyngeal insufficiency also contributes to feeding and swallowing problems, allowing liquids and soft foods to escape into the nasal cavities. The physical correction (surgical-prosthodontic) of velopharyngeal insufficiency is the primary management focus. Feeding and speech training, including voice therapy designed to reduce hypernasality, will have little effect until the structural inadequacy has been corrected.

Once structural adequacy is achieved, the speech-language pathologist plays a primary role in helping the child develop normal speech and voice. The articulation errors of the child are primarily phonetic in nature; that is, the structural problems and altered oral physiology create improper speech movements. Children with velopharyngeal problems usually know the normal phonologic rules for the sounds of their language, but what they lack is the physical capability for correct (adult model) production. The speech-language pathologist helps the child to develop correct labial-lingual placements for the production of sounds; a typical problem, however, is that structural adequacy may not be possible until the child has been speaking incorrectly for many years. The later the child's speaking mechanism is surgically or dentally corrected, the more difficult it is through speech remediation

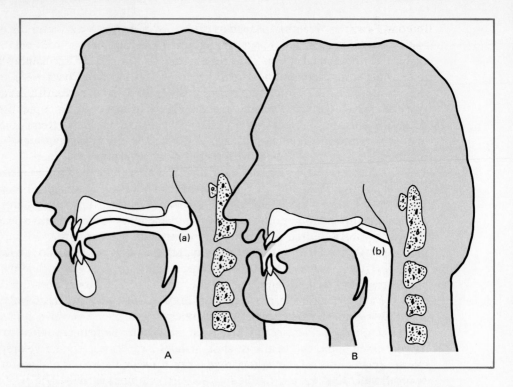

FIGURE 5-5 Two approaches for correcting velopharyngeal inadequacy: in sketch A, we see an obturator-bulb (a) in place: in sketch B, we see an inferiorly based pharyngeal flap (b) obliquing from posterior pharynx across to velum.

to correct faulty speech patterns. The same is true for reducing hypernasality, even though adequate velopharyngeal closure has been achieved. For example, a successful pharyngeal flap in a teenager may not immediately end problems of hypernasality; usually, after the flap operation, the child still profits from some voice therapy designed to establish oral resonance.

Family counseling must begin the day the child with a cleft lip and palate is born. It is important to establish early that with the right surgery, dental management, speech and voice training, the child's problems will become less visible. Normal appearance and normal function more often than not are realistic goals. As these children get older, it is important that they receive some counseling, designed to stress the normal behaviors and situations that they are capable of experiencing. Their normal behaviors are applauded. As structural adequacy develops after successful dental and surgical treatment, the children need continued guidance, as well as speech and voice remediation designed to give them normal communication function. The typical child born with a cleft lip and palate, who receives well-planned, comprehensive treatment, in the teen years will usually have a good appearance, normal speech and voice, and a surprisingly adequate personality.

Cerebral Palsy. There are children who display some motor impairment early in their lives, often from the time of birth, who have **cerebral palsy.** This is not a disease per se, but rather a term used to label a number of motor-sensory conditions that result from damage to or failure of development of the central nervous system. McDonald and Chance (1964) have written that about three in every thousand newborns could be classified as having cerebral palsy. This neurological impairment may occur before birth, during birth, or during the first three years. Therefore, there is often gross motor delay in many aspects of the child's life: crawling, sitting, standing, walking, chewing-swallowing, self-feeding, and talking. The finer the required motor skill, such as talking, the more likely the youngster will experience a problem. In cerebral palsy, the motor deficits may be grossly divided into four types:

Spasticity. Characterized by simultaneous contraction of both primary and antagonistic muscles, producing severe tightness and hypertonicity. Speech prosody is often interrupted by respiratory and voice breaks. Articulation is often severely defective.

Athetosis. **Athetosis** is characterized by a series of involuntary contractions, with flailing of extremities and much facial grimacing. There is marked variability in hypertonicity. Lack of respiratory control causes a monotonic voice, often lacking sufficient volume. Many phonemic distortions.

Mixed. This type of cerebral palsy represents a mixture of both tight spasticity and flailing athetosis, sometimes called **tension athetoid.**

Ataxia. **Ataxia** is characterized by a lack of balance, with severe problems in coordination of movements. Motor behavior is hypotonic. Ataxic speech sounds like the slurred, arhythmical speech of someone inebriated.

The motor-speech problems of the cerebral-palsied child can be classified as dysarthric speech. Since dysarthria manifests itself in problems of articulation, voice, and prosody, we discuss it in much greater detail in Chapters 10, 11, and 12. The term *cerebral-palsied speech problems* continues to be used, implying a motor disorder of speech, developmental in nature; the child with cerebral palsy enjoys few normal developmental experiences, with a marked delay in speech. The treatment of the dysarthria, therefore, experienced by the cerebral-palsied child may be quite different from that provided one who acquires dysarthria after basic, normal speech patterns have been established.

Often the cerebral-palsied child is so physically active with limb contractions and flailing, with constantly changing and unstable head and trunk posture, that speaking appears almost impossible. Therefore, the child must first develop some postural control and some control of extraneous movements before work can begin on the fine motor controls required for speech (Mysak, 1980). For example, learning to sit erect (with or without support) and keeping the mouth in a controlled, closed pattern are often prerequisite behaviors for attempting speech (Boone, 1972). The speech-language pathologist working with the cerebral-palsied child coordinates the speech-language program closely with other treatment specialists, such as the orthopedic surgeon, the physiatrist (a physician specializing in physical or restorative medicine), the physical therapist, the occupational therapist, and the special educator.

Articulation therapy is closely coordinated with feeding training. Speaking ability and chewing and swallowing competence appear often related to the child's developing control of aberrant oral reflexes (Love and others, 1980). For example, helping the child develop enough control of the mouth to open and shut it with some volition would be a most helpful motor skill to have established before working on speech sounds per se. Once gross motor control has been developed, the mildly-to-moderately-involved child can profit from articulation therapy using many of the traditional therapy approaches (detailed in Chapter 10).

For some severely involved cerebral-palsied children, articulate speech is not a realistic goal; for these children, some form of nonvocal communication systems must be introduced. A manually or electronically operated communication board has been found an effective alternate communication system. The child has several stimuli mounted on a board, and selects the appropriate stimulus by indicating it with a hand, a foot, perhaps a head-stick or headlight mounted on a helmet, and sometimes by a differentiated eye gaze. With the improvement of electronic-assistive devices, it is possible to activate stimulus selection by electronic switches attached to the chest wall or to the arm or leg; eye movements have been used to activate stimulus panels on some electronic boards (Broen, 1981; Coleman and others, 1980). Thanks to modern technology, there are assistive communication devices available that will meet the basic communication needs of the most severely handicapped cerebral-palsied child.

VOICE DISORDERS IN CHILDREN

Most of the voices we hear in children during the first five years are perceived by listeners as normal. Occasionally, a baby seems to cry in an inappropriately low-pitched voice or has vocalizations that appear hypernasal. Any deviation in vocal quality, pitch level, or resonance may be but a symptom of an airway or laryngeal disease; for this reason, any preschool youngster with a persistent change in the way the voice sounds should have the benefit of a thorough medical evaluation of the airway and larynx. For the school-age child, we usually say that any vocal (loudness, pitch, quality, resonance) change that persists more than two weeks should also be investigated medically. Let us now look separately at voice problems for preschool and school-age children. They will be discussed in greater detail, with attention also given to adults, in Chapter 11.

Preschool Voice Problems

It is generally agreed that the preschool years may be wisely spent enjoying the various vocal excesses that seem to occur spontaneously, such as crying, laughing, screaming, or yelling. This is probably the only time in life when one can be vocally spontaneous, dramatizing one's emotions with one's voice. It is not necessarily a time, then, for voice therapy. However, a voice that deviates markedly from one's age peers probably needs to be investigated medically. A voice disorder in a very young child can be the early symptom of a serious laryngeal disease, perhaps one that is life-threatening. If the different voice has always characterized the child's vocal efforts, or particularly if a change in voice has persisted more than two weeks, the child should be scheduled for a medical evaluation, including an examination of the nose, throat, and larynx. Depending on the examination findings, the management of the voice problem at this early age will be primarily medical rather than involving voice therapy (Boone, 1983).

Most preschool children tolerate **nasoendoscopy** as well as the six-year-old girl shown in Figure 5–6. When a small, flexible endoscopic tube (3.3 mm) is used, children as young as age three can be examined by a skilled user. The flexible fiberoptic scope is placed through the nose down into the back of the throat, affording the clinician a clear view of the larynx and the airway structures behind and above it. Still photographs can be taken of the nasoendoscopic view, or the physician may couple the endoscope with a television monitor, affording videoendoscopic views of the movement or physiology of laryngeal-airway activity. Once the

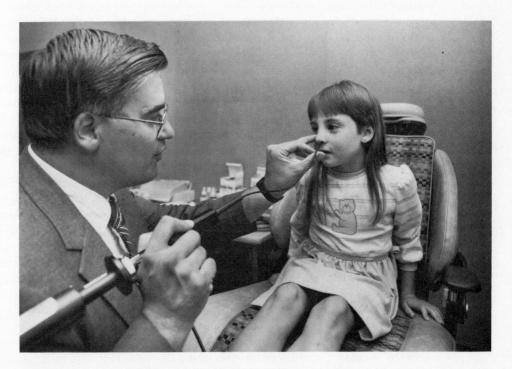

FIGURE 5-6   A six-year-old girl is examined by nasoendoscopy. Used with permission of S. C. McFarlane, University of Nevada Medical School, Reno.

larynx has been viewed, the diagnosis of what is causing the voice problem or airway obstruction can usually be made.

If no structural lesions of the larynx can be identified as possible causes of the dysphonia, a diagnosis is made of **functional dysphonia,** a voice problem related to laryngeal misuse without an organic cause. Instead of an organic problem (such as a tumor of some kind) contributing to the problem, the child is using his or her voice inappropriately; the physiology of phonation is less than optimum, producing a voice that is usually perceived as different (hoarse, lower in pitch, breathy, and so forth). In clinical practice with young children, there do not appear to be too many cases of functional dysphonia. That is, when a young child habitually produces a hoarse voice, it has been our observation that there is usually some kind of physical cause. Typical physical causes of a voice disorder in a young preschooler might include papilloma, granuloma, laryngeal web, vocal-cord thickening, vocal nodules, allergies or infection, and large, infected tonsils.

While the physical causes of voice disorders in children are discussed in Chapter 11, let us consider now the most common voice disorder in young children, dysphonia related to vocal-fold thickening and vocal nodules.

Vocal-fold Thickening and Vocal Nodules. When preschool children continually demonstrate a dysphonic voice (often with low pitch and a breathy hoarseness), they should be evaluated medically. Such a voice in a baby or even a four-year-old signals that there may be some kind of growth obstructing the normal approximation of the vocal folds. Once again, the primary concern with a hoarse voice in a young preschool child is that hoarseness may be the early symptom of what could be a serious airway obstruction. However, more often when the physician views the airway and larynx, early vocal-fold thickening or nodules are identified. Thickening and nodules, as we will discuss in detail in Chapter 11, are membranous tissue changes on the vocal folds that are the result of abuse and misuse. While thickening or nodules may produce a hoarse voice, they are not large enough to obstruct the airway. Therefore, while the symptoms of hoarseness may be annoying, the thickening or nodules are not life-threatening.

Once nodules in youngsters four years of age or younger (we have seen nodules in six-month-olds) have been identified, there are different approaches to the management of the problem. Certainly, surgical removal of the membranous thickening or nodules should not be done (Boone, 1983; Mowrer and Case, 1982). Some speech-language pathologists recommend voice therapy for these additive lesions related to vocal abuse and misuse in preschool children. Parent counseling and working with the child to curb the extreme use of voice (screaming, yelling) have been used with some success (Wilson, 1979). Once the nodules or thickening in the preschool child have been identified, we can discuss the problem with the parents, but in general, we should not start the child in voice therapy. As we have noted in earlier chapters, the voice is often the primary conveyor of emotionality in infancy and the preschool years. Perhaps the young child needs to cry, to laugh, to shriek, to yell. To curb these emotional sounds may indeed be good for the membranes of the larynx but not meet the overall personality needs of the child. By the time the child is five and needs a better voice in school, a voice-therapy program designed to eliminate abuse/misuse (and eliminate the additive lesions) can usually be initiated successfully (Boone, 1980; Wilson and Rice, 1977).

Allergies, Infections, Large Tonsils. The airway and the larynx of the preschool child are small. Allergies and colds that are characterized by an irritation and swelling of membranous tissue are, therefore, particularly bothersome to both the youngster's breathing and voicing. Once again, the primary concern is to maintain adequate breathing, with voice a secondary problem. When the small child is suffering from an allergy or cold, the larynx will be even more sensitive to vocal abuse and misuse, often producing severe vocal symptoms. While temporary voice rest would be helpful, it is usually not possible with the very young child.

Some youngsters suffer from recurring tonsillitis and pharyngitis with the symptoms of fever, sore throat, hoarseness, and often an accompanying otitis media. Their infections are treated repeatedly with antibiotics. Sometimes, after repeated infections, children may require a tonsillectomy and/or an adenoidectomy. After such a surgical procedure, youngsters will temporarily limit velopharyngeal closure movements "in an effort to avoid pain" (Prater and Swift, 1984), resulting in a high-pitched, hypernasal voice. Usually, about two weeks after surgery, the pain is gone and children return to the normal velopharyngeal closure pattern (and normal voice).

School-age Voice Problems

While preservation of the airway is of some concern in all laryngeal pathologies, it becomes increasingly less of a problem as the child gets older. The larger airway can accommodate larger lesions. Still, however, the schoolchild with a changed voice (hoarse, breathy, change of pitch), like anyone who develops a vocal pathology, requires a medical evaluation, with a look at the airway and the larynx. In a national-incidence study of schoolchildren, Hull and others (1976) found that about 3 percent demonstrated phonation disorders. The school speech-language pathologist typically discovers children with voice problems, through a screening program or by teacher or physician referral. The child then receives a voice evaluation that includes a physician's view of the airway and larynx by *laryngoscopy,* a look at the throat and larynx by placing a mirror back in the oropharynx, or by endoscopy. Almost one-third of the schoolchildren with hoarse voices will demonstrate no structural lesion of the vocal folds but are experiencing hoarseness by faulty voice usage (functional dysphonia). The other two-thirds with hoarse voices are found to have thickening nodules-polyps related to vocal abuse-misuse or other vocal pathologies, such as granuloma, papilloma, or web.

Some school-age children continually abuse and misuse their voices, yelling and screaming with daily regularity. The membranes that cover the vocal folds along the glottis begin to toughen (almost callus-like), producing a thickness and sometimes actual nodules; these additive lesions generally form at the same site, the anterior-middle third of the total vocal fold, as shown in Figure 5-7. In fact, a lesion at this

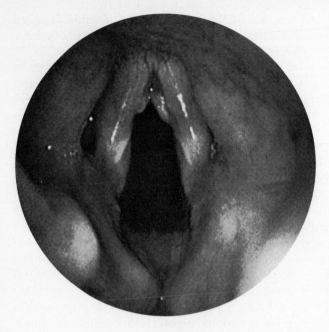

FIGURE 5–7   Large vocal nodules on each vocal fold in an eight-year-old child. Courtesy of University of Arizona Medical Center, Tucson.

anterior site is an indication that it has developed from continuous abuse (throat clearing, yelling) and misuse (loud voice, inappropriate pitch). If these aversive vocal behaviors can be reduced or eliminated, the additive thickening or nodules will usually go away. Toohill (1975) observed that nodules often seen in hyperactive boys seven–eleven years old generally begin to reduce as they become teenagers. It would appear that the social status a young, screaming boy may enjoy by controlling his world with a loud voice may become jeopardized as the boy gets older. The social mores of the teenage male often require that he be "cool," vocally reserved. When the vocal style changes, so does the state of the vocal folds. In the preteen years, there appear to be more boys than girls with vocal lesions related to *hyperfunctional* (too much effort) vocal behaviors. However, in many voice clinics, we now see more teenage girls with nodules related to excessive vocalization in their cheerleading and sporting activities (Boone, 1983; Mowrer and Case, 1982).

Voice therapy designed to reduce vocal hyperfunction in children has had remarkable effects in eliminating such conditions as thickening or nodules and in improving the sound of the child's voice (Boone, 1983; Prater and Swift, 1984; Wilson, 1979). The profession of speech-language pathology has the therapy skills needed to reduce and often eliminate vocal nodules in both children and adults; voice therapy designed to eliminate vocal hyperfunction generally focuses on these four areas:

1. identifies vocal (and laryngeal) abuses and misuses
2. reduces or eliminates the identified abuses/misuses

3. searches with the patient to find vocal approaches that produce voice easily

4. uses the vocal-facilitating approaches in practice and daily living for the patient.

Such a symptomatic approach requires that the child understand what he or she is doing wrong vocally and then substitute easy vocal productions for harmful vocal behaviors.

The treatment of functional dysphonia in children requires an almost cognitive approach to therapy. That is, children must first of all want to change their voices and then understand what they are "doing wrong." Sometimes our explanation to a youngster, such as, "You don't have to talk so loud all of the time," has the immediate and dramatic effect of improving the voice. Of the many therapies provided by the speech-language pathologist for various kinds of communication disorders, voice therapy is probably the one clinical area where dramatic improvement can occur in a relatively short period of time. The state of the art and knowledge in voice remediation are good enough today that no child should have to live year after year with a faulty voice. Management programs for voice disorders are often quick and effective.

FLUENCY DISORDERS IN CHILDREN

The majority of children speak with amazing fluency. Even in the babble and the jargon of the baby, we hear continuous, changing vocal patterns, usually free of any kind of interruption. As the two-year-old child combines words in beginning phrases and sentences, they are said with surprising fluency—surprising because these are often the first combined-word utterances the child has ever attempted. It is not until age three or beyond that we sometimes hear and see an abrupt, observable break in the child's verbal fluency. The breath stops, the voicing patterns cease, and there may be a complete (but temporary) breakdown in communication. These early breakdowns in verbal fluency, which usually occur as the child is generating a sentence of some kind, we will call *disfluency*. They are seen in many normal children and are not classified as **stuttering** behaviors.

One useful way for distinguishing between normal disfluency and stuttering is by identifying the type of speech unit involved in the disfluency (Andrews and others, 1983; Perkins, 1980). For example, children with normal disfluency are more likely to repeat whole words or phrases, such as "I want a, I want a, I want a soda." A child who is stuttering is more likely to make sound or syllable repetitions, such as, "I wa-wa-wa-want a s-s-s-s-s-s-soda." The frequency of the speech disfluency is probably another good way to distinguish between normal disfluency and stuttering. Wingate (1962) found that normal children do not repeat more than 3 percent of their total utterances, while stutterers repeat syllables in 7 to 14 percent of their total utterances. There is also some indication that children who stutter show greater signs of struggle (eye blinking, facial grimacing) than normal children, who may repeat whole words or phrases.

In Chapter 12, some of these distinguishing characteristics are used to develop the following definition: "Stuttering is the involuntary repetition and prolongation of speech sounds and syllables that the individual struggles to end." Most recent definitions of stuttering include the word *involuntary* (Andrews and others, 1983). Since the fluency interruptions are involuntary, the child has no warning that the stuttering is going to occur. It is often the initial sound of the first word of the intended response in which the repetitions and prolongations occur. Stuttering is usually accompanied by struggle. As children experience negative listener reaction to their stuttering, they begin to struggle to end the fluency interruptions by changing the intended word, pursing the lips, facial grimacing, blinking the eyes, and so forth. Often, the secondary things the child does as a reaction to the stuttering become more of a communicative problem than the actual sound repetitions and prolongations.

It appears that about 0.8 percent of school-age children stutter, with a male-to-female sex ratio of three to one. Young (1975) estimated the prevalence of stuttering in school-age children and young adults at about 0.7 percent. In the national-incidence study on speech and hearing disorders, Hull and his colleagues (1976) reported stuttering in about 0.8 percent of the 38,802 children surveyed. There are no data available specific to the prevalence of stuttering in preschool children. It would be our guess, however, that the majority of speech interruptions observed in preschool children are more likely the whole-word repetitions characteristic of disfluency rather than the sound repetitions of stuttering.

In summarizing the recovery from stuttering data, it would appear that the vast majority of school-age children who stutter, experience recovery (normal fluency) before they finish high school. This recovery view is substantiated by the work of Andrews and others (1983), who found that about 78 percent of the children who once stuttered no longer did so. Some children profit from intensive speech therapy, designed to promote fluency, replacing disfluencies with a controlled, easy way of talking. We will consider diagnostic and therapy approaches to the problem of stuttering in children in greater detail in Chapter 12.

Another fluency disorder we discuss in Chapter 12 is **cluttering,** a speech disorder characterized by an extremely rapid rate of talking, often with articulation errors. Fluency is also one of the parameters of the motor speech problem, dysarthria, which we talked about earlier in this chapter and will consider again in later chapters, dealing with articulation (Chapter 10), voice (Chapter 11), and fluency (Chapter 12). The vast majority of children demonstrate normal prosodic voice patterns and verbal fluency in their speech; however, for those relatively few who demonstrate problems in fluency, communicative abilities may be seriously affected.

REVIEW QUESTIONS

Problems in hearing, language, articulation, voice, and fluency in children may be major obstacles to normal development as well as to effective communication. Let us review some questions about children's communication disorders.

1. Describe the effects of moderate-to-severe hearing loss on a child's overall communication.

2. How can learning to sign facilitate the learning of language?

3. What is apraxia of speech?

4. Differentiate between phonologic process errors and phonetic errors of articulation. Is such differentiation necessary in therapy?

5. Why do children with cleft palate often have severe articulation and resonance disorders?

6. Can the motor speech problems of a child with cerebral palsy be classified as a dysarthria? Explain.

7. What is the primary cause of voice disorders in children?

REFERENCES

Alpiner, J., Amon, C., Gibson, J., and Sheehy, P. (1977). *Talk to Me.* Baltimore: Williams and Wilkins.

Andrews, G., Craig, A., Feyer, A. M., Hoddinott, S., Howie, P., and Neilson, M. (1983). Stuttering: a review of research findings and theories circa 1982. *Journal of Speech and Hearing Disorders, 48:* 226–246.

Baker, K., and deKanter, A. (1983). *Bilingual Education: The Effectiveness of Bilingual Education.* Lexington, Mass.: Lexington Books.

Barrett, R. H., and Hanson, M. L. (1978). *Oral Myofunctional Disorders* (2nd ed.). St. Louis: C. V. Mosby.

Boone, D. R. (1972). *Cerebral Palsy.* New York: Bobbs-Merrill.

Boone, D. R. (1980). *The Boone Voice Program for Children.* Tigard, Ore.: C. C. Publications.

Boone, D. R. (1983). *The Voice and Voice Therapy* (3rd ed.). Englewood Cliffs, N.J.: Prentice-Hall.

Broen, P., ed. (1981). *Language, Speech and Hearing Services in the Schools* (special issue on nonvocal communication), *4:* 12.

Chomsky, N. (1957). *Syntactic Structures.* The Hague: Mouton.

Coleman, C., Look, A., and Meyers, L. (1980). Assessing non-oral clients for assistive communication devices, *Journal of Speech and Hearing Disorders, 45:* 515–526.

Eisenson, J. (1971). *Aphasia in Children.* New York: Harper and Row.

Fogh-Andersen, P. (1942). *Inheritance of Harelip and Cleft Palate.* Copenhagen: Busck.

Friel-Patti, S., Finitzo-Hieber, T., Conti, G., and Brown, C. (1982). Language delay in infants associated with middle ear disease and mild, fluctuating hearing loss. *Pediatric Infectious Disease, 1:* 104–109.

Grossman, H. (1977). *Manual on Terminology and Classification in Mental Retardation.* Washington, D.C.: American Association on Mental Deficiency.

Hubbell, R. D. (1985). Disorders of language in children, in *Speech, Language, and Hearing:*

Normal Processes and Disorders (2nd ed.), ed. P. H. Skinner and R. L. Shelton. New York: Wiley.

Hull, F. M., Mielke, P. W., Willeford, J. A., and Timmons, R. J. (1976). *National Speech and Hearing Survey: Final Report*. Project 50978. Washington, D.C.: Office of Education, Bureau of Education for the Handicapped.

Ingalls, R. (1978). *Mental Retardation: The Changing Outlook*. New York: Wiley.

Ingram, D. (1976). *Phonological Disability in Children*. New York: Elsevier.

Jaffee, M. B. (1984). Neurological impairment of speech production: assessment and treatment, in *Speech Disorders in Children*, ed. J. Costello. San Diego: College-Hill Press.

Kirk, S. (1981). Comment on the term dyslexia. *Reading Instruction Journal, 24:* 8–9.

Love, R., Hagerman, E., and Taimi, E. (1980). Speech performance, dysphagia and oral reflexes in cerebral palsy. *Journal of Speech and Hearing Disorders, 45:* 59–75.

Ludlow, C. (1980). Children's language disorders: recent research advances. *Annals of Neurology, 7:* 497–507.

Mantovani, J., and Landau, W. (1980). Acquired aphasia and convulsive disorder: course and prognosis. *Neurology, 30:* 524–529.

Maskarinec, A., Cairns, G., Butterfield, E., and Weamer, D. (1981). Longitudinal observations of individual infants' vocalizations. *Journal of Speech and Hearing Disorders, 46:* 267–273.

Mason, R. M., and Proffit, W. R. (1974). The tongue thrust controversy: background and recommendations. *Journal of Speech and Hearing Disorders, 39:* 115–121.

Mattis, S., French, J., and Rapin, I. (1975). Dyslexia in children and young adults: three independent neuropsychological syndromes. *Developmental Medicine and Child Neurology, 17:* 150–163.

McDonald, E. T., and Chance, B. (1964). *Cerebral Palsy*. Englewood Cliffs, N.J.: Prentice-Hall.

McWilliams, B. J., Morris, H. L., and Shelton, R. L. (1984). *Cleft Palate Speech*. Philadelphia: B. C. Decker.

Mowrer, D. E., and Case, J. L. (1982). *Clinical Management of Speech Disorders*. Rockville, Md: Aspen Systems Corp.

Mysak, E. (1980). *Neurospeech Therapy for the Cerebral Palsied* (3rd ed.). Totowa, N.J.: Teachers College Press.

Naremore, R. C. (1980). Language variation in a multicultural society, in *Introduction to Communication Disorders*, ed. T. J. Hixon, L. D. Shriberg, and J. H. Saxman. Englewood Cliffs, N.J.: Prentice-Hall.

Perkins, W. H. (1980). Disorders of speech flow, in *Introduction to Communication Disorders*, ed. T. J. Hixon, L. D. Shriberg, and J. H. Saxman. Englewood Cliffs, N.J.: Prentice-Hall.

Perkins, W. H. (1984). *Current Therapy of Communication Disorders: Language Handicaps in Children*. New York: Thieme-Stratton.

Prater, R. J., and Swift, R. W. (1984). *Manual of Voice Therapy*. Boston: Little, Brown.

Prather, E. M., Hedrick, D. L., and Kern, C. A. (1975). Articulation development in children aged two to four years. *Journal of Speech and Hearing Disorders, 40:* 179–191.

Rapin, I., and Allen, D. (1983). Developmental language disorders: nosological considerations, in *Neuropsychology of Language, Reading, and Spelling*, ed. U. Kirk. New York: Academic Press.

Sander, E. K. (1972). When are speech sounds learned? *Journal of Speech and Hearing Disorders, 37:* 55–63.

Shelton, R. L., Paesani, A., McClelland, K. D., and Bradfield, S. S. (1975). Panendoscopic feedback in the study of voluntary velopharyngeal movements. *Journal of Speech and Hearing Disorders, 40:* 232–244.

Snyder-McLean, L. (1984). Developmental therapy, in *Current Therapy of Communication Disorders: Language Handicaps in Children*, ed. W. H. Perkins. New York: Thieme-Stratton.

Stark, R., and Tallal, P. (1981). Selection of children with specific language deficits. *Journal of Speech and Hearing Disorders, 46:* 114–122.

Swisher, L. (1985). Language disorders in children, in *Speech and Language Evaluation in Neurology—Pediatric Disorders*, ed. J. Darby. New York: Grune and Stratton.

Swisher, L., and Matkin, A. (1984). Specific language impairment. The method of L. Swisher and A. Matkin, in *Current Therapy of Communication Disorders: Language Handicaps in Children*, ed. W. H. Perkins. New York: Thieme-Stratton.

Toohill, R. J. (1975). The psychosomatic aspects of children with vocal nodules. *Archives of Otolaryngology, 101:* 591–595.

Ventry, I. (1980). Effects of conductive hearing loss: fact or fiction. *Journal of Speech and Hearing Disorders, 45:* 143–156.

Wilson, D. K. (1979). *Voice Problems of Children* (2nd ed.). Baltimore: Williams and Wilkins.

Wilson, F. B., and Rice, M. (1977). *A Programming Approach to Voice Therapy.* Austin, Tex: Learning Concepts.

Wingate, M. E. (1962). Personality needs of stutterers. *Logos, 5:* 35–37.

Wood, M. L. (1982). *Language Disorders in School-Age Children.* Englewood Cliffs, N.J.: Prentice-Hall.

Young, M. A. (1975). Onset, prevalence, and recovery from stuttering. *Journal of Speech and Hearing Disorders, 40:* 49–58.

6

Disorders of Communication in Adults

While most communication disorders in adults are acquired after a lifetime of using normal communicative skills, there are some developmental communication problems that carry over from childhood. Some of the serious problems described in the last chapter, such as cerebral palsy or deafness, continue to influence one's communication for a lifetime. An acquired disorder, however, such as hearing loss, occurs after many years of normal hearing. Most adults enjoy normal language function, except those few with severe developmental language problems or those with acquired language problems, such as aphasia or dementia. The majority of adults exhibit normal phonologic skills, including normal articulation; those with articulation problems usually have some kind of neurological disease that produces a dysarthria. Many adults live with acquired voice problems, such as hoarseness, and never seek professional help to develop normal phonation; other adults may develop serious laryngeal disease, with resulting voice problems, and receive professional help for their problem. Most fluency problems in adults, such as stuttering or cluttering, are carried over from childhood; a few adults acquire a central-nervous-system problem that may result in dysarthria, which usually disturbs their fluency.

There are several classification systems for communication disorders that can be applied to adults. The functional-organic dichotomy is one such classification; for each disorder, a decision is made specific to the etiologic causation of the disorder. An adult, for example, who has always had a frontal lisp (described in Chapter 5) would be classified as having a functional disorder. Someone who always articulated correctly until receiving a massive intraoral burn would be said to have an articulation problem of organic origin. For the functional lisp, the origin of the problem is unknown; the burn-induced organic problem displays a readily identifiable etiology. The treatment for these two disorders would be quite different: for the adult with a lisp, some intensive speech therapy would be the primary treatment of choice; and for the patient with the intraoral burn, the first treatment would be medical-surgical management (perhaps plastic surgery to restore the mouth), possibly followed by speech-pathology procedures. While the functional-organic dichotomy might make some sense for these examples of adult communication disorders, many problems seem to receive the same general treatment regardless of the cause; for example, is the cause of stuttering functional or organic? Regardless of our answer (different speech-language pathologists would provide different responses), our treatment of stuttering is relatively similar.

The developmental-acquired dichotomy is another way of classifying communication disorders. Most of the disorders described in the last chapter were of developmental origin, observable early in the young child's attempts to communicate. Developmental disorders, such as language problems of unknown origin, require early identification and remediation. Efforts are made to help the young child develop normally in as many areas as possible. An acquired disorder, such as a dysarthria, related to a disease like multiple sclerosis, occurs after the individual has had some years of normal overall development and communication. The treatments of communication problems are somewhat varied depending on whether they are developmental or acquired in children, as described in the last chapter. Other than the developmental communication problems that some adults carry over from childhood, the majority of adult communication disorders are acquired; therefore, the acquired-developmental dichotomy has less meaning at the adult level. In each of the clinical parameters (hearing, language, articulation, voice, fluency), there are many examples of acquired problems. The typical high-frequency hearing loss may not occur until advanced middle age. Laryngeal nodules or polyps, dysarthria, aphasia, and injury to the mouth are all examples of acquired problems that compromise communication; each requires the services of the speech-language pathologist, who will have as the therapy target the restoration of communicative function as close to previous (before the disorder) function as possible.

Using the Parameters of Practicum model (see Chapter 1) developed by the American Speech-Language-Hearing Association, let us look at individual communication disorders in adults. We will see that, regardless of causation or etiology, each disorder may be analyzed specific to its effect on hearing, language, articulation, voice, and fluency. Some adults with communication disorders may experience difficulty in only one parameter of involvement, such as articulation. Another person, such as someone with a severe hearing loss, may show changes not only in hearing but in all other four parameters (language, articulation, voice, and fluency). For each parameter of communication disorder, we will look at its cause, prevalence, and treatment, reserving more detailed discussion of the problem for subsequent chapters.

DISORDERS OF HEARING

Normal spoken language requires a normal aural-oral language system. As we have seen, the ability to hear is a basic prerequisite for developing normal language. While the great majority of adults experience normal hearing and normal communication, hearing loss is probably the most common communication disorder in adults, increasing in prevalence as the population gets older. The adult age group seventeen to forty-four years is remarkably free of hearing loss, according to Davis (1970) with only 0.84 of 1 percent experiencing bilateral hearing impairment. The older middle-age group—between forty-five and sixty-four—experiences hearing loss very near the national population average of 3 percent. In the over-sixty-five group, hearing loss increases markedly, with the prevalence figures ranging from 13 to 60 percent, depending on the criteria (frequencies tested and threshold intensities used) that are used to judge hearing as impaired (Hull and Traynor, 1977; U.S. National Health Survey, 1967). Similar to what we observe in children, adults suffer from three types of hearing loss: **conductive, sensorineural,** and **mixed.**

Conductive Hearing Impairment

As described in some detail in the next chapter, conductive hearing losses are usually related to some kind of blockage or lack of transmission of sound from the outer or middle ear to the inner ear. The simplest and perhaps most common conductive loss in adults is related to a buildup of *ear wax* in the ear canal. Often the adult who swims often may complain of a feeling of a stopped ear with some decrement of hearing, related to a combination of water gathering in the ear canal mixing with *cerumen* (ear wax) and forming an earplug. Removal of such a plug results in an immediate and dramatic restoration of hearing. The next most common conductive hearing impairment in adults is related to *otitis media,* an inflammation and infection of the middle ear. Otitis media is often experienced when the individual has symptoms of an allergy or a cold, in which fluids build up in the middle ear and fail to drain properly via the eustachian tube into the nasopharynx. As described in the discussion about children's communication disorders, chronic and recurring otitis media is one of the most prevalent and serious that threatens communication competency in children. In adults, the problem does not usually have a great impact on communication. Middle-ear infection in adults is more likely to be an acute problem characterized by pain and temporary hearing loss than the continuing problem it often is for children. Most adults who experience otitis media, acute or chronic, usually receive effective medical treatment from the **otolaryngologist** (ear-nose-throat specialist), who treats the allergy or infection medically and drains the middle ear surgically, if indicated.

Another conductive hearing impairment (less common than wax buildup and otitis media) in adults may be related to *otosclerosis* or *otospongiosis,* a bony growth around the tiny stapes bone in the middle ear that inhibits stapes vibration. In recent years, there has been a surgical procedure for otosclerosis called a *stapedectomy,* which removes the immobile stapes from the middle ear and replaces it with a prosthesis that plays the stapes's vibratory role in introducing sound through the oval window into the cochlear portion of the inner ear (Goin, 1976).

The primary diagnostic sign on audiological examination that indicates a conductive hearing loss is the *air-bone gap.* Air-conduction thresholds are depressed, while bone conduction thresholds are elevated, indicating that the inner ear and auditory nerve are functioning well. While the sound can travel through the bone to the inner ear, there is some blockage in sound transmission within the outer and middle ear. Fortunately, many such outer- and middle-ear conductive problems in adults can be successfully treated medically and/or surgically. For hearing problems of a conductive type that cannot be medically or surgically treated, the adult patient will usually profit from an audiological evaluation to assess the degree of hearing loss. It can then be determined if the patient would profit from aural rehabilitation, perhaps learning speech reading (watching lips, using auditory cues, watching expressions and gestures). Often the patient is fitted with a hearing aid. Correct hearing-aid fitting requires thorough audiological testing. With careful selection of a hearing aid by an audiologist, most patients with conductive-type hearing losses profit from and tolerate wearing the aid very well.

Sensorineural Hearing Loss

Hearing loss caused from inner-ear damage or disease or from damage to the auditory pathways is known as a *sensorineural* loss. It is this type of hearing loss, usually characterized by a greater loss in higher than lower frequencies, that seems to increase as adults get older. Men show a greater sensorineural loss earlier than women; many men at age fifty show a 35 dB loss at 8K Hz, while women the same age show an average loss of 27 dB (Davis, 1978). Relatively early, at age fifty, a slight high-frequency hearing loss may be seen in the normal population. With increasing age, the prevalence of sensorineural hearing loss increases; this type of loss is often associated with a degeneration of hair cells within the cochlea, which often appears to be a natural consequence of advanced age. This type of high-frequency hearing loss in the aged is known as *presbycusis,* and in terms of numbers of people with the problem represents the most common form of sensorineural hearing loss. Typical patients develop the hearing loss gradually, and are therefore often unaware of its extent. When tested, they are shown to have a high-frequency hearing loss, and often have poorer auditory discrimination than the loss would indicate. Such presbycusic patients often profit from wearing a hearing aid, followed by some aural rehabilitation in which they learn how to use it. Hearing aids that have been purchased casually (such as in a store, without proper fitting) often end up unused. The presbycusic patient who has been seen by an otolaryngologist and tested by an audiologist will usually be able to make a good adjustment to wearing a hearing aid (if one is needed) as a tool that will aid successful communication.

Some adults carry over a serious sensorineural hearing loss from childhood and communicate by the methods they used as children and youth, by oral communication or by sign language, and more commonly by a combination of both oral language and signing. Despite the efforts of many educators of the deaf in the past who attempted to teach aural-oral language exclusively (often to the point of "banning" sign language in schools for the deaf), many deaf children learned signing and freely used it among themselves. So we see deaf adults today who often use a combination of oral speech and signing. Many of these people profit from wearing hearing aids that amplify whatever residual hearing they may have, providing important auditory cues specific to the prosody and melody that characterizes the languages they attempt to speak.

Other causes of sensorineural hearing loss in adults happen as part of the living experience, such as those related to particular diseases and to occasional *ototoxic drugs* (drugs that can damage the ear). Some childhood diseases, such as measles or mumps, when acquired in adulthood often leave the patient with some kind of residual problem, such as a sensorineural hearing loss. Severe bacterial diseases, such as encephalitis or meningitis, may involve the inner ear or parts of the auditory system in the brain, resulting in severe (and sometimes complete) hearing loss. The medical treatment of the overall disease is the primary management during the acute, infectious period; audiologic testing and possible rehabilitation are initiated during the chronic, recovery period after the acute illness. The following quotation cites examples of ototoxicity: "Overdoses of aspirin or quinine can cause hearing loss, although recovery of hearing is common. Some antibiotics can cause permanent sensorineural loss; dihydrostreptomycin, neomycin, kanamycin, and streptomycin are examples" (Hodgson and Matkin, 1985, p. 405). Such ototoxic drugs are used very carefully today, and only when life-threatening diseases must be controlled. Ménière's disease, which includes symptoms of severe *vertigo* (dizziness) and **tinnitus** (internal ear noises) as well as a sensorineural hearing loss, is a dreaded illness involving the hearing mechanism; more often, Ménière's involves only one ear. During its acute phase, however, the severe dizziness that it produces, with its reactive nausea, can be quite debilitating to the patient. Malignant or nonmalignant tumors sometimes involve auditory neural mechanisms, producing a sensorineural hearing loss, among other symptoms, such as pain and facial paralysis. Obviously, the medical-surgical management of such tumors is the primary treatment.

DISORDERS OF LANGUAGE

Other than the occasional language difficulty that someone experiences when in a new language environment (learning a second language, visiting a foreign country), most normal adults experience normal language function in their everyday lives. Most acquired language disorders experienced by adults are of neural origin. That is, until some change in the central nervous system (CNS) occurred, the individual had experienced normal language function. While a whole chapter in this text (Chapter 9) describes language disorders in adults, let us consider at this point the effects on language function caused by aphasia, right-hemisphere disease, mental illness such as schizophrenia, and senile dementia.

Adult Aphasia

It is estimated that about 1 percent of the population of the United States has suffered from strokes, which means that over 2 million Americans have had strokes. Of that number, those who suffered involvement of the left cerebral hemisphere and the right hemisphere would be evenly split. Aphasia is primarily the result of left-hemisphere (which is usually the dominant hemisphere for language regardless of handedness) disease. Patients with left cerebral-hemisphere disease who have aphasia number about 70 percent, which means that there are about 700,000 adult aphasic patients in the United States. Other causes of aphasia other than stroke would include cerebral trauma (accident or gunshot) and occasional cerebral diseases (such as localized brain tumor).

Aphasia is the loss of language (understanding and speaking or writing) after an injury, usually in the left hemisphere, to the brain. It would appear in the normal person that the left cerebral hemisphere is dominant, responsible for acts that require absolute ordering and sequence, such as what we see in language. In language, there is an exact code (verbal symbols and their rules of application) to be followed between sender and receiver; coding and decoding appear to be functions directed by the left hemisphere. The more precise the code (meaning of words) and the more exact the ordering of words (syntax), the more likely this is to be a task directed by the left hemisphere. Right-hemisphere function appears to be more stylistic and employs more uncoded communicative functioning, such as our voicing stress and inflection.

Aphasia occurs in different forms. Goodglass and Kaplan (1972) divided aphasic patients into two general types, the fluent and the nonfluent. The fluent aphasic patients retain verbal fluency, which means that the normal voicing prosodic patterns are retained, even though the patient may have difficulty understanding what others say and will demonstrate problems in verbal expression. The fluent aphasic often demonstrates the jargon, normal voicing communicative patterns we see in the first eighteen months of life. Many of these voicing patterns that portray emotion and affective communication are still present after fluent aphasia. The patient may speak in a jargon, complete with *neologisms* (made-up words that may sound similar to the target word), which, while lacking actual words, carries meaning by its intonation and stress. Other aphasics sound nonfluent, struggling to speak, lacking normal prosodic patterns. They demonstrate serious problems in phonology, and are sometimes unable to say the simplest word. Many of the nonfluent aphasic patients also demonstrate *oral verbal apraxia,* an inability to say a word or even a speech sound with volition (deliberately), but without difficulty saying the same sound or word involitionally (automatically, with no deliberation).

Let us look at the actual spoken protocols of two aphasic patients, each describing a Norman Rockwell picture of a soldier returning home from the war and greeting his family:

Fluent Aphasic (Woman, Forty-nine Years Old, with Wernicke's Aphasia): "Well, the frodlem is gretrching to the places with the famisher stroping by the staris and seeing the crasnoy. He sees his grader and she to the clasbo torsh the fram."

Nonfluent Aphasic (Man, Fifty-seven Years Old, with Broca's Aphasia): (Places his lips tightly together in a posture to say something beginning with /p/). "Pa-pa-a" (shakes his head), "oh, boy, p-p-p-ut, ho-ho-home."

The fluent Wernicke's aphasic speaks in a jargon, with normal-sounding inflection often carrying the meaning of what she says despite the neologistic jargon words. The Broca's patient struggles to say the sounds of individual words, and each word is spoken with some difficulty; normal, prosodic voicing is almost wholly lacking.

We will discuss the different types of aphasia specific to causation and how the patients use language in much greater detail in Chapter 9. The aphasic patient requires detailed speech-language testing to determine his or her residual communication skills. That is, while such patients may have lost much of their previous language proficiency as a result of the brain injury that produced the aphasia, they will still have residual communicative functions. Testing searches for these residual skills, finding out what the patient can still do. Shortly after the onset of aphasia, sometimes while the patient is still in the hospital, being treated for stroke or whatever is the cause of the aphasia, testing begins (some of the tests are described in Chapter 9). The test results will provide a description of the type of aphasia the patient has and how extensive it is, and may often indicate to the speech-language pathologist where to begin therapy.

Speech-language pathology services in the hospital for aphasic patients should begin as soon as they are medically stable. Initial contacts with the family are important for providing counseling and some indication of the long-term prognosis. Therapy efforts may be confined to the individual, sometimes supplemented by self-practice efforts by the patient monitored and guided by the family. When patients return home from the hospital, they are usually seen for aphasia therapy as outpatients, often in a rehabilitation center, where other treatments are available, such as occupational and physical therapies. Some like to have outpatients with aphasia receive both group and individual therapy. The patients seen in Figure 6–1 attend a weekly adult-aphasia support group, where the topics range from discussions of politics to celebrations of birthdays. The individual therapy usually focuses on residual communicative skills, encouraging the patient to use any communicative skills—voice, gesture, and words—to communicate with others.

Right-hemisphere Damage

Although left-hemisphere disease is well recognized as the cause of severe language impairment, as seen in aphasia, the effects on language by right-hemisphere damage are more subtle and less known. Geschwind (1971) reported that among right-handed persons, aphasia occurs in less than 1 percent of those who acquire right-hemisphere lesions. Instead of the dramatic problems of loss of phonologic, syntactic, and semantic function seen in aphasia, the language loss in right-hemisphere disease is perhaps more qualitative. That is, the patient's use of language is changed because of a change in mood, in looking at the world realistically, and in making planned, meaningful responses. The patient's lack of sensitivity to others negatively affects his or her language pragmatics.

The right hemisphere seems to have much to do with the recognition and expression of affect. Schlanger, Schlanger, and Gerstman (1976) studied the perception of linguistic and nonlinguistic emotionally prosodic stimuli with patients with both left- and right-hemisphere damage, finding a marked reduction in the capability of right-hemisphere patients to recognize mood and affect in the voices of others. Clinically, right-hemisphere patients often use voicing, prosodic patterns (described in earlier chapters) inappropriately in their attempts to express their emo-

FIGURE 6–1 An adult-aphasia group. Used with permission of Good Samaritan Medical Center, Pheonix, Arizona.

tions and feelings through the use of voice. Many times, it appears that the emotional message of voicing patterns does not match the linguistic message. This incongruence seems to be what many listeners are reacting to when they judge the affect of right-hemisphere patients as odd.

Wertz (1984, p. 6) has noted that we look in right-hemisphere patients for "spatial perception and body image disorders, visual perception disorders, constructional disabilities, auditory perception disorders, somatosensory disorders, motor impersistence." Any of these faulty behaviors can influence the use of appropriate communication with others. Difficulties in relating one's body (and its parts) to the space around one is a commonly observed symptom of right-hemisphere disease. For example, a man with left hemiplegia (as the result of a right-hemisphere stroke) was recently observed who did not recognize the fact that the left side of his body was paralyzed. We asked him to draw a picture of a man; it is shown in Figure 6-2. It is not unusual to see a left-sided denial (particularly if there is weakness or paralysis on that side) in the drawings of patients with right-hemisphere disease; in contrast, patients with left-brain disease rarely show symptoms of one-sided neglect. Such a perceptual distortion will often jeopardize communication between patients and the others, primarily because the perceptual world of such patients is altered, and is not the same as that of the listeners. While what these patients say or feel may be compatible with their own realities, the lack of correspondence to the reality of those around the patient makes for a disordered communication.

The visual-spatial problems experienced by the patients may lead to direct language problems. In testing how right-hemisphere patients recognized the stories

FIGURE 6-2 Right-hemisphere patient's drawing in response to the command, "Draw a man." Notice the one-sided denial.

depicted in story pictures, Heeschen (1980) found the group to demonstrate measurable syntactic impairment in describing in phrases or sentences the actor-action-object parts of the picture. When talking freely (not in response to the pictures), their language appeared normal. The breakdown in syntax was probably related to not getting the full meaning out of the picture. Another study (Rivers and Love, 1980) looked at right-hemisphere-damaged patients' response to story pictures and found this group to differ significantly from normals in their ability to extract meaning out of story pictures and describe them in well-constructed, spoken story plots. It does not appear to be the modalities of language that are impaired in the right-hemisphere patient, as we see in aphasic patients, but seems rather to be an inability to extract perceptual meaning out of visual presentations. Complicated spoken instructions also seem to give the right-hemisphere patient some difficulty.

Speech-language pathologists work to improve the overall communicative effectiveness of the right-hemisphere-damaged patient. Their language difficulties are quite different from those of the aphasics who have primary difficulties in phonologic and syntactic skills in addition to their obvious semantic problems in word finding. One treatment method is to set up for the patient a language-task hierarchy where particular aspects of the communication are broken down, perhaps in such dimensions as presented by Davis (1983): length of utterance, syntactic complexity, semantic congruity, emotional content, and rate and pauses. Patient performance can be checked out on each of these dimensions and a particular dimension might be isolated for work and communication practice. Communicative performance might be improved by working with patients to make them aware of their own moods and affect as well as those of their listeners; practice can be given in turn taking with others and in describing events and stories.

Because such patients can usually read and speak with relative normality, the verbal modalities of reading and writing make excellent training tools. Since many of these patients neglect their left visual world, written materials that stress that the words begin on the left side of the page are good for practice. There have even been a few reading programs designed for right-hemisphere-damaged patients (Stanton and others, 1981) that basically train visual, perceptual, and sequential organization more than reading per se. Oral descriptions of pictured and tape-recorded events (such as a recording of a sequence of sounds that tell a story) provide excellent practice for the patient to organize the various stimuli into some kind of meaning, followed by practice describing orally the perceived events.

Mental Illness

The most common mental illness that sometimes masquerades as a real breakdown in language is **schizophrenia,** a psychosis characterized by a split-person performance. The affect and language of the same patient may change and shift dramatically, with a suddenness that makes such a shift appear bizarre and sometimes frightening to the listener. Occasionally, schizophrenic patients appear like Wernicke's aphasics or the patient with right-hemisphere disease. Of the three, the Wernicke's patient will demonstrate the best pragmatics, always showing some awareness of the listener and the listener's reactions. On language testing, however, schizophrenic patients will often demonstrate disrupted sequence, with fluctuations in prosody that make the intent of their verbal message difficult to understand. We sometimes see in both the written and the spoken responses of the schizophrenic patient enough neologisms and twisted word order to make the patients appear at times like the fluent aphasic of the Wernicke's type. The superior pragmatic performance (awareness of the listener's response to what is being said) of the Wernicke's patient will clearly differentiate him from the schizophrenic patient, who appears much more focused on her own performance. In his book on aphasia, Darley (1982) has differentiated well the adult aphasic patient from the adult with schizophrenia, describing the psychotic schizophrenic as showing a continual decline in language function, eventually appearing as a patient with dementia.

A thirty-nine-year-old woman with schizophrenia gave this verbal message in response to the presentation of the Rockwell picture of the young soldier returning home from the war:

> "More real than the bricks of the courtyard are the thoughts of the participants who surround all sensual thoughts. Whether there is an eventual get together of the lovers is only limited by the 'gracerlist' motives of each of the participants. Never portray more than the eye can behold."

The perseveration and neologism could characterize the utterance as that of a jargon aphasic patient. A major characteristic of the statement, however, that cannot be observed in our reading of the printed protocol, is that the description of the picture was all given in a rather high-pitched monotone, with little awareness by the patient of how the listener reacted or whether she was understood.

The language problems of the schizophrenic patient seem to increase as the illness continues. While the patient may show some language deficits in specific tasks, such as naming or definitions, the language deficits are best seen when the patient engages in conversation or is asked to describe story pictures, such as the picture of the returning soldier. The disordered language is actually but a symptom of the disordered mind and, therefore, is not a specific language disorder per se. According to Wertz (1984, p. 18), to best appreciate the language differences of schizophrenic patients, "one needs to include tasks that permit the schizophrenic patient to reveal his primary disorder—irrelevance. Conversation and open-ended questions should suffice."

Beyond language testing and possibly differentiating the schizophrenic from aphasic or dementia patients, the speech-language pathologist does not too often play an active role in management and treatment of the adult schizophrenic. In the future, as psychiatric therapy for the schizophrenic is better developed, perhaps the speech-language pathologist will be part of the treatment team, offering some kind of symptomatic language therapy to the patient.

Senile Dementia

As part of a continuing study of senile dementia at the University of Arizona since the early 1980s, we have given some attention to the language performance of the normal aged. In general, we have found that phonology, syntax, and semantics in the language of normal older people are very good; their pragmatics (as one who converses with normal, aged persons quickly finds out) are excellent. Despite some hearing and visual decrements with increasing age, the typical older person communicates quite effectively.

As our older population becomes larger, we are beginning to see more patients with the disease senile dementia. About 5 percent of people over sixty-five have dementia; the prevalence seems to go up with increasing age, with 10 percent among those seventy years and older and about 15 percent of the population over seventy-five. Early dementia is characterized by a loss of memory and increasing disorientation in terms of time and place. In the early stages of the disease, there is great variation in mental clarity within particular parts of the day, as well as fluctuations in mental status from day to day. Examples of this fluctuation may be seen in these brief descriptions:

> Pearl, age seventy-three, parked her car in the lot of a shopping center near her home. Finishing her shopping, she became confused, forgot that she had driven, and asked a clerk in a drugstore to call a cab to bring her home. When she got home, she remembered she had left her car in the parking lot.

> Marvin, age seventy-four, was a well-known artist. On Saturday, he completed an oil painting that he had been working on for four weeks. On Sunday morning, he became confused and painted over his finished canvas. That evening, he called his son in anguish to say he had ruined his painting.

The fluctuation between confusion and lucidity shown in these two patients are typical changes of mental status seen in the patient with beginning dementia. As the disease progresses, there are few or no lucid moments.

The two most common forms of senile dementia are **Alzheimer's Disease** (a progressive cortical deterioration) and **multi-infarct dementia** (many small strokes). Changes in both cognitive and language function begin to be seen. On mental-status examinations that look at the patient's time and place orientation, the patient shows surprising deficits (Mattis, 1976). Our testing has found the senile dementia patient to continue to demonstrate normal phonology, morphology, and syntax even in advanced stages of dementia; however, profound deficits are found in the patients' semantics and pragmatics (Bayles and Boone, 1982). It would appear that those language tasks that are strongly related to cognitive function, such as semantics, are much more likely to give the senile dementia patient some difficulty.

For the first few years of the illness, the patient can usually live at home, profiting greatly from such memory aids as calendars, appointment books, and daily logs. As the disease progresses, the patient will often require placement in a nursing-care facility, eventually requiring total care. The speech-language pathologist's role with the dementia patient is in early identification (some kinds of dementia are treatable), providing suggestions and materials for improving the patient's communication, and eventually counseling members of the family and the staff of nursing homes and hospitals. Although dementia researchers continue to try to find some therapy strategies that might improve the communicative function of the moderately and severely impaired patients, they are at this time still unsuccessful.

DISORDERS OF ARTICULATION

Some adults continue to show evidence of an articulatory problem, such as a lisp, that has been carried over from childhood. Their number is few. In a national-incidence study that looked at various communicative disorders in children (Hull and others, 1976), only half of 1 percent of twelfth-grade children were found to have articulation problems. Since twelfth-graders are in their late teens, we can probably guess that the incidence of adult developmental articulation disorders (articulation problems that are carried over from childhood) remain at about the same level. There are no clear data available that will give us the incidence of acquired adult articulation disorders related to such problems as hearing loss, structural defects (such as loss of tongue), or changes in the central nervous system (as the result of trauma or disease).

It is sometimes believed that an articulation disorder is not as handicapping as communication problems related to changes in language, voice, or fluency. Perhaps for the adult this is not so. In an unpublished study by Langhans and Boone (1975) examining attitudes of unsophisticated listeners toward adult speech problems, it was found that adults with articulation problems were judged as "dumb, less likely to be hired," and in other negative ways. Perhaps because of the relatively reduced prevalence of articulation disorders among adults, listeners know only a few other people with articulation problems with whom to compare the speaker. While they may evaluate the articulation distortions of the preschool child with amusement, the persistence of an articulation defect in adulthood is not tolerated well. Let us look at a few acquired adult articulation problems.

Hearing Loss

Children who were born with severe hearing loss or deafness struggle for a lifetime to develop adequate communication skills; their oral speech suffers from severe problems in articulation, voice, and prosody. As they become adults, their speech difficulties are still present, often characterized by continued problems of articulation, vocal quality and resonance, and prosody. The effects of developmental hearing loss of various levels on communication (including articulation) is described in some detail in the next chapter. The adult who acquires a hearing loss has had a lifetime of normal hearing and normal speech; it takes a severe acquired loss to affect articulation.

The most common acquired hearing loss is the presbycusic-type loss (loss of high-frequency sounds), experienced in various degrees of severity by the majority of people over sixty-five (Hull and Traynor, 1977). While the patient may lose some of the sensitivity that makes the hearing of high-frequency sounds (such as /s/ /ʃ/, and /tʃ/) possible, the typical older patient with presbycusis does not experience the loss or distortion of these sounds in speech. After years of pronouncing sounds correctly, the phonologic system of the individual appears to be highly resistant to breakdown because of incomplete and distorted hearing information. Once normal articulation is acquired, it appears to be less dependent on hearing the auditory signal than it obviously was during the articulatory acquisition phase.

Moderate-to-severe high-frequency losses that may be acquired during an illness that affects the central nervous system will in time change the articulatory productions of the patient. Immediately after acquiring a severe loss, such as during the period of recovery just following meningitis, the patient's articulation may remain intact. Eventually (perhaps within two years), we have seen patients who acquired a severe hearing loss begin to show articulatory deterioration. In Chapter 7, we discuss in some detail the effects of various levels of acquired hearing loss on adult performance. We will also consider the hearing evaluation, the possible fitting of a hearing aid, and other habilitative strategies that will enable the adult with an acquired hearing loss to maintain communicative integrity.

Structural Changes

Obviously, severe problems of the oral mechanisms, such as those related to cleft lip and palate, may affect articulation negatively throughout life. Most such problems, however, receive early medical-surgical-dental treatment, as discussed in the last chapter, enabling the child to profit from intensive speech rehabilitation. Therefore, the typical adult in the United States who was born with a severe problem of cleft lip and/or palate probably has achieved relatively normal speech and vocal resonance by the twenty-first birthday. However, there are many countries in the world in which one can see a number of adults with either unrepaired or inadequately repaired lips and palates who spend a lifetime misarticulating and experiencing severe problems of nasal resonance.

Some adult problems in articulation persist because of various kinds of craniofacial disorders related to disorders of growth of the facial skeleton. The palatal arch may be excessively high or the muscles of the face may be distorted because of some kind of asymmetrical skull growth. Ewanowski and Saxman (1980) present some convincing pictures of orofacial-development disorders, showing individuals with severe underdevelopment or overdevelopment of parts of the face, which may produce malalignment of the speech articulators in such a way as to produce various articulatory distortions that cannot be remediated easily by speech therapy. In Figure 6-3, we see a severe prognathism (extension of the mandible) that was eventually corrected by orthodontia. The patient's intraoral dental alignment was so poor, prior to treatment, that he experienced some difficulty making sibilant consonants correctly. Once he had normal dental alignment, as seen in picture B, he was able to profit from the articulation training provided by the speech-language pathologist.

Perhaps among the more dramatic structural deficits that may have severe effects on articulation is the surgical removal of part or all of the tongue. In 1978, the American Cancer Society reported 15,000 new patients a year with some form of oral cancer. If the cancer is small, it might be treated successfully by radiation therapy; after such small lesions are removed, there probably would be no residual articulation problem. Larger and more persistent tongue lesions may require some excision of tongue tissue. The typical adult patient who has had some tongue tissue surgically removed makes very effective compensations within the mouth and is usually able to maintain normal speech. A few such patients need to be taught compensatory tongue movements by the speech-language pathologist. Occasional tongue cancers require a total **glossectomy** (removal of tongue). Total removal of the tongue obviously produces severe speech problems as well as severe difficulties in chewing

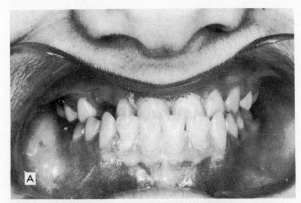

FIGURE 6-3   Dental prognathicism, before (A) and after (B) orthodontia.

and swallowing. The glossectomy patient can often be helped to improve the intelligibility of his or her speech through the combined efforts of the **prosthodontist,** the plastic surgeon (who may be able to do some creative restructuring), and the speech-language pathologist (Skelly and others, 1971). Several years ago, we had a patient who experienced a near-total glossectomy, with only a tongue stub remaining. A prosthodontist created a plastic obturator almost half an inch thick that literally brought his anterior hard palate down to the surface of his tongue stub, enabling the patient to form and produce enough tongue-palatal consonants to be understood. Some patients with glossectomy have to be introduced to various kinds of communication aids, such as a pointing communication board (the patient points to the desired picture or word) or an electronic board that may speak or print the message the patient selects by pressing a key. One such communication board that could be used effectively with the glossectomy patient can be seen in Figure 6–4. The patient can communicate by use of the communication board, by gesture, by learning some kind of sign language, or by writing. For the typical total *glossectomee* (the patient who has had the tongue removed), it is not realistic to have normal, intelligible speech as either a short- or long-term treatment goal. Communication is best fostered by employing these other communication modes.

Another organic problem that might interfere with articulation is excessive forward carriage of the tongue, or tongue thrust. Some adults, often those with excessively large tonsils, carry their tongues high and forward in the mouth, placing pressure against anterior dentition and the alveolar sockets around the incisor area (Barrett and Hanson, 1978). Tongue thrust is seen more often in young children, but occasionally adults are observed with a persistent frontal lisp, such as /θ/ for /s/, accompanied, if not caused, by high anterior carriage of the tongue. Much of the same kind of management explained in the preceding chapter when we talked about tongue thrust and reverse swallowing in children can be used with adults.

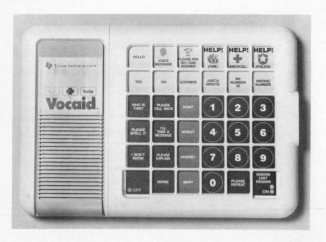

FIGURE 6–4 An electronic communication board. The Vocaid (Texas Instruments). Courtesy of Communication Skill Builders, Tucson, Arizona.

Dysarthria

Dysarthria is a motor speech problem that results from some damage to the central or peripheral nervous system when the patient loses control of the speech muscles as the result of paralysis, weakness (paresis), or incoordination. Dysarthria is the generic name for different motor speech problems that may be caused by a number of nervous-system diseases. An articulation defect is but one of the speech symptoms often associated with dysarthria. Dysarthria may be caused by damage and disease to various sites of the nervous system, resulting in particular kinds of dysarthria. The most common lesions that produce dysarthria involve the *upper motor neuron*. The upper-motor-neuron system begins in the cortex of the frontal lobes, with its axons descending to lower-brain and spinal-column centers; some axons stop at motor nuclei deep within the brain (such as the basal ganglia), and other fibers pass straight through (like the pyramidal tract) to a final nucleus located in the brainstem or spinal column. We will consider in a moment some of the diseases and symptoms of speech associated with upper-motor-neuron disease. The *lower-motor-neuron* system is basically composed of the final nuclei in the brainstem and spinal column and the motor nerves that extend from these nuclei. These final nuclei and nerves that carry impulses to the muscles are known as both *the motor unit* and the *final common pathway* (Darley, Aronson, and Brown, 1975). Another brain area in which damage may produce a distinctive type of dysarthria is the **cerebellum,** a structure that sits astride the brainstem. It plays a major role in coordination, by receiving sensory information from the cerebrum, above; the brainstem, beside it; and the spinal column, below it; and by sending motor-output signals back to these same structures.

The causes of dysarthria are many. Aronson (1980) wrote that lesions that may cause dysarthria "can be classified under the following headings: (1) vascular diseases, (2) infectious diseases, (3) metabolic diseases, (4) tumors, (5) trauma, (6) degenerative diseases, (7) toxins, and (8) cerebral palsy" (p. 412). Upper-motor-neuron lesions can result from all of these conditions and produce such dysarthric symptoms as imprecise consonants, changes in articulatory stress, change in speaking rate, distorted vowels, and changes in voice (pitch, quality, and resonance). Let us consider the case of a twenty-one-year-old who suffered a penetrating head wound to the motor cortex of his right cerebral hemisphere:

> Paul was a Canadian who played ice hockey for an American university. During a practice session when he was not wearing a helmet, he was involved in a serious accident. The skate blade of a teammate pierced his right frontal skull and the motor cortex underneath. He went into a coma with convulsions at the ice rink and was taken to the university hospital. Within a few hours of the accident, he awakened and made efforts to speak. It became obvious that he had some paralysis of the left facial muscles, with his tongue deviating to the left side, producing a moderately severe dysarthria of the upper-motor-neuron type. A speech-language pathologist

worked with Paul within days of his accident, providing him exercises and practice materials to improve his speech. Six months after the accident, only a mild dysarthria continues.

Cortical insults from trauma, such as in this case, usually result in relatively mild dysarthria, often affecting articulation more than rate and voicing changes. In general, the lower the lesion site in the nervous system, the more severe the dysarthria. Some upper-motor-neuron diseases, such as severe strokes or a degenerative disease like multiple sclerosis, can produce moderate-to-severe dysarthria. Diseases that cause lower-motor-neuron dysfunction generally result in severe dysarthria characterized by serious respiratory problems, involvement of the larynx, and difficulty moving muscles of the tongue, velum, pharynx, and mouth.

Some adult patients with severe motor problems, such as having had a stroke in the area of the pons, suffer from **anarthria,** a complete absence of speech because of severe motor involvement. The same involvement that prevents the patient from speaking usually makes chewing and swallowing extremely difficult, sometimes requiring the patient to spend a lifetime on a special diet of liquids and pureed solids. Anarthric patients are sometimes fitted by the speech-language pathologist with some kind of communication aid, such as a pointing alphabet or picture board and various electronic devices that can print out messages or have some kind of synthesized speech output (Yorkston and Dowden, 1984).

DISORDERS OF VOICE

Next to hearing loss, voice disorders are probably the most common communication disorder among adults. The kind of incidence data of voice disorders that we cite for children in Chapters 5 and 11 are not available for adults. However, as you will see in Chapter 11, we make a guess that about 2 percent of the adults in the United States have a phonation disorder and that another 2 percent have a resonance disorder. Remember that a phonation disorder is a problem in the voice as generated at the level of the larynx; a resonance problem is a change in the sound of the voice as it resonates in the various cavities of the head.

Phonation

Many people experience fluctuating problems of voice characterized by breathiness and hoarseness; these are related to difficulties such as allergies and respiratory infections. Such disorders are temporary, and may be more annoying than handicapping. Some forms of **dysphonia** (a disorder of phonation) are often related to structural alterations of the vocal folds, such as nodules or polyps, which are usually the result of prolonged abuse and misuse of the larynx. Other dysphonias are associated with laryngeal diseases, such as granuloma, papilloma, laryngeal web, vocal cord paralysis, or cancer. One can never determine what kind of problem may be causing the dysphonia by listening to the sound of the voice alone; therefore, it is recommended that anyone who experiences a hoarseness for at least ten days, independent of having some kind of allergy or cold that could be causing the problem, should have the benefit of a medical examination by an ear-nose-throat physician, who will examine the vocal cords with a special mirror; this is called *indirect laryngoscopy*. The cause of the dysphonia can then be identified and some kind of treatment program initiated.

Sometimes, after mirror laryngoscopy, no structural change of the vocal cords is observed; the patient's hoarseness, if present, is diagnosed as *functional dysphonia*. The patient's hoarse voice may well be caused by the vocal folds coming together too firmly, with other laryngeal and pharyngeal muscles contracting so vigorously that the larynx is almost shut off.

Some patients have no voice at all. This could be caused by vocal-fold paralysis or be a *functional aphonia* (unable to produce voice despite having a normal laryngeal mechanism). When one or both vocal folds are paralyzed, they are unable to come together sufficiently to produce phonation. Since all voice is produced by the airstream setting the approximated vocal folds into vibration, if they are too far apart (in this case because of paralysis), there will be no voice. It is hoped that the severed laryngeal nerves that cause the paralysis will in time regenerate and the voice will be restored; if nerve regeneration does not take place within nine months of onset, voice therapy and sometimes surgery have been found useful for developing some kind of voice. The patient with a functional aphonia has a totally different problem; after indirect laryngoscopy, his or her laryngeal mechanism is found to have both normal structure and function. However, when the patient is asked to say *eeeh* (this high-front vowel permits the best view) during laryngoscopy, instead of the vocal folds coming together for the phonation position, they may move farther apart. As we will describe in some detail in Chapter 11, symptomatic voice therapy is almost always successful in restoring voice to the patient with functional aphonia.

Perhaps the most dramatic of all voice problems is related to the surgical removal of the total larynx (a **laryngectomy**), which, of course, results in the patient's having lost the laryngeal voice source. Such patients are known as *laryngectomees,* and must develop a new voice source, either by some surgical reconstruction, by using an electronic instrument (Shedd and Weinberg, 1980), or by learning a new substitute voice (Boone, 1983).

Resonance

Another classification of voice problems is resonance disorders. They may be related to faulty oral resonance, perhaps produced by the patient's holding the tongue in an excessively high, anterior position (such as may be heard in the baby-sounding voice) or by the patient with a back focus in tongue carriage (sometimes observed in the deaf speaker). Many deviations in oral resonance are slight and not particularly handicapping. Occasionally, an individual, such as someone whose profession involves the use of the voice—an actor, for example—wants to develop a more normal, oral-sounding resonance. Most problems of oral resonance can be corrected with voice therapy.

The more common resonance problems are related to difficulties involving nasalence; that is, the patient's voice appears to have either too much or too little nasal resonance. Excessive nasal resonance (*hypernasality*) can be either of functional or organic origin. The individual with functional hypernasality elects to speak with greater nasal resonance than the typical speaker; the actor Jimmy Stewart has long fascinated moviegoers with his deliberately hypernasal voice and his somewhat disfluent speech. Some people live in particular regions (such as parts of New England) or speak certain languages (such as Chinese) where increased nasality is the "normal" way to use voice (Boone, 1983). Excessive hypernasality more often than not is caused by structural defects of the *velopharyngeal closing mechanism* (where the soft palate and pharyngeal structures separate the nasal from the oral cavities). Typical structural causes of hypernasality in adults may include cleft lip and palate, paralysis of the soft palate (*velum*) or pharynx, or some kind of trauma to the velopharyngeal area. Voice therapy is usually not effective in remediating hypernasality unless the patient can first experience structural adequacy, either through surgery or from some kind of dental appliance (such as the **palatal lift** shown in Figure 6–5 or an obturator that covers the open palatal defect). Once the surgeon or dentist can achieve structural adequacy for the patient through surgery and/or a prosthesis, the speech-language pathologist is usually successful in lessening the hypernasality through symptomatic voice therapy.

Insufficient nasal resonance (*denasality*) makes people sound as if they have a stuffed nose or "cold in the head." Most cases of perceived denasality are caused

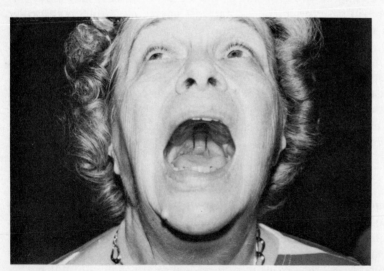

FIGURE 6–5 A woman with a paralyzed palate (caused by a stroke) demonstrates a palatal lift. Without the palatal lift, her voice is hypernasal; the lift gives her adequate velopharyngeal closure and normal voice resonance. Used with permission of University of Arizona, Tuscon.

by blockage in the nasopharynx and nasal cavities, often the result of allergies or severe head colds; sometimes denasality is caused by excessively large adenoid tissue that blocks the flow of air and sound waves through the nasal cavities. The primary treatment of denasality is medical or surgical; voice therapy alone will seldom correct this problem.

The Functional-organic Dichotomy

There has always been some confusion about whether a particular voice problem has a functional or organic cause. We present a listing of various functional and organic phonation disorders in Chapter 11. Functional voice disorders are related to faulty usage of the laryngeal mechanism, perhaps resulting in such problems as functional dysphonia, vocal nodules or polyps, or functional aphonia. Organic voice disorders are more related to a physical cause (such as excessive cigarette smoking); examples of physical causes that contribute to the voice disorder would be granuloma, vocal-fold webbing, or cancer of the larynx.

Let us present a brief case history of two patients with phonation disorders, one with a functional problem and the other with an organically based voice problem.

Eddie, age thirty-eight, is a good example of a functional voice problem. Eddie was a high-school football coach who was known for his loud, ''barking'' voice. After coaching successfully for ten years, he began to experience severe symptoms of hoarseness, particularly as the football season went on. He finally consulted an ear-nose-throat physician, who found that Eddie had ''large bilateral vocal nodules.'' The doctor referred him to a speech-language pathologist, who felt that his nodules were directly related to his repeated yelling and excessive vocal behavior, not only on the practice and playing field, but in almost every situation. Eddie had become known as the ''guy with the booming voice.'' With some counseling and voice therapy that included work on respiration, learning to use the voice easily, and developing optimum voicing patterns, the bilateral vocal nodules eventually disappeared. While Eddie must always closely watch his use of the voice, and in particular avoid excesses of phonation, his voice has returned to relatively normal levels and there has been no return of the vocal nodules.

Helen, age forty-five, smoked three to four packs of cigarettes a day, both at home and while conducting her insurance–real-estate business. She began to experience continuous bouts of hoarseness and coughing. Since much of her work involved talking on the telephone, she became concerned about her voice and coughing problems. On laryngoscopic examination, she was found to have an extensive carcinoma that involved both vocal folds and much of the laryngeal structure above the folds. After minor surgery and radiation therapy were tried without success to reduce the cancerous growths, she received a total laryngectomy. Following her surgery, she received counseling and voice therapy (learning to inject air into her normal esophagus as a voicing source); after six months of esophageal voice instruction, she was able to return to her business and talk well enough that her clients could hear and understand her.

Voice Therapy. Many adults do not receive the voice therapy they need. Voice therapy for children has demonstrated clear results; consequently, children with dysphonic voices, both preschool and school age, receive the diagnostic and therapeutic services they need for the management of their voice problems. Voice evaluations and therapy are far less available for adults. Unless adults experience some dramatic vocal changes (often related to some kind of identifiable disease), those with chronic voice disorders generally go through their adult lives talking with the dysphonic voice. Unfortunately, there are often no funds available for vocal rehabilitation of the adult. Few health-insurance companies will reimburse for voice therapy unless the voice problem is directly related to an identifiable disease (paralysis, cancer). Let us hope that voice therapy for reducing the problems of both dysphonia and resonance disorders in adults will increase in frequency as our society develops a better insurance coverage of adult communication disorders.

FLUENCY DISORDERS

The accent and melody of speech that the individual has used throughout life is obviously well established in adulthood. How smoothly we speak this melody of sounds, syllables, and words in our spoken language is known as *fluency*. All of us at times may show disruptions in fluency (*disfluency*), particularly when we are nervous or tired. The prosodic sound patterns of one's native language are well established in the first two years of life and influence for a lifetime the rate of how fast we speak, our speech accent and rhythm, and the overall stress patterns we use (as discussed in Chapters 2 and 4). We see clearly how deeply rooted fluency patterns are established in the adult when we see someone who is relearning to speak after an operation such as a laryngectomy. A lovely woman, who was known by all as a true southern belle in Atlanta society, had a laryngectomy. As she learned to speak again with esophageal voice, she illustrated well how firmly fluency patterns are established in an adult:

Laura, age sixty-five, had a total laryngectomy and began learning esophageal speech. She learned to inject air into her esophagus and bring it out in an esophageal voice, producing on the direction of her speech-language pathologist monosyllabic words, each beginning and ending with a plosive sound. As she said single words again, we began to realize how much more she prolonged her vowels than her Yankee clinicians. When she began to put words together in a series, her slow rate of speech and excessive vowel prolongations "used up" her esophageal air so fast that despite a good supply of esophageal air, she could only say a few words at a time. Her southern accent came back, now with an esophageal instead of a normal voice, exactly as it had been before her laryngectomy.

Adult fluency patterns are so well established that they are highly resistant to change. Stuttering, which is often the most recognized fluency problem, rarely begins in adulthood. Most adult stutterers stuttered as children. The adult stuttering problem is carried over from childhood. Further, one does not learn to stutter by being around people who stutter. Occasionally, worried graduate students may ask if they are likely to begin to stutter when working with clients who do so. The answer is "no." The adult clutterer has usually experienced a lifetime of cluttering symptoms. The onset of disfluency at the adult level, when it occurs, is usually related to some kind of central-nervous-system disease. Sometimes, after a head injury or a prolonged high fever, the patient will demonstrate some kind of disfluency for the very first time. As we have seen earlier in this chapter, the problem of dysarthria in the adult usually produces some change in fluency.

Stuttering

Curlee (1985) has written that "approximately 0.7 percent of the population stutter and that three to four times more males stutter than do females" (p. 308). In Chapter 12, we review the work of Wingate (1976), who summarized 14 recovery studies, finding that most children who stutter in the preschool years no longer do so at puberty. The prevalence of stuttering among the adult population from the late teens to old age may well be close to the 0.7 percent figure. In a longitudinal follow-up of a number of people over sixty-five, we have been impressed by how few stutterers we have seen in the older population. One man, age seventy, reported, "I stuttered all my life until about the time I was sixty-five and retired. I figured by then, who gives a damn if I stutter or not, so it just seemed to go away." One might speculate that the man's stuttering stopped when he no longer considered it a primary problem. Stuttering does appear to be nurtured and maintained in part by the individual's concern about and intolerance of the stuttering (Travis, 1971). Getting old per se does not appear to lessen stuttering (if indeed the stuttering prevalence is less among older people), but there may be less need to be fluent in the older person. Many older people appear to be remarkably free in what they say and how they say it.

Various definitions of stuttering are presented in Chapter 12. Most apply equally well to children and adults, and usually note that stuttering is heard in involuntary repetition and prolongation of sounds and syllables; they happen without the intent of the speaker. Many definitions of stuttering include the speaker's struggle to end the fluency interruptions. Some definitions include stutterers' expectations and fears that they will stutter in present and future communicative interactions. Stuttering is, then, both the involuntary interruption of fluency (repetitions and prolongations) and behavior (anticipatory and struggle) to prevent or manage the nonfluencies. A brief case history of a nineteen-year-old soldier illustrates these points.

> John Baker had difficulty saying his last name. He usually said it with a repetitive "Ba-ba-ba-baker," and sometimes he would block on the first syllable and say nothing at all. In basic training in the Army, he had to step forward in a lineup of men in his squad and bark out his last name. As the men before him stepped forward and said their names, John became extremely agitated. He knew he was going to stutter when he attempted to say his name. It would not be possible in this situation to change his name (he had done this on occasion to be fluent) or to use some kind of starter phrase that usually enabled him to say his name. So as the sergeant stood in front of him with his clipboard, checking off the men's names, John stepped forward on cue and said, "Baker." He said it with no dysfluency. Inside, he felt good because he had not stuttered. No one—at least, at that moment—knew he stuttered.

The question we must ask about this case is whether John Baker had a problem in this situation. He did not stutter. There were no observable repetitions. To his knowledge, his inner concerns about his speech were not observed or detected by others. It is our belief that John indeed has a stuttering problem (in this situation and in general), and he might well profit from some kind of speech therapy. It appears that the problem of stuttering is not confined only to observable speech disfluencies, but also to the fear of stuttering and the various behaviors the individual may be using to cope with it. Both the evaluation of stuttering and the therapy programs that are used usually focus on the actual stuttering block and the behaviors that are associated with it.

The primary focus in evaluating the adult stutterer is to determine if the problem is truly stuttering, and not cluttering or some other kind of speech disfluency. The type of stuttering (repetitions, blocks, or prolongations) is determined as well as the part of speech where it usually occurs, such as at the sound, syllable, or word level. The social situations are identified where stuttering is likely or not likely to occur, as is the severity of the stuttering in these various situations. As part of the evaluation, Curlee (1985) writes, "Stutterers' self-concepts as people and as speakers and their attitudes toward interpersonal communication in general and speaking in particular are explored" (p. 315). Various attitude scales and self-perception inventories are used at the time of the speech evaluation. The evaluation will often conclude with the clinician employing several clinical probes, such as suggesting that patients reduce their speaking rate by making a conscious effort to prolong vowels; such probes are used to determine the effect of such a clinical technique on modifying the stuttering. Clinical approaches that seem to improve the individual's speech may be utilized in early treatment sessions.

The treatment of stuttering for the adult is highly individualized, determined in part by the performance of the patient and in great measure by the treatment philosophy of the clinician. As we develop in some detail in Chapter 12, three main treatment approaches are used with the adult stutterer: counseling and psychotherapy, modifying the stuttering, and modifying one's overall speech. The relative amount of time spent on each approach is individualized. Counseling is provided in individual therapy and in small groups with other adult stutterers. In each counseling session, some attention is given to putting the stuttering in its proper perspective. Stutterers frequently view stuttering as the most prominent activity in life, dominating and determining the kinds of things they do and the occupations they select, or as the reasons for their failures. Consequently, part of both individual and group counseling is to help the patient put the stuttering in its proper perspective.

The actual modification of the stuttering may take many different forms. One approach is a fluency-shaping one, in which the patient practices producing easy, fluent speech. Wingate (1976) accomplishes this by helping the stutterer develop an easy prosodic flow of speech; this is achieved by slowing down one's speaking rate by extending vowels. The method sets up a regularity-of-speech rhythm. With this easy rhythm, often characterized by gentle onset of words, the stutterer may be able to maintain an amazing fluency, often free of tension and consequently free of stuttering repetitions and blocks. In therapy, some attention is given to modifying the easy way of speaking (slower, with greater vowel prolongation than normal), so that the rate and prosodic melody of speech eventually approach that of the normal speaker. The progress in recent years in helping the adult stutterer increase speech fluency has been dramatic. So many people today have been helped with their stuttering that it is reasonable to suggest that any adult who stutters ought to attempt to improve fluency by speech therapy.

Cluttering

Cluttering is characterized by extremely rapid speech with consonant omissions and distortions. The patient who clutters is difficult to diagnose but is usually distinguishable from the stutterer in terms of rate (stutterers speak more slowly than clutterers), articulation (stutterers have normal articulation), repetitions (the clutterer may repeat whole words), and in tension reactions (clutterers are often unaware of their fluency-articulation problems). Cluttering is relatively rare; very few adults have the problem. The speech rate of one man diagnosed as a clutterer was in excess of 220 words per minute (normal is between 160 and 170 words per minute), and he frequently omitted final consonants in his conversational speech. When asked to read aloud, however, in a loud voice, he immediately approached a normal speaking rate and was judged free of articulatory errors. Unless he was asked to monitor his speech by talking inappropriately louder or with deliberate slowness, he seemed to be oblivious of his cluttering.

The clutterer may have no concern about his fast, sometimes inarticulate speech. In addition to the speech problem, there are often difficulties in reading and writing. The best method of treatment for the rapid speech problem is to treat it holistically; that is, instead of working on respiration and developing an easy rhythm of speech, the patient should be asked to speak more loudly. This artificial increase in intensity seems to have the effect of slowing down the rate and increasing sharpness of articulation. It appears that when the patient intentionally exercises some volition in speaking (such as talking louder), the nervous system functions more normally, resulting in a relatively normal speech product. The associated reading and writing problems in cluttering are much more resistant to direct therapy and instruction; in fact, developing normal reading-writing skills may not be a realistic therapy goal for the clutterer.

Dysarthria

Rate of speech and overall speech fluency are often seriously disrupted by motor speech disorders, as described in some detail in Chapter 12. The type and severity of the problem are directly related to the site of the disease or injury to the nervous system.

The adult patient with dysarthria requires a total speech evaluation that includes assessment of respiration, phonation, resonance, articulation, and prosody fluency. Often the fluency problem is the direct result of not being able to move the speech articulators fast enough for normal speech; speed of alternating movements (**diadochokinesis**) is assessed, as well as how many words per minute the patient can say. Increasing the speed of production, and of tongue movements in particular, is often an attainable goal in therapy, resulting in a slight increase in the speaking rate. Any goal to improve fluency must be consistent with the limitations imposed by the disease and the patient's response to medical-surgical therapies.

REVIEW QUESTIONS

Adult communication problems are many and varied. Let us ask a few questions about some of these problems.

1. What is a useful classification system for studying adult communication problems? Why?

2. What are some helpful habilitation procedures for the adult with an acquired hearing loss?

3. How does the language disorder of aphasia differ from the language problems exhibited by the patient with right-hemisphere damage?

4. What are some organic conditions that may contribute to adult articulation problems?

5. Why do acquired voice problems need to be investigated medically?

6. Is stuttering since childhood treatable in the adult? Explain.

REFERENCES

Aronson, A. E. (1980). *Clinical Voice Disorders.* New York: Thieme Stratton.

Barrett, R. H., and Hanson, M. L. (1978). *Oral Myofunctional Disorders* (2nd ed.). St. Louis: C. V. Mosby.

Bayles, K. A., and Boone, D. R. (1982). The potential of language tasks for identifying senile dementia. *Journal of Speech Hearing Disorders, 47:* 210–217.

Boone, D. R. (1983). *The Voice and Voice Therapy* (3rd ed.). Englewood Cliffs, N.J.: Prentice-Hall.

Curlee, R. F. (1985). Disorders of fluency, in *Speech, Language, and Hearing* (2nd ed.), ed. P. H. Skinner and R. L. Shelton. New York: Wiley.

Darley, F. L. (1982). *Aphasia.* Philadelphia: Saunders.

Darley, F. L., Aronson, A. E., and Brown, J. R. (1975). *Motor Speech Disorders.* Philadelphia: Saunders.

Davis, G. A. (1983). *A Survey of Adult Aphasia.* Englewood Cliffs, N.J.: Prentice-Hall.

Davis, H. (1970). Hearing handicap, standards for hearing, and medicolegal rules, in *Hearing and Deafness,* ed. H. Davis and S. R. Silverman. New York: Holt, Rinehart, and Winston.

Davis, H. (1978). Abnormal hearing and deafness, in *Hearing and Deafness,* ed. H. Davis and S. R. Silverman. New York: Holt, Rinehart, and Winston.

Ewanowski, S. J., and Saxman, J. H. (1980). Orofacial disorders. In *Introduction to Communication Disorders,* ed. T. J. Hixon, L. D. Shriberg, and J. H. Saxman. Englewood Cliffs, N.J.: Prentice-Hall.

Geschwind, N. (1971). Current concepts: aphasia. *New England Journal of Medicine, 28:* 654–656.

Goin, D. W. (1976). Otospongiosis, in *Otolaryngology,* ed. G. M. English. New York: Harper and Row.

Goodglass, H., and Kaplan, E. (1972). *The Assessment of Aphasia and Related Disorders.* Philadelphia: Lea and Febiger.

Heeschen, C. (1980). Strategy of decoding actor-object-relations by aphasic patients. *Cortex, 16:* 5–19.

Hodgson, W. R., and Matkin, N. D. (1985). Disorders of hearing, in *Speech, Language, and Hearing,* ed. P. H. Skinner and R. L. Shelton. New York: Wiley.

Hull, F. M., Mielke, P. W., Willeford, J. A., and Timmons, R. J. (1976). *National Speech and Hearing Survey* (Final Report, Project 50978). Washington, D.C.: U.S. Office of Education.

Hull, R. H., and Traynor, R. M. (1977). Hearing impairment among aging persons in the health care facility: their diagnosis and rehabilitation. *American Health Care Association Journal, 3:* 14–18.

Langhans, J., and Boone, D. R. (1975). "Attitudes Toward the Communicatively Handicapped" (unpublished study, University of Arizona).

Mattis, S. (1976). Mental status examination for organic mental syndrome in the elderly patient. *Geriatric Psychiatry,* ed. L. Ballack and T. B. Karasu. New York: Grune and Stratton.

Rivers, D. L., and Love, R. J. (1980). Language performance on visual processing tasks. *Brain and Language, 10:* 348–366.

Schlanger, B. B., Schlanger, P., and Gerstman, L. (1976). The perception of emotionally toned sentences by right-hemisphere damaged and aphasic subjects. *Brain and Language, 3:* 396–403.

Shedd, D. P., and Weinberg, B. (1980). *Surgical and Prosthetic Approaches to Speech Rehabilitation.* Boston: G. K. Hall.

Skelly, M., Spector, D., Donaldson, R., Brodeur, A., and Paletta, F. (1971). Compensatory physiologic phonetics for the glossectomee. *Journal of Speech and Hearing Disorders, 36:* 101–114.

Stanton, K. M., Yorkston, K. M., Kenyon, V. T., and Beukelman, D. R. (1981). Language utilization in teaching reading to left neglect patients, in *Clinical Aphasiology: Proceedings of the 1980 Conference,* ed. R. H. Brookshire. Minneapolis: BRK Publishers.

Travis, L. E. (1971). The unspeakable feelings of people with special reference to stuttering. *Handbook of Speech Pathology and Audiology,* ed. L. E. Travis. Englewood Cliffs, N.J.: Prentice-Hall.

U.S. National Health Survey (1967). *Hearing Levels of Adults by Age and Sex, United States, 1960–1962* (Series 11, Number 11). Washington D.C.: U.S. Public Health Service.

Wertz, R. T. (1984). Language disorders in adults: state of the clinical art, in *Language Disorders in Adults,* ed. A. L. Holland. San Diego: College-Hill Press.

Wingate, M. E. (1976). *Stuttering Theory and Treatment.* New York: Irvington Publishing.

Yorkston, K. M., and Dowden, P. A. (1984). Nonspeech language and communication systems, in *Language Disorders in Adults,* ed. A. L. Holland. San Diego: College-Hill Press.

7

Disorders of Hearing

Aural-oral language, understanding what others say, and speaking, is a distinctly human ability. Listening to speech and speaking are the most common modes of human communication. A hearing loss can obviously cause severe problems in aural-oral communication. A child who does not hear well or who is deaf will exhibit marked problems in language without receiving special intervention, such as amplification and special language-speech training. A hearing loss in a baby or young child may cause severe delays in overall cognitive growth and language development. An acquired hearing loss developing in later childhood or as an adult may also have devastating effects on one's ability to communicate. We will consider in this chapter the effects on human communication of hearing loss and problems in listening. We will then look at the role of the audiologist in testing hearing in both children and adults. Finally, we will review various hearing habilitative approaches for children and rehabilitative approaches for people who acquire hearing loss after the first few years of life.

There is perhaps no better way to appreciate the effects of hearing loss on effective communication than by describing two actual cases, one a young child and the other an adult.

Jim, age three years, six months, was having problems following spoken directions in his home and was brought by his concerned parents to the university audiologist for a hearing evaluation. The history revealed that the boy was the second of two children, the product of a full-term, normal pregnancy. At the time of birth, however, after a normal caudal presentation, with the normal onset of respiration initiated by a loud birth cry, his breathing stopped. The obstetrician and a pediatric resident in the delivery room assumed the baby had a mucous plug blocking the airway at some point. Unfortunately, the nursery in the new hospital did not have oxygen available. Consequently, the obstetrician was forced to initiate mouth-to-mouth breathing and to stimulate heart action by a direct injection of atropine into the heart musculature. After three minutes of complete anoxia, the baby began breathing normally on his own. Subsequent neonatal behavior was normal.

Toward the end of the boy's first year, his parents became concerned about his lack of attentiveness to sounds. It appeared that often when one of the parents would walk into the baby's room, he would not seem to hear their approach and would react in a startled fashion to their "sudden" presence. It should be noted that both parents worked in a hospital specializing in neurological disorders, and were concerned that their baby might be showing signs of a central auditory problem, perhaps related to his cerebral anoxia at the time of birth. However, in discussing their worries and observations with their pediatrician they were told "not to worry," that the boy's overall development appeared well within normal limits. At the age of two years, the boy's verbal responses were observed to be slower and simpler than those that his sister had showed at the same age. At age three, if he were told, "Take these socks to your room," he would not be able to follow the command. The child would often tilt his head to one side and ask, "What?" If the command were repeated (and sometimes accompanied by a gesture), the child would follow the instructions correctly.

At age three and a half, the father became quite convinced that the boy had a severe learning problem (central in origin and "obviously" related to the three-minute anoxia). As a preliminary step in having the child thoroughly tested for a central auditory problem, the family began its diagnostic search with an audiologist. The boy was quickly conditioned to play audiometry, and it was soon found that he was experiencing "a 40 decibel hearing loss of a probable conductive type"; he was subsequently referred to an otologist, who confirmed the boy's conductive hearing loss and began treating him for an "extensive middle-ear effusion." The parents then began to realize that the child's frequent colds and earaches were all symptoms of his continuing middle-ear infections. Subsequently, the boy had tubes surgically placed in his eardrums to permit middle-ear drainage, and, because his hearing abilities seemed to fluctuate so often, he was fitted with a body-type hearing aid (the year was 1961).

His responses to sound immediately improved, although his comprehension of speech was not as good as his overall performance in all other cognitive and language areas tested. He was subsequently enrolled in a hearing nursery and quickly seemed to "catch up in his aural skills." At age five, when he was about to start kindergarten, the family moved to another city, and the child was placed in first grade. After initially having some difficulty following the teacher's spoken directions, the boy compensated well in visual-motor skills and was able to compete in the first-grade environment. Thanks to a caring teacher who gave him the extra help he needed in acquiring aural language skills and because his hearing problems were now gone, the child successfully completed the first and subsequent grades in school. He now has a doctorate in psychology and is a practicing clinical psychologist.

The case of Jim illustrates many points about hearing loss and its effects on communication. Because of his difficult birth history, with cerebral anoxia, his parents suspected a central auditory problem. His peripheral-hearing difficulties were so subtle, his parents were unable to observe on a day-to-day basis that he had a hearing loss. The effects of the fluctuating hearing loss severely affected developing language, so that he was unable to follow verbal commands like other children the same age. This was particularly noticeable when he started first grade; had his hearing loss not been detected and successfully treated, he might well have been placed in a special classroom for the learning-disabled. Middle-ear hearing loss in infants and young children may fluctuate in severity from day to day. It is difficult for parents to be sure about their observations of loss, and often the pediatrician's approach (as it was in this case) is to minimize parental concern with the typical comment that the child will "outgrow it; let's not be concerned." We will consider later in this chapter the management of young children with fluctuating conductive hearing loss; unfortunately, many such losses are never detected.

Corinne was a fifty-eight-year-old high-school biology teacher when she suffered a severe hearing loss associated with Ménière's disease. The relative suddenness of the disease, which began with severe symptoms of vertigo and dizziness, forced her to stop teaching for about six months. As the acute phase of her Ménière's began to subside, it was found that she had suffered a severe, permanent hearing loss, with a 60 dB average pure-tone loss in the left ear and a 75 dB loss in the right ear. She was fitted with a hearing aid, but her aided discrimination scores could not exceed 30 percent correct with some 40 dB of amplification. Six months after the onset of her hearing loss, her speech remained remarkably intact, characterized by normal articulation and voicing patterns. Some people felt that she spoke a bit slower after her illness than she did before. She was advised to "learn to use her hearing aid" by enrolling in a speech-reading class, and she also received 15 hours of individual auditory training in the audiology clinic of a local university. For the past two years, she has again been teaching biology in the high school; she uses a teacher's aide in the classroom, which she feels enables her "to function as a teacher about as well as I did when I could hear." Despite her severe hearing loss, her speech and voice patterns remain normal.

Most acquired hearing losses in adults come gradually, and are not sudden, like Corinne's. Corinne's story is remarkable in that her severe, handicapping hearing loss has been so well managed that she has been able to return to teaching. An acquired or adventitious severe hearing loss may or may not alter the speech and voice of the speaker (Goehl and Kaufman, 1984), depending on the age of onset of the hearing loss, its severity, and the often-forgotten determination and motivation of the patient. Corinne was determined to do what was necessary to go back to teaching, and she spent long hours wearing her new hearing aid while learning to speech-read (which she learned to do with remarkable skill). The intelligibility of her own speech remained normal.

THE HEARING-HANDICAPPED

One estimate of the total number of people living in the United States with a significant hearing loss is 3 percent (Elliott, 1978). We would include in this figure both children and adults who are either deaf or hard-of-hearing. A social criterion for *deafness,* presented by Davis (1978a), is that "everyday auditory communication is impossible or very nearly so," and is characterized by a pure-tone loss of 90 dB (ISO) or greater over the speech-range frequencies of 500, 1K, and 2K Hz. More often today, a person with a hearing loss greater than 90 dB is classified as having a "profound hearing loss." The term *hearing loss* is used for individuals who experience a loss of sensitivity in the speech range (500, 1K, 2K Hz) greater than 25 dB. Normal hearing may be considered to vary between 0 and 25 dB (Berg, 1970).

We will piece together the reports from several sources to gain a perspective on how many people in the United States have a hearing loss. In the *National Speech and Hearing Survey* (Hull and others, 1976), in a population of 38,568 schoolchildren, grades 1 through 12, hearing impairment (greater than 25 dB loss) was found in 2.6 percent. The majority of these children (1.87 percent of the total sample) had a unilateral loss, with normal hearing in one ear. The remaining 0.73 percent had bilateral losses. Of interest is that the hearing data by grade level show that the greatest number of children with hearing loss are found at the lower grade levels. These data on prevalence of hearing loss in children are similar to those reported by Berg (1970), who, using the 1967 U.S. preliminary census figures, reported these summary data:

Hearing Loss	*No. of Children in U.S.*
26–40 dB	636,975
41–55 dB	353,875
56–70 dB	141,550
71–90 dB	14,155
Total Hearing-Impaired	1,146,555

These data were Berg's projected summaries of the number of hearing-impaired children in the schools (as reported state by state) based on the 1967 census data. While it is difficult to determine an exact incidence of hearing loss in children (in part because of different standards in different states), perhaps the highest figure reported is by Orchik (1981), who wrote, "the incidence of hearing loss in individuals 17 years of age or younger is approximately 3.5 per 1000 persons."

The data on the lowest incidence of hearing loss reported by a U.S. National Health Survey (1967) is 0.84 percent, belonging to the age group seventeen–forty-four years. The 1967 National Health study found that 13.2 percent of the population age sixty-five had a hearing loss. Hull and Traynor (1977) report that presbycusis, the typical high-frequency loss of the aged, may be present in as many as 60 percent of those over sixty-five. Once again, the figures reported and the various estimates of the incidence of hearing loss in the national population vary considerably. Some of the variation in reporting prevalence or incidence is related to using monaural (one ear only) versus binaural (bilateral hearing loss) data or to comparing thresholds for different frequencies. We might conclude this discussion by conservatively estimating that 1.9 percent of the population of the United States of all ages has a hearing handicap greater than 25 dB (Davis, 1978). Projecting this figure to the estimated U.S. population of 230 million, this would mean that over 4,370,000 people among us are living with a hearing handicap.

TYPES OF HEARING LOSS

Hearing losses are generally identified as conductive (involving the outer and middle ear) or sensorineural (usually involving the inner ear). We will consider conductive and sensorineural hearing losses separately as they may occur in both children and adults.

In Children

As we have discussed in previous chapters, the ability to hear is required for normal early language development. Consequently, a hearing loss in a child can have a profound negative impact on developing language and speech.

Conductive Hearing Loss occurs when there is some kind of interruption in the transmission of sound, either in the external ear or, more often, in the middle ear. The most typical conductive loss comes from *otitis media,* when the middle ear becomes inflamed, often leading to middle-ear effusion, the accumulation of fluid behind the eardrum. In the case history of Jim, cited at the beginning of the chapter, we saw the effects of repeated middle-ear infections, with the fluid trapped behind the eardrum, causing repeated moderate hearing loss. It is not uncommon for young children, particularly in the preschool years, whenever they suffer from a head cold or active allergy, to experience middle-ear effusion. Sometimes the child has an ear-ache along with a mild-to-moderate conductive hearing loss; on other occasions, however, the middle-ear infection and resulting hearing loss remain undetected by the family. A typical audiogram of a young child with a conductive hearing loss related to an active problem of otitis media can be seen in Figure 7–1. The child experiences a relatively flat loss that might range anywhere from 15 to 55 dB. At very mild levels of loss, the child will hear all vowels and most consonants, but may miss hearing a few unvoiced (higher frequency) consonants if said with relatively little intensity. The common levels of conductive loss in young children may fluctuate between 35 and 50 dB, with the child hearing almost no speech sounds at normal conversational levels. Early identification and treatment of conductive hearing loss in children is essential. Fortunately, the majority of conductive disorders involving the middle ear can be successfully treated both medically and surgically (Davis and Fowler, 1978). Otitis media treatment may include the administration of antibiotic drugs to control infection, "blowing out the ear" (inflation), surgically excising the eardrum or placing drainage tubes in the drum, and other medical-surgical treatments by the otorhinolaryngologist (ear-nose-throat physician).

Some children suffer from *otosclerosis,* in which bone begins to grow around the footplate of the stapes where it attaches to the oval window. Other children may suffer from *otospongiosis,* a primary bone dycrasia that softens the bone in the middle ear (Goin, 1976). The effect of either the bony growth or bone softening is that the stapes no longer vibrates as it should. The result of this compromise

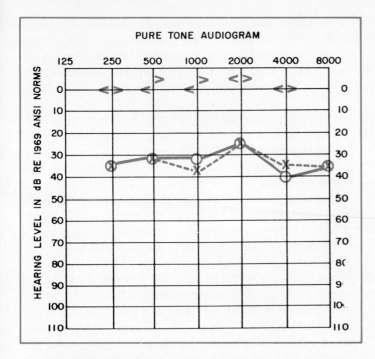

FIGURE 7-1 A typical audiogram of a conductive hearing loss. Erin, age four.

of stapes function is that the transfer of ossicular vibrations is seriously impaired, eventually causing a serious hearing loss. While the otosclerosis often begins at birth, it may be many years (perhaps not until adolescence) before stapes vibration is not possible. If the stapes becomes wholly fixated, hearing losses in some patients have been found to be as much as "50-60 dB for all audiometric frequencies" (Wiley, 1980). The primary treatment of otosclerosis is surgical, with Davis and Fowler (1978) reporting good success with the fenestration operation (which if successful, permits the sound waves to bypass the immobile stapes). Otospongiosis is often effectively treated by surgical removal of the stapes, with a wire or Teflon prosthesis put in its place (Goin, 1976).

Sensorineural Loss in children is less common than the conductive-type loss. In a sensorineural loss, the child has experienced some damage to the hair cells of the cochlea or to the nerve fibers of the auditory nerve (eighth cranial nerve). This type of nerve-damage hearing loss can often be overlooked in the physical examination of a young child, because both the external auditory canal and the middle ear appear normal on examination. The majority of sensorineural losses in children are of *congenital* origin, present at the time of birth. While the mother is carrying the baby she may have a disease (such as rubella) or an injury or be exposed to some form of toxicity (such as noxious fumes). Sometimes the sensorineural hearing loss is passed on through the genes, or the newborn infant may experience a severe anoxia. At other times, there may be a parental Rh incompatibility. A hearing loss acquired after the time of birth would be known as an *acquired* loss. Acquired hearing losses in children are often the result of severe infections, such as meningitis and diphtheria. Children who have already developed normal speech and language before the onset of the acquired sensorineural hearing loss will suffer far less communication interference than the very young child who is still acquiring the aural-oral language system.

A typical sensorineural loss, congenital in origin, can be seen in Figure 7–2. The gradual, sloping high-frequency loss of this moderate hearing loss (41 to 65 dB) tells us that without his hearing aid, the child hears some vowels and only occasional consonants in the speech of others. Unaided, the child can hear his own vocalizations, very loud voices of others at close range, and loud environmental sounds. With his hearing aid, he may be able to hear the different vowels and many of the consonants. His overall voice quality and the prosodic aspects of his speech will be normal. Severe hearing loss, from 66 to 89 dB, requires much amplification and special training to develop and maintain adequate speech and language.

Deafness, characterized by greater than a 90 dB bilateral hearing loss, accounts for about three-tenths of 1 percent of all children in the public schools (Berg, 1970). The term *deaf* carries with it an immediate negative picture of a grossly handicapped person; for this reason, the term ''profound hearing loss'' (90 dB or greater) has been used more often in recent years, and it seems to facilitate a kinder, more objective understanding of the child or adult who for all practical purposes has no

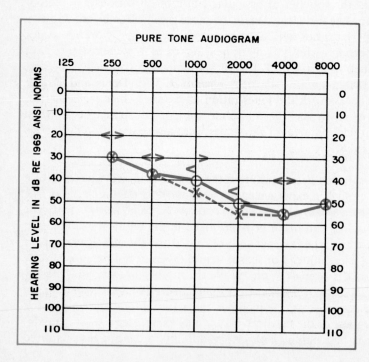

FIGURE 7–2 An audiogram showing a moderate sensorineural hearing loss. Eli, age eight.

functional hearing (Northern and Lemme, 1982). The speech of the child with profound hearing loss may suffer a marked reduction in melody and prosody, with severe articulation defects. Elevated voice pitch, poor vocal quality, and variations in nasal resonance are all possible characteristics of children with profound losses (Boone, 1983). It would appear, however, that a profound hearing loss acquired after the child has developed an auditory language (an adventitious loss) may have only minimal effects on articulation, speech prosody, and voice quality (Goehl and Kaufman, 1984). The severe sensorineural loss that causes deafness, congenital or acquired, is sometimes accompanied by middle-ear problems. However, profound hearing loss can rarely be treated satisfactorily from a medical-surgical point of view.

Rather, the management of such a child requires extensive testing by the audiologist, who searches for a remnant of residual hearing (sometimes at the lowest frequencies of the hearing range) in the hope that the child might profit from high-gain amplification. Special training, including sign language and auditory training, is often required; such training is available in some special classes in selected school districts. Otherwise, children are trained and educated in special schools for the deaf.

As we saw in Chapter 5, there are children who have normal peripheral hearing mechanisms but seem to be unable to listen. Such children are often said to have a *central auditory problem*. For some, the problem in understanding what is said may well be related to an earlier or ongoing peripheral hearing loss. Reichman and Healey (1983) found, in reviewing the literature on learning-disabled children, that these children had significantly greater histories of otitis media than normal-hearing peers. It appears that children who have otitis media for several years are at higher risk of having auditory comprehension problems, even after their hearing disorder has been corrected. It may well be that the child's ability to listen is compromised by a hearing loss in the preschool years. Many children classified as learning-disabled may well have had a hearing loss as one of the primary contributing causes of their inability to understand what they hear. With their faulty hearing, they develop faulty language.

Some children with central auditory problems may actually have a central-nervous-system lesion somewhere in the brain, such as in the cochlear nucleus of the brainstem, in the auditory pathways, the thalamus, or the cortex. Despite our more recent, sophisticated diagnostic techniques (regional cerebral blood flow, CT-scan, PET-scan) for looking at normal and abnormal sites within the central nervous system, it has not been possible to identify discrete lesions in the brain that may be the cause of central auditory problems. When a child (or an adult, for that matter) acquires aphasia, severe problems in auditory comprehension may be part of the receptive aphasia; such acquired lesions in aphasia can be well localized today (Kertesz and others, 1979).

The child with a central auditory problem usually has trouble following and understanding what is said. Some children have demonstrated normal auditory acuity but have difficulty with central auditory processing. As we saw in Chapter 2, in normal development, as the infant-young child matures, there appears to be an increasing ability to process incoming auditory information. The normal infant, for example, is able to pick out the human voice, turn toward it, and attend to it, as early as four months of age (Northern and Downs, 1978). The human species appears to be "wired" so that babies give preferential attention to what they perceive as the human voice. Before they are two years old, they can understand and follow two-level spoken commands. As children learn to comprehend what is said, they must retain the exact order of the words that were spoken long enough to decode their meaning and understand the intent of the speaker and the pragmatics of the interaction. The words "rush" in quickly, and auditory comprehension demands that children pay close attention and develop an ability to comprehend quickly. Understanding the spoken messages that one hears is a complicated and miraculous event. Some children with normal hearing sensitivity cannot master this listening skill, such as certain ones classified as having learning disabilities. Among three types of learning-disability syndromes identified (Mattis, French, and Rapin, 1973; Wiig, 1982) the largest group of children displays problems in aural-oral language, particularly in understanding what others are saying.

In Adults

Hearing loss in adults (let us say, seventeen or older) is usually acquired. Prior to the hearing loss, the individual has enjoyed normal hearing, with normal language and speech. Hearing loss increases dramatically in older age groups. The National Center for Health Statistics, as reported by Davis (1978a), found that in the entire U.S. population, only 0.84 of 1 percent of the population between seventeen and forty-four had a bilateral hearing impairment; 2.94 percent of those forty-five to sixty-four were found to have a hearing loss; and some 13.2 percent of the population over sixty-five showed a bilateral hearing loss.

Conductive Hearing Loss associated with chronic middle-ear infections is far less common in adults than in children. At about the time of puberty, one typically experiences a marked shrinkage of lymphoid tissue, such as tonsils and adenoids, and begins to experience good middle-ear drainage. With adequate ear drainage, the buildup of suppurative matter, which the young child often has with otitis media, does not occur as often in adults. Adults do experience temporary conductive hearing losses secondary to allergic reactions and ear-nose-throat infections. Sometimes flying in an airplane or being at a high elevation while having an allergy or head cold will cause a pressure differential between the middle ear and the atmosphere; the eardrum is retracted and causes temporary ear discomfort and a mild conductive hearing loss. Another conductive-type loss in the adult may be the result of otosclerosis; as in children, the stapes begins to be encapsulated by spongy bone and becomes fixated on the oval window, seriously interfering with the transmission of ossicular vibrations via the oval window into the cochlear portion of the inner ear. With complete stapes fixation, the patient may experience a severe conductive hearing loss, such as seen in Figure 7–3. The patient, a twenty-five-year-old male, experienced a 52 dB average pure-tone loss in the left ear and a 47 dB loss in the

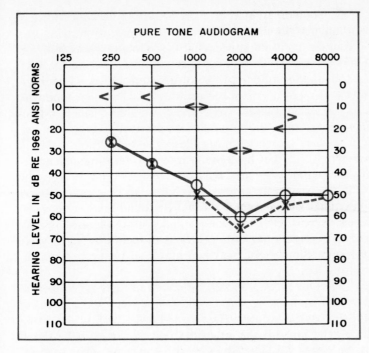

FIGURE 7-3 A severe conductive loss in otosclerosis. Ben, age twenty-five.

right ear. His bone-conduction thresholds were normal except for a drop at 2K Hz, a sensorineural deficit often observed in patients with advanced otosclerosis. This patient experienced a dramatic improvement in hearing by bilateral stapes-immobilization surgery, which basically restored the vibratory capabilities of the ossicular chain in both ears.

Other conductive impairments that are occasionally observed in adults may be related to external ear trauma, which may on occasion damage the external or middle ears. Wiley (1980) cites a case of a twenty-four-year-old man with ear trauma that caused a fracture of the stapes, with a resulting unilateral conductive hearing loss of 45 dB (SRT) in the involved ear. Tumors, benign and malignant, have been found in the external or middle ear, causing conductive hearing loss (Davis, 1978b).

Sensorineural Hearing Loss increases in prevalence as adults get older. Men show a greater sensorineural loss, at a younger age, than women. For example, in our clinical population, men at age fifty showed a 35 dB loss at 8K Hz, while women the same age showed an average loss of 27 dB; at age sixty, the men had an average threshold response of 50 dB at 8K, with women responding at 38 dB at 8K. It may well be that as future populations in the United States get older, there will be greater losses and fewer differences between the sexes (primarily because of today's excessive recreational noises).

Noise-induced Hearing Loss. Sometimes, after attending a noisy rock concert where music was played at high-intensity levels, we experience a temporary hearing loss as part of noise-induced trauma. It would appear that the human ear was not constructed to tolerate the intense noise levels that often characterize our society, such as that of jet engines, the tremendous loudness of a portable tape player with a head set, the noise of rock music at a disco, the pulsations of a jackhammer. One who listens to loud sounds may experience a temporary threshold shift (usually a temporary loss of frequencies higher than those one has been hearing) and a tinnitus (head noises or ringing in the ears). Such temporary losses and head noises should serve as a warning to individuals that they have been exposed to far too much noise. While initial exposure to such loud levels may only produce a temporary loss, the individual should avoid repeated exposures to such noise levels. One cannot overstate the need for using earplugs if one is forced to work around loud noise; also, unnecessary loudness levels in work environments should not be tolerated by employer or employee. Excessive recreational loudness levels should be avoided, since it is well known that continuous loud-noise exposure may lead to severe (and unnecessary) permanent hearing loss.

Noise exposure implies an excessive intensity of sound (dB) over a period of time. The effects of temporary noise exposure can be predicted by the intensity of the noise signal and the time of the exposure (Davis and Fowler, 1978). The actual risk of impairment can be determined if the intensities and duration of the signal are known. Many industries today, aware of the effects of noise on their workers' hearing, have initiated hearing conservation programs, which have resulted in having industrial equipment make less noise and workers wear earplugs or earmuffs while in noisy work environments. The effects of recreational noise have been subject to fewer controls, and many among us listen to loud music repeatedly; band and orchestra playing "night after night should be recognized as a hazardous noise-exposure" (Davis and Fowler, 1978, p. 160).

The cochlea is the primary part of the hearing mechanism that appears to be affected most by continuous noise exposure. Eventually, after repeated noise exposure, the cochlear hair cells are destroyed, creating a permanent sensorineural hearing loss. The audiogram in Figure 7–4 shows the high-frequency loss of a forty-seven-year-old man who used a jackhammer daily in his work in construction. His greatest loss is at 4K Hz, the typical site of impairment from noise trauma, often called the "4,000 Hz notch." At the time this audiogram was taken, the patient had been at his job for 12 years. If he continued using the jackhammer without wearing earplugs in an attempt to attenuate the sound, his high-frequency loss would probably continue to worsen. If he could succeed in reducing the trauma to his ears (by wearing plugs or changing his job), he would probably experience no further progression of sensorineural loss.

Ménière's Disease is another example of an inner-ear problem that may lead to permanent hearing loss (often only in one ear). At the onset of the disease, the patient often experiences severe vertigo (spinning dizziness) and tinnitus. Actually, according to Davis (1978b), the problem of vertigo, tinnitus, and sensorineural hear-

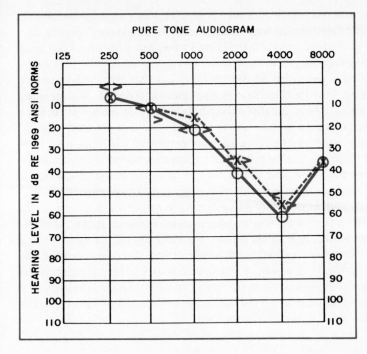

PURE TONE AUDIOGRAM

FIGURE 7-4 A noise-induced hearing loss. Leonard, age forty-seven.

ing loss known as Ménière's disease might be best known as "Ménière's syndrome"; the disorder is usually signaled by a sudden onset of the three symptoms. For the patient, the vertigo is the most distressing. The cause and treatment of Ménière's are not known at this time. Fortunately, the symptoms subside, although the elevated hearing thresholds (often at the lower end of the frequency range) may continue permanently. Unfortunately, the symptoms may return at any time.

Presbycusis is a gradual, high-frequency hearing loss that is experienced to some degree by many older persons. It has been estimated (Sanders, 1978) that 90 percent of adult patients seeking help for a hearing disorder are suffering from presbycusis. Presbycusis may have many different causes and may well be the "cumulative effect of a number of disorders or insults" that contribute to the degeneration of the auditory mechanism (Nadol, 1981, p. 63). Changes begin to take place in the cochlea (particularly at the basal end) during middle age that result in a gradual diminution of hearing sensitivity (primarily IK Hz and beyond). Orchik (1981) describes a second degenerative change that involves a marked decrease in the auditory fibers of the auditory nerve as well as in the auditory pathways leading from the cochlear nucleus in the medulla up to the auditory cortex in the temporal lobes. The axonal-fiber loss is accompanied by a loss of neurons in the various auditory synaptic stations connected by the auditory pathways. This loss of neurons and fibers may well account for the decrease in auditory-discrimination ability that is typically experienced by the patient with a progressive presbycusis. Often the patient with advanced presbycusis experiences not only a high-frequency hearing loss on pure-tone testing, but also a surprising problem of auditory discrimination. The typical patient says to the audiologist, "I know that people are talking to me, but they just don't seem to enunciate." The low-frequency hearing sensitivity stays near normal limits; this enables the patient to hear the voice of the speaker, but the high-frequency loss prevents the patient from hearing the consonants required to decode the message. The patient's attempts to guess at the distorted message are not always successful, and one may experience embarrassment over the inability to comprehend well.

The typical pure-tone audiogram of a sixty-eight-year-old man with presbycusis can be seen in Figure 7–5. This patient experienced a bilateral sensorineural loss that has an average pure-tone loss in the left ear of 22 dB and a 25 dB loss in the right ear. Beyond 2K, he experienced a sharp drop in hearing sensitivity.

An additional problem of many patients with presbycusis is a *narrow dynamic range* (the difference between the threshold of audibility and the threshold of discomfort). Patients with this problem often have difficulty adjusting to hearing aids because of their intolerance of excessive amplification. Freeman and Sinclair (1981) note: "Still unresolved, however, is the question of whether a reduced tolerance level has a physiologic or psychologic basis" (p. 283). Often, patients with a narrow dynamic range require trial periods with amplification and auditory training as a prelude to successfully using a hearing aid.

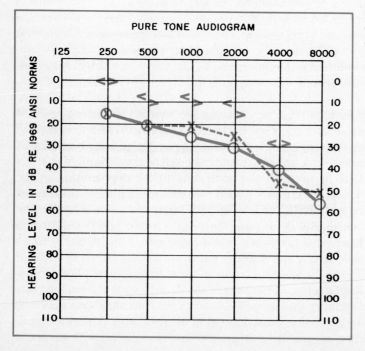

FIGURE 7–5 An audiogram depicting presbycusis. Ralph, age sixty-eight.

HEARING TESTING

There are two primary reasons for the audiologist to test hearing: first, the identification of a hearing loss can lead to the identification of a causative disease (many conditions that cause hearing loss can be medically treated); second, a hearing loss that cannot be medically treated may require habilitative (for the child) or rehabilitative (for the adult) management. Identification of the severity and type of hearing loss through audiological testing is a prerequisite for both medical and habilitative/rehabilitative management. Before we focus on hearing testing, let us consider the people who may be involved in this kind of evaluation:

1. The *audiologist* is a nonmedical professional trained to study hearing and its disorders. These professionals not only provide audiological testing but are trained to design and conduct hearing screening and hearing-conservation programs, conduct auditory training, teach speech reading (and sometimes signing), fit hearing aids, counsel the hard-of-hearing patient and family, and the like. In Chapter 13, we will consider more fully the profession of audiology and the standards of the profession as recommended by the American Speech-Language-Hearing Association.[1]

2. The *otologist* is a medical doctor trained to diagnose and treat (medically, surgically) the diseases of the ear. Most such physicians also treat nose and throat problems and are called *otorhinolaryngologists;* more commonly, they are called *otolaryngologists*. They work closely with the audiologist, who does the majority of the testing and habilitative-rehabilitative work with the hearing-impaired patient.

3. The *hearing-aid dealer* is a business person who sells hearing aids. Often the hearing-aid dealer sees the hard-of-hearing person first; however, there is a national regulation requiring that the patient be referred to an otologist or audiologist for testing before a hearing aid is sold. Hearing aids are prescribed and can be sold in the otologist's or audiologist's office; others are sold by the hearing-aid dealer in an office or store.

Screening Programs

Screening programs are sometimes initiated by the audiologist. Their purpose is to identify particular members of a population who may demonstrate a hearing loss. Perhaps the most common site of successful hearing-screening programs is the public schools; Northern and Lemme (1982) have noted that "63% of all ultimate hearing losses will be identified by screening in kindergarten and 85% by screening at

---

[1]The American Speech-Language-Hearing Association is the professional organization for the profession of audiology and speech-language pathology. The ASHA headquarters are at 10801 Rockville Pike, Rockville, Maryland 20852.

the third grade level" (p. 320). The audiometric screening is provided by a professionally trained person, who tests particular frequencies (such as 1, 2, and 4 K) at specified intensity levels (such as 25 dB); children indicate with a hand signal whether they hear the pure tone. Children who fail the hearing screening are usually scheduled for a full-scale audiological evaluation. In the preschool years, one might question the efficacy of a screening program for nursery-age children who demonstrate some kind of communication lack; at this age, if there is any question about the child's communicative abilities, it is best to provide a more thorough audiological evaluation.

Most hearing-screening programs for young and middle-age adults are found in various industrial hearing-conservation programs. Often, a nurse or audiometric technician is trained to administer various pure-tone frequency sweeps to employees, perhaps testing at the frequencies of 500 Hz, 1K, 2K, and 4K. The decibel level selected for pass-fail on the screening depends in part on the sound level of the testing area. Employees who fail screening are then often referred to an otologist or audiologist for further threshold testing. Screening programs for older people (sixty and beyond) are of questionable value (Hodgson, 1984), since the majority of people would not pass screening criteria; rather, it is recommended that an audiological evaluation be conducted initially. Once identified in an older person, a hearing loss should signal the need for a full audiological and otological examination, so that appropriate treatment or management can be initiated.

Audiological Evaluation

An audiological evaluation usually begins with the audiologist giving the patient a basic pure-tone test. A **pure tone** is a sound that contains only one frequency, which is generated by the audiologist, using an audiometer. Low frequencies (less than 1K) must be tested in a sound-treated room, because the ambient noise level in the typical room is too high. It is a standard audiometric procedure to begin testing threshold at 1K, test higher frequencies, return to 1K, and go down to the bottom of the frequency range (Downs and Northern, 1976). The child in Figure 7–6 is pushing a button to signal that he heard in the headphones the pure tone that was generated by the audiometer. This is known as **air-conduction audiometry,** with the signal usually introduced to the patient via headphones. **Bone-conduction testing** is often done in conjunction with air-conduction audiometry. In bone-conduction testing, a vibrator is placed on the forehead or the mastoid portion of the temporal bone; the sound bypasses the external and middle ears and goes directly into the inner ear. When one ear is being tested, the other ear receives a masking noise. The usual masking sound is a narrow-band noise that so occupies the untested ear that the bone-test signal does not travel across to the ear not being tested. If youngsters have a middle-ear infection, they may well show depressed thresholds for air conduction but normal responses for bone conduction. This difference between the thresholds is called an *air-bone gap*. Such a gap is characteristic of children with middle-ear disease, who typically show depressed thresholds by air conduction but may demonstrate normal responses when the sound is introduced into the inner ear by bone

FIGURE 7-6 A thirteen-year-old boy signals his responses to pure-tone audiometry. Courtesy of Good Samaritan Medical Center, Phoenix, Arizona.

conduction. This often means that the child still has a normal sensorineural system and has the potential for normal hearing, if the middle-ear problem could be cleared up.

To test younger children (often five years or younger) may require using certain kinds of play, such as stacking blocks or dropping a ball in a can, each time they hear a pure tone. Even infants and noncooperative youngsters can usually be conditioned to respond to pure tones, such as by turning their heads toward the presenting stimulus source when they hear the tone.

Another form of audiometry is **impedance audiometry,** where a small probe is inserted at the entrance of the patient's external auditory canal so that a measurement can be made of both the air pressure and air volume within the external and middle ear. Variations in either pressure or volume from normal values may indicate the presence of possible middle-ear disease (such as otitis media).

A different type of audiometry is *Bekesy audiometry,* where subjects trace their own pure-tone thresholds by using a self-recording audiometer. Patients are presented with a pulsed or continuous tone and respond by depressing a switch until the tone is alternately just audible and inaudible. Patients basically plot their own audiograms, a continuous tracing that indicates one's hearing sensitivity to pure tone.

While the documentation of one's hearing capability when listening to pure tones is an essential part of an audiological evaluation, of much practical importance is finding out how well someone listens to speech. In *speech audiometry,* the exact sensitivity level that enables someone to understand speech can be determined. The **speech reception threshold** (SRT) requires that the patient repeat back two-syllable words (such as *cupcake, baseball*) that are presented by the audiologist at as low an intensity level as possible. The intensity level where the patient identifies the words correctly 50 percent of the time is known as the patient's SRT. Another part of speech audiometry is **speech discrimination,** the determination of how well someone can understand speech at intensity levels comfortably above the SRT levels. The usual speech stimuli for speech discrimination are monosyllabic words (*cat-bat; peach-beach*) that sound alike, with only one differing phoneme between the two contrasted words. The words may be presented either through the headphones or in free-field testing (preferably in a sound-treated room). Young children may point to a picture stimulus that represents the word they thought they heard. Older subjects, without an articulation defect, may repeat to the examiner the word they believed was said. The patient's speech-discrimination performance is determined by the percentage of presented stimuli that were heard correctly.

Speech audiometry is particularly important for the child or adult who may need some kind of remedial intervention, such as auditory training or the fitting of a hearing aid. How well such individuals hear speech and can understand what they hear with some amplification often determines the kind of treatment that the audiologist can offer.

With adult patients who are found to have a hearing loss as determined by pure-tone and speech audiometry, it is important to determine the patient's self-evaluation of the hearing handicap (Garstecki, 1981). Patients should be interviewed by the audiologist after testing, to determine how they feel about their hearing handicap. Fortunately, there are a number of hearing-handicap scales available that will provide insights as to how patients view their problem, such as the *Denver Scale of Communication Function* (Alpiner and others, 1971) and the *Hearing Performance Inventory* (Giolas and others, 1979). The effective future management of patients' problems requires this kind of personal attitude scaling, which facilitates audiologists' understanding of patients and their reactions to the hearing loss.

We can appreciate the need for thorough hearing testing as we review the case history of George M. He had purchased a hearing aid at a store, without the benefit of an audiological evaluation, and after much dissatisfaction with his poor hearing, he made an appointment in the otolaryngology department of a local hospital. Much of the dialogue and test results reported here were taken directly from the patient's hospital chart, with his permission.

G. M., eighty-one-year-old-male, retired postal employee. Mr. M. was seen in the ENT clinic for a problem of poor hearing. The patient described his problem and provided this history with very little questioning from the examiner. "I was accusing Minnie [his wife] of talking all the time with mush in her mouth. She up and gets tired of it all and says to me one day, 'George, you are as deaf as a post. Anyone could see that by the way you have the TV on so loud all the time. Don't tell me about mush, you go get yourself a hearing aid.'" The patient took his wife's advice and went to the closest town that had a department store that sold hearing aids. He purchased an in-the-ear aid for about four hundred dollars. The patient experienced much dissatisfaction with the aid, reporting, "The darn thing would just roar back at me every time I tried to use it. Finally, I just gave up, and it's still sitting in our phonograph cabinet. I'm afraid to wear it, it makes me so ornery."

The otolaryngologist found that George was basically free from external or middle-ear disease, and a tentative diagnosis was made of a "sensorineural presbycusis" hearing loss. The patient was referred for audiological testing. In attempts to obtain a history, the audiologist noted, "Patient volunteers his history freely with good evidence of normal cognition, normal language and speech with some tendency to give longer answers than needed." Mr. M. felt that his hearing loss had come on gradually over the years, probably related to his "riding the rail cars as we sorted the mail between cities. I had the Cleveland-to-Chicago run for over 30 years and there were times the cars were so noisy a fellow couldn't hear himself think." Other than his hearing loss and reported problems of indigestion (for which he ate copious amounts of cottage cheese), the patient was in good health and looked ten years younger than his actual age.

Pure-tone testing found Mr. M. to have a bilateral sensorineural hearing loss, with normal hearing in both ears for the frequencies 125, 250, and 500 Hz. Thresholds in his better, right ear were 20 dB at 1K, 35 dB at 2K, 55 dB at 4K, and 70 dB at 8K. Air-conduction and bone-conduction thresholds from 250 through 4K were nearly identical, indicating that the conductive mechanisms of his ears were normal and that his hearing problem was sensorineural, probably related to noise exposure and old age. Speech audiometry began by testing the patient's speech reception threshold, asking him to repeat two-syllable spondee words after the audiologist. At first, Mr. M. misunderstood the task requested and instead of repeating the words, he made up sentences using the words. For instance, for *baseball,* he replied, "They played great baseball in Cleveland." His SRT was 28 dB in the left ear and 30 in the right ear. Speech-discrimination testing found him at 60 dB to discriminate correctly 74 percent of the monosyllabic words presented, a score somewhat lower than one might have predicted from his pure-tone audiogram and SRT. It was postulated that the patient might be experiencing some *phonemic regression* (Gaeth, 1948), when discrimination scores are lower than pure-tone and SRT measures would predict. Older patients frequently display lower discrimination scores than would be predicted, perhaps suggestive of some central-auditory-system deterioration.

It became apparent that the hearing aid the patient had purchased from the store was inappropriate for his loss. He was receiving maximum amplification of low frequencies where he had grossly normal hearing. In an interview in which the test data were interpreted to the patient, Mr. M. exhibited insight about why the previous hearing aid had proved to be unsatisfactory. He was subsequently scheduled for a hearing-aid evaluation and fitted with a moderate-gain instrument that amplified the higher frequencies less than the lower ones. Following the fitting of his new aid, he enrolled in a six-week aural-rehabilitation program, where he learned the care and use of the new aid and reviewed ways of improving overall communication, such as better lighting, speech reading, and learning to take turns talking.

MANAGEMENT OF THE HEARING-IMPAIRED

Let us consider that the child who is hearing-impaired from the time of birth or before normal language development is completed requires hearing *habilitation*. *Rehabilitation* is the term we will use to describe management programs for children and adults who acquire a hearing loss after language and speech have been established. Although there are some similarities between both habilitative and rehabilitative programs, we will also see that there are some marked differences.

Habilitation Programs

Primary consideration must be given to the onset, type, and extent of the hearing loss in young children. Through the audiological evaluation and the medical evaluation of the otologist, the decision is made about whether medical-surgical intervention is possible. With such treatment, can hearing be improved? The audiologist must find out how the child is using any residual hearing and determine the extent of the child's developmental growth (cognitive, language, speech, and functional communication). A useful way to approach an understanding of hearing habilitation of the young child might be to apply some of the normative information we reviewed about listening in Chapter 2 and about language in Chapter 4, relating it to particular levels of hearing loss. In Table 7-1, particular hearing-loss level, language-speech-learning effects, and habilitative-management strategies for each level of loss are listed. Habilitative efforts are quite individualized, depending primarily on the extent of the hearing loss and the age of the child.

Hearing Loss in Children, 15–40dB. Even an identified hearing loss as low as 15 dB should be considered a possible threat to normal learning. Reichman and Healey (1983, p. 276), after summarizing 18 studies that looked at the effects of recurring otitis media on the learning abilities of children, concluded that "fluctuations in hearing due to otitis media (with hearing worse than 15 dB) for half of any six month period during childhood" can have negative effects on learning. Most children with mild hearing losses (15–30 dB) have conductive-type losses that come and go, many times undetected by parents and teachers. When such losses are identified, however, priority should be given to the possible medical-surgical treatment of the disorder. The child in the classroom with such a loss should have the benefit of preferential

TABLE 7-1

Effects of Hearing Loss on Communication and Types of Habilitative Intervention

Hearing loss (500, 1K, 2K)	Communication effects	Habilitation intervention
25–40 dB	Misses hearing many consonants Difficulty in auditory learning Mild speech-language problem	Possible surgical correction Fit with hearing aid Auditory training Needs speech-language therapy
40–65 dB	Speech-language retardation Learning disability Hears no speech at normal loudness levels	Speech-language therapy Special-education placement Fit with hearing aid
65–90 dB	Voice pathology (cul-de-sac resonance & pitch changes) Aural-oral language seriously compromised Severe learning problems	Voice therapy added to speech therapy Hearing aid, with total communication Classroom for the hearing-impaired
90 dB +	Profound hearing loss (deaf) Voice-speech sounds like deaf Severe problems in academic learning	Hearing aid and total communication Voice and speech therapy Classroom (or school) for profoundly impaired

seating. Berg (1970) writes that such children should be taught to develop basic listening competencies, learning to listen critically and watch others closely as part of an auditory-training program. Their hearing-acuity levels should be reevaluated often, so that remediation steps might be taken when hearing sensitivity is down, such as by identification of the better ear (which should be toward the teacher), noting the need for medical treatment, and so forth.

The child with a hearing loss of 25–40 dB should always be fitted with a hearing aid, according to Downs and Northern (1976). Five types of hearing aids may be seen in Figure 7–7: A: the body-type, with cord and receiver (used less today with children who have a slight loss) and ear mold; B: the behind-the-ear aid, with plastic tube and ear mold; C: the eyeglass aid; D: the in-the-ear aid; and E: the ear-canal aid. Such amplification can make a big difference in the child's cognitive development as well as have an obvious impact on language and speech. Speech reading and auditory training should be initiated, with particular emphasis given to the correct articulation of consonants. There is a need for children with mild-to-moderate hearing impairment (25–40 dB) to have developed special language-intervention programs by speech-language pathologists, learning-disability specialists, and remedial-education personnel (Downs, 1981).

Hearing Loss in Children, 40–65 dB. The child with a moderate hearing loss, 40–65 dB, in the speech-range frequencies 500, 1K, 2K Hz should without question be fitted with a hearing aid. The loss may be conductive, sensorineural, or mixed. While

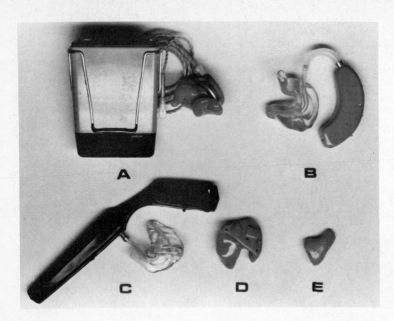

FIGURE 7-7 Types of hearing aids. A: body-type aid; B: behind-the-ear aid; C: eyeglass aid; D: in-the-ear aid; E: ear-canal aid. Used with permission of Hodgson, W. R., ed. (1986). *Hearing Aid Assessment and Use in Audiology Habilitation (3rd ed.).* Baltimore: Williams and Wilkins Co.

primary consideration must be given to possible medical treatment of the ear disorder, the most important problems experienced by the child are severe difficulties in communication, particularly understanding what others say (especially when not immediately visible) and in speech and expressive language. In addition to the fitting and wearing of a hearing aid, the child must be taught speech-reading skills and learn to communicate by watching others closely and using facial expression and gesture, such as the natural gestures used in Amer-Ind (the natural signs of the Native American) as developed by Skelly and others (1975). The Amer-Ind signs are natural ones (such as beckoning someone to come to you) and are not coded-language signs. In adults, such signs come naturally as part of communication; in children, the signs must be taught by example.

The greater the hearing loss in such children, the greater the tendency to show some alterations in prosody and some changes in voice. Some of the methods developed by Ling (1976) for application with the child with severe hearing loss should be used. Ling would place emphasis in moving forward in articulation training, working, in effect, for speed of production and automaticity. Ling wrote, "Training hearing-impaired children toward automaticity through phonetic (non-meaningful) speech development may greatly speed the process of acquisition and also reduce the need for correction at the phonologic level, when emphasis should be on communication rather than on the mechanism of production" (p. 89). Emphasis should also be given to helping the child develop suprasegmental voicing patterns that approach the prosodic patterns heard in normal speech. If children are to develop good oral speech, productions that well represent their expressive language, some emphasis must be placed on developing the vocal patterns and prosodic melodies of normal speakers.

Hearing Loss in Children, 65–90 dB. Such a severe loss before language acquisition will have profound effects on the developing communication system of the young child. Even with amplification, the child will demonstrate impairment when trying to follow and understand the speech of others. The voice and speech may be characterized by the "sound of the deaf child," which includes a back pharyngeal focus in resonance, some hypernasality, fluctuations in pitch level, a slowing down of prosodic patterns, and moderate defects in the articulation of vowels and consonants (Boone, 1983; Ling, 1976; Monsen, 1978). The later the hearing loss (at this severe level) is detected, the more difficult it is for the child to profit from amplification.

The child needs special-educational placement designed for the severely hard-of-hearing. For speech and voice training, the child needs to work with a speech-language pathologist who is especially trained to deal with the severely and profoundly hard-of-hearing child. While the primary focus should be on training the child to achieve functional aural-oral communication skills, the child should be placed in a total-communication program, where signing may be learned as a supplementary communication mode (Downs and Northern, 1976; Northern and Lemme, 1982). For years, there was a controversy between the strictly oralist approach to teaching deaf children to communicate and a manual approach that encouraged the child to communicate by using sign language. While there are still "pockets" where only an oral or a manual approach is used with the severely or profoundly (deaf) hard-of-hearing-child, most special educators use a total-communication approach, where both aural comprehension-oral expression and signing skills are taught. Attempts in oral schools not to permit signing were usually thwarted by the students learning to sign among themselves. It does appear that part of a total communication approach that includes American Sign Language (ASL) teaches the child a fast language system that uses body and hand gestures as symbols for words and ideas. The limitation of using sign language, of course, is that one can only communicate with other people who know the same signing system, such as ASL.

More and more audiologists, speech-language pathologists, and special educators are recommending the total-communication approach with severely hard-of-hearing children. It includes auditory training, speech reading, speaking, finger spelling, sign language, Amer-Ind, and reading-writing. It would appear that the more communication modes available to such children, the more settings in which they will find themselves able to communicate.

Primarily, efforts should be made, however, to develop aural-oral language skills by working to produce automatic articulatory production (avoiding the prolongation of vowels and overarticulation of consonants that often typify deaf speech) and developing normal prosodic voicing patterns. Children with severe hearing loss require the use of much visual feedback, such as letting them see their breathing patterns on an oscilloscope or watch their voicing patterns on the screen of a spectral playback device. With emphasis given to the "sound" of the deaf child's speech, it is often amazing how normal-sounding such speech can become. By using what residual hearing there is, coupled with good speech-reading skills, the child may be able to communicate effectively with the normal-hearing world.

Hearing Loss in Children, 90 dB +. The child with a hearing loss 90 dB or greater is more often classified today as having a profound hearing loss but is still often referred to as a deaf child. It is very doubtful that such a profound hearing loss (once identified) can be corrected medically or surgically. At as early an age as possible, the child should be fitted with a hearing aid, so that any residual hearing can be amplified and used. Consequently, *high-risk registers* for deafness have been set up in many hospitals, so that hard-of-hearing and deaf babies can be identified through hearing screening in the newborn nursery (Downs and Northern, 1976). As early as possible, deaf babies are fitted with hearing aids (which a trained audiologist is able to do). Once the baby is fitted with a hearing aid, a special auditory training program is developed for the family to use at home, doing whatever possible to expose the baby to a hearing world.

The young child with a profound hearing loss needs to be placed in a pre-school training program developed for such youngsters. A typical hearing-nursery program will often make heavy use of powerful amplification devices, such as group auditory trainers, inductance loop amplification, or carrier-wave transmission (Ross, 1972). Such devices may enable the children (with their own hearing aids removed) to experience and hear environmental play noises and the voices of others in the nursery. Language training blends amplification with play experience and extensive use of visual and tactile play materials. Speech and voice training begin with children developing a feel for the "forward-moving" aspects of speech, attempting to use normal voicing and prosodic patterns as much as possible.

Similar to the child with a severe loss, the older child with a profound loss probably would best profit from a total-communication approach. Such a program would include voicing-prosodic training, signing and finger spelling, speech reading, and auditory training. Educational training would be best received in a special class (or school) for the profoundly hard-of-hearing. There is a need for parents and educators to individualize programs for the profoundly hard-of-hearing child, avoiding the stigma of the label of "deafness," which seems to carry with it a view of limitation and "being different." However, application of modern technology specific to amplification and the use of modern educational techniques for handicapped children have done much to improve the communicative function of children with profound hearing loss.

Rehabilitation Programs

The individual child or adult who already has normal speech and language and acquires a hearing loss will usually require some kind of hearing rehabilitation. We shall see, however, that such problems are quite different from those of the child with a developmental hearing loss. Prior to suffering a sudden, devastating hearing loss secondary to a serious, acquired illness, such as encephalitis or meningitis, children experience a normal life. Their parents and families interact with them in a normal manner and applaud their early developmental achievements, including their struggles to speak and formulate language. Undoubtedly, they acquire normal language function and are able to express themselves by blending voice and speech as their primary mode of communication. Their communication skills are well established. The effects, therefore, of an acquired hearing loss will slowly take their toll on communicative function. The acquired hearing loss is a hidden deficit from many of the people around such children. They still look the same, and those around them will often expect them to function just as they did before the hearing loss. Such children will need amplification and must learn to listen to and watch closely the communication of others. Therefore, rehabilitation attempts must focus almost as much on the environment as on the child; the family will need counseling, the child will require a special educational setting, with teachers and other personnel who understand the limiting effects of an acquired hearing loss.

Adults who acquire a hearing loss have had a lifetime of normal educational, psychological, social, and vocational experiences. Rehabilitation attempts, therefore, focus on helping such patients to regain their previous level of functioning as much as possible. Let us consider a three-point hearing-rehabilitation program that we might use for the typical adult or child who acquires a hearing loss:

1. The fitting of a hearing aid
2. An aural-rehabilitation program
3. Psychological counseling

The Fitting of a Hearing Aid. Most older children and adults who acquire a hearing loss are fitted with a hearing aid as part of their rehabilitation. While we discussed hearing aids and looked at a few examples (see Figure 7–7) in our discussion of child-hearing habilitation, let us consider the fitting of a hearing aid in greater detail. For example, the older person may experience a gradual presbycusis hearing loss, almost unaware of a deteriorating hearing sensitivity. Such individuals may attempt to amplify the acoustic signals coming to them by focusing the sound waves; this is done by cupping the hand behind the ear, a gesture that people seem to use naturally in situations where they feel they cannot hear optimally. This gesture actually functions as a primitive hearing aid. Fortunately, the modern hearing aid can provide the hard-of-hearing with the amplification needed to hear the sounds (speech of others, environmental noises, music) that could not be heard well without it.

Up until the 1930s, ear trumpets were commonly used as hearing aids. They were tapered horns (usually of metal) with a large opening at one end to capture the sound, and a small opening that fit in the ear, concentrating the acoustic energy. Most early ear trumpets were designed to conceal the fact that they were hearing aids, and were often shaped to resemble some kind of environmental object (a book, a candle, a vase, a hat). Those who were hard-of-hearing could pose with the neutral-shaped object (such as a vase) and quickly place the small end in the ear when they wanted to hear what was said. It would appear that, from the very beginning in using such assistive devices for minimizing the effects of hearing loss, an important factor was concealment. Hearing aids have never enjoyed the acceptability of eyeglasses. While society has seemed to accept the fact that a large segment of our population is visually handicapped and needs to wear corrective lenses, this same acceptance seems to be lacking for a hearing loss that is severe enough to warrant the wearing of a hearing aid. Consequently, hearing loss is often something the individual wishes to hide.

The wearable electronic body-type hearing aid became available in the early 1930s. The wearer was able to hide the amplifier somewhere in his or her clothing, with a wire bringing the amplified sound into the receiver that was fitted on an ear mold worn in the external ear canal. Up until the 1960s, most hearing aids were of the body type. In all such hearing aids, the amplifier (much smaller today than the vacuum-tube hearing aids of the 1950s) is attached to one's clothing, with the receiver hooked up to an ear mold and worn at ear level. This separation of amplifier from receiver made it possible to generate more acoustic output than other types of instruments, while avoiding the problem of acoustic feedback. For example, the squealing hearing-aid receiver is usually doing so because of acoustic feedback, caused in part by the proximity of the amplifier to the receiver. Fortunately, modern hearing aids have drastically reduced the acoustic-feedback problem. The ear-level hearing aid, particularly the eyeglass hearing aid, was the most popular one worn by adults in the 1960s. The internal components of the eyeglass aid were housed in the temple of the eyeglass frame, once again disguising the amplification device. A plastic tube then conducted the sound into the ear mold, worn in the ear. As technology improved, smaller and smaller transistor hearing aids were made. Small, ear-level hearing aids are worn entirely behind the ear, once again with a plastic tube conducting the sound into the ear.

Further technological improvements have made the hearing aid even smaller, permitting the development of the in-the-ear aid and, more recently, the in-the-ear-canal aid. A special ear mold is developed to which the in-the-ear aid is attached. When the in-the-ear aids first came out, they were only low-gain instruments for people with mild losses; with improved amplification power, such aids are usable by most adults who acquire a hearing loss (Freeman and Sinclair, 1981). When President Reagan publicly started to wear an in-the-ear-canal hearing aid in 1982, the popularity of this type of aid increased markedly. The in-the-ear or the in-the-ear-canal aid can be worn by many adults with acquired hearing loss; it meets our societal desire to ''hide'' both the hearing loss and the hearing aid, still providing, however, the needed amplification.

Before selecting the new hearing aid, the patient must be counseled that all hearing aids have some limitations. The best hearing aid will not enable the person to have normal hearing. Because the hearing aid is an amplifier system, the patient must be counseled that it will amplify many sounds, those one may want to hear and the competing sounds one might prefer not to hear. The relatively poor quality of speech reproduction should also be explained and demonstrated to the patient.

With proper fitting, however, and follow-up aural rehabilitation (in which the patient can learn to use the hearing aid), most aids are worn and provide real benefits.

As mentioned previously, hearing-aid selection for the patient with an acquired loss should begin with an otologist's examination, primarily to determine if any kind of medical-surgical treatment of the hearing problem is possible. The audiologist is the professional of choice to do the audiological testing and fit the hearing aid. A decision is made as to whether the patient will wear a single aid or binaural aids (an aid in each ear). Whenever possible, patients should be fitted with binaural aids, which are a great help in sound localization. The audiologist then makes the needed ear molds. The exact fitting of the ear mold is important. Freeman and Sinclair (1981) have written that "the rejection of a hearing aid by a hearing-impaired individual may not be the result of an adverse reaction to amplified sound, but rather may result from a poorly fitted earmold" (p. 292). An ill-fitting ear mold can result in pain or soreness, squealing, and a "plugged" feeling in the ear. Once the ear mold is fitted satisfactorily, actual hearing-aid selection can begin.

It is best to try on the same model aid that the patient might eventually purchase. There is enough variability in hearing-aid performance that the same brand of hearing aid and even the same model might produce variable acoustic output. Variability of aid, however, is less a problem today than it was a few years ago. The choice of hearing aid is often determined today by computer-assisted selection procedures. There are computer programs that can match the patient's hearing characteristics with the amplification characteristics of various hearing aids. Several hearing aids are tried on the patient and evaluated for overall effectiveness. Insertion-gain instruments, which can measure the actual output of the hearing aid at the eardrum of the patient, can determine the gain and distortion of the instrument, offering a precise and immediate check of the hearing aid's frequency response and output for the patient (Computer System CCI-10, 1984). Then the patient is queried about both discomfort and the most comfortable loudness levels. The hearing aid that is selected is usually the one that gives the best gain, best improves the ability to hear speech, and provides amplification free of discomfort to the user.

An Aural-rehabilitation Program. Most people who acquire a hearing loss, particularly those in whom it develops gradually, have adjusted to it over time. The radio and television have been played much louder (usually to the annoyance of other family members). An amplifier may have been put on the telephone. The common complaint is usually that others do not speak as distinctly as they should, and that members of the family (particularly women and children, with higher-pitched voices) have "forgotten how to enunciate." Such individuals become increasingly reluctant to ask others to repeat themselves, speaking a little louder; consequently, they make errors following directions, have difficulty following stories and jokes, and react slowly or not at all to various environmental sounds such as ringing telephones and doorbells. Hearing testing and the fitting of the hearing aid are important beginning parts of an aural-rehabilitation program, according to Garstecki (1981), who wrote that such rehabilitation included "(1) hearing evaluation, (2) hearing aid evaluation and orientation, (3) speech and hearing conservation, (4) assessment and remediation of speech, voice, and language disorders related to hearing impairment, (5) assessment and remediation of auditory, visual, and manual communication and linguistic skills, (6) measurement and modification of room acoustics, and (7) education and counseling of hearing-impaired individuals and significant other persons" (p. 268).

The person with an acquired hearing loss under 50 dB should not experience any real deterioration in articulation or voice. This would be particularly true for the patient with a mild to moderate loss who has been fitted with a hearing aid. The patient with an acquired hearing loss from the severe to the profound level might well profit from conservation activities designed to maintain normal speech, voice, and fluency. The older the patient is at the time of acquiring a hearing loss, the more years have passed during which normal speaking has been part of communication. The speaking motor experience is deeply rooted and is somewhat resistant to deterioration when patients are no longer able to monitor auditorily what they are saying. However, there is some evidence (Goehl and Kaufman, 1984) that articulation and voice changes do not necessarily occur in all patients who acquire severe-to-profound hearing losses. There are patients who do begin to show some articulation decline, particularly on high-frequency consonants such as /s, z, ʃ, and tʃ/. Some effort can be made in rehabilitation to helping these patients develop a proprioceptive or kinesthetic awareness of the production of particular consonants as a compensation for their inability to hear them being said. The voicing changes that might be experienced by patients with severe-to-profound losses include the production of a posterior focus in oral resonance (apparently caused by posterior tongue retraction), some hypernasality, and variations in pitch level (Boone, 1983). By using some kind of spectral analyzer coupled with an oscillographic display, such as provided on a Visi-Pitch, it is often possible for the patient to practice the maintenance of normal voicing patterns. A typical practice task might be for the audiologist or speech-language pathologist to provide a normal voicing pattern (visualized on a split screen) and then ask the patient to produce the same pattern (as displayed on the lower half of the split screen). Working to maintain a normal prosodic rhythm of speech is also facilitated by using some kind of visual feedback device, such as a spectrographic display, that provides, for example, real-time feedback for the patient.

A big part of aural rehabilitation is to help the patient develop maximum skills in overall communication. While speech reading and auditory training will receive much focus in rehabilitation, the patient must learn to use nonauditory cues to facilitate communication, such as "linguistic, situational, and visual cues" (Wier, 1980). Much spoken language is highly predictive. Phonologic and syntactic rules pretty well dictate how we say things and in what order the words appear; the patient who cannot hear the complete verbal signal can often, therefore, guess phonologic and syntactic components with some degree of success. The guesswork is lessened if the patient couples the fragments of the spoken message heard with common sense. When the patient is aware of the situational context, the verbal guesswork is often greatly reduced. Visual cues include watching the lips of the speaker (hence the word *lip-reading*) and looking at facial expression and hand and body gestures.

With older patients, the listening-watching aspects of communication practice are sometimes difficult. The typical older patient, with a slower reaction time, may require that verbal stimuli be presented at a slightly slower pace. If the patient has more time to respond, the response is more likely to be correct. There are occasional older patients with a cognitive decline, such as a patient with Alzheimer's disease (see Chapter 10), who may profit greatly from wearing a hearing aid but be unable to participate in the structured activities of an aural-rehabilitation program. It should be noted, however, that even patients with senile dementia often present—superficially, at least—spoken responses that are characterized by normal phonology and syntax (Bayles, 1979). Being old (or even having dementia) does not negate the possible benefit the patient may derive from using a hearing aid.

Psychological Counseling

Important insights were gained in understanding the psychological problems experienced by adults with severe-to-profound hearing loss from a study by Fusfeld (1955), who asked 100 deaf adults to list the disadvantages and advantages of being deaf. Let us look at his general findings by paraphrasing these conclusions:

Disadvantages
1. Inability to hear warning sounds
2. Miss day-to-day social mingling
3. Educational limitations
4. Difficulty understanding the problems in an employment setting
5. Feelings of inadequacy and frustration
6. Recreational limitations (music, plays, radio, and television)

Advantages
1. Mental rest and response; "freedom from discourse."
2. Develop close, enduring friendships
3. Inner calm and poise
4. Sensitivity to vibrations

It is important for patients to realize that many of the feelings they experience after acquiring a hearing loss have indeed a basis in reality. The normal speaking world puts a premium on aural-oral language. If you are slow or inaccurate in responding to what has been said, you are likely to be considered unintelligent. Consequently, the hard-of-hearing often develop a monologue-type communication, "holding the floor" with their own verbalizations, not practicing the give-and-take (turn-taking) that is characteristic of normal communication. Any alteration in speaking ability may also be viewed falsely as a symptom of intellectual inferiority. If, because of the acquired hearing loss, the patient is speaking differently, this should be pointed out to the patient.

Ramsdell (1970) has pointed out that there are three psychological levels of hearing: social, signal or warning, and the auditory background of daily living. The possible verbal limitations imposed by the hearing loss (particularly before the fitting of the hearing aid) can be socially overwhelming. For this reason, group therapy is often recommended as the preferred vehicle for aural rehabilitation; the shared experiences of the people making up the group can help each individual develop a perspective about the hearing problem, realizing he or she is not alone. Others feel the rejection, suspect that they are being ridiculed, or have moments of depression. With amplification and development of overall communicative skills, the patient may begin to feel much more socially viable. Also, hard-of-hearing support groups, such as those promoted by the *National Association of Speech and Hearing Action*[1], can offer guidelines for acceptance and rehabilitation, recommend professional speakers in the community (audiologists, otolaryngologists, speech-language pathologists), and give the patient the feeling of belonging to a group made up of other normal people with a similar handicap.

REVIEW QUESTIONS

Hearing disorders can seriously compromise effective communication. Let us review a few issues about hearing loss and its management.

1. How can hearing loss affect a developing natural language?

2. Differentiate between a conductive and a sensorineural hearing loss.

3. What is the most common kind of hearing problem in children? How does it affect speech and language?

4. Can most hard-of-hearing people profit from amplification? Explain.

5. What is presbycusis? How can it be managed?

6. Describe an aural-habilitation program for children with hearing losses of 45–60 dB.

REFERENCES

Alpiner, J., Chevrette, W., Glascoe, G., Metz, M., and Olsen, B. (1971). "The Denver Scale of Communication Function" (unpublished study).

Bayles, K. A. (1979). "Communication Profile in the Geriatric Population" (unpublished doctoral dissertation, University of Arizona).

Berg, F. S. (1970). Educational audiology, in *The*

[1]National Association of Speech and Hearing Action (NASHA), 10801 Rockville Pike, Rockville, Maryland, 20852.

Hard of Hearing Child, ed. F. S. Berg and S. G. Fletcher. New York: Grune and Stratton.

Boone, D. R. (1983). *The Voice and Voice Therapy.* Englewood Cliffs, N.J.: Prentice-Hall.

Computer System CCI-10. (1984). Bernefon, Inc. 1299 U.S. Route 22 East, Mountainside, N.J. 07092.

Davis, H. (1978b). Abnormal hearing and deafness, in *Hearing and Deafness,* ed. H. Davis and S. R. Silverman. New York: Holt, Rinehart and Winston.

Davis, H. (1978a). Hearing handicap, standards for hearing, and medicolegal rules, in *Hearing and Deafness,* ed. H. Davis and S. R. Silverman. New York: Holt, Rinehart and Winston.

Davis, H., and Fowler, E. P., Jr. (1978). The medical treatment of hearing loss and the conservation of hearing, in *Hearing and Deafness,* ed. H. Davis and S. R. Silverman. New York: Holt, Rinehart and Winston.

Downs, M. P. (1981). Contribution of mild hearing loss to auditory language learning problems, in *Auditory Disorders in School Children,* ed. R. J. Rosser and M. P. Downs. New York: Thieme-Stratton.

Downs, M. P., and Northern, J. L. (1976). The management of hearing loss, in *Otolaryngology,* ed. G. M. English. New York: Harper and Row.

Elliott, L. (1978). Epidemiology of hearing impairment and other communicative disorders, in *Advances in Neurology,* Vol. 19: *Neurological Epidemiology,* ed. B. Schoenberg. New York: Raven Press.

Freeman, B. A., and Sinclair, J. S. (1981). Hearing aids for the elderly, in *Aging Communication Processes and Disorders,* ed. D. S. Beasley and G. A. Davis. New York: Grune and Stratton.

Fusfeld, I. S. (1950). Counseling for the deafened, in *Special Education for the Exceptional.* Vol. 2: *The Physically Handicapped and Special Health Problems.* Boston: Porter Sargent.

Gaeth, J. A. (1948). "A Study of Phonemic Regression Associated With Hearing Loss" (unpublished doctoral dissertation, Northwestern University).

Garstecki, D. C. (1981). Aural rehabilitation for the aging adult, in *Aging Communication Processes and Disorders,* ed. D. S. Beasley and G. A. Davis. New York: Grune and Stratton.

Giolas, T. G., Owens, E., Lamb, S. H., and Schubert, E. D. (1979). Hearing Performance Inventory. *Journal of Speech and Hearing Disorders, 44:* 169–195.

Goehl, H., and Kaufman, D. K. (1984). Do the effects of adventitious deafness include disordered speech? *Journal of Speech and Hearing Disorders, 49:* 58–64.

Goin, D. W. (1976). Otospongiosis, in *Otolaryngology,* ed. G. M. English. New York: Harper and Row.

Hodgson, W. (1984). Personal communication.

Hull, F. M., Mielke, P. W., Willeford, J. A., and Timmons, R. J. (1976). *National Speech and Hearing Survey: Final Report.* Project 50978. Washington, D.C.: Office of Education, Bureau of Education for the Handicapped.

Hull, R. H., and Traynor, R. M. (1977). Hearing impairment among aging persons in the health care facility: Their diagnosis and rehabilitation. *American Health Care Association Journal, 3:* 14–18.

Kertesz, A., Harlock, W., and Coates, R. (1979). Computer tomographic localization, lesion size, and prognosis in aphasia and non-verbal impairment. *Brain and Language, 8:* 34–50.

Ling, D. (1976). *Speech and the Hearing Impaired Child: Theory and Practice.* Washington, D.C.: Alexander Graham Bell Association for the Deaf.

Mattis, S., French, J. H., and Rapin, I. (1973). Dyslexia in children and young adults: Three independent neuropsychological syndromes. *Medicine and Child Neurology, 17:* 150–163.

Monsen, R. B. (1978). Toward measuring how well hearing-impaired children speak. *Journal of Speech and Hearing Research, 21:* 197–219.

Nadol, J. B., Jr. (1981). The aging peripheral hearing mechanism, in *Aging Communication Processes and Disorders,* ed. D. S. Beasley and G. A. Davis. New York: Grune and Stratton.

Northern, J. L., and Downs, M. P. (1978). *Hearing in Children* (2nd ed.). Baltimore: Williams and Wilkins.

Northern, J. L., and Lemme, M. (1982). Hearing and auditory disorders. In *Human Communication Disorders: An Introduction,* ed. G. H. Shames and E. H. Wiig. Columbus: Charles E. Merrill.

Orchik, D. J. (1981). Peripheral auditory problems and the aging process, in *Aging Communication Processes and Disorders,* ed. D. S. Beasley and G. A. Davis. New York: Grune and Stratton.

Paparella, M. M., and Davis, H. (1978). Medical and surgical treatment of hearing loss, in *Hearing and Deafness,* ed. H. Davis and S. R. Silverman. New York: Holt, Rinehart and Winston.

Ramsdell, D. A. (1970). The psychology of the hard-of-hearing and the deafened adult, in *Hearing and Deafness,* ed. H. Davis and S. R. Silverman. New York: Holt, Rinehart and Winston.

Reichman, J., and Healey, W. C. (1983). Learning disabilities and conductive loss involving otitis media. *Journal of Learning Disabilities, 16:* 272–278.

Ross, M. (1972). *Principles of Aural Rehabilitation.* New York: Bobbs-Merrill.

Sanders, J. W. (1978). The successful hearing aid user. *Otolaryngologic Clinics of North America, 11:* 187–193.

Skelly, M., Schinsky, L., Smith, R., Donaldson, R. C., and Griffin, J. M. (1975). American Indian Sign. *Archives of Physical and Medical Rehabilitation, 56:* 156–160.

U.S. National Health Survey (1967). *Hearing Levels of Adults by Age and Sex, United States, 1960–1962.* Public Health Service Publication Number 1000, Series 11, Number 11. Washington, D.C.: Public Health Service, United States Department of Health, Education, and Welfare.

Walden, B. C., Demorest, M. E., and Hepler, E. L. (1984). Self-report approach to assessing benefit derived from amplification. *Journal of Speech and Hearing, 27:* 49–56.

Wier, C. C. (1980). Habilitation and rehabilitation of the hearing impaired, in *Introduction to Communication Disorders,* ed. T. J. Hixon, L. D. Shriberg, and J. H. Saxman. Englewood Cliffs, N.J.: Prentice-Hall.

Wiley, T. L. (1980). Hearing disorders and audiometry, in *Introduction to Communication Disorders,* ed. T. J. Hixon, L. D. Shriberg, and J. H. Saxman. Englewood Cliffs, N.J.: Prentice-Hall.

8

Disorders of Language in Children

Language enables normal children to find out about the world beyond their own experiences. By understanding and using word symbols, children can learn about the experience and thoughts of others, past and present. Therefore, children with a language disorder not only have difficulty learning the aural-oral and visual-graphic code; they may experience problems in various aspects of cognitive development. In this chapter, we will describe the symptoms displayed by preschool and school-age children in their use of language. The importance of identifying possible causes of language delay, such as hearing loss or mental retardation, will be discussed as we consider some of the recognized deterrents to normal language acquisition. We will see that the language evaluation focuses on observing and describing the child's use of language and its content, the child's play and interaction with others, and the integrity of the child's sensory and expressive-motor systems, all leading to a prognosis and possible plan for language remediation. Finally, we will look at various approaches to improving language function and use in both the preschool and school-age language-impaired child.

TWO BOYS WITH A LANGUAGE PROBLEM

Before acquiring language, the child must experience the world by touch, taste, sight, smell, and sound, a world somewhat bound by these sensory modalities. Through the use of coded word symbols (language), children soon find that language can represent objects, as well as the thoughts of others, without the requirement that they actually be part of the event. For the child with a language disorder, the limitation of verbal experience appears to limit the living experience. Let us look now at the case histories of two boys with a language disorder, one at the early preschool level and one in his early teens. Beyond our descriptions of the language and speech behavior of each child, we will comment on the possible limitation imposed on each boy by his communication disorder.

Tom. Three Years, Nine Months. Although Tom was evaluated for language and speech when he was two years, nine months old, and found to have a significant language delay, it was not possible for him to begin any kind of formal language program. A year later, he was reevaluated to determine his overall language functioning, believed by his parents to be significantly delayed. Because he cried when we attempted to separate him from his mother, she remained in the room, and we were able to complete receptive language testing, an oral examination, and a parent-child language sample. Tom was unwilling to repeat any verbal stimuli after the examiner; his mother volunteered that Tom repeated words readily after his older brother and suggested that perhaps the brother could be part of the next evaluation session. The second session of the evaluation was conducted using the brother as the speaking model (following the directions of the examiner), and Tom cooperated very well.

Two standardized tests, the *Peabody Picture Vocabulary Test* (Dunn and Dunn, 1965) and the *Sequenced Inventory of Communication Development* (Hedrick and others, 1975), were administered, which found Tom to be functioning in receptive language skills about six to eight months below his chronological age. Observation of parent-child and child-child interactions suggested that Tom comprehends the conversational input, simple commands, and intonational cues of other speakers. He demonstrated problems, however, in understanding words specific to such concepts as location and singular-plural.

Tom's expressive language was characterized by one-word utterances (he made 65 utterances during the evaluation). There were only two instances of word combinations, such as "here boy." He used single words in combination with simple gestures and vocalization to request, draw attention to an object, name, protest, command, or comment on an action. He did use rising intonation to convey questioning. Semantically, his single words coded location, possession ("my"), and existence. Tom was observed to acknowledge input from others, but only on one occasion did he take two turns commenting on a particular topic with the examiner.

His phonologic development was assessed by analyzing spontaneous single-word responses and imitative responses on items from the *Goldman-Fristoe Test of Articulation* (Goldman and Fristoe, 1969), imitating the responses provided by his older brother. Many of his word productions were characterized by single or repeated vowels, such as "ee" for "puppy" or "ah-ee" for "daddy." He used the following consonants in monosyllabic CV words: /m, b, w, j, h/. The following consonants were used in the final position of CVC words: /k, p, f, r, n/. Error patterns were characterized by frequent consonant deletions. In addition, he used /h/ for fricative targets (/ho/ for "phone"), blend reduction (r/dr, w/tr), reduplication (ba-ba/bottle), and assimilation (gak/duck, bap/cup). Tom spoke only in single words, probably to accommodate his listeners because of his multiple articulation errors.

A peripheral examination of oral mechanisms found him to have normal structures and normal function for making speech sounds. However, nonspeech tongue movements (imitating tongue movements) were judged to be limited. It was our feeling that tongue coordination was less than what we usually see in children of the same age. His overall articulatory ability was that of a child under two years of age. Phonologic problems, however, could not be directly related to any lingual incoordination.

Minnesota Child Development Inventory (Ireton and Thwing, 1972) and the *Developmental Activities Screening Inventory* (Dubose and Langley, 1977) indicated an overall developmental level of about 22 months. Areas of gross motor, self-help, socialization, and conceptual comprehension were between 20 and 30 percent below age level. He showed difficulty in matching objects, understanding quantities, and fine-motor skills (copying a circle or a cross). While attention span was judged to be very good, we did not observe any imaginative play.

Tom was judged to be functioning about 20 months below his chronological age in speech and expressive language. Occasional developmental skills and play activities appeared appropriate for his age. It was our impression that no single factor could account for Tom's delayed communication development. It might well have been that a combination of three factors (social-emotional immaturity, delayed conceptual skills, and slight neurological dysfunction, as seen in poor tongue imitations) caused the marked delay in the development of overall communication skills. His poor speech performance seemed to limit his attempts at interaction with the people around him. His social-linguistic behavior was characterized by an unwillingness to produce any verbal behavior on command and a limitation in the establishment of rudimentary conversational skills (turn-taking, self-initiation). It was concluded, therefore, that his expressive limitations should receive priority in overall management. He subsequently enrolled in a daily speech program, where he made impressive gains in improving articulatory skills; he also attended a daily preschool program that placed great emphasis on stimulating cognitive growth.

We might speculate that the discrepancy between his speaking ability (age twenty-three months) and his overall cognitive and receptive language abilities (age thirty-six months) may contribute to the perception of his overall immaturity. Furthermore, in the future, as he speaks with greater success (after therapy) and others are able to understand him more easily, he may begin to participate more freely in the communicative process. One might further speculate (such speculations are hopes that ordinarily are not communicated to parents) that as his language enables him to participate easily in normal human communication and interaction with others, his cognitive and receptive language skills may eventually approximate his chronological age.

Peter, Fourteen Years, Six Months. Peter has had many special evaluations throughout his life and has been in special-education classes since first grade. He was referred to the university speech-language clinic by his public-school speech-language pathologist for an overall "communication effectiveness evaluation." A *Clinical Evaluation of Language Function* (CELF) (Semel and Wiig, 1983) found Peter capable of comprehending language at a level commensurate with his cognitive-academic achievement. Language-sampling and word-association subtest scores on the CELF found that both syntax and semantic functions were grade-appropriate. In essence, his language content and form were adequate. What seemed problematic was poor use of language pragmatics, characterized by his using a very low voice, avoiding eye contact with everyone, and employing long delays in responding to what others said to or asked of him.

The long delays in response were evaluated on a word-association subtest (exploring the possibility of a word-retrieval problem). He did display some difficulty generating words. However, he displayed no formulation difficulties or delayed responses when the word topic was of high interest to him. As a Michael Jackson fan, Peter could answer questions quickly and completely, with some animation, whenever he described the Jackson family tour that was coming to his city. The contrast in verbal style between speaking about test stimuli and about topics in which he had a real interest suggested to us that his delayed response and low vocal intensity were deliberate response modes.

Attempts at role-playing with Peter were not successful. He said, "I can't talk all these different ways." We could not determine if his difficulty in role-playing was related to an inability to take the perspective of others or if his problems were simply related to his inhibition and shyness. When asked, "Why do you speak so softly?" his eyes began to tear, and the question was not pursued.

It was clear that Peter has been the object of much concern on the part of his parents and teachers, and has undergone much testing. The language problems that he experienced earlier in life appeared to be gone, and he demonstrated normal receptive-language and normal expressive-language functions, with the important exception of pragmatic skills. He was a marginal communicator, as characterized by his low voice volume and long delays before responding. These behaviors seemed to influence negatively other people's perceptions of Peter. However, when discussing high-interest topics, his communication and overall affect appeared appropriate. It was our opinion that his overall communication effectiveness could not be improved by a speech-language pathologist. Rather, it appeared that an assessment of his social-emotional status by a clinical psychologist or psychiatrist was needed. Such an evaluation might explain why he used his particular communicative style and whether or not he might require counseling or psychotherapy.

Every now and then, we see a child like Peter. Although his early phonologic-syntactic-semantic language problems resolved over time with special training, he began to develop a troubled affect. He was used to being viewed as someone who had trouble communicating. Despite the fact that he had developed relatively normal language systems, he could not use them effectively because of the discomfort and insecurity he experienced when talking to others.

We see in these case studies, one with a language disorder and one without, that both boys demonstrate problems in communication. The ability to relate meaningfully to other human beings begins, as we have discussed in previous chapters, in the first few months of life. We communicate our feelings as babies through our voicing patterns, our body postures and facial expressions, or our turn-taking. Both Tom and Peter apparently had no real difficulty in their preverbal communication. When they began to acquire language, they had difficulty learning and using the symbols of language. Tom had real problems making his mouth work with the facility needed to speak like other boys the same age. He consequently cut down the number of words he wanted to say, so that his listeners might understand him. His speech (the expressive side of aural-oral language) was so impaired that he withdrew from talking to anyone but his accepting older brother. Tom's overall language was poor. His communication was ineffective.

Peter had experienced great difficulties acquiring and using the symbols of language as he grew up. Before he went to school and in his early school years, he experienced repeated problems understanding what others said; he had even greater difficulties learning to read. It was difficult to put words together in sentences, and he kept the number of words spoken at one time to a minimum. His writing attempts in his early school years were very poor. However, with years of special education and training in various language skills, his language abilities began to approach normal levels. But for so many years he had experienced difficulties using spoken language, he began to "know" he was going to have difficulty communicating. Consequently, he began to look away from others as he spoke to them in a quiet voice. He spoke only when he had to do so. His language pragmatics (his *use* of spoken language) suffered. While his overall language problem had apparently been successfully resolved with training, his communication problem remained and seemed to grow. He communicated feelings of inadequacy in most of his interactions with others.

Language is part of communication. While there are some predictable outcomes that we learn in communication (such as when I cry, you often give me relief of some kind), nonverbal communication modes are not particularly rule-bound. The communication of our feelings or our moods does not require verbal symbols. However, we can become much more efficient in our expression of emotion when we begin to use the same verbal codes as our listeners. The emotional noises we may make (sighs, whining, crying, using a happy voice) are inexact and often interpreted differently by various people. Our language system, with its many words, offers much greater specificity. To use the language code, however, we must follow the same rules for using the language as the people around us. For the great majority of infants and young children, this language code is easily acquired. As we have seen in earlier chapters, the human being appears to have a propensity, a species-specific ability, to acquire language with only a minimum of difficulty. And language for children becomes exciting to use as they begin to experience the world beyond their immediate experiences.

LANGUAGE DISORDERS IN THE PRESCHOOL YEARS

In Chapter 4, we saw that the acquisition of the various dimensions of language follows a rather predictable time sequence. Infants turn their heads toward environmental noises at particular ages, their suprasegmental vocalizations mature and become more complex as they physically mature, and the first word is spoken across cultures at about twelve–thirteen months. The pamphlet developed by the American Speech-Language-Hearing Foundation (Figure 8–1) is based on the premise that certain decoding or receptive language functions emerge in a predictable sequence in the normal child, with encoding or expressive language also coming out at predictable time periods. The pamphlet was designed by the Foundation for doctors' waiting rooms and pediatric clinics, where families sit and wait for their appointments.

FIND YOUR CHILD'S SPEECH AND HEARING AGE

check one		HEARING and UNDERSTANDING	CHILD'S AGE	TALKING	check one	
√ YES	√ NO				√ YES	√ NO
		Does your child hear and understand most speech in the home? Does your child hear and answer when first called? Does your child hear quiet speech? Does everyone who knows your child think he/she hears well (teacher, baby-sitter, grandparent, etc.)?	5 YEARS	Does your child say all sounds correctly except perhaps s and th? Does your child use the same sentence structure as the family? Does your child's voice sound clear, like other children's?		
		Does your child understand conversation easily? Does your child hear you when you call from another room? Does your child hear television or radio at the same loudness level as other members of the family?	2½-4 YEARS	Does your child say most sounds, except perhaps r, s, th, and l? Does your child sometimes repeat words in a sentence?		
		Does your child understand differences in meaning ("go—stop;" "the car pushed the truck—the truck pushed the car")? Can your child point to pictures in a book upon hearing them named? Does your child notice sounds (dog barking, telephone ringing, television sound, knocking at door and so on)?		Does your child use 200-300 words? Does your child use 2-3 word sentences? Does your child ask lots of "why" and "what" questions? Has your child's jargon and repeating disappeared? Does your child like to name things?		
		Can your child follow two requests ("get the ball and put it on the table")?	1½-2 YEARS	Does your child have 10-15 words (by age 2)? Does your child sometimes repeat requests? Does your child ask 1-2 word questions ("where kitty? go bye-bye? more?")? Does your child put 2 words together ("more cookie")?		
		Has your child begun to respond to requests ("come here;" "do you want more")?		Does your child say words (8-10 words at age 1½; 2-3 words at age 1). (Words may not be clear).		
		Does your child turn or look up when you call? Does your child search or look around when hearing new sounds? Does your child listen to people talking?	9 MONTHS-1 YEAR	Does your child enjoy imitating sounds? Does your child use jargon (babbling that sounds like real speech)? Does your child use voice to get attention?		
		Does your child respond to "no" and her/his name? Does your child notice and look around for the source of new sounds? Does your child turn her/his head toward the side where the sound is coming from?	6 MONTHS	Does your child's babbling sound like the parent's speech, only not clear? Does your child makes lots of different sounds?		

FIGURE 8-1 A developmental language scale developed for parents to rate the receptive and expressive language skills of their children. Courtesy of American Speech-Language-Hearing Foundation and Psi Iota Xi Sorority. *How Does Your Child Hear and Talk?* Rockville, Maryland: National Association for Hearing and Speech Action (1983).

A mother, for example, could compare her child's performance with the normative behaviors listed in the pamphlet for a particular age. Certain language skills in normal children are usually present by certain ages. There have been innumerable investigations that have looked at the orderly acquisition of language skills in the normal child (Crystal, 1969; Lock, 1978; McNeill, 1970; Morehead and Morehead, 1976). In summarizing much of the normative work in child language, Lenneberg (1967) concluded that, across cultures, there was a certain predictability to the emergence of single words, phrases, and sentences in the normal child.

Perhaps a good working definition of a language disorder in the preschool child would be the *inability to understand or speak the language code as well as age peers in the same community.* Young children with a language disorder have, in effect, failed to develop and use language with the proficiency of their age peers. Hubbell (1984) has pointed out that the child with a language impairment may be deficient in two aspects of language: language as a social process and language as a cognitive process. If the use of language as a socialization tool is impaired, children may experience difficulties listening to and understanding the spoken language of others; their attempts to answer back with various forms of language and sounds will be thwarted by listeners not being able to understand them. This reduction of effective language between children and the people around them may color negatively their interactions with others; because they do not understand well and because others do not understand them, many of their behaviors may be perceived as different from those of their age peers.

The language impairment may well lead to some cognitive impairment. Since youngsters' perceptions and experiences of the world around them are often facilitated and shaped by the language they hear and speak, with limited language ability, children may experience some cognitive limitation. For example, normal children playing with sand begin to feel its various textures (fine and dry versus wet and coarse) and if there are others around them, they are likely to hear comments about these differences in the sand's texture. If they understand language appropriately for their age, they may have experienced for the first time in their lives some cognitive appreciation of sand differences. Language-impaired youngsters may also have fleetingly noticed the sand-texture differences, but, because they could not understand what was being said about the sand, failed to develop the concept that dryness (or wetness) contributed in part to the texture. The words we hear and use can have a great shaping effect on overall cognitive development (Whorf, 1956). If we do not understand or use the words well, we may experience some lack of cognitive growth.

There are many different kinds of children who have language disorders for various reasons. In the 1950s, the audiologist and the speech-language pathologist used to place much diagnostic emphasis on attempting to find the cause, or *etiology,* of the child's language disorder. As a profession, we put more emphasis on identification of causation (hoping to eliminate the cause) than we did on actual language treatment. With the great growth of behavioral and operant psychology in the 1960s, much more emphasis was given to changing the child's behavior by direct teaching or training than was given to looking for the etiology of the problem. Behavioral approaches lent themselves well to the identification of the child's faulty language syntax, with training efforts used for direct syntactic modification. Much of the evaluation and training focus in the early 1970s was on the study of lexical manipulations and semantics, with little attention given to possible causation of the disorder. In the late 1970s and early 1980s, the focus was given to pragmatics, the use of language in the interactions between child and listener. More recently, there has been an increase in phonologic analysis as part of the language evaluation. While we look closely today at the language performance (phonology, syntax, semantics, pragmatics) of the individual child, there appears once again to be some appreciation for identifying possible causal factors. Let us discuss briefly some of the etiologies and conditions that might contribute to a language disorder in a young child.

Hearing Loss

We basically learn our aural-oral language through hearing other people speak and hearing ourselves make vocal and verbal responses. As discussed in the last chapter, hearing loss can have devastating effects on the learning of language. The earlier and/or more severe the hearing loss, the greater the effects.

The mild-to-moderate hearing loss (usually of the conductive type) in a young child is often difficult to detect. Such a child may fluctuate between normal hearing and a hearing loss, presenting a real learning barrier to developing language. Even losses as low as 25 dB, according to Downs and Northern (1976), should be corrected by having the child fitted with and wearing a hearing aid. Moderate-to-severe losses, which usually have a sensorineural component, will require not only amplification but special language-speech training. Because the child with a moderate-to-severe hearing loss acquires language through special training (rather than by a natural process, exposure), special efforts have to be made to expose this child to various experiences as part of overall cognitive stimulation.

The child with a hearing loss and a language disorder not only has to have necessary medical treatment and probable amplification for the hearing loss, but may require some kind of auditory perceptual training after the hearing aid is provided. Eisenson (1984) writes that "auditory perception is almost invariably impaired" in children with language disorders. Both auditory discrimination and the ability to sequence speech sounds (or remember their sequence) may be associated with hearing loss; however, many times, children with normal hearing demonstrate auditory-perceptual problems as part of a language disorder. We may suspect that many of these children had a hearing loss in their early years (they now demonstrate normal hearing) that helped create the language problem in the first place (Reichman and Healey, 1983). If hearing loss is detected as a possible deterrent to normal language development, it is helpful to detect it as early as possible. Early medical intervention (in some cases), amplification, and special training will often accelerate language development in the young child with a hearing loss.

Mental Retardation

Language learning is a complex task. A child who is developmentally slow in all phases of development will also be slow in the acquisition of complex language skills. Before children can acquire language, they must have cognitive experiences specific to the objects, events, and feelings of their world. They must realize that objects and conditions exist beyond their own immediate experiences. As Morehead and Morehead (1974) have written, the child must eventually differentiate "between himself and reality." It would appear that this differentiation between self and world is a basic big step in one's cognitive development. Once this differentiation begins, the child may be "ready" to use verbal symbols to represent his or her reality. Retarded children are slower to make this separation between self and the world than are normal children. Consequently, they are slower to use verbal symbols to represent things beyond their immediate selves.

Most retarded children are slow in all developmental areas: motor skills, socialization, self-care (such as toilet training), and language. The *Minnesota Child Development Inventory* (Ireton and Thwing, 1972), a developmental profile, will usually reveal for the retarded child a relatively flat-function curve in the areas looked at in this parental questionnaire: general development, gross motor, fine motor, expressive language, comprehension-conceptual, situation comprehension, self-help, and personal-social. The typically retarded child on the *Minnesota* would score at approximately the same delayed developmental age across all abilities.

Retarded children are slow to acquire language. They often remain at the prelinguistic stage longer than other children, using vocalization, facial expression, and gesture for communication. The onset of the first words is at a later chronological age. Morphology, syntax, and semantics will be delayed, although the content and form may not differ too markedly from that of a younger normal child (Schiefelbusch, 1967). As in normal children, however, there is much fluctuation among the retarded in the acquisition of particular language features. For example, some children seem to have a surprisingly large vocabulary, and others use rather advanced grammar forms. In general, the pragmatics, or actual use of language, among retarded populations appears like that of much younger children, probably because the pragmatic abilities of the retarded cannot exceed their cognitive limitations.

Childhood Aphasia

There are occasional children whose language difficulties appear to be part of a developmental aphasia. Their numbers are not many. Eisenson (1984) defines the aphasic child in part by exclusion: the child is not mentally retarded, the child is not deaf or hard-of-hearing, the child is not autistic (which we will describe later in the chapter). There is a marked discrepancy between the child's poor verbal abilities and all other areas of relatively normal functioning (cognitive, social, self-care, and so on). In this way, aphasic children do not appear as "retarded shadows of their age peers" (Eisenson, 1984). Although it is difficult to pinpoint a particular area of the brain that, if damaged, appears to produce symptoms of developmental aphasia, it does seem that the child with aphasia has some kind of neurological dysfunction (Eisenson, 1984; Ferry, 1981).

Some children acquire aphasia. Such a youngster demonstrated normal language prior to experiencing some kind of accident (such as a left-hemisphere head wound) or illness (such as a thrombosis in the left middle cerebral artery); following this the child has acquired aphasia, or a loss of language. The anatomic site of the brain lesion and the cause of the lesion is much easier to determine by the neurologist in acquired than in developmental aphasia. Consequently, the diagnosis of developmental aphasia is usually made after studying the child's poor linguistic performance.

Most children who demonstrate aphasic-like symptoms show marked difficulties in auditory perception and in processing auditory verbal information (Emerick and Hatten, 1979). More often, the child can process nonverbal environmental sounds with no difficulty. Eisenson (1984) reports a number of studies at the Institute for Childhood Aphasia, at Stanford University, over the years that have found aphasic children demonstrating defective auditory memory and problems in speech discrimination and temporal ordering (recognizing sounds and words in a particular sequence). The auditory verbal problems experienced by aphasic children prevent them from participating in the normal verbal interactions of most children.

Semantic difficulties typify children with aphasia. They struggle to retrieve a particular word. This word-finding problem (**anomia**) is a common characteristic of both developmental and acquired aphasic children. As such children increase their recognition and spoken vocabularies, they begin to combine words. At this point, they will usually be observed to have markedly severe syntactic problems (Morehead and Ingram, 1973). Because of aphasic children's relatively normal overall cognitive abilities, they make very good use of the language that they have. Most aphasic children seem to function amazingly well in their pragmatics; similar to adult aphasics, they use gesture, facial expression, and other visual cues to get their ideas and needs across to the people around them.

Children identified as having developmental aphasia will usually require some kind of specialized training program that will focus on their mastery of the language code. Some may also have apraxia and dysarthria, which make it even more difficult for them to develop normal speech.

Minimal Brain Damage

Some children show a language delay and other behavioral symptoms that cause the neurologist to label them as having "minimal brain damage." Such children may show difficulties in self-control, as seen by their hyperactivity, distractability, and violent shifts in emotionality (Kenny and Clemmens, 1975). Occasionally, such a child may show "hard" neurological signs, such as hemiparesis (one-sided weakness); more often the child shows "soft" signs, such as hyperactivity. These are the children who may have difficulty learning language because of problems in auditory perception or auditory sequencing. By the time they are old enough to go to school, they may still be demonstrating real problems in their mastery of aural-oral language. Unfortunately, such children are then introduced to the graphic language system (reading and writing), often before they have mastered the basic language skills of listening and speaking.

These early difficulties in understanding language, spoken or written, may lead to the child's being classified in school as having "specific learning disability." We see the term "minimal brain dysfunction" in the definition of specific learning disability listed in the *Federal Register* (1977, p. 65083):

> . . . a disorder in one or more of the basic psychological processes involved in understanding or using language, spoken or written, which may manifest itself in an imperfect ability to listen, think, speak, read, write, spell, or to do mathematical calculations. The term includes such conditions as perceptual handicaps, brain injury, minimal brain dysfunction, dyslexia, and developmental aphasia. The term does not include children who have learning problems which are primarily the result of visual, hearing, or motor handicaps, of mental retardation, of emotional disturbance, or of environmental, cultural, or economic disadvantage.

Emotional Disturbance

Babies' sense of well-being must help to nurture those first sounds of contentment they make in their first six months. The early experiences of some children, unfortunately, are charged with the excesses of emotion. The people around the child may present a world of unpredictable emotionality. From the beginning, some infants seem to be unlike the usual baby. Unpleasantness may begin to characterize their environment. Some children fail to develop normal aural-oral language because their environment does not seem to meet their needs (this can be caused within children or by those in their environment). Sometimes, children do not experience the thrill of having loving parents reacting to their first words, or perhaps the early struggle to say a single word or to put several words together simply does not seem to be worth the effort. Delayed language is sometimes part of an emotional disturbance.

Autism

A primary characteristic of **autism** (a severe affective disorder) is seen in children's lack of communication with other people. Typically, such children demonstrate unusual behaviors, such as holding one hand above the head and using the other hand to pull on the fingers, perhaps making sounds as they do so. On occasion, such children will repeat another person's comments in an echolalic fashion many seconds after the original words were spoken. Or phrases or sentences the child has heard (such as a commercial jingle) will be repeated for hours or days. Although the language of autistic children may lack intention (they speak more to themselves than to others), their phonology and syntax often sound normal. Phonemes may be produced without distortion, and words may be used in the correct order and with correct grammar. Suprasegmental voicing patterns, however, are often abnormal, with sweeps in pitch level (such as high to low) and increased duration of vowels. It appears as if these children are playing with their vocal apparatus and with words. Accordingly, the semantic meaning system is questionable, with the child seeming to say things without a particular intent to communicate. The use of language patterns most of the time is self-serving and self-stimulating, with little attention given to the listener.

According to Fay and Schuler (1980), no cause of autism is known at this time. Some years ago, we thought the autistic child to be the product of uncaring parents and raised in an "emotional refrigerator" (Kanner and Eisenberg, 1955). A number of autistic children seemed to be the products of professional parents, in a home that often lacked spontaneity and fun. A later etiological explanation of autism was provided by Rimland (1964), who argued that the child's social withdrawal may be the result of a reticular-system (a system vital for sensory storage) dysfunction in the brain. It was Rimland's opinion that the child had a problem with sensory storage and that each encounter was indeed new for the child, since he or she had no sensory memory of previous events. The etiologic view of autism from a psychiatric outlook (Kanner) and the organic reticular-deficit view (Rimland) were used by Brown (1978), who looked at 100 autistic young adults (autistic from childhood, with a present mean age of 22.3 years); she found a high correlation between "Kanner ratings" and "Rimland ratings" on these young autistic adults. The Brown study suggests that there well may be a relationship between a neurological deficit (poor reticular function) and parental reaction to the odd behaviors exhibited by such a young child.

The long-term follow-up and eventual outcome after therapy for autistic children over the years has not been encouraging. We have observed firsthand the young autistic child grow over time into a young adult still showing the same kind of nonintentional communication, more focused on self than on the listener. Some of the more promising behavioral approaches used with these children, such as using stimulus fading techniques and positive-reinforcement withdrawal contingent on incorrect behavior (Lovass, 1968), have not proved to be particularly effective. It would appear, however, that early diagnosis of autism and early therapy intervention produce the greatest chances for some recovery (Bloch, Gersten, and Kornblum, 1980).

Schizophrenia

From a pragmatic point of view, the child with *schizophrenia* shows real deficits in the use of language. Such a child may have perfectly normal phonologic, syntactic, and semantic language functions. The real difference between the autistic child and the one diagnosed as having schizophrenia centers around the intent to communicate; autistic children may direct their sounds and verbalizations toward themselves, while schizophrenics may seek out a listener and seemingly make attempts to convey meanings (DeHirsch, 1967). The catatonic child (one who is totally withdrawn and shows little or no affect) may be the only type of schizophrenic who does not intentionally attempt to interact with others.

The typical schizophrenic child seems to vary in overall affect, at times appearing cooperative and lucid and in other situations showing bizarre, nonmeaningful behavior. The language patterns of such a child often show complex syntactic utterances, with the child's language colored by emotional words accentuated by unusual phonologic stress (accent, duration, loudness). Hicks (1972) describes nonverbal behaviors, including a great variety of facial expressions, such as wooden faces and "staring unseeing eyes." Another characteristic of the schizophrenic child may be aggression toward others, sometimes with a violent acting-out of conflict. Such children in a language evaluation will usually demonstrate intent to communicate, but usually on the terms of their own distorted realities. Their problems in communication are not really the result of faulty language, but rather of a cognitive style that is unlike that of the people around them. Such children's psychopathological behavior may be realistic in response to their internal, distorted worlds. They use the language forms they need to use to respond to those worlds.

Functional Factors in Language Delay

There are particular cases that may contribute to a delay in language function and use. One such factor is illness. Occasionally, children experience devastating accidents or illnesses that appear to influence negatively the development and use of normal language. Hicks (1972) comments that the very ill child will often express conflicts and needs in nonverbal terms, through body movement, facial expression, and voicing. It has long been recognized in hospital pediatric wards that the young child with a serious, confining illness needs therapy in the form of art, crafts, dance, music, and play. The nonverbal communication that such activities offer the patient may do much to release the "locked-in feelings" the child may be experiencing.

As we discussed earlier, normal children learn language primarily through their experiences in their families. Not only do children listen to the narratives and verbalizations of the family members as they do things, but they are active participants in family activities. Children in nursery programs also listen and participate as they learn language through natural processes. Some children live in environments that offer little or none of this exposure to language. We have all read the tragic reports of the child raised in a closet or back room, or of family members who do not talk to one another. More commonly, we may see children who are slow in "learning to talk" (for whatever etiology), who are then treated differently by the family and subsequently isolated from normal language stimulation (Hubbell, 1985). The members of the family may end up talking for such children, anticipating their needs before they have the opportunity to speak.

There are children from particular cultural and social groupings whose speech may demonstrate phonologic and syntactic differences from standard English. Their lexical use of certain words and their sentence length may also vary from standard English. Such children have learned correctly the language code of their family environment and cannot really be judged as having a language disorder. Rather, they may be quite competent in the use of their native language. The Navajo child in northeastern Arizona may be bilingual, learning both Navajo and English in the home. If he suddenly finds himself living in Minneapolis, his language usage might be judged faulty by his non-Navajo listeners in the new city. The black child in Philadelphia may have no problem using black dialect in her neighborhood; however, as she grows up and must compete with children who use only standard English, she may be penalized for her dialectal differences (in both understanding and speaking). Children in many parts of the world are multilingual, using a particular language for a specific situation. Similarly, the black child in Philadelphia can learn both vernacular and standard English, using the language she prefers depending on the situation. For most children, learning two or more languages or dialects in the preschool years (what better age to learn them?) would be relatively easy. There are occasional children, however, who are unable to keep the languages separate and to use any one language with proficiency.

LANGUAGE DISORDERS IN THE SCHOOL YEARS

There are a number of children who demonstrate problems using language in the school-age years. Such children are generally labeled as having a *specific learning disability.* These children are of three types:

1. some acquire a language disorder, such as aphasia, after they begin school;
2. many with language disorders uncovered in the preschool years carry these problems with them when they go to school;
3. some display language problems for the first time when they are challenged by learning to read and write.

All of these children meet the definition of specific learning disability that was defined in The Education for All Handicapped Children Act, Public Law 94-142. By definition, there has to be a significant delay in language usage as determined by accepted diagnostic procedures in special education. Furthermore, there must be a tested discrepancy between the child's language functioning and overall tested intelligence.

The Child with Aphasia

The term *acquired aphasia* is limited to designating the child who developed language normally and then, through some kind of injury to the brain, experienced a noticeable decrement in or loss of language function (Eisenson, 1984). There are very few such children. While in some states such a child will be labeled as having aphasia, in many states the overall educational label might well be specific learning disability. The child with acquired aphasia demonstrates a marked reduction in verbal fluency. In fact, Hécaen (1976) found that among 15 acquired-aphasic children (all with left-hemisphere lesions) whom he studied, 9 of them had symptoms of mutism. Fortunately, the prognosis for recovering language function among children who have acquired aphasia appears very good (much better than among adults). Satz and Bullard-Bates (1981), reviewing the literature on acquired aphasia in children, concluded that 50 to 75 percent make very good language recovery. Along with their school work, these children require intensive individual language therapy.

Children with Early Language Impairment

Infants and toddlers who may demonstrate symptoms of language impairment (which we have been describing in most of this chapter) eventually are old enough to go to school. Except for those who have been found to be mentally retarded, there may be a marked discrepancy between tested intellectual ability and tested and functional use of language. Children demonstrate problems in understanding what is said and what they attempt to read, as well as in word finding and phrase-sentence formulation. For the majority of children who are classified as learning-disabled, Wiig (1982, p. 261) has written that "40 to 60 percent" of them experience a "language disorder syndrome." Such children may also experience localized problems in writing-drawing or in most visual-motor tasks.

If children with language disorders could be identified in the preschool years and provided with early intervention, there might be fewer such children with language problems at school age. Mason (1976) reported that about one-third of all children who demonstrated language delays before they went to school in Edinburgh were having significant problems in reading and spelling two years after starting school. Many such children were thought to have only phonologic problems in the preschool years, sometimes demonstrating inordinate difficulty acquiring the rules of phonology and proficiency in sound production. In the early school years, it may become apparent that some of these same children have problems in morphology; the child seems at times unable to hear parts of words that may be unstressed or may have difficulty understanding word endings. Consequently, plurality, gender, and verb changes may all be used incorrectly. Or the children may have difficulty understanding word meanings or problems with word retrieval; their lexicon is frequently found to be lacking. These problems in semantics, coupled with difficulties in morphology, often result in many syntactic errors. As people around such children use sentences that are more structurally complex, the children may demonstrate difficulty remembering what was said. They will be unable to develop syntactically complex sentences and will often use a simpler form. If asked to repeat a complex sentence, they will do what they can to simplify its construction and still maintain what they think is its message. The following sentence reduction was made by a ten-year-old boy with a language disorder:

MODEL: "Becky drove the white Buick with the fancy blue seats to her uncle's house by the cactus farm."
BOY: "Becky drove the blue Buick to the uncle's farm."

Educators often designate various labels for the language problems these children may exhibit: problems in auditory sequencing, an auditory processing problem, or a central auditory problem (to name a few). Such problems may be viewed broadly (generically) as language disorders that often cut across the various language processes of phonology, morphology, syntax, semantics, and pragmatics. The child with such a language delay is entitled to special education management to be provided by the local school district, according to the provisions of PL 94-142. The school programs for such children may include a special classroom for the language-impaired child, or, more likely, special language therapy with the speech-language pathologist, while the child continues to attend a regular classroom (main-streaming).

Children who Show Language Impairment after Starting School

Many children masquerade their marginal language abilities until they go to school (Wood, 1982). They have learned to hide their problems of comprehension, they speak very little, and their relatively normal cognitive ability helps them participate well in home and play situations. Suddenly, they find themselves listening to one person in a noisy, distracting classroom, they are forced to learn a new language system (reading and writing), and often are asked to read aloud in front of their classmates. Children whose oral skills that were barely adequate in one-person interactions may become overloaded in the multi-person school environment. Some children are able to mask their language limitations during beginning reading by memorizing words, playing the role of the class clown, or being silent. Such children may exhibit greater communicative competence (nonverbal behaviors may be well developed) than language competence (Rees, 1978).

Language competence requires thorough assessment. Using the approach of *form, content,* and *use* (Bloom and Lahey, 1978), specific areas of language competence must be determined. By looking at the form or structure of children's language, we must find their knowledge of the phonologic, syntactic, and morphologic rules of the language. Expressive problems in form may show in the child's problems in letter or sound formation, difficulty in correct grammar usage, and problems in formulating sentences; receptive difficulties are observed in the child's inability to recognize sounds, problems in understanding the meaning of grammatical constructions, and problems in understanding sentence types and complexity (Wood, 1982). Content problems experienced by the school-age child may be seen in the inappropriate choice of words to convey meaning and in the inability to understand the meanings of others (spoken or written). Disorders of use or problems in pragmatics are seen in the child's inability to use language appropriately in social context and discourse.

A language disorder can permeate all aspects of children's experience in the classroom. Obviously, a language disorder may limit the ability to speak or write like their peers and seriously limit their ability to understand what is said or written.

Less obvious is the impact a language disorder may have on the ability to learn and do mathematics. Carlson, Gruenwald, and Nyberg (1980) have written that to do mathematics successfully, one must utilize a language symbol code. We learn mathematical processes (addition, subtraction, multiplication, division) by using a language code. Beyond basic mathematical-calculation processes, most math problems are presented within a verbal context, requiring concepts of shape, space, and time as ready tools to be used in problem solving.

EVALUATING THE LANGUAGE OF CHILDREN

Some children with language disorders are viewed by their families as "talking different" but are not considered to have a problem that needs investigation or treatment. Other children may have relatively normal language but be viewed by their parents as having a problem in "saying things." Children with a typical language disorder are usually viewed as talking very little, with family members not very aware of any language-comprehension problems they may be experiencing. However, with increased public-information programs about language disorders (see Figure 8–1) and greater awareness by physicians, nurses, and psychologists of language disorders and what can be done about them, children with such difficulties are referred to audiologists and speech-language pathologists at younger ages.

Most language evaluations are conducted by speech-language pathologists (clinicians) in a setting that allows them to interview the parents and provides a natural play environment for the children. The first and primary task for the clinician is to determine whether or not a language disorder really exists. This is best determined by observing and measuring, when possible, the child's current content, form, and use of language. Such observation measurement is best obtained by observing the child first in a free-play situation and then in a structured testing situation; one without the other can often provide a false view of the child's actual language abilities. If a language disorder has been found, one purpose of the evaluation is to determine if there are any ongoing problems (such as hearing loss) that could be corrected that might be contributing to the difficulty. Once it is established that a language disorder is present, a prognosis for possible improvement must be established and, most importantly, a plan developed that specifies various remediation approaches. Let us review some of the steps of a child's language evaluation.

The Case History

Usually before the child makes the first visit to the speech-language clinic, the parents and child's physician have completed some case-history forms. By reviewing these forms before seeing the child, the clinician can make some determination of the child's overall cognitive and physical growth. Details of the birth and early developmental history have obvious relevance for acquiring an understanding of the young child. When the parents first noted that there was a possible problem in communication will have relevance. Many audiologists and speech-language pathologists use the *Minnesota Child Development Inventory* (Ireton and Thwing, 1972), a 320-item questionnaire that the parents are asked to fill out before the speech-language evaluation is made. A clear picture of the child's overall function is provided by the *Minnesota* as parents answer each statement with "yes" or "no" specific to the child's past and present behaviors; among the 320 items are statements such as:

> 154. Uses two hands to pick up large objects.
> 155. Turns pages of picture books one page at a time.
> 156. Uses both gestures and words to communicate.

Obviously, the use of such an inventory provides much more information about the child's functioning than would be obtained from interview or direct observation.

Most speech-language clinics require that the child's physician also complete a brief form describing the past and present physical status of the child. Sometimes elaborate forms are used and sometimes a simple topical form, such as the one in Figure 8–2, is completed by the pediatrician or family doctor before the formal evaluation takes place. In this particular example, we see the physician's concern about the child's continuing problem with otitis media and a description of past treatment for the ear infections (antibiotics and tubes in the drums). Some focus on the child's hearing status would be an important part of the evaluation. Much case-history information can be completed by the parents and the physician and sent to the speech-language pathologist before the language evaluation begins. By sending such information in advance, the clinician can spend far less time during the evaluation interviewing the parents and more time observing and testing the child.

Observation

One of the most valid ways of assessing a child's language usage is to observe him in a free-play interaction, particularly with other members of his family. Consequently, the clinic testing room for young children should first of all be a playroom. Designated play areas with attractive toys should be available for the child at the time of the evaluation. Perhaps one of the best evaluation strategies is to begin by putting the child and the parent(s) and any siblings who might have come along together (without the clinician) in the playroom. Such a room should be equipped with a one-way observation mirror and a good-fidelity sound system, so that the clinician can watch closely from the observation room the interactions between all of the family members. I might say to the child and parents, "Let's go in here and play for a while. Just have a good time doing whatever you want to do. I'll be watching [parents should be told when they are being observed] to see how ——— talks and understands what you say. So just go ahead and play. This will give us a good idea how he uses words." We may spend ten minutes behind the glass watching

THE UNIVERSITY OF ARIZONA SPEECH AND HEARING CENTER
Room 308B, Speech Building – Phone: 621-1826
Tucson, Arizona 85721

FORM 1 – MEDICAL EXAMINATION (Please send this form directly to the above address)

NAME _T.R._____ TELEPHONE _862-4170____

ADDRESS _3614 E. Octille Blvd._ DATE OF EXAMINATION(S) _6-18-84_

MAJOR PROBLEM _Delayed Language_____ BIRTHDATE _4-4-80_

Medical history and findings pertinent to the communicative disorder, including
problems in early development, significant illnesses or injuries, medication,
and previous or planned surgery.

HISTORY:

① Otitis media (treated ξ tubes ξ antibiotics
                                      as needed)
② Middle ear effusion (ear aches)
③ Diarrhea (19-24 mos. periodically)

CURRENT PHYSICAL STATUS:

① Normal Physical development
② Does not follow directions ξ speaks out
                               at CA level.

RECOMMENDATIONS:

   Eval. for language ξ intelligence ξ
                         socialization

Examining Physician __RRWhite_____
Address __PNl_____ Telephone _884-3600_

FIGURE 8-2 A physician's-referral form.

the child-parent-sibling interactions, paying close attention to the child's responses. Of particular interest may be how the child seems to relate to other family members. Do they take turns in communicating? Is the mood a happy one? What kind of attention is given the child by the parent(s)? Many clinicians use an observational rating form that allows them to look for specific behaviors; others prefer to take a general look at the family interactions, getting a feeling of the *gestalt,* or an appreciation of the total functioning of the family unit.

Some of the observational time behind the mirror focuses on the child's play. In play, we often see clearly the interrelationship between cognition and language. Watching the child at play and hearing the words he uses as he plays can provide the clinician with some documentation as to how the child functions as compared with other children. Westby (1980) developed a symbolic-play scale that allows the examiner to look at child play and make some determination of its developmental level. For example, in her scale at the Stage V level (twenty-two to twenty-four months), Westby lists these typical play behaviors:

_____Represents daily experiences; plays house, is the mommy, daddy, or baby; objects used are realistic and close to life size.
_____Events short and isolated; no true sequences; some self-limiting sequences; puts food in pan, stirs, and eats.
_____Block play consists of stacking and knocking down.
_____Sand and water play consists of filling, pouring, and dumping.

How children play tells us much about their overall cognitive abilities. By observing their play, we see how they view the world. Normal children (those without a language disorder) use language at pretty much the same level as that of their cognitive play; that is, as they think and experience the world through play, they use the receptive and expressive language levels that are commonly observed in normal children the same age. Using Westby's *Symbolic Play Scale* (1980), the normal child at Stage V (using the same level we cited before) would show both the play behavior and the language functions of the child twenty-two to twenty-four months. As mentioned earlier in this chapter, a strong indication of a language disorder exists when there is a marked discrepancy between children's overall cognitive functioning and their knowledge and use of language.

It is imperative, therefore, that clinicians observe children closely regarding their use of language. A gross assessment can be made of language functions (phonology, syntax, semantics, pragmatics) as children play with their mothers and other members of the family. This observation of children's functional use of language will guide the clinicians in their use of further diagnostic probes and often dictate the kind of testing that will be done. For example, for children who seem to pronounce all of their words with relative clarity for their age, clinicians may be able to eliminate most of the phonological testing in the language evaluation. Leonard (1982) recommends the use of the "nonstandardized probe," which will enable clinicians to look at particular children's language pragmatics as they use language in different ways with the people around them.

Testing

The clinician will use both informal testing and formal testing. As part of the evaluation, the clinician will set up play interactions with the child that will sample particular language behaviors. Some determination can be made as to how well the child understands what is said. For example, while building a block tower, the clinician starts to make a stack with three blocks (leaving the other blocks in a box on the floor). She then says, "Uh-oh, I don't have any more blocks. Where are the rest of the blocks?" The child lets the clinician know (by voicing or by speech or by gesture) that the rest of the blocks are in the box. Or comprehension can be tested by asking the child to do something. Getting the child to say particular things on an informal basis is more difficult. For this reason, we often use imitation as a means of listening to the phonology and syntax of the child. When children begin to make errors in imitation, they may well be demonstrating some of their language problem. Starkweather (1983) has written that "more information is derived from errors the child makes in attempting to imitate sentences beyond his or her capacity than from the level at which correct imitations stop" (p. 314).

When possible, the language evaluation should be audio- or video-recorded, permitting much of the observation and scoring of the child's responses to take place after the evaluation is completed. The delayed scoring of an audio or video tape allows the clinician to determine phonologic competence in using voice and rhythm and in articulation. Syntax and word choice can be studied. The mean length of response (or number of words per utterance) has had a long use in children's language evaluations (Brown, 1973) and can readily be scored on video playback. The interaction of the child and the clinician is often best studied "after the fact," by video playback. It should be remembered that the language behaviors obtained in the clinic will usually show the child using poorer language forms, generally resulting in our underestimating the child's language capacity (Scott and Taylor, 1978). Anything that can be done to make the evaluation session more like a "real-world" play situation will usually result in more valid test behaviors by the child.

However, as useful as comparing children to themselves can be (which is what we do in our informal testing), it is necessary in the evaluation to administer some standardized tests that provide normative data to which we can compare each child. The speech-language pathologist must decide which tests to use for evaluating the specific language-impaired child. It is hoped that the tests selected have been developed to include reliability and validity data as well as other psychometric data (adequate sample size, a defined standardization sample, and so on). Unfortunately, McCauley and Swisher (1984) found that most of the common standardized tests used in the language evaluation of preschool children failed to meet many of these psychometric criteria.

Many tests and subtests of larger tests are often employed in studying the receptive-language function of a young child. Perhaps one of the most common tests of vocabulary recognition is the *Peabody Picture Vocabulary Test* (Dunn and Dunn, 1965). The child looks at four pictures, one of which is named by the examiner. The child then points to the picture she thinks is best represented by the word that was spoken. The *Peabody* (PPVT) is strictly a test of vocabulary recognition and has norms specific to how many words a child should recognize at a particular age. The PPVT is often wrongly used as a measure of the child's verbal intelligence. Another vocabulary test that also has age norms is the *Full Range Picture Vocabulary Test* (Ammons and Ammons, 1948). Other tests of receptive language function that rely heavily on vocabulary recognition are the Auditory Reception subtest of the *Illinois Test of Psycholinguistic Abilities* (Kirk, McCarthy, and Kirk, 1968) and the vocabulary subtest of the *Stanford-Binet Intelligence Scale* (Terman and Merrill, 1960). Many receptive-language tests require that the child act out some kind of sequence to match what the examiner says or point to the picture that best represents some kind of syntactic manipulation of words. The Carrow *Test for Auditory Comprehension of Language* (1973), the receptive portion of Lee's *Northwestern Syntax Screening Test* (1969), and DiSimoni's *The Token Test for Children* (1978) are examples of tests with age norms that purport to show how children understand spoken language.

It is often difficult to conduct a language evaluation of young children that requires them to speak. Our case study of Tom in the beginning of this chapter was a good example of a child who was too reticent to speak to the examiner; he only spoke through his intermediary, his older brother. It is surprising, however, how the experienced and well-trained speech-language pathologist can coax valid speech responses from children who usually prefer to be silent with strangers. Often, the most valid responses from children are the informal, spontaneous utterances they make at play. It is sometimes possible to administer a formal test that can provide age norms specific to the child's expressive language. The expressive section of the *Northwestern Syntax Screening Test* (Lee, 1969) is such a test. Another kind of expression test is an elicited-imitation test, where the examiner says a phrase or sentence and the child repeats it. The *Stephens Oral Language Screening Test* (Stephens, 1977) is an imitation test in which, if the child cannot imitate a sentence, it is assumed that she may not be able to use that particular language form in everyday life. The *Stephens* can provide clues to the child's morphologic and syntactic performance.

It is always important for the examiner to remember that children's response on a particular item of a test is but an indication of their performance (this is what they do). Performance does not equate with one's underlying ability or competence. Naremore said it well: "In one sense, all language tests are tests of language performance, which show what a child can do on a particular set of test items at a particular time" (1980, p. 170). Most of our test data (measuring children's performance) underestimate their true level of competence. During the evaluation, children may give us only a glimpse of their true language competence.

Other Tests

Most language evaluations require testing children's hearing, looking at their peripheral oral mechanisms (structure and function), and a measure of intelligence (perhaps through performance rather than words).

As we discussed in the last chapter, many children experience a significant delay in language development from having a hearing loss. In fact, the most common cause of language delay in children is from either a conductive or a sensori-neural hearing loss. The language evaluation, therefore, must include pure-tone audiometry. The child responds to a number of pure tones at various frequencies and an audiogram is plotted. For very young or immature children who cannot signal their responses, play audiometry is used for testing. Children are usually conditioned to drop a block in a can or place a peg in a pegboard each time the tone is heard. For children with a measurable loss, the audiologist may wish to determine speech-reception thresholds (the intensity level at which 50 percent of the words can be repeated correctly) and the ability to discriminate words comfortably above threshold.

The language evaluation must also include a peripheral oral examination, requiring the speech-language pathologist to examine and make judgments about the structure and function of the child's oral mechanisms. Very few children with language disorders seem to have a significant problem with their tongues or other oral structures. As we will discuss in Chapter 11, organic deviations in the mouth (such as tongue-tie) rarely contribute in any significant way to the speech problems of children related to phonologic errors (Bernthal and Bankson, 1981).

Children with a language disorder often show a marked discrepancy between verbal and performance abilities as measured by tests of intelligence. It is such children's poor language performance that causes them to be sent to the audiologist or speech-language pathologist. Intelligence tests for children have been developed that require little or no language; they are known as nonverbal performance intelligence tests. The *Columbia Mental Maturity Scale* (Burgemeister, Blum, and Lorge 1972) was developed for the intelligence testing of young children with severe cerebral palsy who might be unable to participate in verbal-intelligence testing because of severe motor disability. The *Leiter International Performance Scale* (Leiter, 1978) and the *Raven Coloured Progressive Matrices* (Raven, 1978) are examples of non-verbal intelligence tests that are often used by clinicians in language evaluations. Perhaps the tests of intelligence for children that are most used and best standardized are the *Wechsler Intelligence Scale for Children, WISC-R* (Wechsler, 1974) and the *Revised Stanford-Binet Intelligence Scale* (Terman and Merrill, 1980). Both the *Wechsler* and the *Stanford-Binet* have verbal and performance sections that may show discrepancies (in favor of performance intelligence) of function in a child who is being examined for language difficulties. Full-scale intelligence tests are often added to language evaluations when the examiner feels that the child's overall cognitive functioning needs to be determined. Formal intelligence testing is time-consuming and is often best done by the clinical psychologist who is trained in psychometric testing. If such a psychologist is not part of the evaluation team, the speech-language pathologist makes the appropriate referral, usually deferring final decision-making specific to the child's overall language status until the intelligence testing is completed.

The Evaluation Report

It is hoped that, as a result of the language evaluation, the clinician will be able to describe the status of the child's language. The description will be based on how the child performed. From the performance, however, some inference can be made about the child's overall language competence. The language evaluation will provide a description of how the child uses language. It is also hoped that out of the evaluation will come some identification of possible problems (if there are any) that may be contributing to the cause and maintenance of the language disorder; for example, a hearing loss may have been detected that could be treated medically and possibly eradicated. Or an emotionally charged home situation may be uncovered that might require the professional intervention of the social worker or the psychologist or psychiatrist. The case history, the observations, the intelligence-speech-language testing should all have contributed to a clear understanding of what is the child's language problem. A statement of prognosis (the predicted outcome following treatment and management) must be made in the conclusion of the evaluation report. Finally, a remediation plan must be established and discussed with the parents. The plan must be realistic (recognizing the resources available in the community), and various options should be discussed with the parents, such as a preschool nursery, perhaps a special class with other children with language impairment, maybe individual or group language-speech therapy, or perhaps counseling in conjunction with a home program.

LANGUAGE THERAPY FOR CHILDREN

After language assessment has found the child, whether preschool or school-age, to need some kind of language therapy, the speech-language pathologist must decide on a remediation program. Like other forms of remediation therapy, a careful baseline is determined for a particular language area. A clear view of the child's present performance is a prerequisite for effective language therapy. Not only is assessment required before therapy begins, but there is a need for continuous assessment throughout therapy. Each treatment session, therefore, includes a probe, looking to see how well the child is using the particular language process being taught. A terminal behavior is then determined by the clinician, who designs specific steps for the training session to take the child, it is hoped, from baseline behavior to the terminal product. For each step of the program, specific stimuli and task need to be specified in advance.

While there are some children who only need to work on language expression, the majority of children with language disorders need work on total language function, which includes both receptive and expressive processes. There is some controversy as to what to train first: expressive or receptive functions. The behavioral approach to language training puts emphasis on the children's making some kind of response, with the clinician shaping the child's spoken language patterns (Lovaas, 1968; Gray and Ryan, 1973). As we will see, making a response by imitation and repeating what the clinician says, plays a prominent part of the behavioral approach. Others (Bloom and Lahey, 1978; Snyder, 1979; Winitz, 1976) present a strong argument for putting an early emphasis on receptive-language tasks coupled with play activities, which seems to tie language to more of a normal-process approach. Comprehension and receptive-language functions may be facilitated by varying the presentation of the spoken linguistic signal, such as by deliberate changes in stress, intonation, and rate. Another decision must be made as to whether language training will be provided in individual, tutoring-type sessions or as part of learning in a group with other children (language-disordered or normal).

A Process Approach

The process approach to language remediation is perhaps best facilitated in a group setting. The children are exposed to a number of natural experiences that may include dimensions of language coupled with particular play activities. A nursery playground was constructed at the University of Denver to meet the training needs of children with language disorders. The playground was built by first digging a large hole, filling it with sand, and placing a number of varying-height jumping poles around it. The dirt from the hole was then mounded so that a tumbling hill ("the mountain") could be constructed. A tunnel was dug and lined with cement, with a walkway built through it. A slide was placed on the side of "the mountain"; the rest of the mound was planted with grass. The playground was loaded with spatial things to do (climb, jump, dig, go through, go under, slide). As the children played, the clinicians would narrate what was happening, giving emphasis to particular word forms or combinations. Instructions and comments were given, with stress markers for particular words, such as, "Uh-oh, Billy fell *down*." Very little emphasis was put on having the children make responses; that is, asking them to say things. Of some interest here is that graduate students would write down the verbalizations of both children and clinicians; sometimes, children would be heard to use a verbalization that had been heard in the group four or five months earlier. Such children would often demonstrate a language form in order to communicate when they were ready to use it, with no direct prompting from the clinician.

In the process approach, attempts are made to follow normal developmental sequences and schedules as much as possible. The training environment is manipulated to put heavy emphasis on a particular area of content and form. For example, in the nursery playground, we might have been working on the prepositions *in* and *out;* activities were planned that enabled the child to participate in going in and out of the tunnel, requiring that the clinician repeat phrases and short sentences that stressed these two words. The repeated presentations of the words with the tangible events would, it was hoped, lead to the child's making "inductions" about how the word was used and what its meaning was (Bloom and Lahey, 1978). The words selected for such stimulation in the group should be those that have high utilization value for the child, such as *no* or *none*. Rather than look at pictures or have the child play a passive, watching role, it is perhaps better to encourage the child's active participation in the ongoing events (Leonard, 1975). The child listens and plays, but may not be required to say anything.

Input training should encourage the child's verbal response but not necessarily require it. When some kind of response task is built into the training session, the rate of stimulus presentation can be determined by the correctness of the child's response rate. The rate of verbal presentation will vary with the individual child, as will the preferred modality of presentation (auditory, visual, signing). Finally, in the process approach, the child must be given opportunities to use language in functional-pragmatic situations. The hope is that some "awareness therapy" is built in that not only gives children some success as speakers but begins to teach their "rights and responsibilities" in successful communication (Simon, 1981).

The Behavioral-Learning Approach

The behavioral approach to teaching language to children with language disorders has had success with the autistic or mentally retarded. Such an approach lends itself well for extinguishing an aversive or wrong kind of language behavior. If the child, for example, is using "me," instead of "I," as the subject of a phrase or sentence, the speech-language pathologist might design a program to extinguish the use of "me" as the subject pronoun. First, a baseline would be taken on the "me/I" usage. The child would begin to receive no stimulation or would receive no positive reinforcement whenever the "me" was used. Perhaps the "I" would be presented as a model for the child to repeat as a subject-verb phrase, such as "I go." Each correct response would receive a positive reinforcement, using classical operant-conditioning principles. Aversive behavior is best extinguished by not presenting positive reinforcement after it occurs; correct and desired behaviors that are positively reinforced have a much higher chance of being repeated (Mowrer, 1978).

The behavioral approach to language teaching requires that the child make some kind of response. Therefore, imitation and modeling have been two common procedures used in therapy. In imitation, the clinician presents the verbal model, such as "I go." The child's immediate task is to repeat this. Such a task does not involve the child as much as it might, and consequently, imitations are usually coupled with visual or real-life situations. The clinician presents the imitative model as the child is involved in an activity; for example, a tray of cookies is placed on the table, and the clinician says, "I want a cookie. Billy wants a cookie. Can Billy say, 'I want a cookie?'" Billy's immediate task is to respond with "I want a cookie." If he does so, he receives the cookie (immediate reinforcement), and if he does not make the repetition, the cookie is not given to him. The modeling for his imitation might be repeated as needed. The imitation approach as a preferred method for helping a child generalize and use language functionally has been questioned (Rees, 1975) for its focus on immediacy, perhaps inhibiting at times the child's learning of language rules, which might be viewed as a requisite for language-usage generalization.

Modeling lends itself to behavioral teaching approaches. The child observes the clinician or someone else produce some kind of linguistic feature. The child is instructed to listen closely to the model and then attempt to use the "same way of talking" when we begin the lesson. Perhaps the child is working on *wh-* questions. The clinician presents a brief narrative followed by several *wh-* questions, with emphasis given to the *wh-* words and perhaps the verb that follows. The child listens to the clinician's narrative. The child then asks a *wh-* question. If this is done correctly, some positive reinforcement is given. If not, no reinforcement is given and the instructions for listening to the model may be repeated. The procedure is repeated.

The advantage of the behavioral approach is that it enables the clinician to focus on particular dimensions of language. A teaching session can then be constructed listing specific target behaviors (goals), and procedures developed for reaching the target. Success criteria can be established for each dimension being taught. A high success rate, perhaps in excess of 80 percent, is often a necessary requirement for promoting generalization. We have found behavioral approaches in language therapy to be most effective with children with severe language disorders; that is, with those children who may say very little. Such an approach can zero in on what a child is able to do and by **successive approximation** (step-by-step success) shape the child's simple language utterances into more advanced forms. For the child who is beginning to use spontaneously complex language forms, the behavioral approach may be somewhat limiting. At this point, we might switch to a process or an interactive approach. When the child is ready to work on pragmatics of language, the best teaching approach is probably an interpersonal-interactive one, where the reinforcement is not provided by the clinician but by the feeling of success the child experiences upon making a successful communication.

The Interpersonal-Interactive Approach

In the interpersonal-interactive approach, the focus of the session is on the intent of the speaker and the use of language in the interaction. The primary goal of language and speech usage is to develop communication competence. When we want to ''get the message'' across to someone else, how competent are we at doing so? While the imitation and modeling of the behavioral approach have their place in the early training of children with language disorders, the final goal has to be for the child to be able to use language as a tool in communication. This interpersonal-interactive approach might well be called the pragmatic approach (Wiig, 1982).

Attempts are made in therapy using this approach to use real-world communicative situations. Children put to use the form and content previously learned in spontaneous verbal situations (the complexity and availability of which may be well controlled by the clinician). They begin to learn that it is important that their verbal messages be listener-oriented (as contrasted to the early, egocentric practice in saying things). They soon learn that to get the message across, they must be coherent and fluent in their use of adult lexicon and grammar. Part of therapy using the interaction approach is to help children become somewhat self-evaluative in developing an awareness of their effectiveness; video-tape playback has been found, for example, to be an excellent tool for helping them to appreciate their communicative effectiveness.

Other Approaches

There are some children with severe motor disabilities for whom spoken communication is not a realistic goal. Such children might profit from some exposure to and practice using some form of augmentative communication system. The child is still the sender of the message, and the other person is the receiver. What is needed is some kind of message vehicle. One such form is a coded system, such as the Bliss Symbol System (Archer, 1977), or one of the manual-sign-language systems. There are visual and audio display augmentative aids available today, such as the visual display on a lapboard or on an electronic-language tray (using numbers, words, pictures). With a microcomputer, it is possible to attach a small terminal and output mode (print-out or speaker) to the patient or wheelchair, which permits some user mobility and produces a response that the listener can usually understand.

Sometimes direct counseling is needed for both the child and the parent. The child with the problem needs to know and experience a few areas of success. In counseling sessions, the child might be told he has "the most beautiful blue eyes" or that she's "the fastest runner in the school." It is important to find some asset of these children and let them know that you are aware of it. This may offer a self-image "boost" that will help to offset the verbal-behavior problems requiring such children to have special language therapy. The frustration and anger these children may experience may be vented in the counseling session.

Parents often feel very guilty about the child's language delay. We hear them make remarks such as, "If I had taken him in earlier for a hearing test . . . " or "If only we hadn't just left Stacey with Grandma. . . . " Counseling is often necessary to provide the parents with a perspective on the problem and their role toward it and the child. We have found that parent counseling is often facilitated in a group, where members can offer one another support as well as provide specific management strategies for use in the home. The counseling session, individual or group, can range from an unstructured session that allows parents to vent their concerns and feelings, to having an "expert" come in and discuss a specific topic. Parents may require direct advice on how to react to the child's utterances, perhaps including instructions as to how to make expansions or to provide narrative modeling with no request for the child to say things. Siblings often need some guidance on how to relate; with a little guidance, brothers and sisters can often play important roles in language training and practice within the home.

REVIEW QUESTIONS

Language disorders in children can have serious effects on overall development. Let us review a few questions about these problems:

1. How does a language disorder differ from a communication disorder?

2. Is a child's language development and function a good predictor of the child's overall development? Explain.

3. How can delayed language skills lead to cognitive deficits?

4. Discuss some of the etiologic conditions

that might contribute to problems in acquiring normal language skills.

5. How can we test language pragmatics?

6. What is a process approach to language therapy?

7. What are some of the advantages and disadvantages of a behavioral approach to language training?

REFERENCES

Ammons, R. B., and Ammons, H. S. (1948). *Full Range Picture Vocabulary Test*. Missoula, Mont.: Psychological Test Specialists.

Archer, L. (1977). Blissymbolics—A nonverbal communication system. *Journal of Speech and Hearing Disorders, 42:* 568–579.

Bernthal, J., and Bankson, N. (1981). *Articulation Disorders*. Englewood Cliffs, N.J.: Prentice-Hall.

Bloch, K., Gersten, E., and Kornblum, S. (1980). Evaluation of a language program for young autistic children. *Journal of Speech and Hearing Disorders, 45:* 76–89.

Bloom, L., and Lahey, M. (1978). *Language Development and Language Disorders*. New York: Wiley.

Brown, J. L. (1978). Long-term follow-up of 100 "atypical" children of normal intelligence, in *Autism: A Reappraisal of Concepts and Treatment,* ed. M. Rutter and E. Schopler. New York: Plenum Press.

Brown, R. (1973). *A First Language: The Early Years*. Cambridge, Mass.: Harvard University Press.

Burgemeister, B. B., Blum, L. H., and Lorge, I. (1972). *Columbia Mental Maturity Scale*. New York: The Psychological Corporation.

Carlson, J., Gruenwald, L., and Nyberg, B. (1980). Everyday math is a story problem: the language of the curriculum, in *Topics in Language Disorders,* ed. K. Butler and G. Wallach. Rockville, Md.: Aspen Systems.

Carrow, E. (1973). *Test for Auditory Comprehension of Language*. Austin: Urban Research Group.

Crystal, D. (1969). *Prosodic Systems and Intonation in English*. Cambridge, England: Cambridge University Press.

DeHirsch, K. (1967). Differentiating diagnosis between aphasic and schizophrenic language in children. *Journal of Speech and Hearing Disorders, 32:* 3–10.

DiSimoni, F. (1978). *The Token Test for Children*. Hingham, Mass.: Teaching Resources.

Downs, M. P., and Northern, J. L. (1976). The management of hearing loss, in *Otolaryngology,* ed. G. M. English. New York: Harper and Row.

DuBose, R. F., and Langley, M. B. (1977). *Developmental Activities Screening Inventory*. Boston: Teaching Resources Corporation.

Dunn, L. M., and Dunn, L. M. (1965). *Peabody Picture Vocabulary Test*. Circle Pines, Minn.: American Guidance Service.

Eisenson, J. (1984). *Aphasia and Related Disorders in Children* (2nd ed.). New York: Harper and Row.

Emerick, L., and Hatten, J. (1979). *Diagnosis and Evaluation in Speech Pathology*. Englewood Cliffs, N.J.: Prentice-Hall.

Fay, W., and Schuler, A. (1980). *Emerging Language in Autistic Children*. Baltimore: University Park Press.

Federal Register, 42 (Dec. 29, 1977): 65083.

Ferry, P. C. (1981). Neurological considerations in children with learning disabilities, in *Central Auditory and Language Disorders in Children,* ed. R. W. Keith. Houston: College Hill Press.

Goldman, R., and Fristoe, M. (1969) *Goldman-Fristoe Test of Articulation*. Circle Pines, Minn.: American Guidance Service.

Gray, B., and Ryan, B. (1973). *A Language Program For The Nonlanguage Child*. Champaign, Ill.: Research Press.

Hécaen, H. (1976). Acquired aphasia in children and the ontogenesis of hemispheric specialization in children. *Brain and Language, 3:* 114–134.

Hedrick, D. L., Prather, E. M., and Tobin, A. R. (1975). *Sequenced Inventory of Communication Development*. Seattle: University of Washington Press.

Hicks, J. S. (1972). Language disabilities of emotionally disturbed children, in *Principles of Childhood Language Disabilities,* ed. J. V. Irwin, and M. Marge. New York: Appleton-Century-Crofts.

Hubbell, R. D. (1985). Disorders of language in children, in *Speech, Language, and Hearing Normal Processes and Disorders,* ed. P. H. Skinner and R. L. Shelton. Reading, Mass.: Wesley.

Ireton, H. R., and Thwing, E. (1972). *Minnesota Child Development Inventory*. Minneapolis: Behavior Science Systems.

Kanner, L., and Eisenberg, L. (1955). Notes on the followup studies of autistic children, in *Psychotherapy of Childhood,* ed. P. H. Hoch and Zubin, J. New York: Grune and Stratton.

Kenny, T. J., and Clemmens, R. L. (1975). *Behavioral Pediatrics and Child Development*. Baltimore: Williams and Wilkins.

Kirk, S. A., McCarthy, J. J., and Kirk, W. D. (1968). *The Illinois Test of Psycholinguistic Abilities* (rev. ed.). Urbana, Ill.: University of Illinois Press.

Lee, L. L. (1969). *Northwestern Syntax Screening Test*. Evanston, Ill.: Northwestern University Press.

Leiter, R. G. (1948). *Leiter International Performance Scale*. Washington, D.C.: Psychological Service Center.

Lenneberg, E. (1967). *Biological Foundations of Language*. New York: Wiley.

Leonard, L. (1975). The role of nonlinguistic stimuli and semantic relations in children's acquisition of grammatical utterances. *Journal of Experimental Child Psychology, 19:* 346–357.

Leonard, L. B. (1982). Early language development and language disorders, in *Human Communication Disorders,* ed. G. H. Shames and E. H. Wiig. Columbus, Oh.: Charles E. Merrill.

Lock, A., ed. (1978). *Action, Gesture and Symbol: The Emergence of Language*. New York: Academic Press.

Lovaas, O. I. (1968). A program for the establishment of speech on psychotic children, in *Operant Procedures in Remedial Speech and Language Training,* ed. H. N. Sloane and B. D. MacAuley. Boston: Houghton Mifflin.

Mason, A. W. (1976). Specific (developmental) dyslexia. *Developmental Medicine and Child Neurology, 9:* 183–190.

McCauley, R. J., and Swisher, L. (1984). Psychometric review of language and articulation tests for preschool children. *Journal of Speech and Hearing Disorders, 49:* 34–42.

McNeill, D. (1970). *The Acquisition of Language*. New York: Harper and Row.

Morehead, D. M., and Ingram, D. (1974). The development of base syntax in normal and linguistically deviant children. *Journal of Speech and Hearing Research, 16:* 330–352.

Morehead, D., and Morehead, A. (1974). From signal to sign: a Piagetian view of thought and language, in *Language Perspectives—Acquisition, Retardation, and Intervention,* ed. R. Schiefelbusch and L. Lloyd. Baltimore: University Park Press.

Morehead, D., and Morehead, A., ed. (1976). *Normal and Deficient Child Language*. Baltimore: University Park Press.

Mowrer, D. E. (1978). *Methods of Modifying Speech Behaviors*. Columbus, Oh.: Charles E. Merrill.

Naremore, R. C. (1980). Language disorders in children, in *Introduction to Communication Disorders,* ed. T. J. Hixon, L. D. Shriberg, and J. H. Saxman. Englewood Cliffs, N.J.: Prentice-Hall.

Raven, J. C. (1978). *Raven Coloured Progressive Matrices*. New York: The Psychological Corporation.

Rees, N. (1975). Imitation and language development: issues and clinical implications. *Journal of Speech and Hearing Disorders, 40:* 339–350.

Rees, N. (1978). Pragmatics of language: applications to normal and disordered language development, in *Bases of Language Intervention,* ed. R. Schiefelbusch. Baltimore: University Park Press.

Reichman, J., and Healey, W. C. (1983). Learning disabilities and conductive loss involving otitis media. *Journal of Learning Disabilities, 16:* 272–278.

Rimland, B. (1964). *Infantile Autism*. New York: Appleton-Century-Crofts.

Schiefelbusch, R. L. (1967). The development of communication skills, in *Language and Mental Retardation,* ed. R. L. Schiefelbusch, R. H. Copeland, and J. O. Smith. New York: Holt, Rinehart, and Winston.

Scott, C. M., and Taylor, A. E. (1978). A comparison of home and clinic gathered language samples. *Journal of Speech and Hearing Disorders, 43:* 482–495.

Semel, E. M., and Wiig, E. H. (1983). *Clinical Evaluation of Language Function.* Columbus, Oh.: Charles E. Merrill.

Simon, C. S. (1981). *Communicative Competence: A Functional-Pragmatic Approach to Language Therapy.* Tucson: Communication Skill Builders.

Snyder, L. (1979). "Pragmatic abilities of children with learning disabilities." Paper presented at the Language Disorder Symposium, University of Denver, Colorado.

Starkweather, C. W. (1983). *Speech and Language.* Englewood Cliffs, N.J.: Prentice-Hall.

Stephens, M. I. (1977). *Stephens Oral Language Screening Test.* Peninsula, Oh.: Interim Publishers.

Terman, L. M., and Merrill, M. A. (1980). *Stanford-Binet Intelligence Scale* (3rd rev.) Boston: Houghton Mifflin.

Wechsler, D. (1974). *Wechsler Intelligence Scale for Children—Revised.* New York: Psychological Corporation.

Westby, C. (1980). Assessment of cognitive and language abilities through play. *Language, Speech, and Hearing Services in the Schools, 11:* 154–168.

Whorf, B. (1956). *Language, Thought, and Reality.* New York: Wiley.

Wiig, E. H. (1982). Language disabilities in the schoolage child, in *Human Communication Disorders: An Introduction,* ed. G. H. Shames and E. H. Wiig. Columbus, Oh.: Charles E. Merrill.

Winitz, H. (1978). Full time experience. *Asha, 18:* 404.

Wood, M. L. (1982). *Language Disorders in School-Age Children.* Englewood Cliffs, N.J.: Prentice-Hall.

9

As we have seen, language and speech behaviors become well established in early childhood. We carry our established communicative behaviors into adulthood. In this chapter, we will consider acquired language disorders in adults. We will discuss briefly the language problems one encounters when suddenly confronted with a new language environment. We will then discuss the problem of aphasia, its evaluation and treatment. The language problems of patients with right hemisphere disease will be presented. Finally, we will consider the dramatic dissolution of language seen in the patient with dementia, such as Alzheimer's disease.

Disorders of Language in Adults

EXPOSURE TO A NEW LANGUAGE

The evidence is overwhelming that the optimum time to learn new language is in the preschool years. Many people who live in small countries bordered by several other countries learn three or four languages. They not only are fluent in their *native* tongue (the first language they learned), but can comprehend and speak other languages with equal fluency, keeping them separate and thinking in the language they are using at the time. Lenneberg (1967) has proposed that there is a biologic readiness for the acquisition of language that has its upper limits in the early teen years. After that, the acquisition of other languages becomes much harder. Many of us have experienced the difficulty of learning a new language in the adult years and know firsthand the frustration of attempting to comprehend the "rapid" speech of the foreign speaker or the awkwardness of altering our English prosodic patterns to match those of the new language.

For adults who find themselves in a totally new language environment with minimal or no advanced preparation, speech is out of the question as a method of communication. Some of the nonverbal behaviors discussed in earlier chapters must be used, for the most part. If we were suddenly to be placed in Russia with no English guide, the language we heard would have no meaning and our English responses would go unheeded. We would keep our speech interactions to a minimum. Only the suprasegmentals we used would have some communicative value; that is, accent, pitch changes, syllable duration, loudness variations, and melodic flow might communicate some meaning. But without words, the meaning is gross, inexact in focus. Our body language, facial expressions, and gestures would probably be our best mode of communication. If we needed to make a specific point to someone who spoke only Russian, we would be forced to use a Russian-English dictionary and point to the Russian equivalent of our English words. The actual words provide a specificity of meaning that no gesture or sound can communicate.

APHASIA

Aphasia is the loss of language function after an injury to the brain. It has many possible causes, but perhaps the two most common are stroke and accident. Since we established earlier that language tends to lateralize to the left hemisphere of the brain, most patients with aphasia have experienced left-cerebral-hemisphere damage. We will first discuss the causes of aphasia, particularly how they may relate to the symptoms the patient may be experiencing, and then consider the various kinds of aphasia and related disorders that may be present. Finally, we will discuss the diagnosis-evaluation and management of the patient with aphasia, which are of most importance to the speech-language pathologist.

The Causes of Aphasia

The most common cause of aphasia is a cerebrovascular accident or **stroke.** A stroke is an interruption of blood flow to the brain. The brain requires a continuous renewal of arterial blood flow, bringing oxygen to the brain. There are three primary arteries carrying blood to the brain, the left and right carotid arteries and the basilar artery posteriorly (which is actually a composite extension of the two ascending vertebral arteries). Most strokes are related to an obstruction (thrombosis) forming within one of these primary arteries. Other strokes are obstructions of blood flow within the arteries of the brain caused by an embolus (a clot travels into the cerebral arteries from another part of the body, obstructing the flow of blood). Some strokes are caused by arterial hemorrhages. In summary, the three types of cerebrovascular accident (stroke) are thrombosis, embolus, and hemorrhage. Any of them may cause aphasia, but primarily when the damage is to the left cerebral hemisphere of the brain.

Aphasia has been studied over the years by neurologists, neuropsychologists, linguists, and speech-language pathologists. Early neurologists viewed aphasia as a motor-sensory disease, and this dichotomy in function continues to influence our study of aphasia. Neurologists have established that motor functions appear to be controlled by the anterior part of the brain (as seen in Figure 9–1, anterior to (e) the fissure of Rolando), with sensory functions found to be posterior to that fissure. This motor-sensory model led to a viewpoint termed **cerebral localization,** which specified that bits of behavior were related to the function of relatively discrete areas of the brain. Consistent with this belief, early neurologists introduced the concept of expressive aphasia's being caused by frontal lesions, with receptive aphasia caused by posterior cerebral lesions.

The classical concept of language localization probably began with a paper by Broca (1960) in 1861 in which he presented two cases of aphasia after autopsy. Each case had a lesion in the third convolution of the left frontal lobe, which he felt was responsible for the two patients' experiencing severe expressive aphasias before their deaths. This was the first recognized paper asserting that a specific lesion in the brain could cause a particular language deficit. Broca's patients were described as understanding spoken language well without having the ability to speak. An opposite kind of aphasia was described by Wernicke (1977) in 1874, who demonstrated that lesions to the left posterior temporal lobe could produce devastating problems in understanding the spoken word; he described the speech of these patients as sounding like jargon. These two early papers by Broca and Wernicke established the arguments of cerebral localization, saying that, when destroyed, a spe-

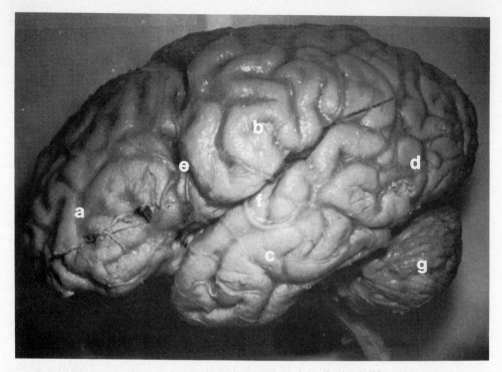

FIGURE 9-1 A photograph of the left cerebral hemisphere. Structures noted include: A: frontal lobe; B: parietal lobe; C: temporal lobe; D: occipital lobe; E: fissure of Rolando; F: Sylvius fissure; G: cerebellum. Used with permission of University of Nevada School of Medicine, Reno.

cific area of the brain could cause a specific deficit of function. While there have been over one hundred years of subsequent studies challenging the concept of localization, the work of Geschwind (1979) and Goodglass and Kaplan (1972) continues to sort aphasia patients into expressive (anterior lesions) and receptive (temporal-posterior) categories.

Although modern localizationists may still attribute particular language functions to certain areas of the brain, we know also that the brain functions as a whole. Recent brain exploration using regional cerebral blood flow has added to our knowledge of cerebral function (Meyer and others, 1980). During these blood-flow studies, the patient inhales a Xeon gas, which distributes itself within the blood vessels of the brain. It is then possible to monitor the densities of blood within particular areas of the brain, using radiographic techniques. The patient is asked to do a particular task, such as snapping one's fingers or reciting the alphabet. Such an activity results in greater blood-flow densities in the corresponding area of the brain that may play an active role in that function. In general, these activation studies have given some credibility to the view of both localization and nonlocalization. While certain areas of the brain appear vital for particular functions, there is much contribution by other areas of the brain. Localization of language function is substantiated today by our realization that language does appear to lateralize to the left hemisphere of the brain; within that hemisphere, however, there is not absolute specificity of area for a particular function. A summary view of language function today related to cerebral localization might be that the absolute specificity of word (lexicon) and sequence (syntax) appears to require active left-hemisphere participation. The right hemisphere might have much to do with tonality of language and with spontaneous and overlearned language functions (such as automaticisms).

Types of Aphasia

We have just mentioned the writings of Broca and Wernicke, who described types of aphasia that still bear their names. The categories and names for aphasia are many. We have difficulty naming the type of aphasia for someone else when we wander far from our behavioral descriptions of the patient. Using the categorizations of Goodglass and Kaplan (1972), fluent and nonfluent, this writer currently uses these subtypes to label and describe aphasia patients, as seen in Table 9–1. One of the best ways of illustrating these various types of aphasia is to provide a brief description of actual cases, showing each type.

1. Broca's or Motor Aphasia. This patient exhibits a severe phonologic problem (can often say nothing), with relatively normal language comprehension. In addition to aphasia, Johns and Darley (1970) have described the oral-verbal apraxia we often see in these patients. One such patient stands out clearly. The only thing this forty-four-year-old woman could say after her stroke was "shoe." All early therapy attempts at introducing other words resulted in marked mouth posturing, characterized by almost random attempts to imitate sounds or words after us. Eventually, she spontaneously developed the phrase "damn shoe," which she used for all spontaneous utterances. One day she attended a football game at the Los Angeles Col-

TABLE 9–1

Types of Aphasia

Nonfluent aphasia
Broca's or motor aphasia
Transcortical motor aphasia
Fluent aphasia
Semantic or anomic aphasia
Wernicke's or jargon aphasia
Conduction aphasia
Global aphasia

iseum, and yelled "damn shoes" throughout the game. Finally, an irritated football fan sitting below her could stand it no longer. Thinking that she was calling one of the opposition players a Jew, he yelled up at the patient, "Okay, he's a Jew. Let's get on with the game!" Unfortunately, the perseverative words of these patients often get literally translated. The Broca's aphasic cannot repeat a word model provided by someone else.

2. Transcortical Motor Aphasia. These patients struggle to produce an utterance, often eliminating function words, such as articles and conjunctions. They speak telegraphically. Melodic, prosodic flow of speech is lacking. However, these patients can repeat a verbal model. Such patients generally have fairly good language comprehension. A thirty-two-year-old woman suffered a cerebral embolus related to a lifetime problem of cardiac disease. A clothing designer and model, she spoke of her work during our interview in this way, "Well, New York. Clothes. Trying, clothes, planning, trying, selling. Nothing, so modeling. Now, nothing" (looking at her paralyzed right arm and leg).

3. Semantic or Anomic Aphasia. Usually these patients have mild-to-moderate receptive-language losses, which is seen in their inability to understand spoken language or written materials as they did before their problem. They exhibit a great deal of difficulty in word finding. Their speech may sound fluent until the moment of searching for words. A fifty-five-year-old attorney with semantic aphasia told us about his former practice: "The, uh-h-h, trials for the defendants were never done in the uh-uh, in the uh-h. Well, we had their trials in the uh, in the Superior Court." Patients usually know what they want to say but have trouble finding the words. If someone else provides a choice of words, the patient can select the correct one. The patient can repeat a word model spoken by someone else.

4. Wernicke's or Jargon Aphasia. This represents the classical Wernicke's aphasia, with the patient exhibiting moderate-to-severe problems in auditory comprehension and with a fluent speech pattern that sounds like jargon. Such patients often write the same way they sound; such jargon writing is known as paragraphia. A recent jargon-aphasic patient, a sixty-six-year-old retired airline pilot, provided this history: "There costumed gressed with American Airlines for the gressed for over thirty years ina gressed correction of stresses and gressed langings from New York to Los Mengress." This was a typical utterance, given quickly, with good prosodic flow and no apparent awareness by the patient that he was speaking this way.

5. Conduction Aphasia. Clinically, we do not see very many conduction aphasic patients. When we do, they make a lasting impression. Such patients often demonstrate near-normal comprehension. As they start to speak, they have trouble saying a specific word. Because of difficulties repeating, they have a lot of difficulty correcting a faulty utterance despite the modeling of the correct word by members of the family or the clinician. An eighty-year-old retired physician used to have high-level conversations with this writer about medicine. This is one of our recorded conversations:

BOONE: What about therapy for arthritis?
PATIENT: About arthritis? Well, we try to keep the patient as mobile as we can. Sometimes we put them on stech, no, I want to say steshals, no—
BOONE: You put them on steroids?
PATIENT: Yes, we put them on stehoids; no, that's not it. We put them on an antiinflammatory thing. It's steroids, that's what it is.
BOONE: What is it?
PATIENT: Well, they might profit from steshaloids.

One can well imagine the frustration experienced by such a patient, who attempts to articulate what he knows and is unable to make self-corrections.

6. Global Aphasia. Patients with global aphasia have a profound problem understanding and speaking. Reading and writing functions are also completely lacking. While such patients may be oriented to time and place, their perseverative, meaningless speech makes most communication impossible. A fifty-eight-year-old woman with global aphasia, a university professor before her stroke, tried to communicate by saying, "Fudafudaka. Fuda. Fuda, fuda, fuda, fudakataka." She appeared totally unaware of her own bizarre responses and, fortunately, of the enormity of her problem.

Other Problems Associated with Aphasia

Most aphasic patients have had damage to the left cerebral hemisphere from such causes as a stroke, trauma to the head, and occasional cerebral diseases (such as a brain tumor). The same lesion that causes the aphasia can produce a number of other symptoms. Let us consider separately some of the more common ones.

Hemiplegia. A left-sided cerebral lesion may commonly produce a right hemiplegia (paralysis) or a right hemiparesis (weakness). A lesion in the left cerebral motor cortex or its descending tracts can affect the extremities on the opposite side (motor-tract fibers cross over to the other side in the medulla of the brainstem). This is why a lesion in the left hemisphere affects the arm and leg on the right side of the body. Most aphasics, particularly those with expressive-language problems related to frontal-lobe damage, experience motor involvement on the right side. Through the cooperative efforts of physical and occupational therapy, the hemiplegic patient can usually learn to ambulate, be independent in self-care activities, and often can return to work.

Hemianopsia. A left-hemisphere lesion will sometimes cause a right-visual-field defect, called right hemianopsia. The patient is unable to see in the right visual field.

The optic impulses from the left half of each eye go to the left hemisphere, and those from the right half of each eye go to the right hemisphere. The curvature of the eyeball and its lense is such that the left half of each retina picks up what we see on the right side. A television screen for an adult aphasic with right hemianopsia might look very much like the drawing in Figure 9-2. What is in the right side of the picture is missing. It is relatively easy for most patients with hemianopsia to develop skills that compensate for their field defect, primarily by moving the head from side to side in order to view the lateral extremes of a visual presentation.

Intellectual Deficits. That part of intelligence that has a verbal component may be reduced after a brain injury that produces aphasia. We cannot get a true look at the patient's intelligence if we use a verbal intelligence test. Therefore, aphasic patients are best evaluated by using the performance section of such an intelligence test as the *Wechsler Adult Intelligence Scale* (WAIS) (Wechsler, 1980) or the *Coloured Progressive Matrices* (Raven, 1962). These performance tests, which correlate very well in normal subjects with the full administration of the WAIS, by lacking verbal instruction and not requiring verbal response, do not penalize the aphasic patient, who must struggle with trying to understand what is said and cannot respond with verbal facility. While many aphasic patients may show a slight intellectual deficit related to their left-sided cerebral lesion, they appear as a group to be far better off intellectually than their poor language performance might indicate. In fact, aphasic patients with left-hemisphere damage seem to perform better intellectually than those with right-hemisphere damage who do not have aphasia. We shall talk later in this chapter about patients with right-hemisphere damage.

Seizures. The majority of aphasic patients neither have nor develop epilepsy. Those who do usually experienced some kind of traumatic injury. Petit mal seizures (they produce only temporary spasms or loss of attentiveness) and grand mal seizures

FIGURE 9-2 The patient with a right hemianopsia (right-field defect) when looking straight ahead cannot detect images in the right field.

(which produce major muscle contractions and often a loss of consciousness) are usually seen only in patients who have had cortical damage caused by an external injury to the brain. Modern medications are so effective today in the control of seizures that patients suffering from them are not seen very often in speech and language clinics.

Dysarthria. The typical aphasic patient does not have a significant problem with dysarthria. Dysarthria is a motor speech problem related to neuromuscular impairment of the muscles that affect respiration, phonation, resonance, articulation, and the rhythm or prosody of speech. Patients with bilateral cerebral lesions and/ or those with low lesions in the cerebrum or brainstem may experience profound dysarthrias. Because most aphasic patients have experienced a relatively high cerebral lesion, usually in the left hemisphere, the motor systems for normal speech are not too extensively involved. When aphasic patients experience dysarthria, it is usually a mild slurring of speech. We shall discuss dysarthria in far greater detail in Chapter 10.

Apraxia. Some patients with aphasia also experience an apraxia of some kind. Apraxia is the inability to execute a voluntary movement (such as not being able to blow on an unlit match) despite being able to demonstrate normal muscle function when executing an automatic motor act (such as blowing out a lit match as the flame is brought toward the mouth). Apraxia of speech is sometimes seen in aphasic patients (sometimes the same lesion that produces aphasia can produce apraxia). The author remembers a man with speech apraxia who could not repeat or read aloud the word *God*. In his frustration, he would say automatically, "Oh, for God's sake." There was no way he could say the word *God* as an isolated response. There are many other forms of apraxia, such as the inability to initiate gait (for example, some patients with Parkinsonism cannot walk through doorways) or to make isolated finger or hand movements on command. There is nothing wrong with the strength or innervation of the patient's muscles; rather, the patient has lost the ability to sequence muscle movements on a voluntary basis. The diagnosis of apraxia can only be made for the patient who demonstrates the dramatic contrast between volitional incompetence and normal motor behavior for automatic acts.

The Evaluation and Management of the New Aphasic

The patient who comes into the hospital with an acute stroke and aphasia is usually referred to the speech-language pathologist as soon as the physician judges the patient to be medically stable. In acute-care hospitals, it is not unusual for the speech-language pathologist to be asked to see the new patient within 72 hours of admission. How the patient appears to understand what is said and how the patient speaks will tell the clinician much about the type and severity of the aphasia.

Usually, during the first visit, speech-language pathologists begin by reviewing patients' charts to determine how well they are doing. Nurses' notes tell much about how patient and family are reacting to the situation. Physicians' and other specialists' reports will describe the patients' status from the time of admission to the time of the present examination. The first visit is relatively brief, and focuses on determining how well patients are functioning in terms of aural-oral language and how they and their families seem to be coping with the aphasia. The families are given a pamphlet to read about aphasia. During the follow-up visit, family members can ask questions about aphasia and the patients' possible recovery.

Most aphasics have some residual language skills. They can still understand some of what is said, some of them have some residual reading skills, a few can write several words, and the speech patterns will be determined primarily by the type of aphasia (nonfluent or fluent) they have. The reason for the speech evaluation is to identify the residual language skills, which is the first step in initiating the patient's rehabilitation program. During the acute phase of recovery, perhaps the first month to six weeks after the onset of the aphasia (Kertesz, 1979), it is important that the patient experience intensive language rehabilitation. There is a period of spontaneous recovery, which seems to last about six months. It would appear that the cause of spontaneous recovery is primarily physiological (brain circulation improves in response to medical control, there is less swelling of offended areas of the brain, and the like) (Davis, 1983). The spontaneous-recovery period is an excellent time to begin intensive therapy, focusing on the stimulation of all existing or residual language functions. The relatively rapid success experienced in the spontaneous period provides strong motivation for the patient. After six months, patient gains are probably directly related to therapy. As a prelude to therapy, however, it is necessary to evaluate thoroughly the patient's residual language skills. Since the focus of subsequent therapy will be on exploiting what the patient can already do (teaching the patient nothing new), speech and language evaluations are necessary for determining residual ("can do") language skills.

Several different diagnostic tests may be used for testing the adult with aphasia. A functional evaluation of the patient can sometimes be made by asking the individual to follow a few tasks presented by the clinician, rather than administering a full-scale evaluation. An example of such tasks would be to ask the patient to count from 1 to 20 or name some of the objects in the room. Simple baseline data taken by the perceptive clinician can often provide the opportunity to set up a training therapy session, starting where the patient's residual skills allow him or her to function. The advantage of administering simple evaluation tasks, rather than full-scale standardized tests, in the beginning sessions with the patient is that the tasks take less time and can be altered or stopped before the patient experiences too much failure. Keeping the patient motivated in the early testing situations is a challenge to the most experienced clinician.

At the time of the first testing, it is wise to inform the patient what you are doing. Years ago, I visited a new aphasic patient, and, after introducing myself (he was confused enough when I told him my name was Daniel Boone), I forgot to tell him what we might be doing. Thinking he might have an apraxia or some other problem that would interfere with his ability to repeat after me, I asked him, without any warning or advance explanation, to say the word *apple*. He replied very quickly, "What is this fixation or penchant you have for apple? It doesn't seem to me to have the slightest relevance to my problems.'' I have never forgotten the lesson this man taught me; that is, always preface your testing with a brief introduction, explaining who you are and what you are planning to do.

Language Tests. *Functional Communication Profile* (FCP) (Sarno, 1975). There are 45 communicative behaviors rated on the FCP, divided into five categories: understanding (auditory), reading, speaking, movement (including gestures), and other (writing and arithmetic). The great advantage of this scale is that it does not require direct administration to the patient. Rather, the examiner completes a rating scale by observing the patient in normal, day-to-day activities or questioning family members about how the patient functions in the various activities measured on the scale. We have used the FCP with chronic aphasic patients, some of whom have had aphasia for over eight years. We observe how the patient functions. Any change in the scale, either a decrement or an improvement, can offer feedback as to how the patient is doing.

Communicative Abilities in Daily Living (CADL) (Holland, 1980). Although the CADL is administered directly to the patient, like the FCP, it provides a measure of the patient's functional abilities. The CADL looks at natural language activities with a testing style that approximates normal communication. Real-life situations are developed, such as visiting the doctor in the office or making a stop at the gas station. Besides looking at specific language functions (listening, speaking, reading, writing), the advantage of the CADL is its emphasis on pragmatics of language. How does the patient play roles? What kind of social conventions are used? Does the patient exhibit humor and react to absurdity? Since both the FCP and CADL offer measures that look at functional use of language, it is interesting to see how the two measures compare. Holland reports in the manual of the CADL (1980) that her CADL correlates at a 0.87 level with the full administration of the FCP. Because the FCP does not involve the patient in testing and because the CADL proves to be enjoyable to give (both for patient and examiner), we often use both instruments as part of our evaluation of the adult aphasic patient.

Boston Diagnostic Aphasia Examination (BDAE) (Goodglass and Kaplan, 1972). The BDAE is a complete aphasia-evaluation text that looks at one's ability to speak, conversational and expository language, auditory comprehension, reading, and writing. The BDAE differs from other aphasia tests in that it was designed not only to isolate the type of aphasia, but it also can lead the clinician to identify the site of the brain damage. Perhaps the biggest problem with the BDAE is that it takes from two to three hours to administer to the typical patient. Figure 9-3 shows a severity rating and profile of speech characteristics taken from the BDAE that we find very useful in the clinic. The BDAE is the only standardized aphasia examination that allows the examiner to describe how the patient speaks, as shown in Figure 9-3, which was completed for a fluent Wernicke's-type aphasic.

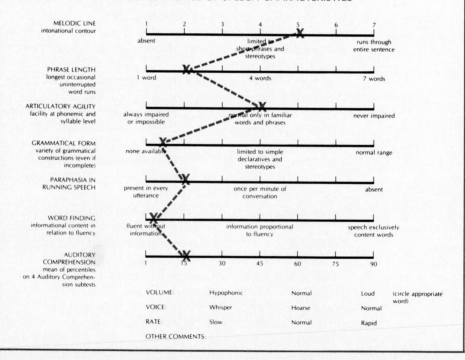

Patient's Name _____ Date of rating _____

Rated by _____

APHASIA SEVERITY RATING SCALE

0. No usable speech or auditory comprehension.

1. All communication is through fragmentary expression; great need for inference, questioning, and guessing by the listener. The range of information that can be exchanged is limited, and the listener carries the burden of communication.

2. Conversation about familiar subjects is possible with help from the listener. There are frequent failures to convey the idea, but patient shares the burden of communication with the examiner.

3. The patient can discuss <u>almost all everyday problems</u> with little or no assistance. Reduction of speech and/or comprehension, however, makes conversation about certain material difficult or impossible.

4. Some obvious loss of fluency in speech or facility of comprehension, without significant limitation on ideas expressed or form of expression.

5. Minimal discernible speech handicaps; patient may have subjective difficulties that are not apparent to listener.

RATING SCALE PROFILE OF SPEECH CHARACTERISTICS

MELODIC LINE
intonational contour

1   2   3   4   5   6   7

absent   limited to short phrases and stereotypes   runs through entire sentence

PHRASE LENGTH
longest occasional
uninterrupted
word runs

1 word   4 words   7 words

ARTICULATORY AGILITY
facility at phonemic and
syllable level

always impaired or impossible   normal only in familiar words and phrases   never impaired

GRAMMATICAL FORM
variety of grammatical
constructions (even if
incomplete)

none available   limited to simple declaratives and stereotypes   normal range

PARAPHASIA IN
RUNNING SPEECH

present in every utterance   once per minute of conversation   absent

WORD FINDING
informational content in
relation to fluency

fluent without information   information proportional to fluency   speech exclusively content words

AUDITORY
COMPREHENSION
mean of percentiles
on 4 Auditory Comprehen-
sion subtests

1   15   30   45   60   75   90

VOLUME:	Hypophonic	Normal	Loud	(circle appropriate word)
VOICE:	Whisper	Hoarse	Normal	
RATE:	Slow	Normal	Rapid	

OTHER COMMENTS:

FIGURE 9–3 A rating scale of severity and speech characteristics of a jargon or Wernicke's aphasic patient. Taken from the *Boston Diagnostic Aphasia Examination (Goodglass and Kaplan, 1972).*

The auditory-comprehension section of the BDAE has been found to be very helpful in determining how well the patient understands what is said.

Minnesota Test for Differential Diagnosis of Aphasia (MTDDA) (Schuell, 1965). The excellent and thorough auditory disturbances section of the MTDDA helps the clinician to assess in some depth how well the patient understands what is said. It takes an average of three hours to complete. The MTDDA has 537 separate scoring items, which are distributed among five sections: auditory disturbances, visual and reading disturbances, speech and language disturbances, visuomotor and writing disturbances, and numerical relations and arithmetic processes. Although Schuell believed that there was an underlying unidimensional language deficit in all aphasic patients, she differentiated individual performance and placed the patient into one of seven categories (Schuell, 1974). Prognosis was established according to the particular category of the patient. *Minnesota* was the first comprehensive test for adult aphasia, and after over 30 years of usage, it is still respected and often used.

Porch Index of Communicative Ability (PICA) (Porch, 1967; 1981). The PICA presents an innovative multidimensional scoring system that permits 16 gradations of scoring for each of the 180 responses on the test. That is, instead of judging whether the patient's response to a stimulus item was correct or incorrect, the examiner categorizes each response by assigning it a score ranging from 1 (no response) to 16 (normal, complex). It takes between one and two hours to administer the 18 subtests of the PICA, which is quicker than either the BDAE or the MTDDA. The multidimensional scoring system gives the PICA a sensitivity for detecting change in patient performance over time; if performance does change (improves or deteriorates), PICA scoring profiles will show it. Porch (1981) has explained how patient scores can be used for both establishing prognosis and planning actual treatment steps.

Western Aphasia Battery (WAB) (Kertesz, 1982). The newest of the aphasia tests is the WAB. It offers an Aphasia Quotient (AQ), which can be used to make a prognosis and classify the patient; the AQ is determined by administering a number of talking and listening items to the patient. The AQ section of the test can be completed in about an hour. Additional data about the patient can be gathered by giving additional subtests, including those of reading and writing and the *Coloured Progressive Matrices* (Raven, 1962), a test of performance intelligence; these additional tests yield a Performance Quotient (PQ). A composite score, the Cortical Quotient (CQ), can be established by scoring all the subtests. The various kinds of aphasia can be derived from the patient's AQ score, while the total CQ is found to help differentiate a patient with aphasia from one with dementia (a topic we will discuss toward the end of this chapter).

Other Tests for Aphasic Patients. The Token Test (DeRenzi and Vignolo, 1962) and *The Revised Token Test* (McNeil and Prescott, 1978). Recognizing that an auditory-comprehension problem is common in aphasic patients, the *Token Test* was created to measure its extent. Patients listen to a series of spoken commands that require them to manipulate tokens. A much more sophisticated version of the test is the *Revised Token Test,* whose administration and scoring techniques are similar to those used on the PICA (a similar 16-point multidimensional scoring system is used). We often use one of these to supplement our testing of the patient's auditory comprehension.

Reading Comprehension Battery for Aphasia (RCBA) (LaPointe and Horner, 1979). This includes ten subtests that begin at the single-word level and progress up through paragraphs. It enables the aphasic patient's reading ability to be tested by requiring only simple, pointing responses.

Audiometric Testing. Any evaluation of an aphasic patient requires an audiometric testing of his or her hearing. In general, aphasic patients demonstrate the same hearing sensitivity as their age peers without aphasia. However, if, as we have seen in earlier chapters, hearing sensitivity begins to decline in the middle forties, the older aphasic age group (the majority of strokes occur after age sixty-five) ought to have a hearing test. Only by audiometric testing can the clinician sort out what is a central auditory problem related to aphasia and what may be an intelligibility problem related to beginning or advanced presbycusis.

Intelligence Testing. The aphasic patient usually has a focal cerebral lesion, as opposed to the more diffuse-type lesions seen in patients with senile dementia. The aphasic patient experiences a disproportionate loss of verbal ability, as compared to overall cognitive functioning. In contrast, the patient with diffuse brain damage experiences a loss of total intellectual functioning. The aphasic patient functions relatively well on performance intelligence tests; these are standardized to sample one's cognitive skills without using verbal instructions (which would penalize the aphasic with auditory-comprehension deficits) or requiring verbal response (obviously a deficient area for the aphasic patient). Among the more commonly used performance intelligence tests with aphasics are the performance section of the *Wechsler Adult Intelligence Scale* (Wechsler, 1980), the *Coloured Progressive Matrices* (Raven, 1962), and Koh's Blocks from the *Arthur Intelligence Scale* (Arthur, 1968).

The use of a nonverbal intelligence test can provide much useful information about the patient, particularly in establishing prognosis and long-range vocational goals. For example, a twenty-two-year-old man was in an automobile accident that left him with a severe left-hemisphere lesion with a resulting right hemiplegia, right hemianopsia, and a moderately severe nonfluent aphasia. On the performance section of the *Wechsler Adult Intelligence Scale,* he scored an IQ of 126. On the verbal section of the same test, he was so involved verbally (because of his aphasia) that he could not be tested. He was subsequently placed in a vocational-rehabilitation program that trained him to be a computer specialist. One year later, he was working as a computer technician despite a profound and persisting expressive aphasia. Not until he was tested and found to have superior intellectual skills on performance measures was he thought to have any vocational potential.

The Rehabilitation of the Adult Aphasic

It should be remembered that successful rehabilitation of the aphasic is helped by developing and encouraging communication. The linguistic dimension is but one part of communication. The recovery process requires the efforts of physicians, physical and occupational therapists, nurses, psychologists, and speech-language pathologists—all working with the patient and patient's family. While the speech-language pathologist plays a vital role on the team, everyone must work together to optimize recovery from aphasia. The patient will usually experience some lessening of physical problems within six months of onset. For example, directed by the physician, the physical and occupational therapists work to keep the paralyzed limb as functional as possible by actively assisting the patient to move the involved limb or do stretching exercises to prevent contractures. Early in the rehabilitation, the focus is on helping the patient learn to use the uninvolved extremities for self-care; much emphasis in therapy, therefore, is put on functionally using the good arm and leg in self-care activities (bathing, dressing, feeding).

Both the patient and family usually profit from counseling and the psychological support provided by the psychologist or medical social worker. Survival of the family unit as it was before the CVA or accident is very important. Not long ago, an Arizona rancher made a mockery of his wife's condition after a stroke by saying, "She's got it in her head to keep this gimp going around. I told her to get the hell out of her wheelchair and take up where she left us. She'd either do that or by God, we weren't going to let her come home." Thinking that he was offering her encouragement, the poor woman had become so depressed over her continuing hemiplegia and aphasia that our rehabilitation focus was in working with the patient's husband and two young-adult children to create a home atmosphere in which her chronic condition would be accepted. (A follow-up visit to the patient's ranch indicated success, finding a caring home and apparent acceptance by patient and family of her persistent problem of right-sided weakness and aphasia.)

The primary goal in aphasia rehabilitation is to improve aural-oral language. The patient's continuing problems of auditory verbal comprehension and talking are the two that seem to bother patients and family members the most. The speech-language pathologist may use reading, writing, and mathematics activities in the speech-therapy sessions, but often in conjunction with spoken-language practice. In general, we use the language modalities that seem to work the best. We might expand upon identified residual skills and stay away from deficient areas. For example, for the man who no longer can name objects but can repeat words after someone else, we would avoid naming practice and instead encourage the patient to repeat the names after us. It would be our hope that the repetition drill would allow the patient to experience verbal fluency, perhaps in time minimizing his difficulty in naming.

Aphasia Therapy. What works in therapy for one patient may not work well with another. Certain approaches may be used more by some speech clinicians than others. Let us discuss some approaches to aphasia therapy, illustrating each by its application with particular patients.

Group therapy. Some language therapy can take place in small treatment groups. However, the real benefit of aphasia group therapy is in maintaining communication skills and providing the patient with some support and understanding. Rather than conduct didactic-type groups (for the teaching of a skill), I have found that social groups that can function as spontaneously as possible meet the needs of aphasic patients who have chronic, lifelong aphasia. Aphasia groups at the University of Arizona very much resemble the format of Johnny Carson's "Tonight" show. The group leader and an assistant will develop a theme for the group and encourage as much interaction among the patients as possible; in a successful group, three or four separate conversations may be going on at the same time. Communication is encouraged in the group, including the use of all the expressive language one might have and supplementing that with affective voicing, laughter, and tears. While the patients are in the group, spouses meet with a clinician in another room (or view the session through an observation room window while the clinician asks questions, comments, or listens). From the clinician's perspective, group therapy is extremely difficult to conduct. The clinician must know the language levels (and frustrations) of each patient, keep the general backgrounds in mind, and appear spontaneous and reactive to whatever may occur without warning in the group.

Family group. A family support group appears to be an excellent way of helping its members to cope with the problems that begin after a family member has aphasia. In the group, the spouses of the patients share insights and support one another. A new patient in a group appeared to have a great sense of humor, provoking amusing situations with his few comments and laughing heartily when something funny occurred. In the family group, his wife described a totally different person at home. He was hypercritical of everything she tried to do, vented much anger at her and their youngest son, who was still living at home, and showed none of the quick humor he displayed in the aphasia group. Other spouses in the family group were quick to point out that the public person was often markedly different from the private one. Where he was comfortable and where loved ones were accepting, it was possible for the patient to demonstrate his frustration and anger over his situation. As he began to recover and experienced some success working part time, his anger at home was reported to have lessened. How one family has coped with a particular problem often serves as a group model for how other families may or may not handle the same kind of situation.

In addition to the family group, some family members profit greatly from individual counseling, whether from a psychologist, a social worker, or the speech-

FIGURE 9–4   A woman with aphasia works with the speech-language pathologist. Used with permission of University of Arizona, Tucson.

language pathologist. All 21 spouses in a study looking at the need for family counseling for spouses of aphasic patients (Linebaugh and Young-Charles, 1978) felt that such counseling was needed and of benefit to them. Throughout the United States, there are a number of support groups for aphasic patients and their spouses called "Stroke Clubs," sponsored by the American Heart Association. One such club, in Tucson, Arizona, has over 60 active members (patients and spouses) attending its weekly meetings. Asking one wife who never misses a meeting why they come every week, she answered, as most of the spouses would, "This is one place we can go where people know what our troubles are. We don't have to say anything, really; they just accept us."

Individual direct therapy. Most individual therapy provided by the speech-language pathologist is of the stimulus-response type (see Figure 9–4). After a stimulus (auditory or visual) is presented, the patient is usually required to make some kind of response. Many times, the experienced clinician presents multiple stimuli to the patient, who listens and reads simultaneously, before requiring a response of some kind. The nonfluent aphasic patient who generally has good receptive-language skills will often spend most of the therapy time practicing saying things. The fluent patient who may have moderate-to-severe receptive-input problems will require much more auditory-comprehension and reading practice. In most direct individual therapy, the patient's correct responses do not receive positive reinforcement by the clinician on any kind of fixed basis. The clinician uses such verbal reinforcers as "good" or "okay" as needed, to keep the patient motivated and working. In effective therapy, however, we have found that the clinician should present material that the patient is able to respond to with about 80 percent accuracy (Boone and Prescott, 1972).

A programmed approach to therapy. In a programmed approach, the patient is exposed to a series of sequenced events that have been preplanned by the clinician. A correct response is reinforced, and the patient moves on to the next stimulus. One advantage of a programmed approach is that the patient can often work alone, not requiring the active participation of the speech-language pathologist. Many software programs have been developed for aphasic patients, in which the patient sits before a computer and responds directly to the commands programmed into it. A severe syntactic-type aphasic was observed working on a program that was designed to improve syntax. The program worked like this:

COMPUTER: Let's work to say THE in front of different words. We see the word
　　　　　CUP and its picture. We want to say THE CUP. What do we want to say?
　　　　　a. CUP
　　　　　b. THE CUP
PATIENT: a.
COMPUTER: No, you are wrong. CUP is wrong. We want b. THE CUP.

We can quickly see how such a simple program might be a real challenge to the patient with a moderate-to-severe aphasia. It is also apparent that such programs might be a real insult to other patients. One would only have to role-play, changing places with a patient, to appreciate the utter devastation one would experience if one's language function were reduced to such a basic level.

There are other kinds of programmed approaches besides computer software. The typical sequenced workbook, such as the one developed by Keith (1977) *Speech and Language Rehabilitation: A Workbook for the Neurologically Impaired* or Brubaker's (1978) *Workbook for Aphasia,* present patient self-practice materials in a sequenced manner. The *Say the Word* program developed by Boone and Campbell (1985) presents a sequenced auditory program on a series of audio cassettes. The patient's task on the program is to listen to what is said and repeat it. The order of the stimuli is preprogrammed, providing each word unit in both the spoken and written form.

Promoting aphasics communication effectiveness, PACE. The focus of the PACE program (Davis and Wilcox, 1981) is to encourage the patient to communicate by whatever means. A natural conversational situation is set up, so that both the clinician and the patient are equal senders and receivers of the message. They simply take turns sending the clues of a hidden message. The stimulus cards depicting situations and actions are kept face down, while the sender attempts to portray what is on the card without actually naming the stimulus picture. The sender may use speech, gesture, writing, noises, or pantomime, any modality desired, to get the message across. Feedback is provided by the speech-language pathologist as the receiver, which gives the patient direct feedback relative to his or her success in communication. PACE has proven to be a most enjoyable and useful therapy method.

Melodic intonation therapy. Melodic Intonation Therapy (Sparks and Holland, 1976) is a programmed approach that presents intoned phrases and sentences for the patient to say. It is particularly effective for the patient who has a severe expressive problem, usually a nonfluent type of aphasia. The patient is asked to listen and watch the clinician as a phrase such as "Good morning" is said with exaggerated stress regarding frequency, loudness, and duration. In many ways, the "Good morning" sounds as if it were sung. The patient then produces the phrase in unison with the clinician. Eventually, the patient can produce the phrase alone. It promotes verbal fluency and prosody perhaps better than any other approach the author has used in therapy. Its developers present specific steps in their program, requiring that the patient experience success at each step before moving on to more advanced ones.

Recovery from Aphasia. Most aphasic patients show some recovery of language function. During spontaneous recovery, lost language functions begin to return, whether or not the patient has had therapy (Culton, 1969; Kertesz, 1979). It has been our experience, however, that as soon as the patient can participate, individual and group therapy should begin. The patient's progress can be dramatic at this time, providing an opportunity to use maximally all language functions as they return. Many severely damaged aphasic patients remain functionally more involved than their physical problem may indicate. In 1954, a rehabilitation hospital was opened in Cleveland, and about 200 people were inherited in the beginning who had been custodial patients in the same facility for between 5 and 25 years. Those with communication problems were severely involved. After assessing these patients and having volunteers converse with them every day, a number of them began to function at much higher verbal levels than they had initially. The functional aspect of their problem, the "cerebral cobwebs from years of disuse" got swept away with some activity. They could (and did) function much better with a little bit of human contact and encouragement.

Our philosophy, then, in aphasia rehabilitation is to push patients maximally, so that all of their abilities will be used as these functions are returning. The efficacy question (Is therapy for aphasia beneficial?) was asked by Darley in 1972. Many studies have attempted to answer that question, using single-subject design (Rosenbek and others, 1979) and group comparisons (Wertz and others, 1981). In general, these two studies and several others looking at treatment have found that therapy has positive effects. On various comparison tests, such as the PICA or the *Boston,* experimental subjects (patients receiving therapy) posted better linguistic improvement in subsequent testing than control subjects. Other benefits from the speech-language pathologist's treatment are harder to quantify but are commonly reported: the patient and family accept the limitations imposed by the disability, and the patient is communicating maximally (gesture, single words, whatever) to get the message across and is using language modalities (listening, speaking, reading, writing) at the highest functional level.

Recovery from aphasia begins as soon as the patient is medically stable. We teach the patient nothing new. Rather, we facilitate the return of previously established language functions at as high a level as possible by family counseling, group and individual speech-language therapy, and by providing an atmosphere of hope.

THE LANGUAGE DEFICITS OF PATIENTS WITH RIGHT-HEMISPHERE DAMAGE

While the overwhelming number of patients with aphasia have had damage to the left cerebral hemisphere, patients with right-hemisphere damage may also demonstrate language deficits. Their deficits, however, are quite different from aphasia. Right-hemisphere-damaged patients often show severe motor-spatial problems, with occasional severe cognitive deficits. Their language problems do not show the phonologic or syntactic deficits of aphasia but rather semantic and pragmatic ones related to their problems in cognition. For example, the typical right-hemisphere-damaged patient may display real difficulty performing on the visual-spatial tests of the *Wechsler Adult Intelligence Scale* (Wechsler, 1980), such as block design, object assembly, and picture arrangement.

When such patients are given verbal instructions to manipulate objects in space, their confusions in performance cause them to look as if they did not understand the commands. For example, a twenty-two-year-old man with closed-head trauma (on the right side) was given this instruction: "Take the big key and put it on the bottom of the box." He took the three keys that were on the table and attempted to stack them on top of one another in the bottom of the box. Asked what he was doing, he replied, "Well, the keys are bigger than each other and the little one isn't going to fit by itself." Evaluating both his receptive-input performance and his spoken language, we might conclude (incorrectly) that he had a fluent aphasia. In his case, this twisted motor response was not very different from his verbal response. His basic problem was the motor-spatial confusion that is often seen in patients with right-hemisphere disease.

Right-hemisphere-damaged patients display problems in recognizing symbols used in various mathematical computations, such as addition or subtraction signs. The international traffic signs that show spatial direction by using figures in various symbolic configurations (such as a left-turn arrow with a diagonal line through it, which means, in effect, "no left turn"). It is our clinical experience that patients with right-hemisphere lesions display real confusions in driving, reacting incorrectly to traffic signs with various drawings on them that stand for some kind of spatial event. The spatial limitations of these patients are even worse when the patient also has left hemianopsia. Typically, patients suffering from right-hemisphere disease with left hemianopsia deny their left-visual-field defect and react to it by simply not seeing what is in the extreme left field. They also have no awareness of the problem, as shown in Figure 9–2. The field defect, combined with a central problem of spatial-motor dysfunction, produces some very strange and incorrect patient responses.

When the patient is given verbal directions that require central cognitive function to answer (such as "The smaller blue car is newer than the big one. Which car is older?"), the patient will display real problems in answering. When the words have spatial cognitive referents, they may lack meaning for the patient (Caramazza and others, 1976). Wapner, Hamby, and Gardner (1981) have found that right-hemisphere patients have difficulty following subtle shifts in language and as a group have great difficulty understanding the punch line of a joke. As a group, they show a deficit in their reactions to humor.

Only recently has the speech-language pathologist began to play a rehabilitative role in helping the patient with right-hemisphere disease to respond more appropriately. The patient with closed-head trauma and right-hemisphere damage is beginning to be seen more regularly in speech-language clinics. A growing number of evaluation batteries have been developed for assessing the motor-spatial deficits of these patients. Our therapy attempts are reserved for helping patients structure the spatial world with cueing, and developing an order to things in the everyday environment. Reading aloud and describing story pictures (skills that the intact left hemisphere of the patient should be able to do) often can help the patient develop some verbal success.

THE LANGUAGE PROBLEMS OF SENILE DEMENTIA

The normal older person speaks and uses language very well. Deterioration (related to disease) of both hearing and vision in an aged person may obviously cause problems in the understanding of the spoken and printed word. These decrements in acuity do not explain totally the comprehension deficits that are sometimes part of normal aging. There may be some slowing in response time, some difficulty switching quickly to a new stimulus, as well as a problem of short-term memory. However, the normal aged person is a good talker, often speaking with an elaborateness that younger people do not use, sounding almost as if one is "playing with words." Lexicon and vocabulary (after a lifetime of usage) are probably at their peak of development (Obler and Albert, 1981). It may well be that the elaborate responses of older persons are in part a compensation for the slight decrement in comprehension they may be experiencing. It might be concluded that older people speak better and have a better vocabulary than younger people, with slightly poorer comprehension and slower responses.

The great majority of older people demonstrate normal language. When we say that someone is suffering from "senility," we are talking about the disease state of dementia. Senile dementia is a disease, and is not a part of normal aging. About 5 percent of those sixty-five or older have senile dementia. The incidence grows dramatically with increasing age; 10 percent of the population over seventy has it, 15 percent over seventy-five, at which time the incidence seems to level out. What causes senile dementia?

Types of Dementia

Although we know that different types of dementia exist, we do not necessarily know their cause or how to prevent them. When dementia begins in an aged person, it is usually one of three types: Alzheimer's, multi-infarct dementia, or subcortical dementia.

Alzheimer's Disease. The symptoms of this disease show up slowly, with some problems of memory and confusion. Patients often exhibit good memory for remote events but begin to show deficits of immediate and short-term memory. In the early stages of the disease, the patient's language appears quite normal, with normal phonology and syntax. Subtle language changes (which we will describe) begin to appear. The diagnosis of Alzheimer's disease is made from the patient's behavior specific to problems of time-and-place orientation, distractability, mood changes, memory deficits, and overall intellectual deterioration. There are various medical tests that the physician can use to diagnose Alzheimer's disease, but the diagnosis must always be presumptive. The causes of Alzheimer's are a series of cortical plaques, nerve tangles, and vacuoles, which can only be confirmed by an autopsy. The diagnosis is perhaps best made by administering psychological tests and some difficult language tests (Bayles and Boone, 1982). About 70 percent of all older patients with dementia have the Alzheimer's type. The speech-language pathologist can often play an active role in helping to diagnose Alzheimer's disease by administering speech-language tests.

Multi-infarct Dementia. About 20 percent of the patients with senile dementia have the multi-infarct type, experiencing many tiny strokes throughout the cortex. The patient shows the same problems of confusion and forgetfulness that we see in the Alzheimer's type. Regional cerebral blood flow, which was described earlier in talking about aphasia, has been found helpful in identifying patients with multi-infarct dementia, finding diffuse areas of the brain that appear to receive no blood after the patient has had many small strokes. The role of the speech-language pathologist is to evaluate the patient's speech and language and provide counseling for the family.

Subcortical Dementia. About 10 percent of the patients with senile dementia have progressive subcortical lesions related to such degenerative diseases as Huntington's chorea or Parkinson's disease. Along with the changes of mentation seen in the other types of dementia, these subcortical patients usually have some motor disturbance in gait, arm movements, or speech (causing dysarthria). They may demonstrate an altered rate of speech, weak vocal intensity, and problems in pitch and speech articulation. In addition to the dysarthria, on language testing they will show some severe deficits in semantic and pragmatic language functions (Bayles and Boone, 1982). The speech-language pathologist aids not only in the diagnosis of subcortical dementia but may play a helpful role in diminishing some of the effects of the dysarthria. As with the other types of dementia, counseling the patient and family has also been found to be helpful.

Language Problems

Measures of intelligence, such as the block design and similarities subtests from the WAIS, have been found to be useful in the early identification of dementia. Other psychological tests, such as the Mental Status Questionnaire (Goldfarb, 1975) and forward-backward digit span, have been found useful in documenting the early mental changes of the patient. In recent years, language tests have been found helpful in identifying these early mental changes. Because the dementia patient may speak with normal phonology and syntax, it has often been assumed that the dementia patient has no linguistic deficits. They can be seen, however, when the patient is asked to perform semantic and pragmatic tasks. This description of a retired secretary illustrates a mild-to-moderate dementia:

> Alice, age seventy-three, lived with her widowed sister, who was five years younger. In the past year, the sister had noticed some real mental changes in Alice, such as forgetting where she was when they went out, forgetting appointments, and continually wearing her white dress gloves inside and outside the home. When asked why she always wore the gloves, Alice replied (with clear speech and normal syntax), "I'm not showing my hands to the winds anymore, and we never know who might be dropping in." Thinking that she might be sensitive to her aging spots, her sister did not pursue the question. Alice's behavior further deteriorated when she began taking down the curtains or stripping the beds when her sister was not there to stop her.
>
> She was subsequently evaluated at the University of Arizona, and Alice was found to demonstrate some real language confusions. On tests of disambiguation, she was asked to think of several meanings for each of the sentences she was given by the examiner. Here are a few examples of the statements and her replies:

EXAMINER: Tell me what this sentence could mean. "The shooting of the police was awful."

ALICE: Well, the police are always shooting when they have to do the shooting. This time, they shot again.

EXAMINER: Can you think of another meaning of the sentence?

ALICE (pointing her gloved hand as if it were a gun): They are shooting again if they have to.

EXAMINER: Okay, let's try another one. See if you can find two meanings to what I am going to say. Listen now. "Visiting relatives can be a nuisance."

ALICE: Well, the relatives are a nuisance when they are the only people in the world that one can never forget. I never had an aunt or an uncle that was a problem.

CLINICIAN: Okay, that's one meaning. Can you think of another one for "Visiting relatives can be a nuisance"?

ALICE: Well, like I said, they are never a nuisance if the relatives are the relatives. The world is easy enough for the ones who make it easy for anyone like a relative. If that's what you wanted, you'd have to ask my sister about it.

Alice used good grammar. Her speech was free of dysarthria or any kind of word substitution. The form of her language was good, but it lacked meaning and specificity. She made many other errors on the language battery and had much difficulty on performance intelligence tests, such as the Raven and the block design. She was diagnosed as having beginning dementia, probably of the Alzheimer's type. Alice was followed over time, and her dementia worsened, to the point where her sister was no longer able to keep her at home. Some five years after the onset of her confusion, she was still in a nursing home.

Interestingly enough, dementia patients can make phonologic and syntactic corrections in the speech of others when asked to do so. If we asked a patient with moderate-to-severe dementia to repeat what we said (and we had built into it an intentional error) such as: "The two boys was taking a bath," we would very likely get back: "The two boys were taking a bath." If we modeled: "We goes to shoot the wabbit," we very likely would hear the patient making the correct response: "We went to shoot the rabbit." Grammatical and phonological capabilities appear to be deeply rooted, and even after the ravages of dementia, the patient seems to maintain grammatic and phonologic competence (Avakian, 1973; Bayles, 1979). As the senile dementia progresses, grammar and phonology remain surprisingly intact.

Management of the Dementia Patient

Most forms of senile dementia are not medically reversible. However, the hope is that the patient's confusions may be related to a condition that can be treated, and for this reason, early identification of the dementia is essential. It would appear, from early investigations of Obler and Albert (1981) and Bayles and Boone (1982), that how the patient responds on speech and language tests will aid in the diagnosis of dementia specific to severity and type. The speech-language pathologist and audiologist should play an important role in working up the patient who is beginning to show early signs of dementia.

Once the diagnosis is established, the speech-language pathologist can work directly with the patient and members of the family. Helping the patient structure his or her world by use of especially marked calendars, keeping diaries and notebooks, and developing schedules specific to time and place have all been found helpful. One patient brought in a diary, and the entries describe his love of gardening and his increasing confusion:

> May 28. I dug the trenches deeper around the roses and the water ought to hold in them better. I bought three trellises to hold the bloom. If we don't have any hot weather this year, we will have a good crop. I saw the doctor today and he confirmed I was going crazy.
>
> December 22. Laura for Christmas. The flower of ponsette is out. My mind is not for holidays.
>
> Febary 12. Cant work for rains. Never bloomed.

In the beginning stages of the disease, the patient can be encouraged to keep a detailed diary and schedule of events. The family is counseled to keep things as much the same as possible, help the patient organize time-and-place schedules, simplify verbal instructions, and expect (tragically) for the patient to become increasingly unaware of most activities. In their confusion, patients will sometimes attempt to argue with family members. The best advice we can give the family is to avoid such confrontations, changing the mood and the topic whenever possible.

The therapy and counseling provided by the speech-language pathologist has no effect on the physical progression of the disease. Rather, these services only help the patient and family to manage a difficult problem as easily as possible. In the advanced stages of the disease, it is usually necessary for the patient to be placed in a nursing-care facility. It has been our experience that when the condition deteriorates enough to warrant nursing-home placement, the patient is accepting and makes no protest.

REVIEW QUESTIONS

In adults, most language disorders are acquired after they have enjoyed years of normal language use. Such disorders are usually related to changes in the brain related to stroke or dementia. Let us consider some questions about language disorders in adults:

1. Why is aphasia more than a "disorder of talking"?

2. Why is aphasia in most persons the result of left-hemisphere disease?

3. What differences in receptive-language and expressive-language function do fluent and nonfluent aphasics show?

4. What are some of the other symptoms that aphasia patients may experience?

5. How does a functional communication profile for an aphasic patient differ from a standardized aphasia examination?

6. How can families of aphasic patients participate in the language-rehabilitation program?

7. What kind of language difficulties do right-hemisphere-damaged patients show?

8. How can we differentiate aphasia from senile dementia?

REFERENCES

Arthur, G. (1968). *A Point Scale on Performance Tests, A Manual*. New York: The Psychological Corporation.

Avakian, H. (1973). Isolation of the language area: neurolinguistic implications. *Dissertation Abstracts International, 34* (1-a): 296.

Bayles, K. A. (1979). "Communication Profile in the Geriatric Population" (Unpublished doctoral dissertation, University of Arizona).

Bayles, K. A., and Boone, D. R. (1982). The potential of language tasks for identifying senile dementia. *Journal of Speech and Hearing Disorders, 47:* 210–217.

Boone, D. R., and Campbell, M. (1985). *Say the Word*. Tucson: Communication Skill Builders.

Boone, D. R., and Prescott, T. E. (1972). Content and sequence analysis of speech and hearing therapy. *ASHA, 14:* 58–62.

Broca, P. (1960). Remarks on the seat of the faculty of articulate language, followed by an observation of aphemia, in *Some Papers on the Cerebral Cortex,* trans. G. von Bonin. Springfield, Ill.: Charles C. Thomas.

Brubaker, S. H. (1978). *Workbook for Aphasia: Exercises for the Redevelopment of Higher Level Language Functioning*. Detroit: Wayne State University Press.

Caramazza, A., Gordon, J., Zurif, E. B., and Deluca, D. (1976). Right-hemisphere damage and verbal problem solving behavior. *Brain and Language, 3:* 41–46.

Culton, G. L. (1969). Spontaneous recovery from aphasia. *Journal of Speech and Hearing Research, 12:* 825–832.

Darley, F. L. (1972). The efficacy of language rehabilitation in aphasia. *Journal of Speech and Hearing Disorders, 32:* 3–21.

Davis, G. A. (1983). *A Survey of Adult Aphasia*. Englewood Cliffs, N.J.: Prentice-Hall.

Davis, G. A., and Wilcox, M. J. (1981). Incorporating parameters of natural conversation in aphasia treatment, in *Language Intervention Strategies in Adult Aphasia,* ed. R. Chapey. Baltimore: Williams and Wilkins.

DeRenzi, E., and Vignolo, L. A. (1962). The Token Test: a sensitive test to detect receptive disturbances in aphasia. *Brain, 85:* 665–678.

Geschwind, N. (1979). Specializations of the human brain. *Scientific American, 241:* 180–199.

Goldfarb, A. I. (1975). Memory and aging, in *The Physiology and Pathology of Human Aging,* ed. R. Goldman and M. Rockstein. New York: Academic Press.

Goodglass, H., and Kaplan, E. (1972). *The Assessment of Aphasia and Related Disorders*. Philadelphia: Lea and Febinger.

Holland, A. L. (1980). *Communicative Abilities in Daily Living* (CADL). Baltimore: University Park Press.

Johns, D., and Darley, F. L. (1970). Phonemic variability in apraxia of speech. *Journal of Speech and Hearing Research, 13:* 556–583.

Keith, R. L. (1977). *Speech and Language Rehabilitation: A Workbook for the Neurologically Impaired*. Danville, Ill.: Interstate Printers and Publishers.

Kertesz, A. (1979). *Aphasia and Associated Disorders: Taxonomy, Localization, and Recovery*. New York: Grune and Stratton.

Kertesz, A. (1982). *Western Aphasia Battery*. New York: Grune and Stratton.

LaPointe, L. L., and Horner, J. (1979). *Reading Comprehension Battery for Aphasia*. Tigard, Ore.: C. C. Publications.

Lenneberg, E. (1967). *Biological Foundations of Language*. New York: Wiley.

Linebaugh, C. W., and Young-Charles, H. Y. (1978). The counseling needs of the families of aphasic patients, in *Clinical Aphasiology Conference Proceedings,* ed. R. H. Brookshire. Minneapolis: BRK.

McNeil, M. R., and Prescott, T. E. (1978). *Revised Token Test*. Baltimore: University Park Press.

Meyer, J. S., Sakai, F., Yamaguchi, F., Yamamoto, M., and Shaw, T. (1980). Regional changes in cerebral blood flow during standard behavioral activation in patients with disorders of speech and mentation compared to normal volunteers. *Brain and Language, 9:* 61–77.

Obler, L. K., and Albert, M. L. (1981). Language changes in the elderly aphasic and the dementing patient, in *Acquired Aphasia,* ed. M. T. Sarno. New York: Academic Press.

Porch, B. E. (1967). *Porch Index of Communicative Ability*. Vol. 1: *Theory and Development*. Palo Alto: Consulting Psychologists Press.

Porch, B. E. (1981). *Porch Index of Communi-*

cative Ability. Vol. 3: *Administration, Scoring, and Interpretation* (3rd ed.). Palo Alto: Consulting Psychologists Press.

Raven, J. C. (1962). *Coloured Progressive Matrices,* Sets A, Ab, B. London: H. K. Lewis.

Rosenbek, J. C., Becher, B., Shaughnessy, A., and Collins, M. (1979). Other uses of single-case designs, in *Clinical Aphasiology Conference Proceedings,* ed. R. H. Brookshire. Minneapolis: BRK.

Sarno, M. T. (1975). "The Functional Communication Profile Manual of Directions," Rehabilitation Monograph 42. New York: New York University Medical Center.

Schuell, H. M. (1965). *Minnesota Test for Differential Diagnosis of Aphasia.* Minneapolis: University of Minnesota Press.

Schuell, H. (1974). *Aphasia Theory and Therapy. Selected Lectures and Papers of Hildred Schuell,* ed. L. F. Sies. Baltimore: University Park Press.

Sparks, R., and Holland, A. L. (1976). Method: melodic intonation therapy for aphasia. *Journal of Speech and Hearing Disorders, 41:* 287–297.

Wapner, W., Hamby, S., and Gardner, H. (1981). The role of the right hemisphere in the apprehension of complex linguistic materials. *Brain and Language, 14:* 15–33.

Wechsler, D. (1980). *Wechsler Adult Intelligence Scale.* New York: The Psychological Corporation.

Wernicke, C. (1977). The aphasia symptom-complex: A psychological study on an anatomic basis, in *Wernicke's Works on Aphasia. A Source Book and Review,* trans. G. H. Eggert. The Hague: Mouton.

Wertz, R. T., Collins, M. J., Weiss, D., Kurtzke, J. F., Frieden, T., Brookshire, R. H., Pierce, J., Holtzapple, P., Hubbard, D. J., Porch, B. E., West, J. A., Davis, L., Matovitch, V., Morley, G. K., and Resurreccion, E. (1981). Veterans Administration cooperative study on aphasia: a comparison of individual and group treatment. *Journal of Speech and Hearing Research, 24:* 580–594.

10

Disorders of Articulation

We have all known someone who has difficulty pronouncing speech sounds. More often, we see this in a young child who may have a developmental articulation problem. Such a problem is related to the child's faulty learning of the rules of speech production, and may thus be classified as a phonological disorder. Some children have a structural problem, which may be caused by cerebral palsy or a cleft palate, that prevents them from producing sounds correctly. Adults also may have articulation disorders, either developmental or acquired. An example of a developmental articulation disorder in an adult is a lateral lisp carried over from childhood, often persisting (if not corrected) throughout adult life. Sometimes adults acquire an articulation problem after an accident or a disease (such as a stroke). Regardless of the person's age or the cause of the difficulty, an articulation disorder can have a serious impact. Fortunately, most disorders of articulation can be successfully treated by speech-language pathologists.

As we have seen, many of the phonemes of all languages are babbled randomly by infants. The sounds are fleeting and carry no meaning. The babble jargon and voicing prosody during the first year of life are relatively random, rather than rule-bound, and their production does not require any precision. It is not until babies begin to say their first words that listeners require them to use some articulatory precision. Without such precision, the early word attempts are not understood. In the beginning, babies often say the vowels of the target words correctly. The consonants that are most easily produced (see Chapters 2 and 3) are usually those utilized in the first words. During the first three years of life, typical babies thrill their listeners when they say recognizable words, often chained together in the proper syntactic order. During these years, articulatory precision is usually of little concern.

As the child gets older, society becomes less tolerant of deviations in articulation. A boy three and a half years old may be considered cute when he substitutes /w/ for /r/, as in "I want a wabbit." At age 13, if still making that substitution the child would be the victim of much teasing by his classmates. The adult world is even more intolerant of continued articulatory errors. For example, a thirty-three-year-old woman with a frontal lisp, when applying for a job, might well experience rejection by a prospective employer when she says, "I wonder what your thenior people get in the way of thocial benefith." Some articulation defects, such as this one, seriously interfere with intelligibility; other articulation errors may have less impact on the clarity of the intended message.

In this chapter, we will see that many children with developmental articulation errors are best aided by the speech-language pathologist, who would approach their problem from the perspective of phonology. Certainly, children with many developmental articulation errors (they cannot say the sounds that their age and social peers can) may well have a phonological disorder, meaning that they have not learned the rules of phoneme application. Rather than work on individual phonetic production in speech therapy, the children may learn the rules for applying a particular sound. For example, the plural /s/ is actually produced as /z/ when following a final vowel or voiced consonant; in the utterance, "bats and cobs," the phonetic transcription (using the ITPA symbols presented in Chapter 2) would be /bæts and kɑbz/. The normal English speaker has learned the phonologic rule for voicing the plural consonant when following a vowel or voiced consonant.

There are children who make phonetic errors. The child who persists in making a single error, such as the w/r substitution or the θ/s frontal lisp, may know the phonological rules but be unable to apply them because of faultily-learned motor patterns. Similarly, children or adults with a faulty muscle system may continue to produce target phonemes incorrectly because they cannot direct the components of speech production (respiration, phonation, resonance, articulation, prosody) into a timed, precise phonemic production. Faulty rule-learning is not the problem here.

Through observation and testing, the speech-language pathologist must determine whether an articulation disorder is phonological (related to faulty rule-learning) or phonetic (related to improper muscle action). Let us look at the cases of two children. The first, a four-year-old boy, has a developmental phonological disorder. The second is a fifteen-year-old boy with cerebral palsy, which prevents him from making correct phonetic productions.

Robbie. At age four, Robbie was brought to a university speech-language clinic by his concerned parents. The parents, most other family members (including three older siblings), and neighbors had difficulty understanding him. He was found to have normal hearing, normal cognitive ability, and normal speech mechanisms at the time of the speech evaluation. His articulation errors were many. In the initial position of a word, he could say correctly: m, p, b, t, d, n; in the medial position, he said correctly: m, p, b; he produced no final consonants correctly. Most of his consonant errors were actually omissions (he left the sounds out completely), although he made a few consonant substitutions (substituting another sound for a target sound): t/k, d/g, t/f, b/v, t/θ. Of the 25 English consonants, he made only six of them correctly; most of his vowel sounds were produced correctly. His overall attempts at conversation were restricted to two- or three-word utterances, many of which were not intelligible. He appeared to keep his mean length of response to two or three words as a conscious gesture to accommodate his listeners; he apparently had learned that if he said more than that, no one would understand him.

Because Robbie could say six consonants correctly in the initial position, a phonological approach to his problem focused on making him aware that many words had consonant endings that he could say. At the start of therapy, the stop consonants that he could produce correctly (/p, b, t, d/) were presented at the beginning and the end of a word. The phonological approach was to teach him the place in a word to say the sound. In therapy, he was soon able to produce most of the six target sounds (the ones he could say at the evaluation) at both the beginning and the end of a word, such as pop, top, mop, Bob, tub, mom, Pam (his sister), and so forth. Saying two words in a rapid series, in which the last consonant of the first word and the first consonant of the second word were the same, such as "mom-mop," seemed to facilitate the production of the omitted consonant in the medial position. Later therapy sessions included working on phonetic sounds that Robbie should have been making correctly; not only was production practiced in therapy, but some phonological instruction was included, providing him with the rules for applying his newly acquired sounds.

Eric. Eric was born with cerebral palsy of the tension-athetoid type. At fifteen, he was confined to a wheelchair, had some stabilizing restraints to restrict his flailing arms, but was able to use speech as his primary mode of communication. When talking to strangers, who could not readily understand what he attempted to say, he used an electronic communication board. This alternative mode to oral communication was helpful when it was important for him to make specific needs known. At the time of his speech and language evaluation, Eric was found to have normal hearing, average intellectual ability, a sixth-grade reading-comprehension level, no ability to write, and one- or two-word speech utterances (characterized by many vowel and consonant distortions).

Initially, his speech therapy had a dual focus. First, he worked to extend his expiratory control, with and without voice. Second, by using a sling under his chin, he was able to restrict the excessive opening of his mandible. The work on extending vowel durations was successful, increasing his /i/ duration, for example, from two to eight seconds. Improved expiratory control enabled Eric to say three or four words on one expiration with only minimal training. Vowel distortions were markedly reduced when he wore the chin sling; after ear training, it was possible to produce correct vowels at least 70 percent of the time when practicing monosyllabic words. Eric continued to work with his speech pathologist to increase the precision of production of all the stop plosives. Direct work on the motor aspects of articulation has had dramatic effects on improving Eric's speech.

TYPES OF ARTICULATION ERRORS

In Chapter 3, we studied the speech mechanisms required for the production of normal speech; and in the preceding chapter, we considered the consonants, vowels, and diphthongs of our English speech patterns. We also learned that our spoken words are strung together in a running prosodic-melody flow. We say these sounds quickly. It is often in the rapid production of sounds required in normal speech that articulatory errors become most noticeable. Whether heard in a single syllable, a single word, or in phrases or sentences, such errors are known as **misarticulations**. There are four forms of misarticulations: **omission** errors (*fi'* for *fish*); **substitution** errors (*fith* for *fish*); **distortion** errors (*filsh* for *fish*); and **addition** errors (*fisha* for *fish*). In the example of the distortion error, the /ʃ/ has been lateralized which in its phonemic transcription would be written as /ʃ̂/; a phonetic transcription would be written as [ʃ̂]. The reader will note that the phonemic designation of an utterance uses the /–/ markers while phonetic transcription uses the [–] (Grunwell, 1981).

Omissions

When small children leave the endings off many words, they seriously interfere with comprehension by others. While omissions may occur anywhere within the word, they are more often observed in the final position. A particular sound or a whole class of sounds may be omitted. Occasionally, a young child will put no endings on words. Shriberg (1980) has noted that consonant deletion, known as a "syllable-simplification process," is a natural part of phonological development. Most other programs (Hodson, 1980; Ingram, 1981) that look at articulation errors from a phonologic-process point of view recognize the omitted consonant, often in the final position, as compared with the productions of adult speech, as a process of simplification.

Children who make many omission errors are perceived by adult listeners as having a severe articulation problem. Most children seem to pass through the omitted-consonant stage rather quickly; it would appear that children with various phonetic-production problems, perhaps related to cerebral palsy or a degenerative central-nervous-system problem such as muscular dystrophy, continue to make omission errors. Later in this chapter, we will see how such errors are often successfully treated from a phonologic-process point of view (working on the general process of omission rather than on individual sounds or phonemes).

Substitutions

The most common articulatory errors heard in the speech of young children are known as substitution errors. One phoneme is substituted for the target phoneme. As we shall see later in the chapter, there is logic or predictability to the substitution error; the incorrect sound is usually similar in many ways (in terms of distinctive features) to the target sound. For example, the child who says, "I tee the white wabbit" has used two common substitutions heard in the speech of children with articulatory errors of substitution. The /t/ substitution is also a voiceless sound and is made near the same spot in the front of the mouth as the /s/; the /w/ has many production similarities to the target sound, /r/.

Until children acquire a particular sound of the adult phonemic system, they often replace it with a sound they have had some success in making. Many of the substituted sounds are spoken earlier developmentally than the target sound. For example, if four-year-olds cannot make an /s/, they might well substitute a sound that they can make, such as /t/. Substitution is perhaps the most common articulatory error in the child who demonstrates a general developmental phonological disorder.

Distortions

As we saw in Chapter 2, the production of a sound must be relatively on target to be perceived by listeners as correct. The *allophone,* the slight variation of a sound that still sounds like the target sound, is even more varied when the sound is classified as distorted. In a distortion error, the target sound is produced with some noises added to it, although not enough to be classified as a substitution or an addition. One of the most common distortions and among the easiest to identify (although very difficult to correct) is the lateral lisp, in which the target /s/ or /z/ phonemes sound slushy (the /s/ or /z/ sounds like it has an unvoiced /l/ as part of its production).

In order to record distortion errors correctly, the International Phonetic Alphabet includes a number of **diacritics** (modified phonetic symbols) used to describe the distorted error (Shriberg, 1980). Examples of diacritic symbols that represent distortions would be the mark for a lateralized lisp, such as (ˆ), and the word *sun* said with such a lisp would be transcribed as (ŝʌn). A retroflex error, marked as (ˏ), would be used to note the production of a sound when the tongue is curled back too far toward the pharynx, such as making the word *sun* sound like (ʂʌn). Distortion mistakes may be seen as developmental phonologic ones or, at later ages, often as fixed phonetic errors (faulty positioning of the articulators).

Additions

A fourth type of articulatory error is an addition mistake, in which the individual adds an extra sound to one already correctly produced. We might hear an individual with an addition-error saying "boata" as phonetically transcribed as /botə/. In most cases, the addition error is the unstressed /ə/, occurring after a final consonant. Most such errors appear to be phonetic in nature, with the individual adding a voicing dimension to a word, sometimes unable to stop the flow of air (voiced or voiceless) at the end of it. Occasionally, a child with cerebral palsy will continue to make voicing additions.

CAUSES OF ARTICULATION DISORDERS

It is often difficult to isolate a specific cause of an articulation problem. The great majority of young children who have difficulties pronouncing their words basically do not differ emotionally, mentally, or physically from their age peers. In most cases of developmental articulation disorders, children's overall communicative abilities are limited primarily by their problems of articulation, so that to listeners they may sound younger than they are. In such children, this would be classified as a developmental phonological disorder, probably related to a faulty rule-learning system. Hull and his colleagues (1976) found in their national-incidence study of communication disorders that about 1.9 percent of the 38,802 children tested were found to have an articulation disorder. Before we consider developmental phonologic disorders in some detail, let us discuss some causative factors that may contribute to faulty learning of articulation.

Hearing Loss

We saw in Chapters 2 and 7 the importance of the hearing mechanism in normal communication. Human communication is primarily an aural-oral interaction. A conductive or sensorineural hearing loss can seriously impair the aural reception of language. Some young children with articulation delay have had a series of middle-ear infections each of which caused a hearing loss. As discussed in Chapter 5, a frequent cause of a developmental communication problem (articulation and language) is hearing loss. Certain children simply cannot hear some of the phonemes. Without adequate auditory sensitivity and the ability to perceive correctly what is heard, it is clear those with such a hearing impairment experience real difficulty in producing the speech sounds they cannot hear. In sensorineural hearing loss, the child or adult might well hear the vowels and low-frequency consonants in others' speech but have difficulty hearing high-frequency sounds (see Chapter 2), such as /p, t, s, θ, ʃ/.

Perceptual Causes

For many years, speech-language pathologists have worked on auditory-discrimination training as part of articulation therapy. Van Riper and Irwin (1958) suggested that children with a functional articulation problem should be tested first to see if they can discriminate between their incorrect sounds and the correct target sounds. For example, the boy who says, "I tee the baby" may not be able to discriminate /t/ from /s/ in the speech of others; or he may be able to discriminate the speech of others but find himself unable to do so in his own speech. Although a number of studies have found faulty auditory discrimination to be significantly related to articulation skills in young children (see Locke's excellent review of the topic [1980]), there is no clear indication which one precedes the other. There is evidence that infants eventually make phonetic distinctions in listening to the prosodic speaking patterns of the people around them; the ability to produce the first words is some evidence of capacity to discriminate the phonetic patterns of a particular word. The many years children spend listening to the speech of others may well establish listening and auditory discrimination ability before first attempts are made to produce target phonemes correctly. However, there is some counter-evidence that, for some children, the ability to produce a sound correctly may be a precursor to being able to discriminate it correctly. For the majority of children with articulation errors, some auditory-discrimination testing (contrasting the incorrect sound and the target sound) is usually warranted in therapy.

Oral-sensory functioning has been investigated relative to its role in articulation (Ringel and others, 1970; Shelton, 1971), finding that performance in somesthetic testing is somewhat related to articulatory proficiency. One such test, seen in Figure 10–1, is for **oral stereognosis,** the ability to recognize the shapes of small objects placed on the tongue (McDonald and Aungst, 1970). Although some studies have found that problems in oral stereognosis may accompany articulation difficulties, defects in oral stereognostic ability have not lent themselves to corrective-

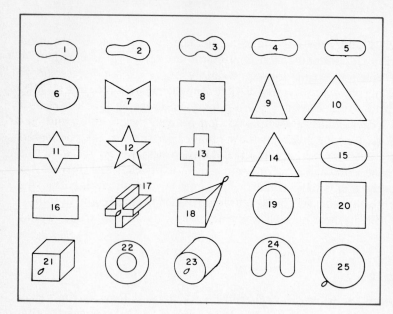

FIGURE 10-1 Twenty-five items from an oral stereognosis test. Twenty-five of the original oral stereognosis items used in the abbreviated oral stereognosis test by McDonald and Aungst (1970). Shown by permission of McDonald, E. F., and Aungst, L. F., An abbreviated test of oral stereognosis, in *Second Symposium on Oral Sensation and Perception,* ed. J. F. Bosma. Springfield, Ill.: Charles C. Thomas.

therapy programs. That is, if someone has an articulation problem related to a deficit in oral-sensory ability, the speech-language pathologist must work around the problem, rather than attempt to remediate the sensory deficit directly. It would appear that many speakers with articulatory defects related to diminished oral-sensory abilities may also have associated oral-motor difficulties.

Oral-Motor Difficulties

In recent years, there has been increased interest in the motor aspects of speech production, particularly related to subtle influences on articulation by such disorders as oral verbal apraxia and dysarthria. Both conditions are related to a pathology in the central nervous system. Some children with severe articulatory problems, characterized by awkward mouth posturing in attempting to produce a simple word, may well have oral verbal apraxia (Macaluso-Haynes, 1978; Yoss and Darley, 1974). Such children may give evidence that the word is known (older patients with acquired apraxia may be able to write what they cannot say) but be unable to sequence the movements of the speech articulators in the proper order to say the word. Older patients who acquire apraxia can be observed to struggle to say a word after being asked to do so, without being able to produce it; however, they may say the same word quickly and free of articulatory error in an automatic situation. For example, a forty-four-year-old man was asked to name a dam in a picture; he struggled with "It's d-d-drol, d-d-dor, d-d-dror. Oh, damn it, I can't say it." *Dam* could not be said volitionally, but the *damn* came out articulated perfectly. Such is the dramatic contrast in apraxia of speech between volition and involition. Characteristic of oral verbal apraxia is its inconsistency; the more focal the request on the "volitional ladder," the more difficult it is to say the word.

Dysarthria

Dysarthria is a motor speech disorder that is caused by a lesion or lesions somewhere in the central nervous system. The kind of dysarthria the patient experiences is usually related to the site and extent of the cerebral lesion (Darley, Aronson, and Brown, 1975). Darley and his associates have identified six types of dysarthria, each of which is related directly to a lesion site. For example, a more common type is *spastic* dysarthria, often related to a unilateral lesion somewhere high in the nervous system (such as that caused by a stroke that knocked out some of the fibers of the pyramidal tract, discussed in Chapter 3). The opposite motor speech problem is **flaccid dysarthria,** caused by a lesion very low in the nervous system (such as one caused by trauma or disease of the brainstem and spinal column). Dysarthria of any type may result in changes in articulation, voice, and prosody. We shall consider dysarthria in more detail later in this chapter and in other chapters.

Oral-Structure Deviations

It is very easy to blame an articulation problem on a repaired cleft lip or an absent tooth. In reality, many structural problems of the mouth, such as losing your two upper front teeth, may have only temporary effects on speech. Since speaking is basically an aural-oral event, speakers are able to use their ears to supply the "inner" model of how the word ought to sound; we soon learn compensatory movements (to make up for the problem caused by the oral defect) and produce our words to match the inner model. Bernthal and Bankson (1981), after reviewing many research reports that looked at the relationship between an oral defect and the presence of an articulation problem, concluded that such a defect does not necessarily play an important part in producing defective speech. Many children with some kind of oral defect demonstrate normal speech. Let us consider, however, some structural problems of the oral mechanism that may contribute to articulation difficulties.

Severe oral-structural problems related to **cleft lip and palate** may contribute greatly to articulation problems. At the University of Arizona clinic, this author sometimes sees a youngster (or even a young adult) who comes from Mexico with an unrepaired cleft lip and/or palate. The articulation and resonance problems of these children are tremendous. Most such children in the United States are fortunate enough to have had a series of repairs to lip and palate, often coupled with orthodontia and prosthetics, so that they become structurally adequate and can develop normal articulation. As far as articulation is concerned, the nasal consonants and vowels produced by those with cleft palate are pretty much intact, with severe articulation problems observed in the production of fricatives, affricates, and stop plosives (Spriestersbach, 1965).

On rare occasions, tongue abnormalities contribute to articulation problems. A common treatment for articulation disorders at the turn of the century (before the profession of speech-language pathology existed) was to clip the *lingual frenulum,* the small piece of tissue that anchors the anterior tongue to the floor of the mouth. When this tissue is too tight, the tongue tip cannot be elevated, and when the tongue is protruded, the tip has an indentation in the middle, giving it a heart-shaped appearance. Rarely is such a configuration the cause of an articulation problem. If the speech-language pathologist determines that the lack of tongue-tip elevation is contributing to an articulation problem of such high front consonants as /l, r, s/, it will be recommended that the lingual frenulum be cut (a surgical task perhaps best done by the otolaryngologist). Tongue size is sometimes blamed for an articulation problem. The tongue may be too small (*microglossia*) or too large (*macroglossia*). While extreme deviations in tongue size may cause problems in producing sounds, most speakers adjust well to their tongue size and make the compensatory movements required for normal speech. Sometimes the patient with cancer of the tongue must have part of the tongue removed (*hemiglossectomy*) or all of it (*glossectomy*). Such a procedure can have devastating effects on articulation, although Skelly and her associates (1971) have reported programs and management approaches that permit the patient to speak with some degree of articulatory precision. Another tongue problem, **tongue thrust,** is characterized by excessively anterior carriage of the tongue (pushing against the upper incisors during the initial phase of swallowing), and is sometimes accompanied by lateral distortion of sibilants (s/s) or frontal lisps (θ/s). The tongue-thrust controversy (whether speech-language pathologists should or should not provide therapy for tongue thrust when there is no accompanying articulatory problem) continues. There do appear to be some youngsters who present a relatively front focus of the tongue that adversely affects both swallowing and articulation. Barrett and Hanson (1978) have described a myofunctional approach to the problem, retraining tongue positioning.

Dental abnormalities are sometimes blamed for articulation problems. Once again, the direct relationship of malocclusion or absent teeth to an articulatory defect is difficult to establish. Shelton and others (1975) studied X-ray cephalometric and other oral data and found them to have little or no relationship to articulation improvement after speech therapy. There are some people, however, with severe dental problems whose defect contributes to articulation problems. Children who lose their two front teeth in the first grade experience only temporary speaking problems; the tongue seems to adjust well to the open space. Much more serious is the case of children who have a collapsed maxillary arch, with barely enough space to accommodate the tongue, and then undergo orthodontia to expand the maxilla. The braces and other appliances they may be required to wear might seriously interfere with tongue movements needed for the production of consonants. Severe problems of **occlusion** (relationship of lower molars to upper molars) occasionally result in dental-alignment difficulties severe enough to influence speech articulation negatively.

Faulty Phonologic Processes

Although there may be a number of physical and structural issues involved in articulation disorders, the effect of such disorders is to contribute to the faulty learning of phonological processes. In considering the examples of some problems that influence articulation, we could say that a physical or structural disorder would not necessarily result in an articulation problem. Only in extreme structural problems, such as in the glossectomy patient, do we see a direct correspondence between the severity of the physical problem and the severity of the articulation disorder. Shelton and McReynolds (1979) have written that "the popular practice of searching for *the* cause of functional articulation disorders has not proven productive" (p. 12). Rather, let us view articulation problems in many children as the natural attempt to simplify the complex adult articulatory productions into sounds that they are able to produce.

In his theory of natural phonology, Stampe (1973) recognized that children's earliest productions of adult words are not random in terms of approximation or error, but seem to follow some distinct processes. He further proposed that the infant has some inborn limitations that prevent the correct production of the adult model in beginning speech. These limitations (physical, mental, experiential) begin to lessen as the child matures and goes through a number of "mental operations called phonological processes" (Dunn, 1982). Borrowed from Stampe (1973) and Dunn (1982), **phonologic process** is the term we will use for the various processes children employ in simplifying the adult model of sound production. Many of the articulatory errors we hear in children's speech are related to these simplification or phonologic processes.

The correctness or incorrectness of an articulatory production is determined by comparing it with the adult production which is considered the standard of the language. Shriberg and Kwiatkowski (1980) wrote that "the phonology of a language is comprised of components and rules in three areas: (1) an inventory of phonemes, (2) distributional rules and sequence rules, and (3) phonetic change rules" (p. 274). As far as the phonemic inventory of a language is concerned, some sounds may be harder to hear (contrast the difference) and more difficult to produce. In terms of a process of simplification, children say what they can, and use these "can do" productions (which adults may consider right or wrong) for their target sounds. The distributional and sequential rules for phonemic use appear to be acquired over time, through use, and not from direct training. For example, we learn that certain phonemic combinations are possible, such as that many words start with *bl* but that none begin with *lb*. From the simplification-process point of view, children learning the adult language avoid many consonant combinations in the beginning, and by the time they have learned a particular rule of consonant combination and sequence (from hearing these sounds made in the speech of others), they may have the phonetic skill to say it. The rules of phonetic change are related to changes in the production of sound when it is adjacent to particular other sounds (vowels, for example, are shorter when surrounded by voiceless consonants), where the word is positioned in the sentence, and how the particular sound or syllable is stressed (loudness, pitch, duration).

The phonologic-process approach to articulation recognizes that it is difficult for young children to master the adult phonetic forms of language. Children simplify the sound-production task by employing various natural processes, such as leaving off final consonants or simplifying the production of blends by leaving

Natural Phonological Processes	Examples	
	ADULT *WORD*	*CHILD* *WORD*
SYLLABLE-SIMPLIFICATION PROCESSES		
Deletion of the final consonant	*ball*	"ba___"
Deletion of the unstressed syllable	*away*	"___way"
Cluster reduction	*stop*	"___top"
ASSIMILATION PROCESSES		
Regressive (backward) assimilation	*doggie*	"goggie"
Progressive (forward) assimilation	television	"televivon"
SUBSTITUTION PROCESSES		
Stopping—fricatives are replaced by stop-plosives	*shoes*	"tood"
Fronting—palatal and velar sounds are replaced by alveolar sounds	bake	"bate"

FIGURE 10–2 Some natural processes in normal phonological development. Used with permission of Prentice-Hall. From Shriberg, L. D. (1980). Developmental phonological disorders, in *Introduction to Communication Disorders,* ed. T. Hixon, L. Shriberg, and J. Saxman. Englewood Cliffs, N.J.: Prentice-Hall.

out one of the consonants. Shriberg and Kwiatkowski (1980) have summarized these natural phonologic processes well, basing their work on materials discussed by Ingram (1981). Their work is summarized in Figure 10–2. Children must produce the sounds of a language for a number of years before they achieve phonetic mastery of it.

The early voicing patterns discussed earlier (in Chapters 1, 2, and 3) are the infant's first generated sounds, somewhat independent of the adult voicing models. It is not until infants are about six months old that they seem to hear the prosodic patterning of the adult forms around them, eventually incorporating them into their own repertoire of random sounds. There is some suggestion (Ferguson and Farwell, 1975) that close examination of infants' prelinguistic utterances will reveal "sound-alikes" to particular phonemes of the adult language, especially jargon vowels and real speech vowels. For children to produce words recognized as such by listeners, they must spend time listening to the sounds and the words of people around them. What children hear is related to their communicative environment and the adequacy of their hearing equipment. For example, they won't be placed in a tank with porpoises, and even if they were, their hearing mechanisms would not permit them to pick up the high-frequency utterances of their porpoise friends. Similarly, what they do try to say is seriously limited by their speaking equipment and their relative lack of sophistication in using it. As Locke (1983) noted: " . . . all languages must be producible and perceivable, and therefore consistent with the production and perception capabilities of humans'' (p. 340).

We see, therefore, that our ability both to hear and to speak the sounds of a language develop slowly in the normal youngster. It takes the normal child almost seven years to master the phonemes of the parent language (Sander, 1972). Part of this time is spent listening to the contrasts between various phonemes, and may also be spent attempting to produce the phonemes of the adult language, but in a logical order (easy to difficult). Perhaps quite naturally, young children simplify the acoustic and production features of the sounds to fit their repertoire of receptive and expressive skills. From a phonologic-process point of view, children's faulty productions (in the sense that they differ from the adult model) may well be products of their need to simplify and approximate the adult speaking model. It would appear that the majority of articulation disorders classified as "functional" could well be approached by viewing them from a phonological process perspective. We shall view how such an approach works in both the evaluation and therapy of someone with an articulation disorder.

EVALUATION OF ARTICULATION DISORDERS

Every now and then, a child or an adult is identified as having an articulation problem. The individual may be a preschooler whose parents have difficulty understanding what he says; or it may be a youngster in third grade who persists in saying /w/ for /r/; or it may be a middle-aged woman who is beginning to show the first symptoms (an early dysarthria) of a degenerative neurological disease. All of these people would require some kind of formal assessment of their articulatory abilities, particularly if some kind of therapy program were to be initiated. Let us first consider a screening program, the kind that might be used in the public schools to identify children who were not producing their phonemes with the accuracy of their age peers.

Articulation Screening

Most articulation screening programs are used in the public schools, particularly in kindergarten and the first few elementary grades. We might hope that their goal is to identify those children whose articulation problems would not go away as a result of natural development, but instead might require the services of the speech-language pathologist. Such programs are typically set up in the fall, and all new children in the particular school district (kindergarten and other grades) meet with the speech-language pathologist for a brief screening. It might focus on naturalistic dialogues with the children, observing not only their articulation but their overall language function, voice quality, and speech fluency. Unfortunately, many young children are so reticent about talking to the speech "stranger" that a natural conversation is often impossible. Therefore, it is usually necessary to structure the screening so that a maximum amount of information can be obtained from a relatively brief speech sample.

It should be noted that certain speech sounds are stressed in the screening program, usually those that young children typically mispronounce throughout the early primary years. Perhaps the most common articulation errors identified during screening programs are distortions and substitutions for /s/ and /z/ and the common w/l and w/r substitutions. The focus of the screening program is to identify the children who misarticulate, not to identify the reason for the problem or study the possible phonologic-simplifying processes involved.

Ideally, the screening test should identify those children who will outgrow their problem with maturation and those with articulation problems who need remediation training. There have been a few predictive tests, such as Van Riper and Erickson's *Predictive Screening Test of Articulation* (1969) and McDonald's *A Screening Test of Articulation* (1968), that help identify the child who needs speech therapy. For example, on the Van Riper and Erickson screening test, a particular cut-off score has been found that seems to indicate which children may need therapeutic assistance. Unfortunately, speech-language pathologists in the schools often find that identifying children who "need" therapy does not necessarily satisfy the parents who want their five-year-olds who make an /r/ substitution to begin therapy, whether the screening test indicates a need or not. More and more often, screening programs are heavily supplemented by teacher and parent referrals to the speech-language pathologist for a full speech evaluation.

Articulation Evaluation

Articulatory precision in the production of the phonemes of a language naturally facilitates communication. Any formal articulation evaluation should begin by engaging the child (or adult) in a real-world conversation. The conversation may be between the client and other children, between parent and child, or, when needed, between clinician and child. Most speech clinics have testing suites (which should look like playrooms for young children) that have observation mirrors, permitting the clinician to observe the child in as natural a communication setting as possible. A conversation during spontaneous play will often reveal how the child actually talks out of the testing situation. With an adult client, an actual conversation about topics that might be of mutual interest to clinician and client will reveal the client's actual communicative ability, offering information about articulation proficiency as well as about voice, language, and fluency. The experienced and well-trained speech-language pathologist is able to observe the client's productions systematically and make a useful summary statement based on the observations relevant to the articulatory adequacy, specifying type and number of errors, place of error, and so forth. It is possible, however, that observation of play and conversation will not reveal all of the client's articulatory errors, nor will conversation alone provide the diagnostic information that a more structured evaluation will include. However, the evaluation begins with free play and conversation, which then leads to more formal testing.

Hearing and Listening Testing. Audiometric testing, at least as a screening measure, should be part of every articulation evaluation. By taking a case history, the clinician must determine if there has been or continues to be a hearing problem. As we saw in Chapters 2 and 7, various levels of hearing loss can have devastating effects on developing language, particularly in the sound-contrasting aspects of phonology. The client's ability to discriminate between phonemes is an important part of the evaluation. Overall auditory discrimination ability can be determined by using, for instance, the *Goldman-Fristoe-Woodcock Test of Auditory Discrimination* (1969) or the *Washington Sound Discrimination Test* (1971); they require the child to point to a picture that represents one of the contrasting words being said. For example, two simple words are pictured, such as *peas* and *peach,* that vary from each other primarily by having a different final consonant (although the duration of the vowel may vary also, as in this example). The child's task is to point to the picture named.

Peripheral Oral Evaluation. A peripheral oral evaluation provides the speech-language pathologist with information relative to the adequacy of oral structure and function. As we discussed earlier in this chapter, sensory losses, structural defects, and faulty movements of the articulators and resonance structures (velum and pharynx) can all contribute to faulty articulatory production. The oral peripheral form (see Figure 10-3) requires the clinician to make a judgment about various structural areas of the vocal tract and how well they may function. The particular form pictured has been completed for an adult man with normal articulation who has a voice problem (Boone, 1982). The slight departures from normal described for this man apparently do not contribute in any way to faulty articulation. His oral *diadochokinesis* (rapidity of alternating movements), like other parts of the peripheral oral examination, was found to be within normal limits.

The advantage to the speech-language pathologist of using a form to summarize the data from the oral examination probably lies in the need to be complete and systematic. The form, in effect, provides a checklist for each part of the oral mechanism in terms of structural and performance adequacy. For the patient with dysarthria or a major structural defect (such as a cleft palate), a more detailed and supplementary examination obviously would be required.

The Articulation Inventory. Many commercially available articulation tests provide the clinician with a ready inventory of the client's misarticulated sounds. Most such tests can identify not only the actual sounds produced incorrectly, but the place in the word where the error occurs (initial, medial, or final position) and the type of error that exists (omission, substitution, distortion, or addition). A typical articulation inventory will include a scoring sheet that looks like the completed one in Figure 10-4. Katie, the six-year old whose articulation profile is shown, demonstrates errors in producing /s, z, l, r, θ, ð/, sounds that other children her age generally make like the adult model. She is able to make a few of the sounds cor-

SECTION 4
Oral Peripheral Evaluation

Check (✔) if normal.

Describe any abnormality.

	STRUCTURE	FUNCTION
Lips	*normal*	*normal*
Teeth	*Slight overjet and prominent incisors.*	*He's sensitive about his big teeth.*
Tongue	*ok*	✔
Hard Palate	*normal*	✔
Velum	*Moves well; somewhat reddish.*	✔
Pharynx	*Reddish (dry?)*	*Appears excessively dry; mild irritation.*
Nose	✔	✔
Mandible	*Class III occlusion*	*Slight overjet; movement restricted.*

Diadochokinetic Rate*:

SYLLABLE	REPETITIONS	NUMBER OF SECONDS
pʌ	20	*4*
tʌ	20	*5*
kʌ	20	*5*
pʌtəkə	10	*4*

Velopharyngeal Competence:
       Oral reading of *Explorers of Space* or *The Duck-Billed Platypus* or
       Oral reading of *Moons and Planets* or *Miss Jane Marple*

Comments: *Read Explorers and Moons with normal resonance.*

FIGURE 10–3 An oral peripheral evaluation form. Used by permission of C. C. Publications, Inc., Tigard, Oregon.

ARTICULATION TEST

Name **Katie C.**   Age **6·8**

KEY: Sound produced correctly (✓); substitution (write phonemic symbol of sound substituted--e.g., w/r); distortion (D); sound addition (write symbol of sound added).

SOUND	STIMULUS	I	M	F	STIMULABILITY
p	put, happy, up	✓	✓	✓	
b	bag, baby, tub	✓	✓	✓	
m	mitten, hammer, home	✓	✓	✓	
t	toy, bottom, hot	✓	✓	✓	
d	dog, radio, sad	✓	✓	✓	
n	nut, many, pin	✓	✓	✓	
k	car, cookie, sock	✓	✓	✓	
g	girl, wagon, big	✓	✓	✓	
f	foot, coffee, leaf	✓	✓	✓	
v	valentine, T.V., cave	✓	θ/ð	θ/ð	
s	soap, bicycle, bus	θ/ð	θ/ð	θ/ð	NO
z	zoo, easy, nose	θ/ð	θ/ð	θ/ð	
ʃ	shoe, dishes, fish	D	D	D	
ʒ	measure, garage		D	D	
dʒ	jump, magic, cage	D	D	D	
h	house				
θ	thin, nothing, bath	f	f	f	NO deep testing?
ð	that, mother, breathe	v	v	v	
j	yellow, onion	✓	✓	✓	
w	wall, bow-wow	✓	✓		
r	run, parrot, bear	w	w	u	ra-ra-ra ok✓
l	lap, jelly, pill	w	w	u	la-la-la ✓
ŋ	sing			✓	
br-	brown	bw			
bl-	black	bw			
tr-	train	tw			
tw-	twin	✓			
fr-	frog	fw			
st-	stove	θt			additions (dropped) ✓
str-	string	θtw			
sw-	swim	θw			NO
sl-	slow	θw			NO

FIGURE 10-4 An articulation test for Katie, age six years, eight months. During stimulability testing (providing her with correct spoken and visual models), she could produce the /r/ and /l/ phonemes correctly.

rectly in the medial position, suggesting that she does have some capability for normal sound production. *Stimulability* testing and deep testing would follow the formal articulation test to see whether, under the special conditions of those tests, the incorrect sounds could be produced correctly. Both tests will be discussed shortly. A phonologic-process evaluation (considered later in the chapter) might follow, particularly if stimulability and deep testing were unsuccessful in eliciting correct phonemic productions.

One of the most used articulation tests is *The Templin-Darley Tests of Articulation* (1969), which contains 176 items, each is a picture representing a particular sound. The pictures are named spontaneously by younger children; older children can read single words or sentences aloud. Scores are recorded, similar to those seen in Figure 10–4, using the following notations:

    ✓ for a sound produced correctly
    __ for a sound omission
    w/r for a sound substitution
    D for a sound distortion
    m-t for a sound addition

Other tests used in evaluating articulation compare an individual with the adult model as well as with age peers. These include *The Fisher-Logemann Test of Articulation Competence* (1971), the *Photo Articulation Test* (1969), and the *Goldman-Fristoe Test of Articulation* (1969). None of these tests is standardized, but each presents a collection of pictures designed to elicit the desired words that contain the phonemes to be tested. Following the administration of the formal articulation test, the speech-language pathologist summarizes the total number of errors, error type, and position within the word where the error occurred. Certain incorrect sounds will be selected for further testing.

Stimulability. An important part of the articulation evaluation is to see how well the client can produce incorrect sounds when they are presented by the clinician as repeated auditory, visual, and tactile models. Snow and Milisen (1954) found that *stimulability,* hearing and watching the correct production of a sound in a syllable, often facilitates its correct production. For those children who were found to be stimulable, the prognosis for correction was much better than for those who were not. After the formal articulation test is completed, the speech-language pathologist selects several incorrect sounds to determine if the client is stimulable for that sound. If, for example, the /l/ sound were selected, the clinician would repeat "la, la, la" three times, allowing the client to listen and watch the production of the sound (and to touch the mouth, if needed). The client is then asked to say "la." If the client can then produce the sound (previously tested as an error) correctly, the child is said to be stimulable. Consequently, the stimulable sounds are often selected as the first ones in articulation therapy, since the client has some capacity for making the sound correctly.

Deep testing. For some children, stimulability testing may not result in the successful production of the incorrect sound. In the clinician's quest to find the correct production as a beginning place in therapy, *A Deep Test of Articulation* (McDonald, 1964) can be used. The **Deep Articulation Test** is based on several motor theories of speech production. Stetson (1951) pointed out years ago that the isolated phoneme exists only on the scoring sheet of an articulation test; rather, the consonant or vowel in question is always tested in combination with another phoneme, in effect creating the syllable. The sound in isolation does not exist. Theories of *coarticulation*, as developed by MacNeilage (1970), state that no particular phoneme is produced as an independent movement but is highly influenced by the phonemes that precede or follow it. For example, in the word *tramp*, the lips are closing for the /m/ and /p/ as the tongue is gliding down to produce the /r/; the velum is dropping for the /m/ as the /t/ is being produced, and so forth. Phonemes are produced in a rapid sequence and blend into one another.

McDonald's *Deep Test of Articulation* is based on the principle that any target sound is heavily influenced by adjacent and overlapping sounds. In the *Deep Test,* the test pictures are presented in pairs. The test searches for a facilitating context that permits the correct motor production of the incorrectly produced phoneme.

In clinical work, this author first administers some type of articulation inventory. Sounds that have been identified as errors are then presented under conditions of stimulability. If this fails to elicit correct production, deep articulation testing is introduced. It is a rare individual, whose phonologic problem may be functional or organic, who cannot produce the incorrect phoneme correctly, at least, in one phonetic context using the *Deep Test of Articulation*. Once a facilitating phonetic context can be identified, it becomes the clinician's job in therapy to introduce a series of similar-word contexts to help the child produce the sound correctly. If the /t/ were found to influence the correct production of /s/ when it preceded the /s/, the clinician would develop a number of word couplets such as *bat-sun, hat-sun, beet-sun, heart-sun,* and so forth. Articulation therapy could then begin.

Phonologic-process analysis. As young children branch beyond their early consonant-vowel productions in an attempt to match adult articulation models, they engage in a process of simplification. As Dunn (1982) has written, "The term phonological process, however, is frequently used as a way to describe the systematic simplifications observed in child speech" (p. 147). The articulatory productions of young children who make articulation errors are systematic and seem to be the result of the same processes that normal children use (Ingram, 1981). It would appear, however, that children with articulatory errors persist in using simplification processes beyond the time when their age peers use them (Grunwell, 1980). To test a child's use of phonologic processes, it is important to have a method of identifying the different processes that are used, control for the number of times a process can occur, and identify the actual number of times that it has occurred. There are several such phonologic-process-analysis tests commercially available that clinicians use, particularly with young children who show developmental articulation disorders.

The *Phonological Process Analysis* (Ingram, 1981) analyzes the child's errors by a set of processes and determines which of the following specific simplification processes occur:

1. final consonant deletion
2. reduction of consonant clusters
3. syllable deletion and reduplication
4. fronting of palatals and velars
5. stopping of fricatives and affricates
6. simplification of liquids and nasals
7. other processes

No pictures or test stimuli are prepared for the Ingram *Analysis*. The clinician provides the actual test stimuli. Sixty-seven consonants are tested, either by sampling the child's speech via a continuous speech sample or by using a formal articulation test that looks at phoneme production in the three positions (initial, medial, final). The *Analysis* summary sheet provides the clinician with information about sounds within one of the seven processes, position within the word, and the frequency of occurrence of the error. If a process pattern is identified, it can become the focus of therapy.

In Weiner's *Phonological Process Analysis* (1979), 136 "elicitation pictures" are used with the child, who is asked to make responses in two ways: single words imitated after a short delay, and phrases imitated after a short delay. The Weiner "Process Profile" sheet summarizes these phonologic-process data for each child:

1. syllable structure processes
    deletion of final consonants
    cluster reduction
    weak syllable deletion
    glottal replacement
2. harmony processes
    labial assimilation
    alveolar assimilation
    velar assimilation
    prevocalic voicing
    final consonant devoicing
3. feature contrast processes
    stopping
    gliding of fricatives
    affrication
    fronting
    denasalization

gliding of liquids
vocalization

A beginning place in therapy can often be related to a particular simplification proc-ess that has been identified. Rather than teach a child the correct production of a specific phoneme, a whole class of phonemes can sometimes be treated by changing the child's application of a particular rule (such as deletion of final consonants).

Other tests using the phonologic-process approach include Compton and Hutton's *Compton-Hutton Phonological Assessment* (1978), Hodson's *Assessment of Phonological Process* (1980), and Shriberg and Kwiatkowski's *Natural Process Analysis* (1980). Another linguistic approach to the evaluation of an articulation defect, one that translates easily into therapy, is the distinctive-feature approach.

Distinctive-feature analysis. Each phoneme (consonant and vowel) has one or more features that distinguish it from other phonemes. The features of the incorrect sound are compared with those of the adult-model sound, in the hope that a particular feature error could be corrected. Two examples of a feature error would include substituting a voiceless production for a voiced production, such as /t/ for /d/ (the voicing feature), or using a /t/ for a /k/ (a placement feature). If one were going to make a feature-contrast analysis between two phonemes, it might look like the one we see in Table 10-1. A distinctive-feature list has been included, and is applied to the consonants /s/ and /t/, which are two sounds that are often confused among young children (who usually substitute the /t/ for /s/). We see that all phonemes share seven common features (no wonder the simpler /t/ is often used, instead of the more complex /s/). The two consonants differ from each other in only three ways. The feature analysis lends itself to direct use in therapy.

Language testing. The majority of children who display defective articulation ap-pear to have a functional problem that may well be classified as a phonological

TABLE 10-1
A Distinctive-Feature Analysis Between /s/ and /t/

Feature	/s/	/t/	
high	−	−	
back	−	−	
low	−	−	
anterior	+	+	
coronal	+	+	
voice	−	−	
continuant	+	−	differ
stop	−	+	differ
nasal	−	−	
strident	+	−	differ

disorder. Locke (1983) wrote an excellent article explaining the treatment of speech sound disorders, in which he noted: "It seems we need a single, generic term for disorders involving the sounds of a language. Rather than invent a new word, my own practice has been to call them *phonological disorders* since the sounds of a language are properly a part of its phonology" (p. 340). A phonologic problem may be but a symptom of an overall language difficulty. At the time of the articulation evaluation, the speech-language pathologist should certainly make a gross determination of the child's overall adequacy of vocabulary usage and recognition, use of syntax, and morphology. For this reason, a phonological examination should include a detailed history of language and speech development and provide an opportunity to observe the child's use of spontaneous language. If there is any concern about the child's language usage, some formal language testing (such as that presented in Chapter 8) should be included.

In older children with isolated articulation defects, such as the persistence of a lateral lisp, an associated language problem is often less likely to be found. Rather, the child exhibits a phonetic problem related to executing speech movements with the precision required for production of the adult model. Similarly, the adult patient who acquires an articulation problem (perhaps as part of a dysarthria or from a loose denture) will not also exhibit an associated language problem.

When evaluating the younger child with an articulation problem, it is probably wise to include some kind of sample language measure. Speech-language pathologists will often administer a measure of vocabulary recognition, such as the *Peabody Picture Vocabulary Test* (Dunn, 1965) or the *Test for Auditory Comprehension of Language* (Carrow, 1973). A low score on one of these measures might give some evidence that the presenting articulation problem is only a symptom of an overall language problem.

ARTICULATION THERAPY

Let us now consider several approaches to articulation therapy. Speech-language pathologists work with children and adults with articulation disorders in many ways. Earlier in the chapter, many possible causes of faulty articulation were reviewed. We could probably find as many advocates of particular approaches to therapy as there are causes of a problem. Causation, which is difficult to identify, rarely can be treated directly as a first step in the management of an articulation problem. That is, if a hearing loss were identified as a possible cause of a developmental articulation problem in a child, correction of that loss (sometimes possible in a conductive loss) will not magically cure the faulty articulation. It may still be necessary to make the child aware of the desired target behavior, work directly to modify the articulation, and develop strategies for generalization of the newly acquired pattern into everyday speech.

The decision to begin therapy is usually made by comparing children's articulation with that of their peers. The question about treatment would be: "With some kind of remediation training, could we improve the child's articulation?'' The most effective speech-language pathologists working with articulation disorders may well be those who are familiar with different approaches and employ the one most appropriate for the individual with the defect. The least effective clinicians, in this author's opinion, provide the same remediation steps for all their clients. The diagnostic-evaluation data should have provided the information needed to plan individualized treatment. Let us consider briefly what is done in articulation therapy, dividing the topic in two: acquisition training and generalization training.

Acquisition Training

Helping the child or adult acquire the target model sound is common to all forms of articulation therapy. To do this, according to Van Riper and Emerick (1984), clients first must be aware of the target sound and "recognize how his misarticulations differ from those target sounds"; these two clinicians write that the second goal of therapy is to produce and establish the target sounds. Van Riper and Emerick break therapy down into four steps, the first three of which are part of sound acquisition: sensory/perceptual training (if needed), correcting, stabilizing, and transferring. The four steps are used to teach the isolated sound, the sound at the syllable level, the sound at the word level, and the sound at the sentence level.

Many speech-language pathologists approach the acquisition phase of articulation therapy by teaching *progressive approximation* (moving slowly with the child from the best production of the target sound to the actual target), *auditory stimulation* (listening to the sound and imitating it), and *phonetic placement* (showing the child the physical steps for making the sound). Some clinicians use the deep approach, or key-word method, of therapy; the clinician searches with the child (perhaps using the McDonald *Deep Test,* 1964) to find a phonetic context in which the target sound is produced correctly. Winitz (1975) advocates the context method of articulation therapy, combining the context search with distinctive features and other phonological patterns. Therapy begins where the client is, shaping the child's on target productions by using behavioral methods.

There are many commercially available behavior-modification programs available for working with children with articulation disorders. They offer a number of attractive therapy materials that are designed to make the learning task interesting and fun for the young child. At the time of the evaluation, the speech-language pathologist establishes a baseline of what the child is able to produce. For example, a particular target sound is selected, and the number of productions the child is able to say correctly, either spontaneously or by prompting, is established as the child's baseline for that sound. The treatment program for that sound then begins, following the systematic presentation of a particular program. The child is given an occasional prompt (a helping suggestion) to aid in production tasks, and as the typical program progresses, the clinician fades out (doing less and less). A particular sound is usually taught to a particular success level (percentage correct); for example, the child who makes an /r/ error must produce that sound correctly 80 percent of the time before going on to the next (usually more difficult) task in the program.

An operant conditioning approach can be used with phonetic placement, progressive approximation, or when learning distinctive features. As children do a specific therapy task correctly or reach a particular level of success (such as 80 percent correct), they receive positive reinforcement of some kind. Children at the preschool level may be given candy or chips that can be turned in for a prize at the end of the session. Older children can be given points for successful responses and have their total scores add up for some kind of payoff. For teenagers and adults, correctness of articulatory responses (reacted to positively by the clinician and others in the school or family) usually serves as adequate positive reinforcement. In a behavioral approach using reinforcement, the clinician takes a baseline of the target sound, presents a sequence of programmed steps, and reinforces responses in some way. Clients dictate their own progress in therapy. They move along in the program as they make correct responses. The following six innovative articulation programs are appropriate for use with children: Collins and Cunningham (1982); Haney and Peterson (1984); McLean et al. (1976); Mowrer (1974); Waters (1981); and Worthley (1981).

Shriberg and Kwiatkowski (1977) have developed a natural-process approach to sound acquisition. Instead of focusing on sound production, the clinician views the child's errors as the output of phonological rules that differ from adults'. Accordingly, articulation training in such an approach would focus more on when to say the target sounds than on sound production per se. The clinician attempts to isolate a particular simplification system that the child may be using, such as deletion of final consonants. The therapeutic focus would be on presenting the child with a cognitive awareness that words do indeed have endings, and, further, that the sounds at the beginning and in the middle of words often appear at the end as well. Rather than working on a specific consonant, such as /t/, that the client may be omitting at the end of a word, the child listens to and practices producing many consonant endings to words. One serious limitation of this approach is that the simplifications that are uncovered in the process analysis do not always lend themselves to therapy procedures that a child is able to follow. McReynolds and Elbert (1981) have written that, although traditional methods in articulation and distinctive-feature training have reported data regarding sound generalization beyond therapy, these data are lacking in the literature describing generalization from the phonologic-process approach.

Generalization

The goal of articulation therapy is to use the newly corrected sound in real-life situations. It must be recognized, however, that the production of a new sound is a fragile bit of behavior. It needs special attention to be utilized in actual speech, without which it can be lost. The older the child (or the longer the wrong pattern has been used), the more difficult it is to replace the sound with a new target sound. Before a new one can be used correctly in the real world, it must be nurtured and strengthened in therapy.

One excellent way to strengthen a new sound is to produce it in a rapid series at the syllable and word level. For example, if one were acquiring the /s/

sound and could produce it in a few words, those words would be repeated in a rapid series; for instance, *soup, soup, soup, soup, soup, soup*. Rapidity of production approaches the way sounds are produced naturally in conversational speech. From the point of view of motor skills, we must remember that conversational speech represents a series of overlapping coarticulations for each word, and each word in conversation must be placed in an absolute sequential order in relation to other words. Conversation requires such a complicated oral motor plan that it seems remarkable that anyone is able to do it correctly. We see, then, that attempting to generalize a sound, incorporating it in such a rapid sequence of events, might be facilitated by learning to produce the sound in a rapid repetitive series.

Van Riper and Emerick (1984) present several ways to stabilize the new sound at the word level, such as finding a number of key words in which the sound can be produced correctly and utilized in actual conversation, simultaneous talking and writing, or providing a signaling technique that requires the child to use a target word the moment a signal is given (prepare to say the sound, and say it the moment you hear a beep or knock).

Stimulus generalization is usually built into operant approaches for acquiring new articulatory responses. For example, as children acquired a new sound, Bankson and Byrne (1972) assigned them points for reading aloud word lists that contained particular target sounds. The more the target word lists were read correctly, the more points the children accrued that could be turned in for prizes at the end of the training session. Van Riper and Emerick (1984) report that such word lists make good practice activities and should be rewarded when spoken correctly and penalized when incorrect (once children have shown they can produce the sound correctly).

Finally, generalization can be facilitated by providing the client with oral reading practice that gives some emphasis to the target sound(s). Such reading should be tape-recorded; the client can then listen (perhaps with the clinician) to the taped playback, using some kind of scoring-listening task that enables client and clinician to listen critically to the new sounds. McReynolds (1982) writes that bringing other people into generalization sessions as critical listeners will sometimes accelerate generalization; however, she notes that we must caution others "not to overdo their help, so that the person does not become overly self-conscious about the problem" (p. 136). Articulation generalization occurs primarily in a practice atmosphere, providing an opportunity to work on a new behavior. Individuals should be treated gently when they make mistakes and given realistic positive reinforcement when sounds are produced well.

DYSARTHRIA

Some people never acquire normal articulation, because of the motor limitations imposed by dysarthria. Other people may have demonstrated normal articulation for years until acquiring a dysarthria or motor speech problem. Let us look at the problem of dysarthria once again, this time from the perspective of faulty articulation.

In an introductory book, particular problems, such as dysarthria, are viewed from different perspectives. The reason we consider dysarthria this way is that it can affect communication in various ways:

1. Phonation may be disturbed, with changes in voice pitch and quality (see Chapter 11).
2. Voice resonance may be altered, with changes in both oral and nasal resonance (see Chapter 11).
3. Speech prosody and rate may be altered (see Chapter 12).
4. Articulation and speech intelligibility may be compromised (Chapter 10).

Motor involvement of the lips, tongue, mandible, palate, pharynx, and larynx could have obvious effects on clarity of articulation. More often than not, the patient with dysarthria is unable to move the speech articulators quickly enough or with the precision required to produce the target phoneme free of error.

As we saw in Chapter 5, children who demonstrate developmental motor problems in their attempts to speak are often classified as having cerebral palsy. Cerebral palsy is defined by Perkins (1977) as a "neurologic disability of children in which the primary symptoms of paralysis, weakness, and incoordination reflect motor damage." Most youngsters with spastic, athetoid, or mixed cerebral palsy show marked delays in achieving the normal articulation of their age peers, requiring many hours of remedial speech therapy. The children's obvious problems—lack of oral motor control and good posture, difficulty using their arms and legs, and faulty head position—all compete against the control needed to develop normal articulation. The articulation errors these children make are phonetic, caused by absent or off-target muscle movements. The speech-language pathologist must work closely with other professionals on the rehabilitation team, including physical and occupational therapists and physiatrist, if speech therapy is to be helpful.

Children may experience other neurological diseases that may cause symptoms of dysarthria. The type and extent of the dysarthria is usually related to the site of the lesion and kind of neurological disorder (Netsell, 1984). Meningitis and encephalitis often cause problems of muscle movement and control, creating a dysarthria that is related to mixed involvement (some flaccidity and spasticity). Bulbar poliomyelitis (rare today) used to leave children with lower motor neuron atrophy of the muscles of articulation. Children may experience an intracranial tumor or be brain-injured in an accident, which often produces muscle spasms and spasticity that might contribute to dysarthria. Degenerative diseases, such as chorea or muscular dystrophy, may begin to alter the articulation of a child who demonstrated normal speech before the onset of the disease.

Of the six types of motor involvement outlined in 1975 by Darley, Aronson, and Brown (flaccid, spastic, ataxic, hypotonic, hypertonic, mixed), all were found to be characterized by imprecise consonants and irregular articulation breakdown. Faulty articulation is a common symptom of dysarthria. Some adults with various developmental neurological diseases have dysarthric speech patterns that are usually well established. Severe problems in articulation may coexist with disorders of phonation, resonance, and rate.

Most adults with dysarthria, however, acquire their speech problem after a lifetime of normal talking. The primary causes of dysarthria in adults are stroke and degenerative diseases, such as multiple sclerosis (MS), amyotrophic lateral sclerosis (ALS), and Parkinson's. Typical stroke patients have a relatively high lesion (cortical or subcortical), usually unilateral, and consequently may experience no or only a mild dysarthria. They might have a slight unilateral facial weakness that causes the lips to pull to the normal good side; the tongue might deviate to the side of the muscle involvement. Such a unilateral weakness of facial muscles and tongue causes only a mild dysarthria. As patients make some overall recovery of muscle function, the dysarthria lessens. The lower the CNS lesion, the greater the probability of a severe dysarthria or an *anarthria* (no speech at all as the result of severe neuromuscular involvement). Occasionally, patients experience a stroke at or near the brainstem, which causes devastating motor speech problems, possibly causing severe difficulties in controlling respiration, moving the velum, and controlling the tongue. Such anarthric patients might have no intelligible speech at all.

Speech therapy for dysarthric patients who have had a stroke is directed toward helping them utilize as much residual motor function as possible, to develop normal-sounding speech. For many years, a few facial exercises have been used in treating patients with hemiplegia (unilateral weakness) that are designed to increase facial symmetry. Patients are asked to alternately purse their lips (as if whistling) and extend them (as in an exaggerated production of *eeh*). Sometimes this is done with light finger resistance preventing the rounding of the lips on the involved side. The hope is that, through spontaneous recovery and the extensive workout of the weakened orbicularis oris and other facial muscles, some restoration of lip symmetry will be possible. Another activity often used with unilateral stroke patients suffering from a mild dysarthria is to practice counting or saying the days of the week as rapidly as possible. The speech-language pathologist determines how many words patients can say in a specific time period; in therapy, the goal is to increase the word count. Often by practice in speeding up the rate, patients' relaxed or functional speaking rate will approximate normal levels with increased intelligibility.

Stroke patients with a lower lesion who have a severe dysarthria may need help from the speech-language pathologist in developing a functional communication system. When possible, direct work on improving speech is the preferred approach. Patients may need help in developing expiratory control of the airstream, perhaps learning to produce a single word or short phrase on each expiration. Since such patients may experience great difficulty making tongue movements, articulatory intelligibility may be aided best by deliberately slowing down the rate of speech. In effect, patients are told to speak only fast enough to produce each word clearly. A palatal lift may be considered as an aid toward directing expiratory airflow through the mouth, which in some cases will improve articulatory precision (Aten and others, 1984). If intelligible speech is not a realistic goal, patients may require some kind of training to use a nonspeech communicative mode (gesture, communication board, an electronic communication board). Patients and their families work closely with speech-language pathologists to develop a working communication system, one that enables the patients to be understood.

REVIEW QUESTIONS

Let us review some of the key points about disorders of articulation:

1. Are children's articulation performances compared to the normal adult articulation standard? Why?

2. Distinguish between phonologic-process errors and phonetic errors. Would a different therapy approach be used for each?

3. Discuss typical articulation errors (omissions, substitutions, distortions, additions) from a phonologic-process point of view.

4. How can hearing loss contribute to faulty articulation?

5. List some physical problems that can contribute to phonetic errors.

6. How can phonologic-process analysis be used to remediate articulation errors?

7. What is the difference between acquisition and generalization in articulation training?

REFERENCES

Aten, J. L., McDonald, A., Guitterrez, R., and Simpson, M. (1984). Efficacy of modified palatal lifts for treatment, in *The Dysarthrias,* ed. M. R. McNeil, J. C. Rosenbeck, and A. E. Aronson. San Diego: College-Hill.

Bankson, N. W., and Byrne, M. C. (1972). The effect of a timed correct sound production task on carryover. *Journal of Speech and Hearing Research, 15:* 160–168.

Barrett, R. H., and Hanson, M. L. (1978). *Oral Myofunctional Disorders* (2nd ed.). St. Louis: Mosby.

Bernthal, J. E., and Bankson, N. W. (1981). *Articulation Disorders*. Englewood Cliffs, N.J.: Prentice-Hall.

Boone, D. R. (1982). *The Boone Voice Program for Children*. Tigard, Ore.: C. C. Publications.

Carrow, E. (1973). *Test for Auditory Comprehension of Language*. Austin, Tex.: Urban Research Group.

Collins, P. J., and Cunningham, G. W. (1982). *Articulation Modification Programs*. Tigard, Ore.: C. C. Publications.

Compton, A., and Hutton, S. (1978). *Compton-Hutton Phonological Assessment*. San Francisco: Carousel House.

Darley, F. L., Aronson, A. E., and Brown, J. R. (1975). *Motor Speech Disorders*. Philadelphia: Saunders.

Dunn, C. (1982). Phonological process analysis: contributions to assessing phonological disorders. *Communicative Disorders, 7:* 147–163.

Dunn, L. M., and Dunn, L. M. (1965). *Peabody Picture Vocabulary Test*. Circle Pines, Minn.: American Guidance Service.

Ferguson, C. A., and Farwell, C. B. (1975). Words and sounds in early language acquisition. *Language, 51:* 419–439.

Fisher, H. B., and Logemann, J. A. (1971). *The Fisher-Logemann Test of Articulation Competence.* Boston: Houghton Mifflin.

Goldman, R., and Fristoe, M. (1969). *Goldman-Fristoe Test of Articulation.* Circle Pines, Minn.: American Guidance Service.

Goldman, R., Fristoe, M., and Woodcock, R. W. (1969). *Goldman-Fristoe-Woodcock Test of Auditory Discrimination.* Circle Pines, Minn.: American Guidance Service.

Grunwell, P. (1980). Developmental language disorders at the phonological level, in *Language Disability in Children,* ed. F. M. Jones. Lancaster, Pa.: MTP Press.

Grunwell, P. (1981). *The Nature of Phonological Disability in Children.* New York: Academic Press.

Haney, S., and Peterson, M. (1984). *The Haney-Peterson Articulation Program.* Tigard, Ore.: C. C. Publications.

Hanson, M. L. (1976). Tongue thrust: another point of view. *Journal of Speech and Hearing Disorders, 41:* 172–184.

Hixon, T. J., Shriberg, L. D., and Saxman, J. H., eds. (1980). *Introduction to Communication Disorders.* Englewood Cliffs, N.J.: Prentice-Hall.

Hodson, B. W. (1980). *The Assessment of Phonological Processes.* Danville, Ill.: Interstate Press.

Hull, F. M., Mielke, P. W., Jr., Willeford, J. A., and Timmons, R. J. (1976). *National Speech and Hearing Survey.* Colorado State University, Fort Collins, Colo.: U.S. Department of Health, Education and Welfare; Office of Education, Bureau of Education for the Handicapped.

Ingram, D. (1981). *Procedures for the Phonological Analysis of Children's Language.* Baltimore: University Park Press.

Locke, J. (1980). The inference of a phoneme perception in the phonologically disordered child: a rationale, some criteria, the conventional tests. *Journal of Speech and Hearing Disorders, 45:* 431–441.

Locke, J. (1983). Clinical phonology: the explanation and treatment of speech sound disorders. *Journal of Speech and Hearing Disorders, 48:* 339–341.

Macaluso-Haynes, S. (1978). Developmental apraxia of speech: symptoms and treatment, in *Clinical Management of Neurogenic Communicative Disorders,* ed. D. F. Johns. Boston: Little, Brown.

MacNeilage, P. (1970). Motor control of serial ordering of speech. *Psychological Review, 77:* 182–196.

McDonald, E. T. (1964). *A Deep Test of Articulation.* Pittsburgh: Stanwix House.

McDonald, E. T. (1968). *A Screening Deep Test of Articulation.* Pittsburgh: Stanwix House.

McDonald, E. T., and Aungst, L. F. (1970). An abbreviated test of oral stereognosis, in *Second Symposium on Oral Sensation and Perception,* ed. J. F. Bosma. Springfield, Ill.: Charles C. Thomas.

McLean, J. (1976). *Stimulus Shift Articulation Program.* Bellevue, Wash.: Edmark.

McReynolds, L. V. (1982). Functional articulation problems, in *Human Communication Disorders: An Introduction,* ed. G. H. Shames and E. H. Wiig. Columbus: Charles E. Merrill.

McReynolds, L. V., and Elbert, M. (1981). Generalization of correct articulation in clusters. *Applied Linguistics, 2:* 119–132.

Mowrer, D. E. (1974). *First Steps in Writing Instructional Programs for Articulation Improvement.* Salt Lake: Word Making Products.

Netsell, R. (1984). A neurological view of the dysarthrias, in *The Dysarthrias,* ed. M. R. McNeil, J. C. Rosenbeck, and A. E. Aronson. San Diego, Calif.: College-Hill.

Pendergast, K., Dickey, S., Selmar, J., and Soder, A. (1968). *Photo Articulation Test.* Danville, Ill.: Interstate Printers and Publishers.

Perkins, W. H. (1977). *Speech Pathology: An Applied Behavioral Science* (2nd ed.). St. Louis: C. V. Mosby.

Prather, E., Addicott, M., Miner, A., and Sunderland, L. (1971). *Washington Speech Sound Discrimination Test.* Chicago: Stoelting Company.

Ringel, R. L., House, A. S., Burk, K. W., Dolinsky, J. P., and Scott, C. M. (1970). Some relations between orosensory discrimination and articulatory aspects of speech production. *Journal of Speech and Hearing Disorders, 35:* 3–11.

Sander, E. (1972). When are speech sounds learned? *Journal of Speech and Hearing Disorders, 37:* 55–63.

Shelton, R. L. (1971). Oral sensory function in speech production, in *Cleft Lip and Palate,* ed. W. C. Grabb, S. Rosenstein, and K. Bzoch. Boston: Little, Brown.

Shelton, R. L., Arndt, W. B., and Hetherington, J. (1967). Testing oral stereognosis, in *Symposium on Oral Sensation and Perception,* ed. J. Bosma. Springfield, Ill.: Charles C. Thomas.

Shelton, R. L., Furr, M. L., Johnson, A., and Arndt, W. B. (1975). Cephalometric and intraoral variables as they relate to articulation improvement with training. *American Journal of Orthodontics, 67:* 423–431.

Shelton, R. L., and McReynolds, L. V. (1979). Functional articulation disorders: preliminaries to treatment, in *Speech and Language,* Vol. 2. New York: Academic Press.

Shriberg, L. (1980). Developmental phonological disorders, in *Introduction to Communication Disorders,* ed. T. J. Hixon, L. Shriberg, and J. Saxman. Englewood Cliffs, N.J.: Prentice-Hall.

Shriberg, L., and Kwiatkowski, J. (1977). *Natural Process Analysis (NPA): A Procedure for Phonological Analysis of Continuous Speech Samples.* New York: Wiley.

Shriberg, L., and Kwiatkowski, J. (1980). *Natural Process Analysis (NPA): A Procedure for Phonological Analysis of Continuous Speech Samples.* New York: Wiley.

Skelly, M., Spector, D., Donaldson, R., Brodeur, A., and Paletta, F. (1971). Compensatory physiologic phonetics for the glossectomee. *Journal of Speech and Hearing Disorders, 36:* 101–114.

Snow, K., and Milisen, R. (1954). The influence of oral versus pictorial representation upon articulation testing results. *Journal of Speech and Hearing Disorders, Monogram Supplement 4:* 29–36.

Spriestersbach, D. (1965). The effects of orofacial anomalies in the speech process, in *Proceedings of the Conference-Communicative Problems in Cleft Palate. ASHA Report #1:* 111–127.

Stampe, D. A. (1973). "A dissertation on natural phonology." Unpublished doctoral dissertation, University of Chicago.

Stetson, R. (1951). *Motor Phonetics.* Amsterdam: North Holland Publishers.

Templin, M., and Darley, F. (1969). *The Templin-Darley Tests of Articulation.* Iowa City: Bureau of Educational Research and Service, University of Iowa.

Van Riper, C., and Emerick, L. (1984). *Speech Correction: an Introduction to Speech Pathology and Audiology.* Seventh Edition. Englewood Cliffs, N.J.: Prentice-Hall.

Van Riper, C., and Erickson, R. (1969). A predictive screening test of articulation, *Journal of Speech and Hearing Disorders, 34:* 214–219.

Van Riper, C., and Irwin, J. (1958). *Voice and Articulation.* Englewood Cliffs, N.J.: Prentice-Hall.

Waters, B. (1981). *Articulation Base Programs.* Dekalb, Ill.: Northern Illinois University.

Weiner, F. F. (1979). *Phonological Process Analysis.* Baltimore: University Park Press.

Winitz, H. (1975). *From Syllable to Conversation.* Baltimore: University Park Press.

Worthley, W. (1981). *Sourcebook of Articulation Learning Activities.* Boston: Little-Brown.

Yoss, K. A., and Darley, F. L. (1974). Therapy in developmental apraxia of speech, *Language, Speech and Hearing Services in Schools, 5:* 23–31.

11

Disorders of the Voice

Some people spend a lifetime struggling to have a normal voice. Whenever they use their voices a lot, they experience hoarseness or other symptoms that interfere with normal communication. Society is relatively tolerant of people with voice disorders, and it is not uncommon to hear them everywhere. A voice problem may prevent some people from pursuing a career, such as acting, singing, sales work, or teaching. Some voice disorders are symptoms of serious laryngeal disease. We shall consider two types of voice disorders in children and adults: problems of phonation and resonance.

As we saw in earlier chapters, phonation is produced by the airflow passing between the vocal folds, causing them to vibrate. These laryngeal vibrations are perceived as voice, or phonation. Phonation disorders, then, are problems in frequency (pitch), intensity (loudness), and quality. According to a national incidence study testing children across the United States (Hull and others, 1976), about 3 percent of all children have a phonation disorder. The incidence in the total population including both children and adults may be a fraction lower (there are no statistics available). Let us guess conservatively that about 2 percent of the population has a disorder of phonation.

In previous chapters, we saw that the vocal folds produce phonation (the source), but the entire vocal tract contributes to resonance (the filtering of the source sound). Any constricture or mass or change of shape of the vocal tract can cause some filtering of the source signal, contributing to a change of resonance. About 3 percent of the children in the study just cited exhibited resonance defects. However, a large number of these children may well have had colds or allergies that produced stuffed noses with a resulting change in resonance, producing temporary changes of voice resonance rather than the permanent change we might hear as a result of a cleft palate or a palate that is too short to make contact with the pharyngeal wall. Actual statistics are not available for the population as a whole, so let us make an educated guess that 2 percent has resonance defects of some type.

If the incidence of voice disorders (phonation plus resonance) is 4 percent, there must be a vast number of people with voice defects among us. This would include a sizable group for whom the voice problem is only an annoyance, which does not require any kind of remediation. For others, any problem of phonation or resonance might be considered career or personally threatening in some way, and therefore intolerable. On occasion, a voice problem may exist primarily in the ear of a listener; an employer or teacher may point out a dysphonia or resonance defect of which the individual was unaware. Sometimes the voice problem develops as the result of an acquired physical condition (allergy or infection), and is best dealt with by treating the physical condition rather than the voice per se.

It would appear that, of all the communication disorders seen by audiologists and speech-language pathologists, voice disorders are among the most successfully treated. The treatment of both phonation and resonance problems usually requires the combined specialties of the ear-nose-throat doctor (otolaryngologist) and the voice clinician (speech-language pathologist). Before considering phonation and resonance disorders separately, let us examine an actual case for each, including the problem, the specialties involved, and the kind of treatment that was offered:

Catherine, age forty-four, was a third-grade teacher who began to experience increased hoarseness toward the end of each school day. It became so difficult for her to use her voice (phonate) that she could no longer teach. An otolaryngologist found her to have a large unilateral polyp on one vocal fold, with some thickening on the other. Polyps, like vocal nodules, are generally the result of using the voice improperly, so the physician referred Catherine to a speech-language pathologist for "a voice evaluation, and voice therapy if indicated." It was found that Catherine spoke at the very bottom of her pitch range, more loudly than necessary, and "through clenched teeth," with her mandible barely moving. She began a program of voice therapy, in which she learned to use her voice more optimally. After 12 weeks, her unilateral polyp was "markedly reduced, with the other vocal fold now normal." Her voice restored, she returned to the classroom and was able to maintain a relatively normal voice by remembering to keep her pitch and loudness under control and make a conscious effort to open her mouth more while talking (which proved to be a more relaxed way of speaking for her).

Carl was a six-year-old who had received about two years of speech therapy for both an articulation and a language problem. His speech-language pathologist became concerned about Carl's speaking in a monotone, with a continually hypernasal voice. She finally referred him to an orofacial-disorder team. He was seen by an audiologist, a speech-language pathologist, voice scientist, plastic surgeon, and several dentists (including orthodontists and prosthodontists). It was discovered by the team that the boy had large tonsils and adenoids and a soft palate that appeared too short to make adequate pharyngeal-wall contact. It was subsequently recommended that he "first receive a tonsillectomy and adenoidectomy, to be followed by a pharyngeal flap." It was believed by the team that his velopharyngeal closure was structurally too inadequate to permit him to have normal oral resonance. After the proposed flap, speech and voice therapy would have a much better chance of success. Unfortunately, Carl's parents refused to follow the recommendations of the team, and no surgery was performed. The boy is now eight years old, and continues to display a moderately severe vocal-resonance defect; his voice is consistently hypernasal.

PHONATION DISORDERS

Most phonation disorders can be classified as either functional or organic. A functional disorder is usually a faulty voice resulting from vocal abuse and/or misuse. If we abuse or misuse the voice long enough, it may produce actual tissue changes

TABLE 11–1
Functional and Organic Phonation Disorders

Functional	Organic
Traumatic laryngitis	Infectious laryngitis
Functional dysphonia	Granuloma and hemangioma
Functional aphonia	Papilloma
Vocal-fold thickening	Laryngeal trauma
Vocal nodules/polyps	Laryngeal web
Spastic dysphonia	Vocal-fold paralysis
Contact ulcers	Carcinoma
Pitch and phonation breaks	Other physical conditions

within the larynx, such as vocal nodules or polyps. Since faulty use is the cause of the problem, we would still classify the problem as functional. An organically caused vocal problem is related to some kind of laryngeal condition or disease. Table 11–1 lists functional and organic phonation problems, each of which will be considered separately.

Functional Phonation Problems

Let us consider separately each of the functional phonation problems listed in Table 11–1. We will briefly consider the possible cause and typical management of each by both the physician and the speech-language pathologist.

Traumatic Laryngitis. Whenever I give a voice workshop or meet with a new voice class, I ask the students, "How many of you have ever lost your voice or had a severe case of laryngitis?" Invariably, about half the people in the room raise their hands. I have concluded that about half the population experiences occasional traumatic or infectious laryngitis, and the other half never experiences any vocal symptoms. Functional laryngitis is sometimes called **traumatic laryngitis.** It is usually the result of continuous vocal abuse, such as yelling throughout an exciting football game. In the excitement, people yell at high intensity levels (the crowd noise masks their efforts). The membranous edges of the vocal folds are irritated by the continuous yelling, becoming swollen (edema) and reddened. The vocal folds increase in size and cannot come together efficiently to produce a normal voice. The voice becomes very hoarse and in some cases can be lost altogether. The treatment for such a condition is to rest the voice. Keeping quiet is perhaps the best treatment for vocal-fold irritation related to too much effort (prolonged screaming, crying, and the like). After such a rest, the laryngeal edema and irritation usually subside, and the normal voice returns.

Functional Dysphonia. Any problem of hoarseness, harshness, breathiness (or whatever we want to call it) can be classified as a *dysphonia*. Any of these conditions can have many causes. Because many dysphonias may be but symptoms of serious laryngeal disease, we recommend that anyone who has dysphonia, independent of a cold or allergy (where the cause is more obvious), ought to have the benefit of indirect laryngoscopy or endoscopy.

In endoscopy, a lense is placed up the patient's nose, so that it sits behind the uvula, above the throat. This permits a direct view of both the vocal folds and other supraglottal structures. If the patient has dysphonia, and no laryngeal lesion (such as nodules) or dysfunction (such as paralysis) is seen, the diagnosis will be functional dysphonia. The patient would then be thoroughly evaluated by the speech-language pathologist to determine the probable cause or causes of the dysphonia. Learning to use the voice properly through therapy would be the treatment of choice for most patients with functional dysphonia (Boone, 1983; Greene, 1980; Wilson, 1979).

Functional Aphonia. When a patient experiences a complete loss of voice and no physical cause (such as vocal-fold paralysis) can be identified, we classify the problem as *functional aphonia.* The patient keeps the vocal folds apart, always speaking in a whisper. The cause of functional aphonia is different for each patient. For one person, the voice loss might have been part of a severe throat infection of some kind, with the voicelessness persisting beyond the original illness. For another, the problem might have an emotional base. A psychologically traumatic event might have produced the voicelessness initially; the aphonia persists for various reasons. A trial period of symptomatic therapy is warranted for most patients with aphonia. For example, the clinician sees whether the patient can produce a cough. If so, the cough is extended into a prolonged phonation. The patient keeps repeating the cough-induced voice, eventually forming some simple words on the extended phonation. The therapy methods for aphonia are described in detail by Wilson (1979) and Boone (1983). Occasionally, patients appear to need their voicelessness, and they resist symptomatic therapy. Such patients should be referred to a psychologist or psychiatrist.

Vocal-fold Thickening. Some people who continuously abuse or misuse their voices eventually develop a membranous thickening along the glottal edges of the vocal folds. This thickening develops slowly, over time, at the anterior-middle-third junction (the middle of the vibrating muscular portion of the folds). If it occurs day after day, the same kind of vocal abuse that produces traumatic laryngitis can eventually lead to thickening. Unless the abuses are curbed, the thickening will either remain or lead to bilateral vocal nodules. The therapy for vocal-fold thickening is to identify any abuse or misuse, and then reduce the occurrence of such behaviors. For example, a young woman developed bilateral vocal-fold thickening. The only abusive behavior found was her need to clear her throat continuously. Voice therapy focused on making her aware of her throat clearing and the need to reduce it. She drastically cut back on this behavior, the thickening disappeared, and her voice was restored to normal.

Vocal Nodules/Polyps. **Vocal nodules** or polyps occur on the vocal folds at the anterior-middle-third junction, usually as the result of long-term vocal abuse and misuse. Nodules are often bilateral, as seen in Figure 11–1, and vocal polyps are more often unilateral. Nodules are fibrotic, hard growths, which probably develop over time as a protective device by the continually irritated glottal membrane. Nodules can produce severe problems of voice. The mass of the nodules will add mass to the vocal folds, usually lowering pitch; this nodular mass will also prevent the folds from approximating normally together, allowing too much air to escape, which produces symptoms of breathiness and hoarseness. As nodules get bigger, the voice symptoms tend to get worse.

Vocal polyps are usually softer and more pliable than vocal nodules. A soft polyp is less irritating to the opposite vocal fold than a nodule; therefore, polyps are more often unilateral lesions, while vocal nodules tend to be bilateral. There is some evidence (Boone, 1983) that polyps may be the result of a single vocal abuse (such as screaming during a particular event), while nodules seem to be caused by long-term abuse. We are much more likely to see nodules in children, who may make a lot of noise with their voices (Toohill, 1975) throughout their waking hours. Pol-

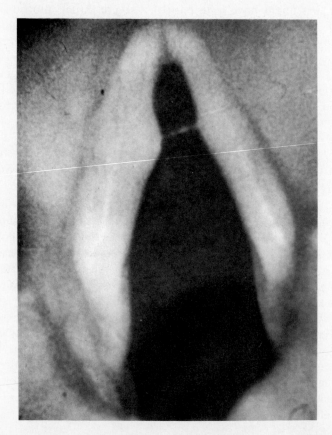

FIGURE 11–1   Bilateral vocal nodules.

yps are more common in adults, who may scream and yell on isolated occasions. The unilateral polyp may cause severe problems of voice characterized by breathiness, diplophonia (a double voice, caused by each vocal fold vibrating at a different rate), and hoarseness.

Voice therapy is the treatment of choice for both vocal nodules and polyps. Therapy must begin by searching with the patient to identify any kind of voice abuse (such as throat clearing) or misuse (for instance, speaking too loudly). Since patients will not usually exhibit the abuse-misuse pattern in the clinic office, it is often necessary for clinicians to observe them directly in those settings where there is some suspicion that the abuse-misuse is occurring. Once the bad vocal behavior is identified, vigorous efforts must be made to curb it. Using the voice in a better manner in voice therapy will not assure success unless vocal abuse and misuse have been drastically reduced. Voice therapy utilizes various approaches (Aronson, 1985; Boone, 1983; Wilson, 1979) for learning to use the vocal mechanism as optimally as possible. Large nodules or polyps, particularly those that have been present for a while, may have to be surgically removed before voice therapy can be started.

Spastic Dysphonia. One of the hardest voice disorders to treat with voice therapy is spastic dysphonia. Although we will consider it as a functional voice problem, the actual causes of the disorder are not known. The patient struggles to get the voice out. The vocal folds apparently approximate so tightly together that the airflow is cut off, resulting in a harsh, strangle-type phonation. The patient may experience a normal voice in some situations, such as in talking to a cat, repeating a memorized verse, or singing. It is no wonder that spastic dysphonia has been described as the "laryngeal stutter" (Luchsinger and Arnold, 1965), with the faulty voice varying in severity according to how the speaker views the listener. The more critical the communicative act, such as giving one's name to a ticket seller on the telephone, the more likely it is that the laryngeal tightness will occur and the voice will be shut off.

Voice therapy for this problem has produced only sporadic results (Cooper, 1977). Attempts to work with the patient to develop a relaxed phonation (by relaxing, chewing, using an open mouth, easy onset) have not been overly successful (Boone, 1983). Taking a different approach, Dedo and others (1978) have developed a different approach to the problem, in which the recurrent laryngeal nerve on one side is surgically severed; this produces a unilateral paralyzed vocal fold (in the paramedian position), which prevents further tight adduction of the folds. The "strangle" voice is replaced by the light, breathy phonation of someone with a unilateral vocal-fold paralysis. The operation is followed by several weeks of voice therapy, designed to give the patient the best voice possible. The Dedo surgical approach is still used for the treatment of spastic dysphonia, although there have been some reports that the tight voice recurs some time after surgery (Aronson and DeSanto, 1981; Wilson, Oldring, and Mueller, 1980).

Contact Ulcers. Contact ulcers are among the few lesions that occur posteriorly along the glottal edge of the vocal folds. Figure 11–2 shows ulcerations that appear

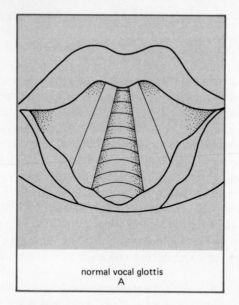
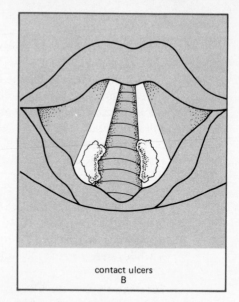

normal vocal glottis
A

contact ulcers
B

FIGURE 11-2   A: The normal inverted-V opening (glottis) between the vocal folds. B: Bilateral contact ulcers at the posterior end of each vocal fold along the glottis.

along the glottal membrane. This type of laryngeal disorder does not occur very often, and is usually found in adult males. The classic cause appears to be speaking with excessive force, voicing at the bottom of the frequency range, and speaking with excessively abrupt glottal attack (sudden initiation of phonation). More recently, it has been observed that many men with contact ulcers also have many gastric symptoms characterized by heartburn and reflux (in which the contents of the stomach and acidity come up into the throat). In any case, most problems of contact ulcers are managed well by voice therapy, sometimes with a physician's assistance in coping with the heartburn and reflux.

Pitch and Phonation Breaks. During puberty, young men often experience an upward pitch break in their voices. They will be voicing normally and will suddenly experience a pitch break (sometimes one or two octaves higher than the original pitch). These kinds of pitch breaks disappear by themselves as the larynx matures. Clinical concern about pitch breaks is reserved for individuals past puberty who experience either an upward or a downward pitch break. Most commonly, the voice suddenly breaks upward, and then returns quickly to the previous pitch. Such breaks indicate that the individual might be better off habitually speaking slightly higher. The voice tends to break in pitch toward the direction it would "like" to be. In any case, once upward breaks become a problem, they often "miraculously" disappear when individuals raise their pitch slightly. Downward pitch breaks are often related to speaking inappropriately high. By lowering your habitual pitch somewhat, the downward breaks can usually be eliminated.

The cause and treatment of phonation breaks vary greatly. The individual will be speaking (often with too much effort) and suddenly have no voice at all. The vocal folds suddenly abduct (separate), and the individual experiences a sudden, often fleeting loss of voice. Some years ago, I worked with a hard-rock disc jockey who used an excessively "hyper" vocal pattern when he narrated the music portion of his program. Once an hour, he read the news for 15 minutes; during the newscast, he began to experience phonation breaks. On one news recording we heard him say, "President Nixon told the Congress that the American [break] . . . for inflation. If the Congress was [break] . . . without recourse." Rather than lose his job because he couldn't read the news, he sought voice therapy. It was found that the phonation breaks appeared to be caused by the excessive force and artificiality he was using to match his voice to the hard-rock format. By becoming aware of this and using an easier vocal pattern during the 45 minutes of talking and music, he was soon able to speak in a regular manner for 15 minutes without experiencing phonation breaks. Therapy for this problem is usually similar; it takes the work out of voicing. Sometimes phonation breaks are caused by a beginning neurological problem, in which the patient is experiencing some changes in the central nervous system. In such instances, the phonation breaks are the early symptoms of a serious neurological disease. The speech-language pathologist is trained to distinguish between breaks related to hyperfunction and those that may have a neurological origin (which usually should be referred to a neurologist).

Organic Phonation Problems

Let us now consider some of the organic phonation problems that were listed in Table 11–1.

Infectious Laryngitis. The same people who experience traumatic laryngitis after only minor abuse or misuse of the voice also often experience an organic laryngitis when they have a cold or allergy. The best treatment for this disorder is voice rest (including *no* whispering) and whatever medical management by the physician is found helpful. No voice therapy is required.

Granuloma and Hemangioma. The most common injury to the vocal folds from external trauma is **granuloma** (a granulated sac) or hemangioma (a blood-filled sac) caused by intubation. During a surgical procedure, for example, a child had a breathing tube put up his nose. It was extended down his throat, pushed into the larynx and between the vocal folds into his trachea. The tube and the resulting granuloma can be seen in Figure 11–3. Once identified, granuloma are closely followed by the physician, and usually go away with no special treatment. Occasionally, large granuloma must be removed surgically. There may be a need for therapy, designed to give the patient the best voice possible with whatever scarred mechanism remains.

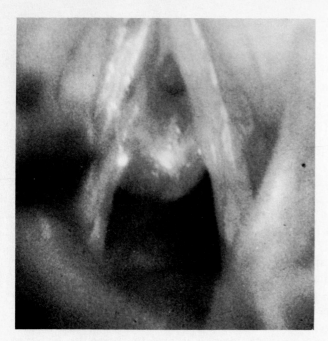

FIGURE 11-3   A vocal-fold granuloma occupies the glottis.

Papilloma. Usually of viral origin, **papilloma** are warty growths found in the warm, moist caverns of the vocal tract. The majority of papilloma are found in young children (usually preschool age), and only about 20 percent of the lesions persist beyond puberty (Kleinsasser, 1979). Of all the laryngeal lesions that may be found in children, papilloma are considered the most serious. They may grow very rapidly in a young vocal tract, posing a threat to the airway; getting adequate air is more serious than the voice problem. Speech-language pathologists in the public schools play an important role in identifying children with such airway lesions as papilloma. If these lesions are present in the larynx, the child may be experiencing some breathiness and hoarseness. All schoolchildren who experience a hoarseness for more than ten days are generally referred to a physician, who will perform laryngoscopy (get a mirror view of the vocal folds). Once a lesion such as papilloma is identified, it becomes a medical-surgical problem; if the papilloma are large enough to obstruct the airway, they must be surgically reduced. The speech-language pathologist would then work closely with the physician in managing the total airway-voice needs of the child. Because papilloma have a tendency to grow back quickly (one child we treated had 26 recurrences of papilloma, each requiring surgery), such children have to be watched closely over time.

Laryngeal Trauma. Although **laryngeal trauma** is seen more often in children than in adults, it can happen to anyone. People have had their larynges battered by having a baseball bat swung against the neck, being hit on the larynx by a baseball, being kicked by a horse, having the larynx crushed during an attempted strangulation, hitting the larynx on the dashboard, steering wheel or the car seat in front. The thyroid cartilage may be fractured, driven back, in part or wholly, toward the vocal-process end of the vocal folds. The immediate problem after injury is usually a lack of airway competence, requiring that the patient have an immediate tracheostomy (an opening through the neck into the trachea) to permit the intake and outtake of air. Therefore, in the beginning, such patients will have a permanent tracheostomy until the larynx has been surgically reconstructed; any attempt at voice (if voice is still possible) requires patients to cover the open tracheostomy with their finger on expiration, so that the airflow may go up through their vocal folds. The traumatized larynx requires surgical reconstruction so that patients can have sufficient valve protection of the airway and an adequate voice. After reconstruction is completed, patients may require voice therapy; after laryngeal trauma and reconstruction, such therapy has been found the most difficult of all voice therapies. It is highly individualized, according to the physical changes and the current needs of the patient.

Laryngeal Web. The membrane that covers each vocal fold sometimes grows across the glottis (opening between the vocal folds). This is known as a **laryngeal web.** Normally, the two vocal folds touch at the point of their origin, at the anterior commissure on the thyroid cartilage. As seen in Figure 11–4, anything that might traumatize the two glottal edges at the same site of approximation might result in the growing of a laryngeal web. The web grows in an anterior-to-posterior direction.

FIGURE 11–4 The larynx of a small child with a laryngeal web.

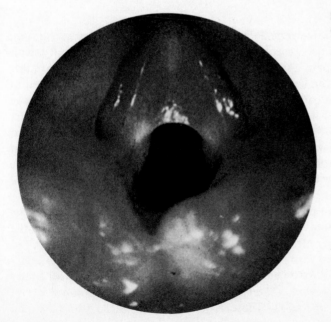

Severe laryngeal infection, laryngeal trauma, or bilateral removal of vocal-fold lesions have been known to cause the growth of webbing. The web must be surgically removed, and a keel (small piece of plastic) placed between the offended edges of the folds until healing is complete. Once this occurs (six to eight weeks after surgery), the keel is removed and voice therapy is often initiated.

Vocal-fold Paralysis. The most common form of vocal-fold paralysis is the unilateral type, which is usually caused by a cutting of the recurrent laryngeal nerve on one side. Nerve trauma is usually the result of a surgical procedure at a site near the nerve (such as a thyroidectomy) or the accidental cutting of the recurrent nerve during neck or chest surgery. In unilateral paralysis, the paralyzed fold is more often in the open, paramedian position. The patient has no voice, or aphonia. Usually, the severed nerve will regenerate within six months, and voice will be restored. Prior to its restoration, a temporary voice may be established by the patient working on respiration, promoting forceful phonation by a technique called pushing, and slightly raising pitch level. If no regeneration of the severed nerve occurs, there are several surgical procedures that have been found helpful, such as injecting the paralyzed fold with Teflon, so that it bulges out to make sufficient contact with the normal fold to produce phonation.

Bilateral paralysis of the vocal folds presents a much more serious problem, often resulting in having both vocal folds paralyzed in an open position. The airway becomes vulnerable without normal vocal-fold valving capability, and some kind of surgical intervention is usually necessary. Bilateral paralyses are usually related to a central-nervous-system dysfunction, such as a stroke (see Chapter 9) or dysarthria, which includes the lack of voice resulting from having both vocal folds paralyzed in the open position.

Carcinoma. The most serious laryngeal disease, of course, is cancer, or **carcinoma,** of the larynx. Besides hoarseness, early warning signs include having difficulty swallowing, neck swelling, and pain. An adult who experiences any of these symptoms for ten days ought to have the benefit of an examination by a physician trained in mirror laryngoscopy, such as an otolaryngologist. If cancer is suspected, a biopsy will be taken. If the diagnosis is confirmed, several treatment options are available. Smaller lesions are successfully treated by radiation therapy alone; some throat and laryngeal cancers can be treated by a combination of radiation, chemotherapy, and surgery; more advanced problems may require the total surgical removal of the larynx (laryngectomy). After total laryngectomy, the patient may also require some follow-up radiation therapy.

The speech-language pathologist often sees the patient just before and/or immediately after laryngectomy. The patient and family are counseled about the loss of communicative ability after surgery and what can be done. Alternatives to the normal voice are reviewed with the patient, such as using a writing pad, "magic-slate," or electronic voice instruments, and learning esophageal speech. Many speech-language pathologists work closely with lay-laryngectomee groups, whose members have had such an operation. These laryngectomees (those who have had the operation) work closely with the clinician, offering encouragement and suggestions to the new patient. The speech-language pathologist demonstrates the use of electronic instruments and provides instruction for the patient learning to use esophageal speech. In esophageal speech, the patient is taught to trap air in the mouth, forcing it to go into the esophagus; as the air comes back up, an eructation (belch) is produced. With training, this can become the new substitute voice. Esophageal speech requires many weeks of training and is facilitated today by occasional surgical changes of the mechanism and by having the patient use various assistive electronic devices (Shedd and Weinberg, 1980).

Other Physical Conditions. There are many other physical conditions that can influence the sound of one's voice. Obviously, we have only to think of the dramatic change in pitch of children's voices as they go through puberty. The hormonal influences on the larynx and its voice productions are enormous. The boy's larynx doubles in size during the pubertal years, with a resulting drop in pitch of about one octave; the female's larynx becomes half again as large in size during puberty, with a resulting drop in pitch of about four musical notes (Kahane, 1983). While the voice pitch remains relatively stable through most of the adult years, there is a continuing lowering of fundamental frequency for both sexes during the working years. After the age of sixty, the female continues to experience a gradual lowering of the vocal pitch. The voice of the male over eighty, on the other hand, gradually begins to be elevated (Honjo and Isshiki, 1980).

When we considered dysarthria in Chapters 9 and 10, it was noted that any changes in the central nervous system may produce changes in the voice, including problems of pitch, loudness, quality, and resonance. The vocal difficulties caused by severe hearing loss and deafness were documented in Chapter 7.

THE EVALUATION OF PHONATION DISORDERS

The successful management of a phonation disorder first requires a thorough evaluation. Voice patients either seek help and come to the voice clinic on their own, or they are identified in some kind of voice-screening program (such as in the public schools). Regardless of how and why a patient comes to a voice clinic, a medical evaluation must be made first. The otolaryngologist exams the patient's ears, nose, and throat for any kind of structural disease or blockage to the vocal tract. Typically, a mirror is placed in the back of the throat (mirror laryngoscopy), and the vocal folds and larynx are viewed by reflection in the mirror. The otolaryngologist then diagnoses the laryngeal disorder, which is usually one of those reviewed in this chapter. For example, during a public-school screening, a nine-year-old boy who was found to be hoarse, was subsequently evaluated at a voice clinic; he was found to have "bilateral vocal nodules, fibrotic and possibly of long standing." This diagnosis tells the speech-language pathologist that the child has hard, fixed nodules that have probably been there for a while, perhaps indicating that long-term voice therapy will be required to eliminate them.

Next, the patient is evaluated by the speech-language pathologist. Before taking a history or any voice measurements, the clinician should get to know the patient as a human being. As I wrote in an earlier publication:

> Engaging the patient in some conversation about himself or herself is an important beginning of the evaluation. With the adult we want to know a bit about the life situation, including occupation, personal interests, hobbies, family and marital status. Inevitably, the clinician will ask the patient, "What is it about your voice that brought you to see us today?" The patient's own description and view of the voice problem can provide insights on how to proceed with the evaluation (Boone, 1983, p. 260).

The clinician takes a complete case history with special attention given to what the patient feels is the cause of the problem, how long the voice problem has been present, and how it may vary throughout the day.

It is of critical importance in the evaluation to make some determination of how patients use the voice in different settings. How they speak in the clinic does not usually represent how they speak on the outside. Therefore, it is vital for clinicians to observe patients in various work and play settings, particularly as the clinician must search for possible vocal abuses (such as yelling) and misuse (such as speaking at an inappropriate pitch). When we work with children, we must visit the playground and perhaps the home; we must enlist the cooperation of parents and friends in an attempt to identify possible voice abuse-misuse. With adult clients, clinicians go to the church, the school, the nightclub, the auction barn, or wherever patients may be abusing and misusing the voice. When possible, it is important to identify firsthand the patient's voice usage.

It is helpful for clinicians to use a rating scale for organizing observations about their patients. Such a scale allows them to view the possible interactions of such vocal parameters as pitch, loudness, quality, nasal resonance, oral resonance, rate, and pitch range under various voicing conditions, including conversation, play, and oral reading. The completed scale of the nine-year-old boy with vocal nodules notes, in summary, that he "uses his voice at the bottom of his pitch range, with a voice that's barely audible, characterized by breathiness and hoarseness." Wilson (1979) uses a number of voice-scaling profiles directly with children, who help complete their own ratings on the *Buffalo Voice Profile, the Buffalo Voice Abuse Profile, and the Buffalo Resonance Profile.* By having children help to complete their own profiles, the evaluation process also begins the therapeutic process of making patients aware of what they are doing.

Now the speech-language pathologist evaluates the patient's oral mechanism, with focus given to the adequacy of both structure and function. A direct view by the clinician of the patient's mouth can do much to determine the adequacy of both structure and function of:

lips
facial muscles
teeth (occlusion and alignment)
hard palate (maxillary arch)
soft palate (velum)
tonsils (fausces)
pharynx

Many speech-language pathologists also use the endoscope to look at the vocal folds themselves.

Particular vocal functions, such as pitch and loudness, are best measured by the use of various instruments as part of the evaluation process. These will be considered next.

Respiration Measurement

The voice evaluation should include some data specific to the patient's respiratory performance. Hixon (1972) has written that four types of respiration measurement are particularly important for the voice patient: driving air pressure, flow through the glottis, lung volume changes, and motions of the body wall. One method, of course, for perceiving the effects of air pressure is to listen to changes in loudness of the patient's voice. The louder the voice, the greater the pressure. The oral pressure may be measured by using a pressure transducer or a manometer; the patient's task is to repeat *pa* into the mouthpiece of the measuring instrument, which permits the measurement of peak pressure. Or the clinician may wish to measure how the patient can generate pressure over a period of time. The patient is asked to blow into a mouthpiece with a small air leak for five seconds; Netsell and Hixon (1978) have written that if subjects can generate five to ten cm H_2O of pressure for at least five seconds, they probably have adequate driving air pressure to produce normal voice.

Since it takes about 100 cc of airflow (volume of air) per second for a subject to produce a vowel, running speech uses up a considerable amount of air volume. Airflow volumes are best measured with the pneumotachometer. The patient wears a mask over the mouth and repeats or reads a passage aloud; the oral airflow is recorded for each part of the utterance. We use about half our volume of air in running speech, and beyond the initial breath that starts our conversational voice, we often take little catch-up breaths that are hardly visible to our listeners. Part of the voice evaluation usually looks at adequacy of overall respiration, often by measuring the patient's **tidal volume** (the amount of air breathed in and out in a normal at-rest breathing cycle) and **vital capacity** (the maximum amount of air that can be expelled from the lungs after a maximum inspiration). The spirometer is used for measuring air volume and capacity.

Many voice patients, particularly those with motor speech problems, may use the muscles of the torso incorrectly for breathing. For example, patients may be pushing out the stomach when they should be tucking it in. Hixon, Mead, and

Goldman (1976) developed a method for studying the movements of the torso by using small magnets, placed on the chest and abdominal walls. The distance between the two magnets on the chest (and/or the abdomen) changes according to the active and passive movements of these structures; the distances between the magnets are plotted on an oscillograph. It is then possible to identify whether particular movements are out of synchrony with one another. Not only can the oscillograph display be used for measuring chest wall-stomach movements, but it can be used in therapy as a feedback device, allowing patients to see the movements of the torso as they speak and sing.

Acoustic Measurements of the Voice

Not many years ago, so few instruments were available to study voice problems that clinicians were forced to use instruments such as the piano or pitch pipe as their primary measuring devices. Today, the frequency of the voice can be documented, in addition to vocal quality, intensity, and sharpness of glottal attack.

Measuring Frequency. Several measurements of voice pitch must be taken at the time of the evaluation. As we discussed in Chapter 4, pitch or pitch range is determined by matching the voice to the notes of a piano. When we measure the actual cycles per second on an instrument such as the Visi-Pitch, we have a measurement of actual frequency. We determine the patient's pitch range by using instruments such as the Visi-Pitch or PM Pitch Analyzer. Patients are asked to sing down to their lowest possible note (we usually repeat this twice) and then to sing up to the highest one without strain (this is usually repeated also). This gives us patients' frequency ranges, the lowest to highest notes. Patients are then asked to display their normal voice by repeating sentences, conversing, and perhaps reading aloud. These same frequency analyzers usually permit a fixed display of patients' running speech-frequency values; clinicians then count the number of the most often-occurring frequency values and determine patients' *modal* or **habitual pitch** (the pitch that occurs most often).

   It has been argued that our habitual pitch ought to be the same as our *optimum* pitch, if we use our voices as we should. Fairbanks (1960) introduced the concept of optimum pitch as the pitch value that is about one-fourth up from the bottom of one's total range. The optimum pitch is perhaps a note or two several notes about one's lowest note and can be produced with less effort. In a voice conference at the Juilliard School of Music, several authors (Bless, 1984; Boone, 1984; Minifie, 1984) concluded that there was no such thing as an absolute optimum pitch. There appears to be no note on which most voicing should be done. It does seem true, however, that you can speak with less strain if you keep your speaking pitch a note or two up from the bottom of your total frequency range. When people speak at the very bottom of their total pitch range, they may experience real vocal strain as they try to use an artificially low voice pitch, one that is so low, they cannot inflect the voice downward.

   A female graduate student was evaluated for a persistent voice problem.

Her lowest note was a D_3 (147 Hz), and her highest was E_5 (659 Hz), which gave her a range of more than two octaves. Yet her measured habitual pitch was found to be a E_3 (164 Hz), only one note up from the bottom of her total range. According to the Fairbanks formula for optimum pitch, using the voice one-quarter of the total range up from the lowest note as a guideline, her optimum pitch would have been G_3 (196 Hz). Although she was not counseled to use a particular note as an optimum pitch, she was shown that using a pitch several notes above her lowest one produced a voice that sounded far less strained. Keeping her voice pitch off the bottom of her total range greatly helped her to develop a better speaking voice.

Measuring Quality. Instruments available for displaying variations in voice quality include the sound spectrograph (Kay Sound Sonograph, or the PM Pitch Analyzer). A tape recording is made of the patient's voice, and the vocal signal is analyzed spectrally, offering a visual display of what is heard. Figure 11–5 shows the typical spectrograms for voices that are considered normal, breathy, and harsh. Spectrographic displays are sometimes helpful in making before- and after-therapy comparisons, enabling one to measure actual changes in spectral display. Two other measurements of quality can be taken, **jitter** and **shimmer.** Jitter can be measured using an adapter device added to the Visi-Pitch, which gives a perturbation value of frequency, a frequency "wobble" around the fundamental. Wendahl (1963) reported that there appeared to be a direct relationship between the amount of measured jitter and vocal roughness perceived by a large panel of judges. Shimmer is similar to jitter, except that it looks at "wobble," or variations in amplitude or intensity of the voice. Listeners hear the measured shimmer as hoarseness or roughness.

Measuring Intensity. To determine the loudness of a voice is to make a perceptual judgment. The measurement of loudness can reveal the sound pressure value or intensity. It is best accomplished during the evaluation by using a sound-level meter. The patient is asked to keep a fixed distance from the sound-level-meter microphone, and the actual sound pressure of the voice is measured in decibels for that fixed distance. The Visi-Pitch can also give relative intensity differences of the voice, and provides useful indicators of the interaction of frequency and intensity for the same signal. That is, someone can speak an eight-second passage and see the interface of both intensity and frequency for it, locked on the storage scope of the Visi-Pitch. In reality, however, intensity varies so much in the voicing situation that a measurement of loudness in the laboratory often has little clinical relevance to what the patient is doing in the real world (such as yelling at a noisy child). Some patients who come to voice clinics, however, do demonstrate problems of vocal loudness; for them, intensity measurements play a primary role in the evaluation.

Measuring Glottal Attack. *Glottal attack* is the term that was used to define the temporal aspect of initiating phonation. Hard, abrupt glottal attack can be heard in speakers from some big cities in the northeastern United States, as opposed to the easy, slow attack of some speakers from rural southeastern states. If excesses

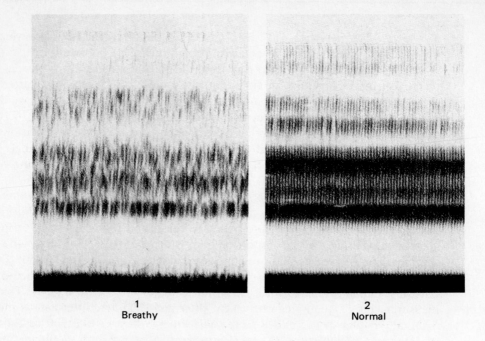

1
Breathy

2
Normal

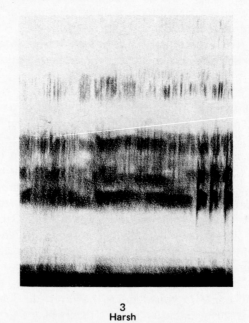

3
Harsh

FIGURE 11-5   Three spectrograms of the same speaker producing the vowel /i/ under three conditions: breathy, normal, harsh. The relative spacing of the formants stays the same as the signal source changes.

of glottal attack were observed at the time of the voice evaluation, the clinician might wish to quantify these onsets of phonation. The Visi-Pitch is useful for quantifying glottal attack; the intensity measurement is used with a two- or four-second display. In hard glottal attack, there is an abrupt initiation of phonation that is characterized by a vertical onset line on the Visi-Pitch scope; easy attack is represented by a gradual upward slope, clearly differentiating the time of onset for a speaker with hard attack and one with soft attack. Although a therapist might very occasionally help a patient to stop using an easy, soft, glottal attack, the usual thrust in therapy is to help a patient change a hard glottal attack to an easier one.

VOICE THERAPY FOR PHONATION DISORDERS

Voice therapy may take many different forms. The kind of therapy one might provide people who simply want to improve their voices might vary markedly from what one would do with a patient who has a paralyzed vocal fold. Voice therapy is highly individualized, according to the physical problem (if any), the length of its existence, how the voice sounds, and how the patient may feel about it. In general, we follow a four-point program in working with both children and adults with voice problems:

1. identify abuse/misuse;
2. reduce its occurrence;
3. search with the patient for the best voice that can be produced;
4. practice facilitating approaches.

Let us consider each of these points separately.

Identify Abuse/Misuse

Voice improvement or voice therapy cannot be successful as long as patients continue to abuse or misuse their voices. For example, a forty-four-year-old man with a unilateral vocal polyp was observed to abuse or misuse his voice in the following ways:

1. Smoke two packs of cigarettes a day (abuse)
2. Constantly clear his throat (abuse)
3. Use over-the-counter decongestants for his "nasal drip" (abuse)
4. Speak at the very bottom of his pitch range (misuse)
5. Yell frequently at his children and dog (misuse)

Most of this patient's abuses/misuses were determined primarily by case history. For voice therapy to be successful, clinicians often must visit patients' various vocal environments in order to validate the identification of harmful laryngeal behaviors. Unless these abuses/misuses can be identified, the voice therapy (working on easy glottal attack, for example) may have little or no effect.

Reduce the Occurrence of Abuse/Misuse

Once laryngeal and vocal abuse and misuse have been identified, the findings must be discussed with the patient. If patients can understand what they may be doing wrong, and if they are at all motivated, they will initiate efforts to curb their abuse/misuse with only minimal prodding by the clinician. This is called the cognitive approach to voice therapy. In discussing the history of the forty-four-year-old man described earlier, the harmful effects on his larynx from his moderately heavy smoking were explained to him. He was shown pictures of a reddened airway made worse by heavy exposure to tobacco smoke. In effect, the patient was told "If you want to get over this vocal polyp problem—and you should be able to with voice therapy—you are going to have to quit smoking." His throat clearing and the fact that it may well have been a habit he had developed were discussed. It was explained: "You have a pair of reddened vocal folds that exude mucus to protect themselves (irritated mucosal tissue exudes its own mucus). When you clear your throat, that mucus is cleared away. The act of throat clearing causes additional irritation, and you clear the newly formed mucus away again. Throat clearing becomes a circular kind of behavior." The smoking and throat clearing were discussed in language the patient could easily understand. When he seemed to realize that he should curb both his smoking and throat clearing, strategies were developed with him to reduce these behaviors. Voice therapy at this stage of the treatment basically meant identifying and developing ways to curb or eliminate abuse.

A cognitive approach to children with voice problems is also used. For example, a nine-year-old boy with bilateral vocal nodules had been identified as using an excessively loud voice most of the time. Voice therapy could not be successful until he made consistent attempts to reduce his loudness. The child was helped to realize that there were different loudness levels possible by being shown pictures that depict five different loudness levels. We encouraged him to speak more often at a "two-loudness level," in which "you don't want to speak loudly enough to wake up the fellow sleeping in the chair." Pictures and stories developed for children are often effective in helping them to understand what they may be doing wrong. Like adults, when they understand how they are abusing and misusing their voices, children usually do what they can to reduce or eliminate such behaviors.

Search with the Patient for the Best Voice

At the beginning of voice therapy, various therapeutic probes are used to determine what voice techniques might be useful. Therapeutic approaches are almost as numerous as the clinicians providing the therapy. In *The Voice and Voice Therapy* (1983), I list 25 facilitating approaches (therapy techniques) that can be used in voice therapy. An example of using a therapy probe would be to take one of those techniques, use it with the patient, and see what effect it has on the voice. For example, in an early therapy session, the clinician might determine the effect on the patient's voice of using the "Open-Mouth Approach." There are six specific steps for administering this approach, and the therapy probe would determine which of them seemed to produce a better voice. If the technique works, it is used in therapy; if it has no effect or seems to make the problem worse, the technique is abandoned and another one is used.

When we talk about helping to produce the best voice, we do not mean necessarily a normal voice. The boy with bilateral vocal nodules has heavily weighted vocal folds, and having him use an easier, more relaxed way of talking will probably produce a voice that is excessively breathy, low in pitch and loudness. In fact, talking in an easy manner may temporarily produce a voice that is judged to be hoarser than before. The easy voice would still be the "best" voice for the child to use as a means to achieve a better-sounding voice. For many problems of vocal hyperfunction (using too much effort for phonation), the early therapy approaches are designed to take the work out of talking, so that in the beginning, the voice sounds worse. As people learn to speak with less effort, the vocal mechanisms are used more efficiently, which results in a better voice. A better voice, or the one that is sought in therapy, is the voice that is similar to that of patients' age and sex peers.

Practice Facilitating Approaches

Once the patient has produced a good target voice, using whatever therapy techniques that work, intensive practice using the new voice is required. It is important in therapy that the patient be able to distinguish clearly between the old phonation pattern and the new one. The clinician needs to present the patient with contrasts between the old and the new voice. Not only may the voice sound different, but it may feel quite different to produce. A successful therapy approach, once a new voicing pattern has been established, is to use negative practice, asking the patient to go back and use the old way of talking. To illustrate voice therapy, here is a summary of a therapy session written for a twenty-two-year old waitress who had a functional dysphonia (no organic changes in the larynx) that was characterized by harshness and hard glottal attack:

> Karna became aware of her problem—hard glottal attack—by listening to her conversation with the therapist on tape. We then played tapes of some famous people talking, and she listened critically and found those who spoke with hard attack and those who spoke with soft attack. For the first time, she noticed the easy attack of people such as Jimmy Carter and Joanne Woodward, as opposed to the hard attack of such individuals as Don Adams and Bette Davis. By imitating the clinician's models, she was able to produce single words with easy glottal attack. We used the Visi-Pitch intensity tracings at a two-second setting to confirm the slope lines of easy glottal attack. Karna finished the session by practicing easy-attack word lists with 95 percent accuracy.

Practice in producing a new voice pattern should not be started until the patient understands how the old and the new voice patterns differ. Successful therapy requires that the patient be provided with lots of feedback. The mirror, audio-tape and video-tape playback, the oscilloscope screens of certain instruments, various digital and dial instruments that tell us the scores or values of a parameter on which we are working are all useful external feedback devices used in voice therapy. Internal feedback is also used. For instance, the therapist may ask the patient, "Does it feel different when you do it that way?" or "Does it still feel scratchy in your throat after you do the reading?"

There is probably no other group of patients with whom the speech-language pathologist works that is more responsive than voice patients. Symptomatic voice therapy works. Voices can often be improved dramatically in a relatively short period of time. The abuse and misuse of the laryngeal mechanisms that eventually lead to vocal-fold thickening, nodules, and polyps can be stopped, resulting in a decrease in the actual lesions and an improvement in voice quality. Many dysphonias related to vocal hyperfunction can be eliminated by guiding the patient into more optimal vocal production.

PROBLEMS OF RESONANCE

As we discussed in Chapter 4, the shape of the normal vocal tract is very much like a capital *F,* as shown in Figure 11–6, Diagram A. To have normal oral and nasal resonance, we must have a normal *F*-tract, capable of shutting off the oral cavity from the nasal cavity with adequate velopharyngeal closure, as well as open coupling between the oral and nasal cavities when nasal resonance is desired. Resonance disorders occur when any part of the open *F*-tract is altered or impeded (see Figure 11–6). Problems of oral resonance occur primarily when the tongue occupies either an excessively high front position (Diagram B) or when it is carried high posteriorly in the oropharynx (Diagram C). Baby-talk resonance is usually produced by excessively high front carriage of the tongue, while cul de sac resonance (Boone, 1983) is produced by high carriage of the tongue toward the back of the pharynx (which we often hear in the voices of deaf speakers). Variations of nasal resonance are shown in Diagrams D and E. The most common resonance defect is hypernasality, characterized by open coupling between the oral and nasal cavities (Diagram D); the patient experiences excessive nasalance, particularly of vowels, and the voice sounds as if it were coming through the nose. Diagram E shows blockage between the oral and nasal cavities, which prevents normal nasal resonance of the three nasal consonants (m, n, ŋ), producing a resonance problem of denasality; patients sound as if they have a severe allergy or head cold and a stopped-up nose.

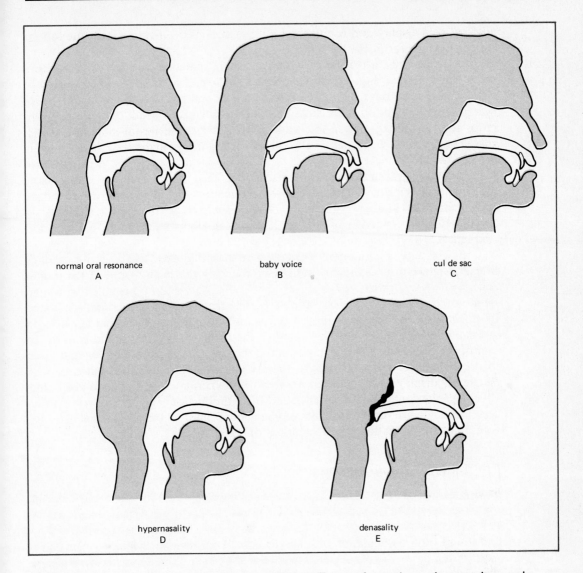

normal oral resonance
A

baby voice
B

cul de sac
C

hypernasality
D

denasality
E

FIGURE 11-6 Variations in the shape of the vocal tract for various changes in vocal resonance.

Problems of Oral Resonance

The oral cavity is the most changeable of the resonating chambers, continually altering its shape by the lowering or raising of the mandible, movements of the tongue, and soft-palate movements with attendant pharyngeal-wall movements. Occasionally, patients display oral-resonance problems caused by having the tongue too far forward or too far in the back of the mouth.

Sometimes, a teacher or employer refers someone with a baby voice to a voice clinic. Rarely do such patients come on their own. If they are motivated to change the front focus of the voice to a more normal-sounding resonance, voice therapy is usually quite successful. The thin baby voice is produced with high anterior tongue carriage, often also causing a lisp or distortion of sibilants, as discussed in some detail in Chapter 10. Therapy is begun by having the patient practice the production of back vowels (/a/, /ɔ/, /o/, /ʊ/, and /u/), which usually produces an immediate improvement in resonance; when the tongue is back and lower, the resonance improves. The back vowel production with the use of the two back consonants, /k/ and /g/, is then coupled. Practice using the back consonants in combination with middle to back vowels will usually produce more optimal oral resonance.

The patient with cul de sac resonance caused by excessive posterior carriage of the tongue can often change resonance focus by producing front-of-the-mouth consonants (/w/, /wh/, /p/, /b/, /f/, /v/, /θ/, /ð/, and /l/) coupled with high front vowels (/i/, /I/, /e/, /ɛ/, and /æ/). The front focus is sometimes facilitated by having the patient make these front sounds rapidly in the beginning, using a whisper or very light voice. The sound of the front voice is in marked contrast to that of the back one, and it is important in therapy for the patient to feel and listen to the difference. When working with very-hard-of-hearing or deaf patients (who frequently display back-focus voice, often with hypernasality), we spend much time "feeling" the contrast between back and front production. Ling (1976) reports success in changing the back resonance of young deaf children to more normal patterns, combining amplification with techniques of direct resonance modification.

Problems of Nasal Resonance

Any alteration of the function or structure of the velopharyngeal-closure mechanism can cause a problem in nasal resonance. The majority of nasality problems are related to excessive nasal resonance (hypernasality), in which there is excessive airflow and sound-wave transmission through the nose. The opposite problem—insufficient nasal resonance (denasality)—is usually caused by some kind of structural blockage that prevents the flow of air and sound waves from passing through the nose (as is required for the normal nasal resonance of /m/, /n/, and /ŋ/).

We can perhaps best understand nasal-resonance disorders by reviewing the velopharyngeal-closure mechanism. The lateral view of resonance deviations in Figure 11–6 shows the structures required for normal velopharyngeal closure. The actual closure point for most subjects is at point X in drawing A, somewhat above the bottom of the uvula (the view we see when we look directly into someone's mouth). Different people have different closure patterns (Zwitman, Sonderman, and Ward, 1974): for some, closure is achieved by velar lifting to make contact with a relatively static pharyngeal wall; for others, the pharyngeal wall bulges forward to meet the lifting velum; for still others, the lateral pharyngeal walls are much more active and move in laterally to "grip" the rising velum and protruding pharynx.

Most normal speakers demonstrate tight velopharyngeal closure, with relatively no air leakage, for all oral sounds in English, and have a velopharyngeal opening only for the nasal consonants.

The majority of persistent nasal-resonance problems are related to hypernasality caused by velopharyngeal inadequacy. A brief review of the embryological development of the hard and soft palate (velum) will help us to see that most of the structural problems causing hypernasality are related to lack of palatal fusion in the sixth to tenth week of fetal development. The fusion of the hard and soft palates develops in an anterior-to-posterior manner, rather like the closing of a zipper (Ewanowski and Saxman, 1980). The anterior part of the mouth, including the midsection of the upper lip, the alveolar process, and the premaxilla, form embryologically by the nasal processes moving down from the nose area and growing into the mouth, forming the upper anterior portion of the mouth (this occurs at six and a half weeks). As the nasal process moves in a posterior direction, the two lateral processes move medially and begin to fuse around the premaxilla (at eight weeks). After the hard-palate fusion is complete, the lateral processes continue to fuse together, moving in a posterior direction, fusing the soft palate, with just a slight clefting of the uvula remaining at the beginning of the tenth fetal week. By the eleventh fetal week, the fusion development of the hard and soft palates is usually complete (Patten, 1971).

Hypernasality. Let us consider the usual causes of hypernasality.

Cleft palate. The most serious problems of hypernasality are usually found in individuals who demonstrate a dramatic lack of palatal fusion, as in cleft palate. Clefts of the palate may also involve the upper lip and alveolar process (unilaterally or bilaterally). Hard-palate clefts may be bilateral, often isolating the premaxilla. As long as a person with a cleft palate has openings of either the hard or soft palate, there is a risk of a massive escape of air and sound waves through the open oral-nasal areas, which may cause perceptual judgments of hypernasality and possible nasal emission (escape of air through the velopharyngeal port for high intraoral pressure sounds, such as /s/ and /z/).

Velopharyngeal inadequacy. In the absense of an overt cleft or sometimes after palatal surgery, the individual may experience velopharyngeal inadequacy causing problems of hypernasality. About 15 to 20 percent of new patients seen in an orofacial clinic were found to have problems of velopharyngeal inadequacy (Pruzansky and others, 1977). Causes of inadequacy may be related to the velum being too short, inadequate in length to make adequate contact with the lateral and posterior pharyngeal walls. Or the velum may not move well enough to permit adequate levation. Sometimes, short velums are observed not to move adequately (they seem to "know" why bother to move because they cannot make contact anyway) but have the capability of moving. Cole (1979) has recommended direct muscle training for individuals with marginal velopharyngeal closure mechanisms; Shelton and others (1971) have used training obturators in an attempt to stimulate more vigorous muscle movement to achieve closure. Velopharyngeal inadequacy is usually related to some kind of structural lack that prevents closure; until this lack is corrected by surgery, or a prosthesis, or by voice therapy, severe problems of hypernasality and nasal emission may persist.

Velar paresis. There are occasional neurological conditions that may result in partial or complete paralysis of the velum. Occasional children are born without adequate innervation of the velum. More commonly a velar paralysis may be found as one of the symptoms of someone who has had a stroke, or a degenerative disease, or a developmental disorder such as cerebral palsy. Many of these problems present palatal involvement that is assymetrical; that is, one side of the velum may be paralyzed with no involvement on the other side. Often the best management of a paralyzed velum is for the patient to have a palatal lift created by a prosthodontist.

Postadenoidectomy and/or tonsillectomy. Many children experience temporary hypernasality following the removal of adenoids, but this usually lasts only four to six weeks (Pruzansky and others, 1977). The problem may be more lasting if the child had been using the adenoidal pads to help achieve velopharyngeal closure before the adenoids were removed; the distance between the rising velum and the pharyngeal wall is too great to permit closure. What had been a problem of nasal blockage (which required the adenoidectomy) becomes the opposite problem, excessive nasal opening. If the difficulty persists, the child might require either a prosthetic appliance or some kind of surgical correction (discussed later in the chapter).

Functional hypernasality. On occasion, we see someone who speaks with excessive hypernasality who can demonstrate normal oral resonance when asked to do so. The actor James Stewart is an example of someone who speaks with functional hypernasality. He has no need to change his voice resonance, and it may that if he did, he would no longer present the speech pattern that characterizes him (and is so attractive to imitators). Since the patient with functional hypernasality has no structural problem contributing to nasality, functional voice therapy, with a heavy emphasis on ear training and modeling, will often have positive effects.

Denasality. Denasality is a lack of sufficient nasal resonance. The voice sounds blocked and muffled, as if the speaker has a severe head cold and cannot breathe through the mouth. The term *hyponasality,* although synonymous with denasality, is unfortunately often confused as *hypernasality,* despite the fact that the two disorders are at opposite poles of the nasal-resonance continuum. Thus, we prefer to use *denasality.* The condition is characterized by insufficient nasal resonance for the three nasal phonemes /m/, /n/, and /ŋ/ and near-total lack of nasal resonance for vowels in the English language. Fletcher (1972) reported, using his Tonar II (an instrument that measures relative oral-nasal resonance), that a voice will be perceived by listeners as having normal oral resonance if the nasal component of the vowels does not exceed 20 percent. Slight nasal resonance, therefore, is part of normal vowel production in English, in which there is far less nasality heard in the normal voice than in many other languages, such as Chinese or French.

Denasality is usually caused by some kind of structural blockage. As shown in the blockage in diagram E (Figure 11–6), blockage occurs anywhere from the nasopharynx up through the nasal cavities through to the nostrils. Common causes of temporary denasality are an allergy and a cold. The patient experiences a swelling within the nasal passages accompanied by a marked increase of mucus, which literally blocks the passage of both airflow and sound wave. More permanent types of denasality are seen in individuals who may experience blockage from enlarged adenoids or growths and tumors that block nasal passages. The obvious primary treatment of denasality is medical-surgical. If the nasal blockage can be reduced, the denasality will lessen. Voice therapy is rarely effective in reducing denasality.

Evaluation of the Patient with Abnormal Nasal Resonance. Many of the case-history items that are used in evaluating the patient with a phonation disorder are also used with the patient who has a resonance problem. Our judgments of nasality, whether it be hypernasality or denasality, usually correspond well to our measurements. Fletcher (1978) reported correlations between nasality judgments when listening to forward-played tapes and nasalance scores on the Tonar II to range from 0.74 to 0.92 (mean of 0.85); those who listened to reverse playback made judgments that correlated with Tonar II measurements of 0.45 to 0.93 (mean of 0.66). We begin our evaluation usually with rating scale judgments made after close listening and visual observation of the patient. Measurements are then made using various instruments:

Articulation. Assessing the individual's articulation is an important prelude to any kind of instrumental evaluation. The articulation test can reveal, for example, if the patient has nasal emission, the escape of noise through the nose when producing high-intraoral-pressure consonants (often observed in someone with velopharyngeal insufficiency). Certain articulation tests are particularly useful with patients who have nasal-resonance problems, such as the *Iowa Pressure Articulation Test* from the *Templin-Darley Tests of Articulation* (1980).

Aerodynamic measures. Special instruments are used for measuring oral and nasal air pressures and flows, such as the pneumotachometer and the manometer. The patient is generally asked to say particular words and phrases into a face mask, particularly those with high-normal intraoral pressures. Or the pressures and flows from the nose may be tested separately from those coming from the mouth. For example, high volumes and pressures of air coming from the nose when the patient is asked to say such words as "Susie eats potato soup" might indicate a problem in velopharyngeal closure. Such measurements are particularly helpful in evaluating the need for surgical or prosthetic correction; once such correction is made, comparative pressure-flow measurements are helpful in evaluating the success of the particular correction.

Acoustic measures. The Tonar II (Fletcher, 1972) is a useful device that measures the relative participation of oral and nasal resonance in the total acoustic signal of the voice. The patient speaks into a split-microphone mask, with one microphone picking up the nasal signal and the other one picking up the oral signal. As previously mentioned, the Tonar II provides a relative acoustic ratio of the oral-to-nasal signal; if more than 20 percent of the signal is found to be nasal, the voice is usually judged to be hypernasal. Other instruments for acoustic analyses include the Visi-Pitch (1980), which can measure frequency, and the spectrograph (Kay Sonograph or the Voice Printer), which offers spectral analyses, including distribution of harmonics and identification of formants.

Visualization instruments. Radiographic studies of the velopharyngeal mechanism can provide data needed about velopharyngeal closure. For example, lateral cine-fluorography can provide cephalometric measurements regarding velar length and movement, pharyngeal depth, tongue height, and other physiologic data (Fletcher, 1978; Skolnick, Glaser, and McWilliams, 1980). The oral and nasal endoscope can provide a direct view of velopharyngeal closure or determine the amount of adenoid-tonsil tissue that may be present.

Treatment of Nasality Problems. As we have discussed various nasality problems, we have considered possible treatments for them. In most cases, close attention must be paid to any kind of structural abnormality (such as a short velum); if such an abnormality can be corrected by dental, medical, or surgical efforts, the first priority is to work for structural adequacy. The speech-language pathologist plays a primary role in evaluating the patient, by observation, tests, and instrumental analyses. A prelude to therapy requires that the patient attempt to a normal oral or nasal resonance by imitating the clinician. As in the stimulability testing discussed in Chapter 10, the clinician provides the model, and the patient attempts to match it. Patients with a resonance disorder who can quickly match a model with a normal production indicate to the clinician that they have adequate structure to do the task some of the time. Voice therapy may be successful in modifying the resonance excesses of patients who are easily stimulable.

Once structural adequacy is established, patients may or may not show a marked improvement in voice resonance. More often, patients continue to demonstrate a resonance problem. For the first time, however, they experience structural adequacy, which permits successful speech and voice therapy. In therapy, the clinician may use ear training, modeling of correct productions, and trial and error in searching with the patient for the best voice. It is vital that patients be given continuous feedback, so that they can see the immediate effects of what they are doing. Such feedback devices as audio and video recorders play an important role in therapy, supplemented by oscilloscope tracings from various instruments used in therapy, such as the Visi-Pitch or a pneumotachometer. Much of the therapy and techniques used to modify resonance are the same ones used for other problems of voice. They are explained in voice texts, such as Aronson (1985), Boone (1983), Cooper and Cooper (1977), Greene (1980), and Wilson (1979).

REVIEW QUESTIONS

Although some disorders of the voice are symptomatic of airway or laryngeal disorders of some kind (organic voice problems), others are related to faulty voice usage (functional voice problems). We have looked at various organic and functional voice disorders and their management. Let us review some key issues.

1. Do you feel that the organic-versus-functional dichotomy in terms of causes of voice disorders is a useful one? Comment.

2. What is vocal hyperfunction?

3. Why is hoarseness considered a danger signal as far as the airway is concerned?

4. What is the difference between laryngeal abuse and voice misuse? Give examples of each.

5. How can we determine velopharyngeal insufficiency?

6. What is a facilitating approach in voice therapy?

7. What are some essential instruments used in evaluating the patient with a voice disorder?

REFERENCES

Aronson, A. E. (1985). *Clinical Voice Disorders* (2nd ed.). New York: Thieme-Stratton, Inc.

Aronson, A. E., and DeSanto, L. W. (1981). Adductor spastic dysphonia: One and a half years after recurrent laryngeal nerve resection. *Annals of Otolaryngology, 90:* 2–6.

Bless, D. (1984). *Transcripts of the Eleventh Symposium Care of the Professional Voice,* ed. V. L. Lawrence. New York: Voice Foundation.

Boone, D. R. (1983). *The Voice and Voice Therapy* (3rd ed.). Englewood Cliffs, N.J.: Prentice-Hall.

Boone, D. R. (1984). *Transcripts of the Eleventh Symposium Care of the Professional Voice,* ed. V. L. Lawrence. New York: Voice Foundation.

Cooper, M. (1977). Direct vocal rehabilitation, in *Approaches to Vocal Rehabilitation,* ed. M. Cooper and M. H. Cooper. Springfield, Ill.: Charles C. Thomas.

Dedo, H. H., Townsend, J. J., and Izdebski, K. (1978). Current evidence for the organic etiology of spastic dysphonia. *Journal of Otolaryngology, 86:* 875–880.

Ewanowski, S. J., and Saxman, J. H. (1980). Orofacial disorders, in *Introduction to Communication Disorders,* ed. T. J. Hixon, L. Shriberg, and J. H. Saxman. Englewood Cliffs, N.J.: Prentice-Hall.

Fairbanks, G. (1960). *Voice and Articulation Drill Book.* New York: Harper and Row.

Fletcher, S. G. (1972). Contingencies for bioelectronic modification of nasality. *Journal of Speech and Hearing, 37:* 329–346.

Fletcher, S. G. (1978). *Diagnosing Speech Disorders From Cleft Palate.* New York: Grune and Stratton.

Greene, M. C. (1980). *The Voice and Its Disorders* (4th ed.). London: Pitman Press.

Hixon, T. J. (1972). Some new techniques for measuring the biochemical events of speech production: one laboratory's experiences. *American Speech and Hearing Association, Report No. 7:* 68–103.

Hixon, T. J., Mead, J., and Goldman, D. (1976). Dynamics of the chest wall during speech production: function of the thorax, rib cage, diaphragm, and abdomen. *Journal of Speech and Hearing Research, 19:* 297–336.

Honjo, I., and Isshiki, N. (1980). Laryngoscopic and voice characteristics of aged persons. *Archives of Otolaryngology, 106:* 149–150.

Hull, F. M., Mielke, P. W., Willeford, J. A., and Timmons, R. J. (1976). *National Speech and Hearing Survey.* Final Report, Project 50978. Washington, D.C.: Bureau of Education for the Handicapped, Office of Education, Department of Health, Education, and Welfare.

Kahane, J. C. (1983). Postnatal development and aging of the human larynx. *Seminars in Speech and Language, 3:* 189–203.

Kleinsasser, O. (1979). *Microlaryngoscopy and Endolaryngeal Microsurgery: Technique and Typical Findings.* Baltimore: University Park Press.

Ling, D. (1976). *Speech and Hearing Impaired Child: Theory and Practice.* Washington, D.C.: Alexander Graham Bell Association for the Deaf.

Luchsinger, R., and Arnold, G. E. (1965). *Voice-Speech-Language Clinical Communicology: Its Physiology and Pathology.* Belmont, Calif.: Wadsworth.

Minifie, F. (1984). *Transcripts of the Eleventh Symposium Care of the Professional Voice,* ed. V. L. Lawrence. New York: The Voice Foundation.

Netsell, R., and Hixon, T. J. (1978). A noninvasive method for clinically estimating subglottal air pressure. *Journal of Speech and Hearing Disorders, 43:* 326–330.

Patten, B. (1971). Embryology of the palate and the maxillofacial region, in *Cleft Lip and Palate: Surgical, Dental, and Speech Aspects,* ed. W. Grabb, S. Rosenstein, and K. Bzoch. Boston: Little Brown.

PM Pitch Analyzer. (Voice Identification, Inc. P.O. Box 714, Somerville, N.J.).

Pruzansky, L., Falzones, S. P., Loffer, J., and Parris, P. (1977). Hypernasality in the absence of overt cleft. *Proceedings of the Third International Congress on Cleft Palate and Related Craniofacial Anomolies.* Toronto, Canada.

Shedd, D. P., and Weinberg, B. (1980). *Surgical and Prosthetic Approaches to Speech Rehabilitation.* Boston: G. K. Hall.

Shelton, R. L., Lindquist, A. E., Arndt, W. B., Elbert, M., and Youngstrom, K. A. (1971). Effect of speech bulb reduction on movement of the posterior wall of the pharynx and posture of the tongue. *Cleft Palate Journal, 8:* 10–17.

Skolnick, M. L., Glaser, E. R., and McWilliams, B. J. (1980). The use and limitations of the barium pharyngogram in the detection of velopharyngeal insufficiency. *Radiology, 135:* 301–304.

Sound Spectrograph (Kay Elemetrics, 12 Maple Avenue, Pine Brook, N.J. 07058).

12

We have considered disorders of hearing, articulation, language, and voice and their effects on communicative effectiveness. We will now discuss disruptions of fluency (rate and rhythm changes of speech) and their effects on communication. Most of our emphasis will be given to the problem of stuttering, what it is, and how we manage it. Then we will consider cluttering, which is also a disorder of fluency, although dramatically different from stuttering. Finally, we will see that the same motor speech problems that alter articulation and voice will more often than not cause alterations in speech fluency.

Disorders of Fluency

STUTTERING

Infants and young children seem to have much practice producing the fluent melodies that they have been hearing in the language around them. The sequence, duration, and melody of their jargon seem to listeners to parallel closely those same dimensions in the parent language. In the normal acquisition of first words (at ten to twenty months), these first words are often "plugged" into the jargon flow; in effect, youngsters preserve the melody flow or prosody of the language they are learning. When children get a bit older (in the third and fourth years), we may see some evidence of struggle as they attempt to grasp an idea they then wish to express with words or as they search for a particular word. During this struggle, fluency may break down, and many normal children will show speech *disfluency,* usually characterized by the repetition of whole words and phrases with occasional interjections, such as *ah* or *er,* used to fill in the pauses. Parents and the others may perceive the child as disfluent, but they generally view this as normal. The struggle to articulate is an accepted behavior that usually results in a disfluency of some kind (a delayed gesture or a repeated word). In general, society is quite tolerant of these kinds of disfluencies in both children and adults.

The disfluencies exhibited by young stutterers vary considerably from the kind we have just described. In stuttering, the youngster will repeat and prolong sounds and syllables, often at the beginning of a phrase or sentence. For the stutterers, the blocks often appear to be involuntary (they seem to just happen), and are often accompanied by muscle tension as the individual struggles to "get out" of the block. It also appears that, over time, the child who stutters develops other tension-appearing behaviors that accompany the repetition and prolongation of sounds and syllables, such as facial contortions or excessive eye-blinking.

Let us describe two children who were seen initially in a speech clinic, each with a problem of disfluency. One boy was found to have normal disfluencies that were explained to the parents and required some brief counseling. The other boy displayed a severe stuttering problem that subsequently required many years of therapy. Each boy was four years old when seen initially.

Dwight. Dwight was brought to the speech clinic by his mother within several weeks of asking his parents one night at the dinner table, "Why, why, why, why,

why do I talk like this?'' The parents had noticed that he frequently repeated words, particularly when he was tired or at mealtimes, but they had never realized that he was aware of it. Speech-language-cognitive-test protocols described the boy to be functioning in the bright-superior range in all areas tested. His speech fluency was the only problem area identified; the evaluation report described his responses in this manner: "Dwight seemed to know much about animals and how they lived, and in the middle of a sentence, he might repeat the word *cub* several times. He frequently repeated the first word of an utterance three to four times. Phrase repetitions were also heard, such as 'we went to the, we went to, we went to the San Diego Zoo, and there was a big, there was a big, a big hippopatamus there, and we saw him go under the water, and he wouldn't, he didn't, want no more, not any, he didn't want to come out.''' A one-year follow-up evaluation found Dwight to be free of excessive word or phrase repetitions, and his overall communicative performance was labeled "verbally gifted."

Andy. Andy's parents were particularly concerned about his speech disfluency because both of them were severe stutterers (they had met in a university speech clinic). When first seen by this examiner, Andy stuttered so badly that he had no functional speech. His parents reported that his early speech and language development had been well within normal limits. They had become concerned about his sound and syllable repetitions when he was about three and a half years old. They felt that he quickly learned to purse his lips in a locked position, close his eyes, and literally not be able to say a word. At the time of our first evaluation, when asked to say something, he struggled unsuccessfully for about two minutes. A recording of that evaluation showed his best speech fluency to be: "Well, wh-wh-wh-wh-wh-wh-wh-where do ya-ya-ya-ya-ya-ya-ya-ya-you leh-lehleh-live?" Most of his disfluency, accompanied by severe facial contortions, was primarily silent prolongations of airflow, renewed innumerable times, with no identifiable word spoken. As part of our diagnostic attempt to see if he would be disfluent in saying nonsense words after the examiner, we each put on a pith helmet, looked at each other in the mirror, and played "jungleeze" (affectionately called "pith helmet therapy" by tolerant and accepting colleagues). I would say in a loud voice, using lots of accent and stress, "Wanga, wanga." Andy would quickly respond with a fluent "Wanga, wanga," imitating the same stress pattern, free of any observable struggle. "Topa toppa tunga" modeled by the clinician was followed quickly by Andy's fluent repetition. We had clearly demonstrated that Andy had the physical equipment to say utterances that had no semantic value. Much of our early therapy efforts were directed toward establishing some fluency using "jungleeze" coupled with some real words. Over the past 15 years, I have followed Andy's progress by corresponding with his mother, who reports: "Andy still stutters, but not as bad as his dad and I do."

The differences in disfluency between the normal speaker, Dwight, who used word and phrase repetitions (normal disfluency) were in dramatic contrast to the severe repetitions and tension blocks that Andy experienced (stuttering) whenever he wished to say something meaningful. Unfortunately, the distinction between normal disfluency and stuttering is not usually this dramatic. It is not easy to distinguish between those who have a normal disfluency that will probably disappear without clinical intervention and those who have a stuttering problem that may require extensive, long-term therapy.

Some Distinctions Between Normal Disfluency and Stuttering

Stuttering has been described by Perkins (1977) as a breakdown in the flow of speech. Perkins goes on to describe five temporal interruptions of speech flow, some of which are sometimes observed in normal speakers and in stutterers:

1. *Sequence:* the order of speech sounds must be exact if meaning is not to be compromised
2. *Duration:* the length of time that any phonetic element lasts
3. *Rate:* the speed with which phonetic elements of various durations are articulated together
4. *Rhythm:* the phonetic patterns of a language are spoken with a flowing rhythm
5. *Fluency:* the smooth pattern which with sounds are articulated together

The speech of stutterers is often characterized by duration changes and rate and rhythm alterations, with frequent interruptions of smooth fluency between one sound and another. In the child with normal disfluency, there is a much more normal flow of speech in the production of a single word than what would be observed in the child stutterer. The latter may take longer to utter single sounds and combinations of sounds; and the production of the word may show a noticeable breakdown in rhythm and fluency. One distinction between normal disfluency and stuttering, then, is the type of verbal utterance in which the disfluency occurs (Andrews and others, 1983; Perkins, 1980) (see Table 12-1). The type of speech unit in which the individual is most likely to produce normal disfluency is the word, phrase, and sentence; stutterers are most likely to stutter on single sounds and syllables.

Normal disfluencies have been well documented in the early speech patterns of young children (Davis, 1940; Metraux, 1950). Beyond using interjections when they are hesitant as they retrieve particular ideas and words, normal children at about the age of three and a half show compulsive repetition of words and phrases. By age four and a half, according to Curlee (1980) who summarized Metraux's findings, normal children usually repeat utterances only when they wish to emphasize something. When we discuss Johnson's diagnosogenic theory of stuttering (1959), we shall see that Johnson felt the disfluencies exhibited by normal children

TABLE 12-1
Dysfluency Judgments Related to Type of Speech Units

normal dysfluency	word repetitions
	phrase repetitions
	sentence repetitions
	hesitations, interjections
stuttering	sound repetitions
	syllable repetitions
	sound and syllable hesitations
	sound and syllable interjections

did not differ from those of children viewed by their parents as stutterers. In his studies, Johnson found that the age of greatest disfluency in the normal child was between the ages of three and a half and four years; however, he did not distinguish between the type of disfluency seen in normal children and that seen in children who stutter.

The frequency of the disfluency is also different for the two groups. Normal children do not appear to repeat as often as stutterers. Wingate (1962) found that normal children do not make repetitions for more than 3 percent of their total speech utterances; children who stutter were found to have a frequency of syllable disfluencies ranging from 7 to 14 percent.

Recent research supports the view that parents can often distinguish between normal disfluency and stuttering (Yairi, 1981); the child's increased repetition and prolongation is often accompanied by some degree of struggle and tension.

Definitions of Stuttering

Exact descriptions and definitions of stuttering vary with the perspective of the individual writer. It is, therefore, difficult to develop an all-encompassing definition of stuttering that will represent all views. There is some agreement on the definition, including a mention of repetition and **prolongation** of speech sounds and syllables. Let us consider a few definitions of stuttering found in the literature.

Wingate (1978), who views stuttering as a "phonetic transition defect," developed this definition: "Stuttering is characterized by audible or silent elemental repetitions and prolongations. These features reflect a temporary inability to move forward to the following sound" (p. 249).

In his summary of definitions in *Stuttering Words,* Fraser (1973) noted: "Stuttering is a communication disorder characterized by excessive involuntary disruptions or blockings in the flow of speech, particularly when such disruptions consist of repetitions or prolongations of a sound or syllable, and when they are accompanied by avoidance struggle behavior" (p. 43).

Johnson (1955), who believed that normal children displayed disfluency and some of them learned to stutter, put focus on the anticipation of stuttering. Among his definitions was: "Stuttering is an anticipatory, apprehensive, hypertonic avoidance reaction" (p. 23). Johnson went on to say that stuttering is what speakers do when they expect stuttering to occur, dread it, tense in anticipation of it, and attempt to avoid doing it.

Perkins (1980) has written that "stuttering is the abnormal timing of speech sound initiation." More recently (1983), Perkins commented on the definitions reviewed by Andrews and others (1983), noting that any definition of stuttering must include the word *involuntary*. Perkins feels that repetitions and prolongations alone seem to appear in the speech of both children with disfluency and children who stutter; normal children repeat with greater deliberation, as opposed to the stutterer, who has an involuntary fluency interruption.

The definition of stuttering provided by the World Health Organization (1977), and commented upon by Andrews and others (1983), was "disorders in the rhythm of speech, in which the individual knows precisely what he wishes to say, but at the time is unable to say it because of an involuntary, repetitive prolongation or cessation of a sound" (p. 227). Once again, we see the important qualifier "involuntary."

Despite the uncomfortable fact that clear definitions of stuttering are elusive, most listeners "know" when someone is stuttering (McDearmon, 1968; Yairi, 1983). Bloodstein (1981) commented in effect that one definition of stuttering is whatever is perceived as stuttering by a reliable observer who has relatively good agreement with others.

Let us add our own definition to the list: "Stuttering is the involuntary repetition and prolongation of speech sounds and syllables that the individual struggles to end." Our definition represents a consensus of most (but not all) of the definitions we have reviewed, stressing three primary characteristics of the act of stuttering:

1. repetition and prolongation of sounds and syllables;
2. involuntary fluency interruptions; and
3. struggle behavior to end the fluency interruptions.

Let us see how our definition might apply to a particular case, Laura, age seven:

Laura's parents report that she has stuttered since she was three years old. At the time of her speech evaluation, she was found to repeat the first sounds and syllables of many words at the beginning of a phrase or sentence. At times, she seemed to posture her mouth and blink, and no sound could be heard. She made no attempt to avoid talking, and would have moments of normal fluency; suddenly, the fluency would end, seemingly without warning. During her stuttering, she would often purse her lips, close her eyes, and appear as if she were trying to push out the word she was attempting to say.

In this brief description of Laura, we find that her involuntary sound repetitions came without warning. As they happened, she did what she could to restore her fluency.

Prevalence of Stuttering

If we take a look at a population at any one time in an attempt to find out how many in the population have a particular problem, we are doing what is known as a prevalence study. Such a study on speech and hearing disorders was reported by Hull and others (1976) after sampling the speech and hearing of 38,802 children, first through twelfth grades, in 100 sites across the United States. For the problem of stuttering, 0.8 percent of the total sample was found to stutter, with a male-to-female ratio of 3:1. The figure is remarkably close to that reported by Young (1975), 0.7, as a prevalence figure for both school-age children and young adults. Morley (1952), studying 33,339 college students over a ten-year period, reported that 0.8 percent of them stuttered. This would mean that there are presently about 1.5 to 1.8 million stutterers in the United States (based on a population estimate of 225 million people).

The incidence of a disorder can be determined over time. A longitudinal study can follow a group of persons over a number of years and determine what percentage of them experience a particular disorder during that time. Some 1,000 children were followed for 15 years in a Newcastle-upon-Tyne study that looked at various aspects of development (Morley, 1972). The incidence of stuttering among these children was about 4 percent, with a male-to-female ratio of 2.4:1. Wingate (1976), in looking at recovery from stuttering in the reports of 14 different authors, found that of the 46,608 people surveyed, 4.1 percent of them had stuttered at one time in their lives (which is almost identical with the Newcastle-upon-Tyne data). Both Morley and Wingate reported that most children began stuttering before the age of five, and the problem disappeared before puberty.

Wingate's summary of the 14 studies found that approximately 80 percent recovered from stuttering. Young (1975) felt this figure was too high. However, Andrews and others (1983) reported that recovery in school-age children is generally to be expected, and that "the best estimate of the probability of recovery by 16 years is 78 percent" (p. 228). It would appear, then, that for the vast majority of children, their stuttering will disappear before they get out of high school. In summarizing the prevalence, incidence, and recovery data on stuttering, Curlee (1980) came to the following conclusion: " . . . if the incidence of stuttering among the general population does approximate 4 percent, a recovery rate of 80 percent would account for a 0.7 percent prevalence of stuttering" (p. 281).

Curlee's conclusions seem to represent the consensus about the number of people who presently stutter. For many years, a much more pessimistic view of stuttering was held. It was felt that early stuttering in a youngster would only compound itself, and that the stuttering and associated symptoms would get worse. The 80 percent recovery data do not support such pessimism.

Also, there are very little data available that show that stuttering begins beyond puberty, particularly if the individual has never before been disfluent. There are very few reports of individuals who begin to stutter in adulthood; some patients who incur some kind of neurological damage from cerebral disease or injury may show extreme disfluencies (usually whole word repetitions), but they differ markedly from the kind observed in stuttering.

The Theoretical Causes of Stuttering

There is probably no clinical area in speech-language pathology that has generated more controversy than our understanding of the causes of stuttering. Many people have different viewpoints. It may well be, of course, that under the broad generic term *stuttering* there exists different subtypes, each with its own cause or treatment. While we may agree that stuttering consists of involuntary repetitions and prolongations of sounds and syllables, we cannot agree why such disfluencies occur. The number of causative theories (listed in Table 12–2) is astonishing. We will discuss each theory and its possible application to the treatment of stuttering.

The left column of Table 12–2 consists of broad headings; in the right column, each theory is given specificity via key words that have appeared in the literature. At one time or another, this writer has subscribed to most aspects of all of these theoretical positions. Let us consider each one separately.

Learning Aspects of Stuttering. Johnson (1959) spent his professional life studying the onset of stuttering. He concluded that the normal disfluencies experienced by many children were often labeled by their parents and other listeners as stuttering. His **diagnosogenic** theory of stuttering was basically built on the belief that stuttering begins by having normal disfluencies labeled as stuttering. During his years of research at the University of Iowa, he was never able to report any biological or psychological differences between stutterers and nonstutterers. For many years, this shaped the belief that people learned to stutter, and that stutterers were no different constitutionally or psychologically from anyone else. As we shall see when we look at organic and linguistic theories, there have since been numerous findings that point

TABLE 12–2
Theories of Stuttering

Learning	anticipatory struggle, diagnosogenic, interactional semantic, approach-avoidance
Psychological	repressed-need, neurotic, personality conflict, substitute symptom
Organic	dysphemia, neurological, laterality, diminished reaction time, laryngeal factor
Linguistic	sound-syllable-word-phrase-sentence, speech-language, central auditory functioning

to differences between stutterers and nonstutterers. The learning-theory approach to stuttering, however, basically said that normal speakers with normal disfluencies experienced negative reactions to their disfluencies and learned to stutter.

This theory recognizes that most children in the threes and fours exhibit verbal disfluencies as they attempt to formulate language. As children acquire a lexicon, they attempt to use their new words in the proper sequential order and with the correct grammar. If children are to be successful in their communications, listeners' responses must be appropriate. When children's verbal presentations are accurate, they are likely to be appropriately responded to by listeners. Fatigue, nervousness, the search for the right idea and words to go with it may all contribute to a disfluency. Children may repeat a word or a phrase as they attempt to be fluent, only to be told to slow down or take a big breath and start over. In some way, listeners communicate an intolerance for the disfluency. Children react by doing something to achieve better fluency and maintain the goodwill of their listeners. They begin to struggle at each disfluency, which results in sound and syllable repetitions. These repetitions receive further negative evaluations from listeners, and we have the beginnings of stuttering. Disfluency with negative listener reaction is the genesis of stuttering, according to Johnson (1959). It is why he believed that stuttering exists in the "ear of the listener." The problem of stuttering, then, is a result of interactions between children and critical listeners. This causative idea is known as the **interaction** theory.

From a learning perspective, we not only learn to stutter, but the amount and kind of stuttering we do can be governed by learning principles. Fluency can be induced by subsequently resaying or rereading a passage. This is known as the **adaptation effect.** The passage is repeated over and over, with a marked improvement (up to 50 percent) in overall fluency over the baseline measure (Bruce and Adams, 1978). Although the repeated practice of a passage produces increased fluency, there may be only minimal generalization to other attempts at talking. Another aspect of stuttering that is consistent with a learning approach to the problem is the **consistency effect.** Certain words are more likely to be stuttered on by particular stutterers; it would appear that they "know" they are going to stutter on a given word, and such "knowing" usually results in stuttering on that word again and again.

The behavioral approach as a treatment mode in speech-language pathology was appropriate for the treatment of stuttering when such treatment was based on a learning model. The premise was that, since you had learned to stutter, you could learn to be fluent. Both children and adults participated in training sessions that used the stuttering behavior as an operant, with a variety of consequences. Sometimes fluency was rewarded positively, in the hope of shaping more fluent speaking (Martin and Siegel, 1966); or stuttering was punished, in the belief that such behavior could be extinguished by verbal punishment (Quist and Martin, 1967). When this author attempted to extinguish stuttering by operant procedures, the involuntary aspect of the disfluency (which is part of our definition) prevented operant-shaping procedures from being wholly effective. Stutterers can anticipate that they are going to stutter, but they never know exactly when the disfluency will occur.

Brutten and Shoemaker (1967) felt that stutterers become apprehensive about stuttering in particular situations, and the apprehension heightens the arousal of the autonomic nervous system, resulting in a breakdown of fluency. They believed that the core of the stuttering was increased stress in anticipation of stuttering. Much of their behavioral therapy involved working with the stutterer to keep arousal and apprehension under control. As one patient said who was receiving this kind of therapy, "I'm learning to keep my cool, and as long as I can do that, I don't seem to stutter." Beyond the core of the stuttering related to autonomic-nervous-system arousal, the rest of the stuttering represents "instrumentally acquired adjustive responses" (Andrews and others, 1983). Stutterers learn this behavior through classical conditioning.

As we saw earlier, Johnson defined the problem as an "anticipatory, apprehensive, hypertonic avoidance reaction." In his view, the fear of stuttering is conditioned over time, and this fear becomes at least as great a problem as the actual stuttering. Sheehan (1970) looked at the anticipatory fear of stutterers and developed his approach-avoidance theory: stutterers are involved in the struggle over whether to speak or not. "Knowing" that they are going to stutter, they begin to use all kinds of avoidance behaviors (grimacing, eye-blinking, noise-making) that they have learned instead of making an easy, open sound or syllable repetition. Sheehan suggests that, without these distracting tricks, "little stuttering would remain."

Psychological Aspects of Stuttering. If we were to ask most people what causes stuttering, they might well respond, "Stuttering is a nervous disorder that is a symptom of psychological problems." Many people today consider stuttering to be a manifestation of an emotional disorder, a view that has had its professional proponents over the years. In carefully controlled studies, no differences have been found between stutterers and nonstutterers on various dimensions of neuroticism (Andrews and Harris, 1964; Andrews and others, 1983; Molt and Guilford, 1979; Prins, 1972).

Just as Wendell Johnson was the leading researcher in the development of the learning theory of stuttering, Lee Travis (1971) is best known for his development of the repressed-need theory of stuttering. In his view, stuttering is but a surface symptom of repressed needs, often a disguised hostility. In their love of making oral noises, their feeding, fascination with urine and feces, need to be dirty and unwashed, and lack of sexual experience, children are often thwarted and restricted (Travis, 1971). Their primitive likes and wants are thwarted by those around them. "The parents not only induced in the child the drives of fear, guilt, and shame as checks on the child's primary drives, but they and their helpers in society perpetuated these checks" (p. 1,020). Stuttering becomes a way of getting around the curbing and the thwarting. The stuttering becomes an acceptable behavior, in place of more primitive urges of eating, sucking, caressing, or fondling.

In a classic chapter, "The Unspeakable Feelings of People with Special Reference to Stuttering" (Travis, 1971), the repressed needs and feelings of adult stutterers are remarkably detailed, as well as their cravings and thoughts. Rather than working directly on the stuttering, Travis and others (Barbara, 1962; Glauber, 1958) recommended psychotherapy, with a heavy emphasis on uncovering the hidden prohibitions under which many stutterers hid. Freeing the patient from such prohibitions seemed to result in greater speech fluency. Travis concluded that "those stutterers who recovered and expressed what we have termed unspeakable feelings and thoughts did enjoy increased speech fluency and less anxiety over speech blocks" (p. 1,032).

Many stutterers, perhaps like the population in general, profit from psychological counseling or therapy. Bryngelson (1971) chastised speech pathologists who become so concerned with the symptoms of a disorder that they neglect the area of the "patient's need to be an acceptable human being." Psychotherapists commonly believe that most patients come for help when their personal misery is intense. The same is true for stutterers. If they seek treatment from a speech-language pathologist (rather than being referred as a result of a school screening or brought to a clinic by parents) because they are miserable about their stuttering, they may well require counseling to develop some degree of perspective about their problem. Such counseling or therapy may well be fear-reducing and permit stutterers to work on directly controlling their speech through symptomatic therapy.

Later in this chapter, we will consider the role of psychotherapy and counseling in helping stutterers to cope with their problem. The focus at present has been on psychological problems that cause the stuttering. Despite the writings over the years by psychologists (Travis, 1970; Wyatt, 1958), psychoanalysts (Glauber, 1958), and psychiatrists (Blanton, 1965) that suggest that the genesis of stuttering may be neurotic needs, there is very little convincing evidence of this.

Organic Aspects of Stuttering. Early studies, in the 1920s and 1930s, began with the belief that stuttering had a physical cause. It was thought that stutterers as a group differed physically from normal speakers. We will consider some of these early studies, most of which were dismissed as invalid by Johnson and his disciples (1959). Interestingly, as Van Riper (1971) noted, the pendulum is beginning to swing back again toward some belief in a constitutional difference [between stutterers and nonstutterers], at least as shown in certain stutterers. Let us consider some of the organic aspects of stuttering that may contribute to its causation or maintenance.

Neurological aspects. The relative miracle of putting expressive language together to form speech requires a combination of cognitive-linguistic mixing, the rhythm of respiratory patterns that produce a prosodic flow of phonations, and a fluent blending of speech sounds, combined with various stress changes (loudness, pitch, and duration). As suggested in earlier chapters, the miracle is that anyone can speak at all. It is no wonder, then, that someone with a nervous system that varies in any way from that of most people might have difficulty orchestrating the rapid sequences required for normal speech. The early investigations of stuttering led quite naturally to considerations of the nervous system as a possible etiologic source of the breakdown in speech fluency.

An early idea was the cerebral-dominance theory of stuttering. It has long been recognized that one cerebral hemisphere (usually the left) plays the dominant role in speech and language. Although this hemisphere may play the lead in the sequencing of sounds and words, the actual execution of these sounds requires a well-coordinated bilateral innervation. The paired muscles of speech must receive their impulses at exactly the same time. The cerebral-dominance theory states that the arrival of impulses at the peripheral muscles is poorly timed. This lack of precise timing is known as **dysphemia.** In the case of stuttering, the flow of nervous impulses to the paired speech musculature might break down with the slightest provocation. The bilateral coordinations that are essential for normal speech would be compromised by one side's receiving innervations to muscles before the other side. As Van Riper (1971) put it, it is very difficult to lift ''a wheelbarrow with one handle.''

In the early days of speech pathology, in 1931, before he embraced the repressed-need theory of stuttering, Travis pursued the cerebral-dominance theory, and found that the brain waves of stutterers showed a cerebral skewing, with the two sides of the brain not in synchrony. West, an early founder of the profession of speech pathology, searched for an organic theory of stuttering that embraced the concepts of dysphemia for a time (1958). In later years, both Travis and West refuted their earlier theories of cerebral dominance. Andrews and others (1983), summarizing years of research on laterality and stuttering, concluded that there was no clear evidence that stutterers as a group had poorly lateralized speech centers or an excess of EEG (electroencephalograph) abnormalities.

Another aspect of central-nervous-system dysfunction as a possible cause of stuttering may be seen in a number of reaction-time studies. Luper and Cross (1978) compared finger-movement reaction times and voicing reaction times in stutterers and normal people, and found that stutterers had slower reaction times for both activities. Hand and Haynes (1983) also found manual and voicing reaction times to be slower in stutterers than in normal speakers. Reich, Till, and Goldsmith (1981) found manual-skill times to be normal in stutterers, but they did find slower vocalization reaction times. A number of studies have looked at vocalization reaction times in stutterers (How quickly can they vocalize after being given a signal to do so?) and found that the stuttering group demonstrated slower vocal reaction times than normal speakers. This consistent finding has led to many other studies looking at timing problems in the innervation of the larynx as a possible cause of stuttering.

Laryngeal aspects. Probably one of the leading exponents of the belief that stuttering may be caused by a disorder of the vocal mechanism is Schwartz (1974), who published a book with a relatively immodest title, *Stuttering Solved* (1976). He believes that the airway dilation reflex (ADR) occurs on expiration while the stutterer is speaking. Normally, the ADR is a rapid opening of the glottis during inspiration because of a rising subglottal air pressure (which will happen reflexively if there is a subglottal obstruction and a need for a greater air supply). As the stutterer speaks, according to Schwartz, the vocal folds may reflexively open, creating the stuttering block. The lack of phonation is suddenly out of synchrony with the speaker, whose mouth is postured to say a certain word. The Schwartz plan to overcome the ADR is to have the stutterer forcefully contract the laryngeal mechanism or deliberately "hypertense postures of the lips, tongue, jaw, etc. to 'release the abducted larynx' or close the glottis to say a particular word" (Starkweather, 1982, p. 9).

Adams (1974) began to suspect that the laryngeal participation of stutterers in the act of speaking was often out of synchrony with the other muscles used for speech. Adams and Reis (1974) found less stuttering when individuals read a passage that was designed to have no voiceless sounds, suggesting that when the on effect of the larynx was "on" without vocal fold abductions, there was better laryngeal functioning. Adams believes that in young children who are beginning to stutter, the genesis of their disfluency may be a laryngeal discoordination with their supraglottal speech movements. As the stuttering behavior becomes more complex, Adams feels, stutterers develop "abnormal respiratory, laryngeal, and articulatory events [and] disruptions in the coordination" of the three systems (Adams, p. 140, 1978).

Both the theoretical ideas and the therapy plans developed by Schwartz and Adams, although from different points of view, seem to point the finger at the larynx as one of the sites that may function differently in stuttering. Other investigators have looked at this component of stuttering (Freeman and Ushijima, 1975; Shapiro, 1980) and confirmed that laryngeal function may be poor during the moment of stuttering, but no more aberrant than the performance of such oral structures as the lips or tongue. In fact, Starkweather (1982) concluded that "nothing in any of these physiological observations supports the idea that laryngeal stuttering is any more likely to cause oral stuttering than the other way around, nor does anything preclude the possibility that oral and laryngeal stuttering are caused by some other variable" (p. 12).

Many systems are involved in the production of stuttering, including changes in respiration, abductions and adductions of the vocal folds, pursing of the lips, and facial grimacing. To look at a particular site that is not functioning well during stuttering is, in effect, to look at the physiology of stuttering; that is, you are looking at the production of what you hear acoustically. The faulty function of a particular anatomical site during stuttering, such as the larynx, does not necessarily mean that that site is the *cause* of stuttering. If the larynx is not functioning properly, one must ask, "Why isn't it?" The answer to that question, which remains unknown, might explain the origin of stuttering.

What seems to help reduce stuttering is to establish some kind of rhythm to the speech-voicing pattern (Wingate, 1976). Any change in vocalization that is tied to controlling and simplifying the stutterer's rhythm seems to improve speech fluency.

Rhythm aspects. It would appear that fluency is dependent on the smooth coordination of respiration, phonation, and articulation. Wingate's thesis in *Stuttering Theory and Treatment* (1976) is that the evidence is overwhelming that the problem is reduced markedly whenever the stutterer "speaks in a more-or-less regular rhythm." Kent (1983) makes a strong case that verbal fluency requires a well-regulated sequential flow of activities. In stuttering, fluency is enhanced by changing the stutterer's temporal sequencing uncertainties, such as choral reading, prolongation of vowels, slowing speech, speaking with a rhythmic pacing (such as that provided by a metronome), and speaking under conditions of delayed auditory feedback. Changing the role of the larynx in speech (such as by the prolongation of vowels) is known to improve verbal fluency (Adams, 1974; Schwartz, 1976); however, it may well not be the voicing changes that produce fluency, but rather the alteration of rhythm that facilitates the fluency.

After tracing the treatment of stuttering over the years, Wingate (1976) found that those treatments that incorporated some aspect of changing the rhythm of speech seemed to be of most benefit to the stutterer:

> Distillation of this wealth of material relating to conditions having a substantial salutary effect on stuttering reveals as the principal agent of each effect an induced emphasis on phonation, implemented most effectively by increase in duration, expressed (at least experientially at this point) through "slowing down," and commonly involving modulation of stress contrasts; in brief, changes in prosodic expression (p. 239).

Many stutterers seem to have a defective rhythmic-monitoring system. The rapid-fire sequencing of sounds and syllables required for the production of normal speech seems to be difficult for many stutterers. Consequently, the slowing down of speech, particularly by extending the duration of vowels, seems to play a facilitative role in the improvement of fluency.

The stutterer seems to need more neural response time to respond on various verbal tasks that require a quick reaction (Adams and Hayden, 1976; Netsell and Daniel, 1974; Reich, Till, and Goldsmith, 1981; Till and others, 1983). These studies generally show that phonatory reaction times for various linguistic and laryngeal-motor response tasks are slower for stutterers than for nonstutterers. There are mixed results in reaction-time studies comparing stutterers and normal speakers on tasks requiring finger or manual responses or other nonspeech activities. The voice-onset findings would be quite consistent, then, with the clinical findings that tell us that slowing the rate of speech improves verbal fluency. Although it is impossible at this time to localize a cerebral deficit in stutterers that is responsible for slower voicing reaction times, the consistency of this finding allows us to postulate that some kind of central deficit in rapid-fire voicing sequence may exist.

Linguistic Aspects of Stuttering. It is only during a linguistic utterance of some kind that we see people stutter. The repetitions and prolongations of sound and syllable have no parallel in other behaviors of the person called a stutterer; that is, we do not observe the stutterer repeating motor movements with the hands or fingers or posturing the mouth in a tension-exaggerated manner unless there is a speech attempt. Stuttering is an event we only see when someone speaks (or attempts to speak).

Earlier in this chapter, we found that a gross differentiation exists between the normal speaker with disfluency and the stutterer in terms of the type of speech unit where the disfluency occurs. Normal speakers display disfluencies by repeating a word or phrase, and may hesitate and make interjections between phrase or sentence units. In contrast, stutterers display most of their difficulty by repeating the first sounds or syllables of words, particularly at the beginning of a verbal unit (word, phrase, or sentence). For stutterers, the disfluency comes involuntarily and suddenly, without warning; the tension observed is usually the result of an attempt to end the stuttering block. Although this block does not represent some violation of phonologic rules (stutterers know the sound they want to make), it does represent a major interference in the normal prosodic-speech flow. The phonology of the language is seriously compromised. Syntax is often violated by stutterers in their attempt to circumlocute the sound they cannot say, and interjections are frequently used in the search for alternate words or phrases that may be free of the sound that is causing the problem. The inefficiency of such verbal productions by stutterers no doubt has serious effects on pragmatic effectiveness.

Table 12–3 records an actual description of a football game by an adult male stutterer to his clinician. Linguistic commentary is included where appropriate. Although categorizing each case of stuttering in Table 12–3 as a linguistic event is a mental challenge, it does not have much meaning. A breakdown in linguistic competence does not cause stuttering. The presence of stuttering, however, seriously compromises the execution of linguistic events, as the table shows.

Beyond the obvious problem of stuttering, there is some evidence that stutterers as a group show certain deficits on linguistic tasks when compared to normal speakers. For example, Bloodstein (1974) has corroborated the typical clinical finding that stuttering most often occurs during pauses between utterances (phrases or sentences); this is when normal speakers also pause to search for words to articulate their thoughts. Stutterers are often most disfluent after these search-pauses. Some

TABLE 12–3
A Linguistic View of a Stutterer's Blocks

Tom said, "S-s-s-s-s-s-s, you want to know, the Chag-chag-chag-chargers gave the g-g-game away. You want to know, S-s-s-s-s--s-san Diego gave the g-g-g-ga—, gave the s-s-s-s to Washington."

S-s-s-s-s-s-s-s	Phonologic breakdown, morphologic deficit (word never said)
you want to know	An interjection, used as filler, in search for alternate way to name team
Chag-chag-chag-chargers	Phonologic breakdown, pragmatics compromised when cannot name city
you want to know	Interjection, poor pragmatics
S-s-s-s-s-s-s-san	Phonologic breakdown, pragmatics compromised
g-g-g-ga—	Wanted to say *game*, phonologic repetition was abandoned, repeated the verb, a breakdown in both morphology and syntax
s-s-s-s	Phonologic repetition is abandoned and object of verb is omitted (he meant to say "score"), sentence as stated had no meaning (omitted word is a semantic violation), message vague (poor pragmatics).

studies (Andrews and others, 1983; Westby, 1979) have reported that stutterers as a group perform more poorly on certain language tasks than normal speakers. Usually, the task involves some speaking response, and stutterers are naturally not going to do as well on such tasks as normal speakers. In reviewing seven studies that looked at the articulation ability of stutterers, Andrews and his colleagues (1983) concluded that stutterers "show three times greater risk of articulation disorder than nonstutterers" (p. 230). This conclusion may explain the clinical observation that too much direct articulation therapy for preschool children will sometimes lead them to disfluency, if not to stuttering. It may well be that these children are just not "verbal athletes," and would find it difficult to handle any kind of linguistic task.

A few reports have noted that stutterers as a group have difficulty with central auditory functioning, particularly on **dichotic listening** tasks. In dichotic listening to verbal messages, listeners attend to competing messages; a different verbal message is given in each ear. Both messages are as alike as possible in terms of duration, intensity, and phase. For example, subjects hear the numbers "one-five" in the right ear and, exactly at the same time, the numbers "four-eight" in the left one. Subjects are asked to respond by saying or writing the numbers they heard. Normal subjects generally show the right-ear effect (the ear contralateral to their dominant hemisphere), which is determined by their hearing more responses in the right than in the left ear. Disregarding the laterality effect (one ear's advantage over the other) several studies (Barrett and others, 1979; Pinsky and McAdam, 1980; Rosenfield and Goodglass, 1980) have reported that stutterers' recognition of competing messages in dichotic listening tasks is poorer than that of normal speakers. These could mean that stutterers as a group have poorer overall language competencies than normal speakers.

Finally, while it may be concluded that some stutterers appear to perform poorly on some language tasks, there is no clear evidence that stuttering is only a symptom of an overall language deficit. Stuttering too often exists in people who demonstrate no other problem in human communication.

The Evaluation of Stuttering

As we discussed earlier in this chapter, if the recovery rate of children who stutter is 80 percent by the time puberty arrives, those who evaluate child stutterers should focus on identifying the type of disfluency and any accompanying struggle. It would be important to be able to differentiate those children who show signs of serious, long-term stuttering and those whose disfluency will go away spontaneously (the state of our "diagnostic art" doesn't yet permit this to be done with accuracy). For older children and adults, besides identifying the type of block and struggle, emphasis must be on sampling stutterers' attitudes toward themselves and stuttering. Clinicians must get to know stutterers as well as the dimensions of their problem.

Evaluating the Young Child Who Stutters. Most young children who display enough disfluency to be viewed as having a problem are brought to a speech clinic by their parents, although a few of them are picked out by speech-language pathologists in the public schools. The speech evaluation of young stutterers should include the following:

1. Observe the spontaneous interactions (verbal and nonverbal) between the children and their parents. (This author usually begins such a speech evaluation by watching child-parent interaction through a one-way mirror.) How do they relate to one another? If speech disfluencies are observed, of what type are they? Do the children exhibit tensions during the moments of disfluency?

2. The Johnsonian diagnosogenic (1959) approach to stuttering obviously had some validity; that is, parental reactions to early disfluency undoubtedly play an important role in how both children and parents perceive it. Clinicians must find out how the parents view the disfluency. Emerick and Hatten (1979) recommend using the Speech Chart, shown in Figure 12–1, as a means of documenting both parental concern and observations.

3. Document children's disfluencies. This is best achieved by making a video recording (or audio recording, if video is not available) of the child's speech at play, in conversation, in choral unison with the examiner, and under conditions of role-playing (as in the pith-helmet therapy with Andy described earlier in the chapter). After the evaluation, the tape should be analyzed in terms of the type of block, frequency, severity, and observable presence of tension (pursing the lips, blinking the eyes, hand movements) during stuttering.

4. Document children's normal speech, particularly the situations that seem to facilitate it. This can be done by using the video tape to identify parameters of disfluency and by interviewing the parents. Find out what facilitates fluency. Is it related to what the child has just eaten or drunk? Is it related to the child's role? To fun and games? To being awake and rested? Obviously, any contexts or situations that can be identified as facilitating fluency might deserve a greater role in children's lives.

5. How aware are children of their disfluency? What do they do to control the problem? What behaviors are used in an attempt to get out of a block?

Most diagnostic evaluations of young children include counseling sessions with the parents, designed to give them information about disfluency and suggestions for incorporating into children's lives those situations that have been observed to promote verbal fluency. For children who make occasional sound or syllable repetitions, with most of the disfluency centered around word and phrase repetitions (relatively free of signs of struggle), the evaluation may be followed by several counseling sessions with the parents and, perhaps, play therapy (with no direct work on speech) with the child. In the section entitled, "The Treatment of Stuttering" (later in this chapter), some of the things that can be done for youngsters who are begin-

SPEECH CHART

What type of speech interruptions did the child have (repeating sounds or words; hesitations, changing his sentences)?	date: .... date:	date: .... date:
Did he appear to be tense or struggle with the speech interruptions?	date: .... date:	date: .... date:
Did he seem to be aware that he was having the interruptions; did he react to them? If so, how did he react?	date: .... date:	date: .... date:
To whom was he talking when the speech interruptions were noted?	date: .... date:	date: .... date:
What was he talking about?	date: .... date:	date: .... date:
What had happened immediately prior to his speaking (was he interrupted, ignored, excited, frustrated, tired)?	date: .... date:	date: .... date:
What was happening--what was the listener doing--when the child was talking? (Did they offer advice, look away, become tense, etc.?)	date: .... date:	date: .... date:

Record number of times:

1. Demand for speech

2. Child told "no" or "don't"

3. Child was interrupted while talking

4. Parental conflict or tension

5. Gave child speech advice, such as "stop and start over," "take a deep breath," "slow down."

FIGURE 12-1 The Speech Chart, a form for parental recording of speech interruptions. Used with permission of Emerick, L. L., and Haynes, W. (1986). *Diagnosis and Evaluation in Speech Pathology.* Englewood Cliffs, N.J.: Prentice-Hall.

ning to show early signs of stuttering (involuntary disfluency with struggle) are out-lined.

Evaluating the Older Child or Adult Who Stutters. In the speech evaluation of the stutterer, we must focus on the type and frequency of the stuttering block, to be sure that the problem is true stuttering, and not another form of disfluency (such as cluttering or dysarthria). The evaluation will usually include the following:

1. A close observation is made of the stutterer's conversational speech. The type of disfluency is noted (repetition; hesitation; interjection; silent, prolonged block). Particular attention is given to the linguistic unit involved (sound, syllable, word, phrase, sentence). Usually, the form of stuttering that has the best prognosis is simple sound repetition; poorer prognosis is usually accorded the prolonged block of the sound or syllable, characterized by tense efforts to get out of the block. Accessory speech features are identified, such as compressing the lips while trying to say the word; ancillary body movements, such as eye blinking, are noted.

2. Most of the observations of the stutterer's speech can be made while taking the history from the patient. The clinician hopes to find out when the stuttering began (usually it is in the preschool years). From there, the typical history includes:
   a. health history
   b. social history
   c. language development (there is increasing evidence that it is often delayed or impaired in stutterers)
   d. family history (Johnson [1959] reported eight studies that found a much higher incidence of stuttering in families of stutterers than those of nonstutterers)
   e. speech-therapy history (if there has been previous therapy, when was it, was it effective, what was done?)

3. Frequency of the stuttering block should be recorded for three kinds of speech: reading, conversation, and repeated readings of the same passage to measure the adaptation effect (a decrease in disfluency is noted for subsequent readings of the same passage). Ryan (1974) has recommended making frequency counts in other speaking tasks such as echoic repetitions of what the examiner says, choral reading, and puppet talk. Sometimes beginning therapy is facilitated by using the speaking tasks with the lowest frequency of occurrence that were identified during the initial speech evaluation.

4. A severity rating is helpful. If therapy is to follow the evaluation, comparisons of severity ratings can often be used as a measure of the therapy's effectiveness and success in generalization. A severity form developed by Wingate is shown in Figure 12–2.

Severity Rating Guide

Overall Rating	Frequency (per words spoken)	Descriptive Assessment		Accessory Features
		Effort		
Very Mild	1/100 (1%)	no perceptible tension		none
Mild	1/50 (2%)	perceptible tension but "block" easily overcome		minimal (staring; eye blinks or eye movement or slight movement of the facial musculature)
Moderate	1/15 (7%)	clear indication of tension or effort; lasts about 2 seconds		noticeable movement of facial musculature
Severe	1/7 (15%)	definite tension or effort; lasts about 2-4 seconds; frequent repeat attempts		obvious muscular activity, facial or other
Very Severe	1/4 (25%)	considerable effort; lasts 5 seconds or more; consistant repeat attempts		vigorous muscular activity, facial or other

FIGURE 12-2   A stuttering-severity guide. Used with permission of Wingate, M. (1976). *Stuttering Theory and Treatment.* New York: Irvington Publishing Co.

5. How patients view the stuttering is important to determine. Their attitudes toward the problem are often revealed when they explain their reasons for seeking treatment. The way they answer certain questions during the interview will often show how they tolerate the stuttering. What they do to control the stuttering (such as pursing the lips or breaking eye contact with the listener) needs to be identified; these accessory learned behaviors often interfere more with effectiveness of communication than does the actual stuttering block.

The Management of Stuttering

Since we established that approximately 80 percent of all children who reportedly stutter no longer do so after puberty (with or without therapy), it is important that the direct modification of stutterers' symptoms be reserved primarily for the remaining 20 percent. In the long run, many disfluent children may benefit more in terms of developing normal fluency if their parents are counseled than by any kind of direct therapy intervention.

Management of Early Disfluency. Young children who are brought into the speech clinic by concerned parents may display a variety of disfluent speech behaviors. Much of the problem may indeed be in the ear of the parents, who have become anxious about what may be considered normal disfluency, particularly as children string words together in their early attempts to express rather complex thoughts in longer verbal units. Or these children may no longer be repeating words and phrases, but sounds and syllables, in an obvious struggle to say things. It does appear, however, as if the best way to manage preschool children is to focus on the parents, helping them to understand normal disfluency and place less emphasis on how children say things. Activities that are identified in the interview as fluency-producing (such as yelling at the dog) are explained to the parents to be desirable verbal events; the parents are encouraged to encourage them in the child's daily life. Most problems of normal disfluency (repetition of words and phrases) tend to go away without any intervention of any kind, usually during the preschool years. The benefit of parental counseling seems to be in buying time, providing children with an atmosphere that is more accepting of the disfluency.

The Treatment of Stuttering. Speech therapy for stuttering in both children and adults may take different forms, depending primarily on the treatment philosophies of the speech-language pathologist. To simplify our understanding of the treatment of stuttering, let us identify three main approaches used with stutterers:

Psychological approach: Counseling and psychotherapy are given to improve the individual's attitude toward the problem, decrease avoidance, and create a better self-image.

Modifying the stuttering: Therapy is given to modify the stuttering blocks, helping the individual to stutter more fluently.

Modifying speech: Therapy is given to use speech free of stuttering by modifying rhythm, rate, and voicing.

Recognizing that speech therapy for stutterers often combines several approaches (such as the psychological approach with one of the other two methods), let us consider each method separately.

Psychological approach. You would not have to stutter for very long before you might develop negative feelings about speaking. Some stutterers go to great lengths to avoid speaking, and begin to employ avoidance behaviors of various kinds (being silent, not using words they "know" will come out stuttered, and so on). Simple sound repetitions begin to be accompanied by accessory behaviors (eye blinking, grimacing). Counseling or psychotherapy may be used to help stutterers see themselves as whole, having a complete life that includes many different kinds of experiences, including stuttering. Such therapy is often helpful in providing stutterers with a perspective on the problem, so that the stuttering does not loom larger than it should.

There are almost no documented reports that claim a psychotherapeutic approach alone will give patients permanent fluency. Rather, counseling and psychotherapy are generally adjunctive to more direct therapeutic approaches (modifying disfluency or extending fluency). For example, many stutterers blame their problem for all their misfortunes. A twenty-nine-year old stutterer told me, "If I didn't stutter, I would have gone on to law school, but no one wants to go see a lawyer who can't even say, 'Your Honor,' don't you agree?" A poor self-image begins to taint reality, imposing itself on every dimension of the patient's life. Counseling and psychotherapy have been found to be most important in providing the stutterer with a better (more realistic) self-concept (Wingate, 1976).

Modifying the stuttering. At the turn of the century in the United States, the primary treatment for stuttering was to work on easy voicing onsets, developing a rhythm of some kind, and maintaining speech fluency. Modifying the stuttering (instead of the fluent speech) developed as an opposite form of therapy, and is still widely used as a treatment for stuttering. In modifying the stuttering, the belief is "that the root of stuttering is in the struggle to be fluent," as described by Perkins (1980). Consequently, most such therapy is of a dual nature: improving your attitude toward speaking, and learning to stutter with less effort and reduced tension.

Van Riper (1973) is best identified as one of the leading advocates of the modification of stuttering. Over the years, he has developed an eclectic approach to stuttering, borrowing from different disciplines, as needed, to develop an individualized therapy approach for each stutterer. What works for one person may not work for another. In his classic text, *The Treatment of Stuttering* (1973), Van Riper presented four steps, which should be tailored to the needs of the individual:

1. *Identification.* Patients must become aware of and identify what they are doing in terms of disfluency, fluency, and associated behaviors.

2. *Desensitization.* Patients gradually learn to disassociate tension and stuttering. A progressive sequence of anxiety-producing stimuli are presented, to which the patient practices an easy, tension-free response. It is the goal eventually to replace the well-established, tense responses with fluent and relaxed ones.

3. *Modification.* Both attitudes (toward self and disfluency) and stuttering are modified in therapy. Direct counseling is given to stutterers, in the hopes of changing their way of living and self-image. Learning to stutter in an easier manner is practiced in therapy (Brutten and Shoemaker, 1967; Gregory, 1973). Van Riper (1973) requires that patients monitor their speech closely (such as speaking with intent), using particular techniques to maintain fluency and decrease the fear of stuttering. These techniques include cancellation and pull-out (see *The Treatment of Stuttering* for elaboration).

4. *Stabilization.* The terminal stage of Van Riper's approach to the modification of stuttering is stabilization. Bringing the stutterer to fluency is not enough. If treatment stops at this point, stutterers may regress and begin to stutter again. Fluency and moments of stuttering may alternate for a while, and counseling can help stutterers to understand this. Direct attempts to extend fluency are practiced during the stabilization phase, using many methods, including easy voicing onsets, slower speech, and choral reading. Van Riper also recommends that stutterers employ some negative practice, actually faking stuttering, deliberately using some of the postures and tremors that characterized the old stuttering (Van Riper and Emerick, 1984). The final work in therapy focuses on stutterers' expectancies, replacing the expectancy of stuttering ("I know I'm going to stutter") with a positive expectancy ("I know I'm going to be fluent").

Modifying Speech. In the treatment of stuttering during the mid 1970s, there was some shift away from its modification and toward the shaping of fluent speech. The fluency-shaping approach came directly out of Skinnerian learning theory (1953), in which a baseline behavior (such as a baseline of fluency) is followed by shaping approaches designed to extend or refine that behavior. One of the early practitioners of fluency shaping was Webster (1974), who established fluency by working primarily on mastering five target behaviors: the stretched syllable, syllable transition, slow change, full breath, and gentle voicing onsets. Webster's patients are required to spend three weeks of intensive, daily training mastering the five target behaviors in sequence. Schwartz (1976) requires massive therapy practice (as much as three months of three-times weekly therapy, two hours per day) to overcome the laryngeal airway problem (Airway Dilation Reflex), which he feels precipitates the stuttering. Schwartz places his emphasis on the preparation for speech, attempting to establish a passive flow of air to initiate an easy-onset voicing.

Wingate (1976) offers a fluency-shaping program that is very compatible with this author's view of voicing, melody, and prosody, particularly as developed in Chapter 2. That is, there is a basic prosodic flow that is used by all normal speakers. In stuttering, this flow is seriously interrupted. To establish more normal fluency, Wingate recommends that the rate of speech be slowed down, primarily by prolonging the length of vowels. As he explains in his monograph, *Stuttering and Laryngeal Behavior: A Review* (1982), Starkweather feels that, although Wingate's vowel-lengthening is effective in reducing stuttering, it is effective also because of the reduced rate of speaking and the regularity of rhythm that is induced. Adams (1974) helps to shape fluency by focusing on the timing and smoothness of voicing onsets, with some attention given to extending the duration and ease of expiratory airflow. Studebaker concludes that, although some stuttering may be precipitated by laryngeal-system dysfunction, some is also the result of an oral-system breakdown (poor coordination of lips, tongue, and jaw).

The fluency-shaping approach often begins by having stutterers use exceptionally long vowel prolongations and speak at a markedly reduced rate. While such speech may sound fluent, it is a long way from normal prosody. It is obviously important that patients be counseled about the "temporary differentness" of their speech. By small increments, this "difference" will be gradually shaped away. The eventual goal—to establish fluent speech—seems to be reached best by working on easy voicing onset, slowing down the rate of speech, and establishing a predictable speech rhythm. This fluency shaping, accompanied by counseling, appears to be used in more clinical settings today than either the psychological or modification-of-stuttering approaches.

CLUTTERING

Another clinical disorder that is characterized by an alteration of rhythm and rate of speech is *cluttering*. The actual incidence or prevalence of cluttering does not appear known at this time, in part because of the vagueness of definition and lack of agreement among authorities as to the dimensions of the problem. Wood (1971) defined cluttering as "rapid, nervous speech marked by omissions of sounds and syllables" (p. 10). This definition gives equal prominence to the symptoms of rapid rate and articulatory errors, and is thus similar to that of Wingate (1978), who defined cluttering as "a fluency disorder of unknown origin characterized by sporadically excessive rate and incomplete and distorted articulation" (p. 268). In one of the few monographs written on the topic, *Studies in Tachyphemia* (1966), Arnold reviewed a detailed European literature, which described cluttering as a disorder that included symptoms of rapid rate, faulty articulation, and related reading and writing problems; all three speech-language problems are often associated with "disorders of lateral dominance."

Clutterers usually speak much faster than stutterers; in fact, the word **tachy-**

phemia (often used as a synonym for cluttering) literally means "rapid speech." Clutterers may be further differentiated from stutterers by their usually slurred and omitted phonemes, lack of awareness of their poor speech, and the fact that they neither avoid nor feel tense about the act of speaking. The additional observation that clutterers often demonstrate an associated language disorder involving reading and writing (Weiss, 1964) further separates them from stutterers, who usually do not appear to have an overall language problem. By combining the views of several different writers, let us redefine cluttering:

> Cluttering is rapid speech characterized by articulatory omissions and substitutions, usually without the speaker's awareness or concern.

Evaluation of Cluttering

Typical clutterers are sent by someone else to a speech clinic, primarily because they are not very concerned about their speech. It is often the classroom teacher who refers a child who clutters, having observed rapid and sometimes unintelligible speech in the classroom. The adult clutterer is often referred by an employer, who hopes to improve the employee's speech patterns.

Three areas are looked at during the speech evaluation: determining the individual's concern about the problem, evaluating rate, and measuring articulation. If there are associated reading and writing problems, they would receive some additional assessment. How the individual feels about the speech disorder is an important finding in establishing the diagnosis of cluttering. During the evaluation, typical clutterers will usually protest that there is nothing wrong with their speech, and state that they would prefer not to be at the clinic.

Some measure of both conversational speaking rate and oral reading rate should be made. Darley (1940) and Fairbanks (1960) both state that normal conversational rate is slower than the oral reading rate, which is about 160–170 words per minute. The patient's conversation and oral reading are timed by counting the syllables spoken per second or words per minute; an elevated speaking rate is the typical finding. A standardized articulation test, such as the *Templin-Darley Tests of Articulation* (1969) or the *Goldman-Fristoe Test of Articulation* (1970), will provide the documentation needed for determining the probable errors of articulation. It would appear that the articulation errors made in cluttering are physiologic in origin, rather than the result of a breakdown in the understanding of phonologic rules.

Treatment of Cluttering

Because clutterers are often oblivious of their speech problem, some time in therapy must be spent developing an awareness of the problem. Letting patients hear a recording of their speech, and contrasting it with a recording of a normal speaker, is often necessary at the beginning of therapy. The following brief dialogue occurred after a seventeen-year old clutterer heard a recording of himself, followed by one of a normal male speaker near the patient's age:

CLINICIAN: You must speak twice as fast as that other kid. Did you hear that?
PATIENT: He donna wanna go fatter than me.
CLINICIAN: Maybe if we just had you talk louder, like this, *"I'm going to speak very loud for a bit."* That sure makes me sound better, doesn't it?
PATIENT: Talin' loud is easy for me. *I tal' loud at home and they all hear me.*
CLINICIAN: Well, let's make a recording of you talking extra loud, and we'll see how that sounds.

Rather than working on the components of rate and articulation, both of which were far from normal in this case, the clinician elected to work holistically on making the patient aware that he could speak better by speaking more loudly. Given a tangible method of changing his speech, the patient could monitor it closely when he spoke more loudly, which would slow down the rate of speech and improve his articulation.

Speaking with a rhythm, such as using the pacing supplied by a metronome, will often have a dramatic effect on the clutterer's speech. It slows down the rate and improves articulation. Another method of slowing rate can be achieved by reading aloud in unison with the clinician, with pauses built in between phrases. The voice therapy-approach, "place the voice" (Boone, 1983), has been found effective with clutterers, as have other approaches, such as chewing, chanting, opening the mouth, and the "yawn-sigh." Wingate (1978) notes that overall-speech-improvement approaches have had some positive effects on clutterers' speech. Despite the existence of the articulation disorder (omissions and substitutions), therapy focusing directly on articulation has not proved very effective unless it is coupled with the primary effort, to reduce the rate of speaking. Speaking more slowly and slightly more loudly often has dramatic effects in improving the articulatory proficiency of the clutterer.

MOTOR SPEECH DISORDERS

Rate of speech and overall speech fluency is often seriously disrupted in motor speech disorders. Both the sensory and motor components of speech may be altered by various neurological diseases that create motor speech disturbances, or dysarthria. The type and severity of the speech problem are usually directly related to the site of the disease, and not necessarily to the type of disease, such as stroke, a degenerative disease (such as multiple sclerosis), an infectious disease, a tumor, or a developmental disorder (such as cerebral palsy). As we have seen in earlier chapters, dysarthria cuts across the parameters of speech, causing problems in phonation, resonance, and articulation. Most dysarthrias also cause serious speech-fluency problems.

Treatment of Fluency in Dysarthria

Obviously, successfully treating the disease that causes the dysarthria would be the treatment of choice. Unfortunately, most neurological diseases that may cause dysarthria are either static (the condition is permanent, such as in cerebral palsy) or progressive (as in multiple sclerosis). A goal to improve fluency must, therefore, be consistent with the limitations imposed by the disease and the patient's response to medical-surgical therapies.

The administration of various kinds of therapeutic drugs may have dramatic effects on the patient's fluency. L-Dopa, for example, for the treatment of Parkinson's disease is a dramatic example of a drug that can improve speech. The Parkinson patient who is successfully treated with it may exhibit a marked reduction in severity of dysarthria, including louder, slower, more articulate speech. In contrast, the spastic interference experienced by the patient with multiple sclerosis may be lessened by muscle relaxants, enabling the patient to speak in sentences, no longer interrupted by spastic contractions that cut off attempts at fluency.

The speech-language pathologist often plays a primary role in helping the dysarthric patient improve fluency. Improving respiration efficiency may improve fluency. This can be done by providing the patient with a normal model for a quick inspiration and prolonged expiration. The patient then tries to match the model, and is provided with feedback regarding relative movements of the abdomen and thorax, using the magnetometer feedback system described by Hixon, Mead, and Goldman (1976). Another method for improving functional respiration to increase fluency is to work on duration; the patient practices extending the expirations of phonemes, both voiceless (such as /f/ or /s/) and voiced (such as vowels). Or the speaking rate may be improved by direct work on increasing diadochokinesis—speed in moving the articulators—in a rapid series of speech sounds. For example, the patient is asked to repeat the speech sounds /pʌtʌ/ as quickly as possible; after timing the number of sounds made in a specific period of time, the patient works on saying the sounds a bit faster. Sometimes, staccato phonation practice, in which discrete and rapid phonations are produced as fast as possible, will provide the patient with greater laryngeal control, permitting a faster rate of speech.

Modifying the fluency of a patient with a motor speech disorder is a highly individualized endeavor. It is occasionally possible, however, to change the rate of speech and encourage more normal prosody by directly working on fluency. Speech-language pathologists work closely with other professionals in their attempts to improve the fluency of the dysarthric patient who may require medication, surgery, an appliance of some kind, or rehabilitation (such as physical or occupational therapies).

REVIEW QUESTIONS

We have seen that interruptions of verbal fluency may be seen in such disorders as stuttering, cluttering, and dysarthria. Let us review some questions about disorders of fluency and their management.

1. What is fluency? What is disfluency? What do we mean by fluency disorders?

2. Differentiate disfluency from stuttering.

3. Write your own definition of stuttering. How does it differ from the author's?

4. Describe several theories on the cause of stuttering.

5. Some theorists believe that the larynx may play a prominent role in stuttering. Explain.

6. What are the three primary approaches to the treatment of stuttering presented in this text?

7. What is cluttering?

8. What are some of the fluency problems seen in dysarthria? Can they be treated?

REFERENCES

Adams, M. R. (1974). A physiologic and aerodynamic interpretation of fluent and stuttered speech. *Journal of Fluency Disorders, 1:* 35–67.

Adams, M. R. (1978). Stuttering theory, research, and therapy: the present and future. *Journal of Fluency Disorders, 3:* 139–147.

Adams, M. R., and Hayden, P. (1976). The ability of stutterers and nonstutterers to initiate and terminate phonation during production of an isolated vowel. *Journal of Speech and Hearing Research, 19:* 290–296.

Adams, M. R., and Reis, R. (1974). Influence of the onset of phonation on the frequency of stuttering, a replication and re-evaluation. *Journal of Speech and Hearing Research, 17:* 752–754.

Andrews, G., Craig, A., Feyer, A., Haddinott, S., Neilson, M., and Howie, P. (1983). Stuttering: a review of research findings and theories circa 1982. *Journal of Speech and Hearing Disorders, 48:* 226–245.

Andrews, G., and Harris, M. (1964). *The Syndrome of Stuttering*. London: Heinemann Medical Books.

Arnold, G. (1966). *Studies in Tachyphemia: an Investigation of Cluttering and General Language Disability*. New York: Speech Rehabilitation Institute.

Barbara, D. (1962). *The Psychotherapy of Stuttering*. Springfield, Ill.: Charles C. Thomas.

Barrett, K. H., Keith, R. W., Agnello, J., and Weiler, E. (1979). Central auditory processing of stutterers and nonstutterers. Paper presented at American Speech-Language-Hearing Association meeting, Atlanta, Georgia.

Blanton, S. (1965). Stuttering, in *New Directions in Stuttering*, ed. D. Barbara. Springfield, Ill.: Charles C. Thomas.

Bloodstein, O. (1981). *A Handbook on Stuttering*. Chicago: National Easter Society for Crippled Children and Adults.

Boone, D. R. (1983). *The Voice and Voice Therapy* (3rd ed.). Englewood Cliffs, N.J.: Prentice-Hall.

Bruce, M. C., and Adams, M. R. (1978). Effects of two types of motor practice on stuttering adaptation. *Journal of Speech and Hearing Research, 21:* 421–428.

Brutten, E. J., and Shoemaker, D. J. (1967). *The*

Modification of Stuttering. Englewood Cliffs, N.J.: Prentice-Hall.

Bryngelson, B. (1971). Speech and personality, in *Handbook of Speech Pathology and Audiology,* ed. L. Travis. Englewood Cliffs, N.J.: Prentice-Hall.

Curlee, R. F. (1980). A case selection strategy for young disfluent children. *Seminars on Speech, Language, Hearing, 1:* 277–287.

Darley, F. L. (1940). "A Normative Study of Oral Reading Rate." Unpublished Master's thesis, University of Iowa.

Darley, F., Aronson, A., and Brown, J. (1975). *Motor Speech Disorders.* Philadelphia: W. B. Saunders.

Davis, D. M. (1940). The relation of repetitions in the speech of young children to certain measures of language maturity and situation factors: part II and part III. *Journal of Speech Disorders, 5:* 235–246.

Emerick, L. L., and Hatten, J. T. (1979). *Diagnosis and Evaluation in Speech Pathology.* Englewood Cliffs, N.J.: Prentice-Hall.

Fairbanks, G. (1960). *Voice and Articulation Drillbook* (2nd ed.). New York: Harper and Row.

Fraser, M. (1973). *Stuttering Words.* Memphis: Speech Foundation of America.

Freeman, F. J., and Ushijima, T. (1975). Laryngeal activity accompanying the movement of stuttering: a preliminary report of EMG investigations. *Journal of Fluency Disorders, 1:* 36–45.

Glauber, I. P. (1958). The psychoanalysis of stuttering, in *Stuttering: a Symposium,* ed. J. Eisenson. New York: Harper and Row.

Goldman, R., Fristoe, M., and Woodcock, R. (1970). *Goldman-Fristoe Test of Articulation.* Circle Pines, Minn.: American Guidance Service.

Gregory, H. (1973). *Stuttering: Differential Evaluation and Therapy.* New York: Bobbs-Merrill.

Hand, C., and Haynes, W. (1983). Linguistic processing and reaction time differences in stutterers and nonstutterers. *Journal of Speech and Hearing Research, 26:* 181–185.

Hixon, T., Mead, J., and Goldman, M. (1976). Dynamics of the chest wall during speech productions: function of the thorax, rib cage, diaphragm, and abdomen. *Journal of Speech and Hearing Research, 19:* 297–356.

Hull, F. M., Mielke, P. W., Willeford, J. A., and

Timmons, R. J. (1976). *National Speech and Hearing Survey.* Final Report, Project 50978. Washington, D.C.: Office of Education, Bureau of Education for the Handicapped, HEW.

Johnson, W. (1955). A study of the onset and development of stuttering, in *Stuttering in Children and Adults,* ed. W. Johnson and R. R. Leutenegger. Minneapolis: University of Minnesota Press.

Johnson, W. (1959). *The Onset of Stuttering.* Minneapolis: University of Minnesota Press.

Kent, R. (1983). Facts about stuttering: neuropsychologic perspectives. *Journal of Speech and Hearing Disorders, 48:* 249–255.

Luper, H. L., and Cross, D. E. (1978). Finger reaction time of stuttering and nonstuttering children and adults. Paper presented at American Speech-Language-Hearing Association meeting, San Francisco.

Martin, R. R., and Siegel, G. M. (1966). The effects of simultaneously punishing stuttering and rewarding fluency. *Journal of Speech and Hearing Research, 9:* 466–475.

McDearmon, J. (1968). Primary stuttering at the onset of stuttering: a re-examination of the data. *Journal of Speech and Hearing Research, 11:* 631–637.

Metraux, R. W. (1950). Speech profiles of the preschool child 18–54 months. *Journal of Speech and Hearing Disorders, 15:* 37–53.

Molt, L. F., and Guilford, A. M. (1979). Auditory processing and anxiety in stutterers. *Journal of Fluency Disorders, 4:* 255–267.

Morley, M. E. (1952). A ten-year survey of speech disorders among university students. *Journal of Speech and Hearing Disorders, 17:* 25–31.

Morley, M. E. (1972). *The Development and Disorders of Speech in Childhood.* Edinburgh, Scotland: Churchill Livingstone.

Netsell, R., and Daniel, B. (1974). Neural and mechanical response time for speech production. *Journal of Speech and Hearing Research, 17:* 608–618.

Perkins, W. H. (1977). *Speech Pathology: An Applied Behavioral Science.* St. Louis: C. V. Mosby.

Perkins, W. H. (1980). Disorders of speech flow, in *Introduction to Communication Disorders,* ed. T. Hixon, L. Shriberg, and J. Saxman. Englewood Cliffs, N.J.: Prentice-Hall.

Perkins, W. H. (1983). The problem of definition: commentary on "stuttering." *Journal of Speech and Hearing Disorders, 48:* 246–249.

Pinsky, S. D., and McAdam, D. W. (1980). Electroencephalographic and dichotic indices of cerebral laterality in stutterers. *Brain and Language, 11:* 374–397.

Prins, D. (1972). Personality, stuttering severity, and age. *Journal of Speech and Hearing Research, 15:* 148–154.

Quist, R. W., and Martin, R. R. (1967). The effect of response contingent verbal punishment on stuttering. *Journal of Speech and Hearing Research, 10:* 795–800.

Reich, A., Till, J., and Goldsmith, H. (1981). Laryngeal and manual reaction times of stuttering and nonstuttering adults. *Journal of Speech and Hearing Research, 24:* 192–196.

Rosenfield, D. B., and Goodglass, H. (1980). Dichotic testing of cerebral dominance in stutterers. *Brain and Language, 11:* 170–180.

Ryan, B. (1974). *Programmed Therapy for Stuttering in Children and Adults.* Springfield, Ill.: Charles C. Thomas.

Schwartz, M. F. (1974). The core of the stuttering block. *Journal of Speech and Hearing Disorders, 39:* 169–177.

Schwartz, M. F. (1976). *Stuttering Solved.* Philadelphia: Lippincott.

Shapiro, A. (1980). An electromyographic analysis of the fluent and dysfluent utterance of several types of stutterers. *Journal of Fluency Disorders, 5:* 203–231.

Sheehan, J. G. (1970). *Stuttering: Research and Therapy.* New York: Harper and Row.

Sheehan, J. G., and Martyn, M. M. (1970). Spontaneous recovery from stuttering. *Journal of Speech and Hearing Research, 13:* 279–289.

Starkweather, C. W. (1982). *Stuttering and Laryngeal Behaviors: A Review* (ASHA Monograph 21). Rockville, Md.: American Speech-Language-Hearing Association.

Templin, M. C., and Darley, F. L. (1969). *The Templin-Darley Tests of Articulation* (2nd ed.). Iowa City, Iowa: Bureau of Educational Research and Service, University of Iowa.

Till, J., Reich, A., Dickey, S., and Seiber, J. (1983). Phonatory and manual reaction times of stuttering and nonstuttering children. *Journal of Speech and Hearing Research, 26:* 171–180.

Travis, L. E. (1971). The unspeakable feelings of people with special reference to stuttering, in *Handbook of Speech Pathology and Audiology* (2nd ed.), ed. L. D. Travis. Englewood Cliffs, N.J.: Prentice-Hall.

Van Riper, C. (1971). *The Nature of Stuttering.* Englewood Cliffs, N.J.: Prentice-Hall.

Van Riper, C. (1973). *The Treatment of Stuttering.* Englewood Cliffs, N.J.: Prentice-Hall.

Van Riper, C., and Emerick, L. (1984). *Speech Correction: An Introduction to Speech Pathology and Audiology* (7th ed.). Englewood Cliffs, N.J.: Prentice-Hall.

Webster, R. (1974). A behavioral analysis of stuttering: treatment and theory, in *Innovative Treatment Methods in Psychopathology,* ed. K. Calhoun, H. Adams, and K. Mitchell. New York: Wiley.

Weiss, D. (1964). *Cluttering.* Englewood Cliffs, N.J.: Prentice-Hall.

West, R. (1958). An agnostic's speculations about stuttering, in *Stuttering: A Symposium,* ed. by J. Eisenson. New York: Harper and Row.

Westby, C. E. (1979). Language performance of stuttering and nonstuttering children. *Journal of Communication Disorders, 12:* 133–145.

Wingate, M. E. (1962). Personality needs of stutterers. *Logos, 5:* 35–37.

Wingate, M. E. (1976). *Stuttering Theory and Treatment.* New York: Irvington Publishing.

Wingate, M. E. (1978). Disorders of fluency, in *Speech, Language, Hearing, Normal Processes and Disorders,* ed. P. Skinner and R. Shelton. Reading, Mass.: Addison-Wesley.

Wood, K. S. (1971). Terminology and nomenclature, in *Handbook of Speech Pathology and Audiology* (2nd ed.), ed. L. Travis. Englewood Cliffs, N.J.: Prentice-Hall.

World Health Organization (1977). *Manual of the International Statistical Classification of Diseases, Injuries, and Causes of Death,* Vol. I. Geneva: World Health Organization.

Wyatt, G. (1958). A developmental crisis theory in stuttering. *Language and Speech, 1:* 250–264.

Yairi, E. (1981). The onset of stuttering in two-year-old children. *Journal of Speech and Hearing Research, 24:* 490–495.

Yairi, E. (1983). The onset of stuttering in two- and three-year-old children: a preliminary report. *Journal of Speech and Hearing Disorders, 48:* 171–178.

Young, M. A. (1975). Onset, prevalence, and recovery from stuttering. *Journal of Speech and Hearing Disorders, 40:* 49–58.

13

The Management and Treatment of Communication Disorders

The focus of this book has been on verbal communication and its disorders. Although we have looked briefly in earlier chapters at both verbal and nonverbal communication, our emphasis has been on communication disorders involving hearing, listening, language, speech, and voice. In the concluding chapter, we will look at the many disciplines that contribute to the management and treatment of various communication disorders. Primary consideration, however, will be given to the audiologist and speech-language pathologist, whose primary professional role is to work with people who have communication disorders.

Throughout this text, we have looked at the management and treatment of various developmental and acquired problems of verbal communication. In this chapter, we will consider the people in various professions who may work with the audiologist and speech-language pathologist to treat children and adults who have a variety of communication problems. For example, a boy born with a cleft palate is probably delivered by an obstetrician, who then works closely with a pediatrician to develop a strategy for the parents to follow in caring for and managing the baby, particularly offering direction for feeding the baby and protecting his airway. Soon, the medical social worker, the plastic surgeon, and possibly the otolaryngologist may play consulting and active roles, helping to provide care for the baby and his family. Often, it is one of these specialists who first refers the child with the communication disorder to the audiologist or speech-language pathologist. Or the specialist in communication disorders may refer the client or patient to another professional specialist for a further evaluation and possible treatment. Table 13–1 lists specialists (in alphabetical order) who work closely with the audiologist and speech-language

TABLE 13–1

Specialists Who May Help in the Management and Treatment of Children and Adults with Communication disorders.

Professional Specialist	Medical Specialist
audiologist	geriatrician
classroom teacher	internist
counselor	neurologist
linguist	ophthalmologist
occupational therapist	orthopedist
optometrist	otolaryngologist
orthodontist	pediatrician
pedodontist	physiatrist
prosthodontist	plastic surgeon
psychologist	psychiatrist
social worker	
special-education teacher	
speech and hearing scientist	
speech-language pathologist	

pathologist to deal with various communicative problems. In the left-hand column are 15 professional specialists (including the audiologist and speech-language pathologist) who may work directly together, and in the right-hand column are listed some 10 medical specialists who may work closely with other specialists in the total management and treatment of someone with a communication disorder.

As we will see, all these professionals have diverse interests and backgrounds. They will be considered in alphabetical order.

PROFESSIONAL SPECIALISTS

Audiologist

The audiologist is a nonmedical professional who is certified by the American Speech-Language-Hearing Association and licensed in most states to test for hearing sensitivity and to administer diagnostic tests to children and adults with various hearing disorders. As we shall see later in this chapter, when we discuss the profession of audiology and speech-language-pathology in greater detail, the audiologist is also trained in the testing and fitting of hearing aids and in providing aural habilitation and rehabilitation.

Classroom Teacher

Hearing and speech services have been provided in the public schools since the early 1900s. Classroom teachers often observe children in their classes who demonstrate some kind of communication handicap, and they make an appropriate referral. The school audiologist or speech-language pathologist is often able to evaluate and possibly help these children referred by the teacher. The audiologist or speech-language pathologist works closely with the teacher to provide the right kind of atmosphere to help such children to do well in the classroom, as well as to lessen the effects of their communication handicap.

Counselor

Many children with hearing and speech-language handicaps and members of their family profit from professional counseling. The counseling psychologist or counselor is a trained professional, with a master's or doctoral degree, who can offer direct suggestions that may improve children's environments. Adults with serious communication handicaps (such as an acquired profound hearing loss or an aphasia after a stroke) often profit from a counseling approach that considers possible vocational changes or modifications in living arrangements. Sometimes the vocational counselor will send patients for a hearing and speech evaluation, to determine whether, with remediation therapy, they might improve their communication skills sufficiently to permit some kind of employment. For example, a young man who had been unemployed for 20 months was sent by his counselor for a hearing evaluation; it was found that he needed a hearing aid. He was fitted with one, and was later able to be placed in a job by his counselor.

Linguist

A linguist is a scientist who studies the content, form, and use of language. A linguist may specialize in a particular aspect of language, such as phonology or syntax. Historically, linguists have been interested in the content and form of language; its actual use and its effects on others has been studied by the psycholinguist. However, with recent increased interest in the pragmatics of language, more linguists are looking at its functional use. Linguists' clinical interests include the application of what is known about normal language development to the child with a language disorder. For many years, linguists have helped speech-language pathologists to understand the linguistic dissolution experienced by adult patients with aphasia.

Occupational Therapist

The **occupational therapist** (OT) is a medical technician who primarily does work prescribed by such medical specialists as the neurologist, the orthopedist, and the physiatrist. The OT often works closely with the speech-language pathologist to help children who may have neuromuscular problems related to such neurological conditions as cerebral palsy, closed-head trauma, or muscular dystrophy. Adult patients with degenerative diseases (such as multiple sclerosis or amyotrophic lateral sclerosis) and aphasia are often seen jointly by the OT and the speech-language pathologist, who work together to make the patient's overall communicative function as good as possible.

Optometrist

The doctor of optometry is qualified to test the function of the eye and to prescribe and carry out the treatment of eye disorders, such as refraction testing or the fitting of corrective lenses. Nonmedical **optometrists** and their medical counterparts, **ophthamalogists,** who also treat diseases of the eye, make many cross-referrals. The optometrist contributes to communicative effectiveness by prescribing and fitting corrective lenses, as well as offering eye exercises for various disorders of the eye.

Orthodontist

The **orthodontist** is a dentist who, after several years of additional training, has been certified by the American Board of Orthodontics and become a member of the American Orthodontics Association. Orthodontia is concerned with the alignment of teeth and the correction of malocclusion. The orthodontist often works closely with the speech-language pathologist in helping children with severe orofacial anomalies, such as cleft palate, and with some adults who have various dental alignment problems that may affect speech articulation.

Pedodontist

A **pedodontist** is a dentist who works only with children. The pedodontist has several years graduate training beyond the basic dental degree and is board certified by the American Association of Pedodontics. Along with the speech-language pathologist, the pedodontist may play an active role in the overall management of young children with severe developmental problems, such as mental retardation or cerebral palsy, where proper dental care may be difficult.

Phoniatrist

There are very few speech and voice scientists in the United States who would call themselves phoniatrists. In many countries, however, a voice scientist who specializes in vocal function and laryngeal disorders may be known as a **phoniatrist** (who may be a physician or a nonphysician). The speech-language pathologist who is particularly interested in voice, the speech-voice scientist, and an occasional otolaryngologist (one who specializes in the larynx) function as phoniatrists in this country.

Prosthodontist

The prosthodontist is a dentist who specializes in the construction and fitting of various dental appliances, such as dentures, obturators, and palatal lifts. The prosthodontist is a dentist who has done additional work in dental prosthetics and is board certified as a prosthodontist. The speech-language pathologist works closely with the prosthodontist (and the plastic surgeon) in the construction of appliances for children and adults who demonstrate problems of velopharyngeal closure. Prosthodontics also help the older population by fitting dentures.

Psychologist

Most **psychologists** enter their profession at the doctoral level, are certified in different specialties, and hold membership in the American Psychological Association. The clinical psychologist may play a primary role in the assessment and treatment of patients with various kinds of communicative disorders. The psychometrician tests patients' mental abilities and functioning. Counseling psychologists may work as closely with families as they do with their actual patients. Areas of specialization include child psychology, neuropsychology, rehabilitation, or of death and dying. The audiologist and speech-language pathologist frequently work closely as a nonmedical team with the psychologist, and together they face difficult diagnostic and remediation problems in managing patients of any age with communicative disorders.

Social Worker

Many agencies and hospitals have **social workers** on staff to counsel both other professional staff members and patients. Social workers have graduate training (usually at least a Master's degree) and are certified by the Academy of Certified Social Workers. Audiologists and speech-language pathologists learn to rely on social workers who can play a primary role in history taking and in providing a complete description of patients and their family environments. For the patient with a severe communicative disorder (such as the adult who has sustained closed-head trauma, followed by a combination of symptoms difficult to treat) the social worker may play a much-needed role in helping the patient and family to develop a realistic perspective on the patient's status and long-term prognosis. Many patients with communicative disorders have a myriad of other problems, and the social worker often knows the most about which agencies may be helpful, as well as about the availability of funds for rehabilitation and other needs.

Special-education Teacher

The special-education teacher (who may be known as a **special educator** or adaptive educator) is a classroom teacher who has had additional graduate training in special education. Many special-education teachers are members of the Council of Exceptional Children, and have special state credentialing that allows them to function as resource specialists in particular school districts. With the advent of Public Law 94-142 (see Chapter 8), the federal government mandated that local school districts must provide handicapped children with the services needed for their education. Accordingly, the special educator is the professional in a school district who can serve as its resource person, providing services needed by children who are emotionally handicapped (EH), mentally retarded (MR), orthopedically handicapped (OR), and by other children who may require adaptive education.

Speech and Hearing Scientist

Speech and hearing scientists play a prominent role in the profession of audiology and speech-language pathology. Although such individuals may belong to other professional organizations (such as the American Acoustical Society), they are also members of the American Speech-Language-Hearing Association. Hearing scientists may focus on the ear's various auditory characteristics and performance, or they may limit their work to acoustical analyses of sound. The work of speech scientists is equally diverse, perhaps involving respiratory physiology, laryngeal function, or the complexities of neuromuscular function required for speech. Although some areas focused on by speech and hearing scientists may appear abstract, and divorced from the clinical arena, many of their scientific findings eventually filter into clinical practice and have direct impact on patients with a communicative disorder. More and more students are studying speech and hearing science as a professional entity in itself (a discipline of inquiry about normal and disordered communication) with no direct clinical training or practicum; their continuing efforts are making significant contributions to our understanding of human communication and its disorders.

Speech-language Pathologist

A speech-language pathologist is trained at the master's or doctoral level, certified to practice by the American Speech-Language-Hearing Association (ASHA), and licensed in most states. Speech-language pathologists are employed in a variety of settings, including public schools, clinics, hospitals, agencies, universities, and private practice. Speech-language pathologists are trained to work with both children and adults who have such communication problems as articulation defects, voice disorders, stuttering, hearing problems, and language disorders of various types. We will discuss the profession of audiology and speech-language pathology and the professional association, ASHA, in greater detail later in the chapter.

MEDICAL SPECIALISTS

Although the majority of communication problems are not health-related, many disorders do require the active involvement of a medical doctor. Let us consider the ten medical specialties listed in Table 13–1.

Geriatrician

Geriatrics, the health care and management of the aged, is a relatively new medical specialty. **Geriatricians** are board specialized in geriatrics. The communicative disorders that they uncover among their patients include hearing loss, dysarthria, aphasia, and the language dissolution shown by patients with senile dementia. Geriatricians function as patient "managers," referring those with problems to the specialists who are best trained to treat them. For example, the patient with a suspected dementia may be referred by the geriatrician first to the neurologist, then to the neuropsychologist and the speech-language pathologist; eventually, the patient and family may be referred to the social worker and the occupational therapist.

Internist

The majority of adult patients are routinely followed by the **internist,** a medical doctor who has a board specialty in internal medicine. The internist looks after people's general health, but also often has a particular medical specialty, such as cardiovascular or pulmonary medicine. The alert internist listens to and watches the adult patient closely for possible problems in communication; for example, a change in hearing or speaking may be the early symptom of a serious disease. The internist may make a direct referral to the audiologist or speech-language pathologist for assessment and possible treatment of the patient's communicative disorder.

Neurologist

The **neurologist** is a physician who specializes in the diagnosis and treatment of neurological diseases. The pediatric neurologist, for example, may specialize in the diagnosis of various neurological conditions that may be interfering with children's normal developmental growth. The neurologist looks closely at the patient's overall neuromuscular function and at communicative function, two areas that are sensitive to change after the onset of a neurological disorder of some type. The neurologist may send to the audiologist and speech-language pathologist patients who have various kinds of degenerative diseases (such as amyotrophic lateral sclerosis), patients with head trauma, or those who have had strokes, producing problems of aphasia or dysarthria. Neurologists work closely with other members of the medical community, such as neurosurgeons, otolaryngologists, oncologists (specialists in treating cancer), and ophthalmologists.

Ophthalmologist

The diagnosis and treatment of disorders of the eye are the primary responsibilities of the ophthalmologist, a physician with a board specialty in ophthalmology. Visual disorders that interfere with sight, such as presbyopia (a reduction in near-vision acuity that begins after the age of forty) or glaucoma (a loss of peripheral visual fields as a result of prolonged high-intraocular pressure), may have an obvious impact on communicative effectiveness. When severe visual handicaps are involved, the ophthalmologist may work with the optometrist, the occupational therapist, or the speech-language pathologist to develop some kind of functional augmentative communication system for the patient.

Orthopedist

Certain children with cerebral palsy or some other severe neuromuscular handicap will require early medical-surgical treatment by an **orthopedist,** a surgeon who specializes in the diagnosis and treatment of muscular-skeletal diseases. Early treatment of such children will often prevent serious skeletal deformities and promote better motor function. Orthopedists are physicians who have had advanced training and a residency in orthopedics. Although they closely direct both the physical and occupational therapists, they also refer patients with hearing and speech problems to the audiologist and the speech-language pathologist for evaluation and possible treatment.

Otolaryngologist

The audiologist and speech-language pathologist work closely with the otolaryngologist, a physician with advanced training in the diagnosis and treatment of the ear, nose, and throat, as well as a residency in the specialty. Because of the involvement of these three sites (ear, nose, and throat), the otolaryngologist is often known as the ENT physician, or sometimes as the otorhinolaryngologist. Many audiologists work closely with the ENT doctor, particularly in the areas of hearing testing, the fitting of a hearing aid, and aural rehabilitation. The speech-language pathologist frequently sees the child with delayed language function whose primary problem is recurring middle-ear infections, requiring the help of the otolaryngologist. The treatment of voice problems, both of phonation and resonance, often requires the close cooperation of the speech-language pathologist and the otolaryngologist.

Pediatrician

Many speech and hearing referrals come from the **pediatrician,** a physician with board certification in pediatrics who specializes in the care and medical treatment of children. The typical pediatrician cares for a youngster from infancy through the late teen years. The hearing problems commonly experienced by preschool children are often routinely treated by the pediatrician; if the problems become severe, a referral is often made to the otolaryngologist, who in turn may seek the diagnostic and habilitative services of an audiologist. Children who appear slow (compared to their age peers) in their use of language and speech may be referred to the speech-language pathologist for evaluation and possible therapy. For the optimal management of children with severe communicative problems, perhaps related to such problems as cerebral palsy or cleft palate, the pediatrician may play a major role on a management team with other professionals (perhaps in an orthopedic clinic or on an orofacial-disorders team). The pediatrician's diagnosis is vital in the early identification of children with various communicative disorders, making appropriate referrals to some of the specialists listed in Table 13–1.

Physiatrist

The **physiatrist** is a medical doctor who has completed a residency and is board certified in rehabilitation medicine. In clinics and hospitals, the physiatrist often heads a rehabilitation unit, which may have a variety of names, including Rehabilitation, Adaptive Medicine, Restorative Medicine, or Physical Medicine and Rehabilitation. Patients with acute or chronic medical problems may have treatments prescribed by the physiatrist in physical therapy, occupational therapy, or vocational training. Some rehabilitation units also include services for patients with communicative handicaps, and the physiatrist will refer such patients directly to the audiologist and speech-language pathologist for evaluation and possible therapy. Otherwise, the physiatrist may refer patients with hearing and speech problems to independent departments of audiology and speech-language pathology (such as may be found in Veterans' Administration hospitals).

Plastic Surgeon

The **plastic surgeon** is a physician who has completed a residency and has become board certified in plastic surgery, a specialty concerned with the repair and restoration of absent, injured, or deformed parts of the body. Deformities of the nose, mouth, jaw, and palate that interfere with normal speech and voice production are frequently corrected by the plastic surgeon. During a procedure, tissue may be transplanted from one site to another. For example, a child with a short soft palate that cannot make the contact with the posterior pharyngeal wall required for normal oral resonance may need a pharyngeal-flap procedure (discussed in Chapter 11); a small piece of tissue is loosened on three sides from the pharynx and bridged across to the short soft palate, in effect producing a structural separation between the oral and nasal cavities. Besides repair of the palate, the plastic surgeon can often surgically correct other anomalies that may interfere with normal communication. Even when structural adequacy of a particular part (such as an injured lip) has been restored by the plastic surgeon, the patient may still require hours of speech retraining by the speech-language pathologist; these two professionals work closely together in an effort to reduce the effects of a communicative handicap.

Psychiatrist

The **psychiatrist** is a doctor who has completed a residency and is board certified in psychiatry, the specialty dealing primarily with neurotic and psychotic mental behaviors. Most mental disorders have a direct impact on individuals' communication effectiveness. Neurotic patients, who are usually aware of their interpersonal struggles, may have difficulty relating to the people around them. Psychotics, such as autistic children, may be unaware of their differences; their communicative problems primarily involve their own realities, which may be quite different from those of their listeners. Psychiatrists may have patients referred to them by a variety of sources, such as pediatricians, neurologists, psychologists, audiologists, or speech-language pathologists. Many psychiatrists refer patients to other specialists who work with patients with communicative handicaps. A referral may be made to the behavioral psychologist, who may design and conduct a behavior-modification program for a patient who has difficulty communicating; or it may be to the speech-language pathologist for the patient who stutters.

AUDIOLOGY AND SPEECH-LANGUAGE PATHOLOGY

To many, **audiology** and **speech-language pathology** combined represent a single profession; the unifying factor is the overlapping needs of those with communicative disorders. For example, patients with a severe hearing loss cannot have their problem split in two, seeing one practitioner for the hearing loss and another for the language-speech-voice effects of such a loss. For some time, the American Speech-Language-Hearing Association (ASHA) has developed documents that speak of one profession. In 1969, the first Legislative Council (after ASHA's governance was reorganized) stated in a resolution that speech pathology and audiology form a single profession (ASHA, 1970). In 1978, the Legislative Council voted that the officers and staff of ASHA refer to *the* profession of audiology and speech-language pathology (ASHA, 1979). In 1981–82, a special Ad Hoc Committee on the Single Profession and its Credentialing was created to study the concept of the single profession; the Committee concluded in its final report (ASHA, 1982) that audiology and speech-language pathology constitute a single profession. The Committee believed that a single profession "now exists," stemming from a common core of study in the discipline of human communication and its disorders. The profession arises from the discipline, offering ameliorative services to those with communicative disorders. These services are provided by two designated areas of practice, audiology and speech-language pathology.

In St. Paul, Minnesota, ASHA conducted a national conference (1984) on undergraduate, graduate, and continuing education, attended by many leaders of the profession. At that conference, the discipline (the area of undergraduate and graduate study) was called "Human Communication Sciences and Disorders," and the single profession was designated as audiology and speech-language pathology (Rees and Snope, 1983). What is lacking at the present time is an all-inclusive generic name for this single profession. In 1970, Goldstein proposed reviving the name *communicology* as the name for the profession, having found the word in early documents of the profession.

SPEECH-LANGUAGE-HEARING CLINICAL SETTINGS

The developmental and acquired communicative disorders described in this book are treated clinically by the audiologist and speech-language pathologist in a variety of settings. Let us look at these settings and describe them briefly.

Children's Clinics

A variety of clinical agencies, with a variety of names, exist to help the child with hearing and speech-language problems. These include, for instance, the cerebral palsy clinic, the crippled children's clinic, the preschool evaluation clinic, and the pediatric evaluation-habilitation clinic. Since most of them treat a great number of children who require some kind of hearing assessment and management, an audiologist is usually employed on the staff. Since most developmental delay in young children is characterized by problems in language development and function, speech-language pathologists play an important role in such organizations. Most children's agencies make heavy use of the team evaluation, in which various specialists examine the child and pool their findings at staff meetings.

Public Schools

Speech and hearing programs in the public schools began as early as 1910 in the United States (Paden, 1970). Problems in hearing and speech were found to influence children's performance in the classroom. Rather than send such children to a local community clinic or hospital, it made sense to have hearing and speech services available in the school. Such services for communicatively handicapped youngsters have grown tremendously over the years. With the passage of two federal laws, speech-language-hearing services are now federally mandated. Public Law 94-142, the Education for All Handicapped Children Act, requires local school districts to provide needed remediation services for all handicapped children ages three through twenty-one; Public Law 95-561, the Educational Amendments Act, provides federal support for improving children's basic educational skills, including listening and speaking. New programs in the schools are able to place greater emphasis on the prevention of serious communicative handicaps, by giving young children the intensive work that may be needed to eradicate speech-language-hearing problems before their severity increases (Marge and others, 1985). Nearly half of the members of the American Speech-Language-Hearing Association work in school settings.

University Departments

Scientific inquiry into human communication, both basic and applied, is conducted in many universities. Those departments that train people for the profession have various names, such as Human Communication Sciences and its Disorders, Speech and Hearing Sciences, Audiology and Speech-Language Pathology, and Communication Disorders. Most of these departments have three functions: clinical training, teaching, and research. Clinical training requires that the university clinic have sufficient number of clinical supervisors to provide demonstration, clinical teaching, and clinical supervision. Most university clinics, therefore, provide clinical services (and the important training for students that comes from providing such services) to both children and adults who have hearing, language, articulation, voice, and fluency problems. The teaching is usually structured so that undergraduates are exposed to a broad array of basic areas (normal communication, science, and so on) with most of the course work in communicative disorders reserved for the graduate years. Clinical training—direct work with clients—is generally reserved for graduate school. Most training programs confer a Master's degree, which is the entry level for employment for audiologists and speech-language pathologists. Research in most departments does not usually cover the entire spectrum of communicative disorders, but is limited to those areas that are of interest to the faculty, determined in part by their training and background.

Community Speech and Hearing Centers

Many of the first speech and hearing programs outside of the public schools in the United States originated in community speech and hearing centers. Many such centers still exist, employing audiologists and speech pathologists (the term *speech-language pathologist* did not appear until 1976, by action of ASHA's Legislative Council). The clientele includes both children and adults, most of whom are referred to this nonmedical speech and hearing agency by community professionals (physicians, dentists, teachers, social workers, psychologists). Most community agencies derive some of their financial support from sources such as the United Way, permitting the agency to make considerable fee adjustments for both evaluation and therapy. Some community speech and hearing centers are affiliated with university programs, such as the Cleveland Hearing and Speech Center, which is affiliated with Case-Western Reserve University, and the Houston Speech and Hearing Institute, which developed ties with the University of Texas Health Sciences Center at Houston.

Hospital Programs

Audiology and speech-language pathology services are offered in many hospitals in the United States. Some of the earliest such programs were established in Veterans' Administration hospitals after World War II. Many community, private, and state hospitals now include these services for both inpatients and outpatients. Also, as a result of federal social-security medical coverage (Medicaid and Medicare), which finance many speech and hearing services, numerous private insurance carriers now include speech and hearing problems (related to physical conditions) as part of their coverage. Audiology is more often found in hospitals as part of a department of otolaryngology; some audiology sections are found in departments of physical medicine and rehabilitation (PM&R). Speech-language pathology services are offered in such departments as otolaryngology, PM&R, neurology, pediatrics, and geriatrics. Sometimes, audiology and speech/language pathology are separate departments, as in Veterans Administration hospitals. Although some hospital programs (particularly those in university hospitals) conduct research into various aspects of speech and hearing science, the majority of hospital programs focus on clinical hearing and speech services.

Private Practice

An increasing number of audiologists and speech-language pathologists are choosing careers in private practice, in effect serving the general public with communicative handicaps very much as the private psychologist does, who works with individuals with emotional problems. Some practitioners do private work only part time, and may spend the rest of the day in some other speech and hearing setting (such as a public school). Most, however, have a full-time private practice. Many patients with chronic impairments of some kind leave the hospital setting much earlier than they did in the past; instead of returning to the hospital as outpatients, they seek out the speech-language pathologist for whatever training they may require. Typical patient populations for the private practitioner include the preschool child with poor speech and language, the child or adult stutterer who may require intensive therapy, the adult with a voice problem, or the patient with a speech-language problem (aphasia, apraxia, dysarthria, central confusion) that was acquired after some kind of neurological insult.

THE PROFESSION'S ASSOCIATION

The speech and hearing profession began in this country in the early 1900s. A relatively complete history of the profession and its association is provided by Paden (1970). A good review of the history may also be found in a chapter by Matthews (1982); an overview of the growth of the profession and its association may be found in Boone's ASHA presidential address (1977). While there are reports between 1900 and 1924 of speech and hearing services provided both in the public schools and in some university clinics, there was no attempt by early practitioners to organize an association of communicative-disorder specialists until 1925. In December of that year, 11 such specialists met at the University of Iowa and founded the profession's first organization, called the American Academy of Speech Correction. The focus was on speech disorders, particularly stuttering and problems in articulation. The group convened annually at the meeting of the National Association of Teachers of Speech (Paden, 1970). In 1935, the organization changed its name to the American Speech Correction Association and met independently, creating its own publication, the *Journal of Speech Disorders.*

During and after World War II, there was great surge of interest in aural rehabilitation, because a number of veterans were returning to civilian life with destructive hearing losses, incurred during combat. The profession broadened its focus (speech correction) and developed the name *audiology.* The individual who provided audiological services was known as the *audiologist.* With the inclusion of audiologists in its ranks, in 1948 the professional association became known as the American Speech and Hearing Association. This name continued until 1978, when it was decided by the Legislative Council (the policy-setting governing body of ASHA) that the word *language* should be included in the title, since the speech pathologist played a primary role in the understanding and treatment of language disorders. The name became the American Speech-Language-Hearing Association (but the logo ASHA was retained).

The organization has grown remarkably, from a membership of 87 in 1935 to over 45,000 in 1986. The majority of practitioners in the area of communicative disorders are members of the organization, although membership is not required for ASHA certification or to receive its journals (*Journal of Speech and Hearing Disorders; Journal of Speech and Hearing Research; Language, Speech, and Hearing Services in Schools; ASHA*). The obvious benefits of membership in and identification with ASHA may be seen in a review of its published goals as an association (*ASHA, Application Booklet,* 1983):

> to maintain high standards of clinical competence for professionals providing speech-language pathology and audiology services to the public;
>
> to encourage the development of comprehensive clinical service programs;
>
> to promote investigation of clinical procedures used in treating disorders of communication;

to stimulate exchange of information about human communication through conventions, publications, and other continuing professional education activities;

to encourage basic research and scientific study of human communication and its disorders.

ASHA created a certification program early in its history, certifying the clinical competence of each designated area of practice. Today, ASHA's Certificate of Clinical Competence (in Audiology or Speech-Language Pathology) is often required for professional employment. ASHA's clinical certificate can be awarded only to those with a "graduate degree or its equivalent in speech-language pathology, audiology, or speech-language and hearing science; or have a graduate degree in an allied discipline and have demonstrated an active interest in the field of communication" (ASHA, 1983, p. 6). Although membership in ASHA is not a prerequisite for the Certificate of Clinical Competence (CCC), certificate holders must adhere to the Association's Code of Ethics (reprinted later in the chapter). To receive the certificate, students in training must be supervised by professionals in speech and hearing who already hold the CCC. Following the completion of the graduate degree, the CCC applicant must spend a Clinical Fellowship Year (CFY) working in an approved clinical setting in audiology or speech-language pathology, under the direct supervision of a clinician who already holds the CCC. Before the applicant begins the clinical fellowship year, an application must be filed with ASHA's Clinical Certification Board, which must approve the site, the type of clinical experience, and the type of supervision the applicant will receive. Beyond the professional organization's certification program, there are other requirements for practice in many states, such as credentialing by a state department of education or an audiology or speech-language pathology license to practice issued by a state licensing board (Flower, 1984). State licensing is basically the state's legalization of the professional standards set by ASHA.

Much of the concern of ASHA and its members is the ethical responsibilities of each practicing member of the profession. The primary purpose of ASHA's Code of Ethics is to protect the public by providing high-quality remediation services for those with communicative disorders. Matthews (1982) writes that individual practitioners may be faced with the following choices when they work as professionals:

(1) What is the appropriate decision as far as the best interest of my client?
(2) What is the best decision in terms of the organization I work for? and
(3) What is the best decision for me personally? (p. 15).

If audiologists or speech-language pathologists have the know-how to provide the services needed by clients or patients, their priority must be to provide the best professional services possible. On occasion, speech-language pathologists may face a clinical problem in which they have had very little training and past experience (such as teaching esophageal speech to a laryngectomee); the patient's best interests

CODE OF ETHICS OF THE AMERICAN SPEECH-LANGUAGE-HEARING ASSOCIATION 1983

(Revised January 1, 1979)

PREAMBLE

The preservation of the highest standards of integrity and ethical principles is vital to the successful discharge of the professional responsibilities of all speech-language pathologists and audiologists. This Code of Ethics has been promulgated by the Association in an effort to stress the fundamental rules considered essential to this basic purpose. Any action that is in violation of the spirit and purpose of this Code shall be considered unethical. Failure to specify any particular responsibility or practice in this Code of Ethics should not be construed as denial of the existence of other responsibilities or practices.

The fundamental rules of ethical conduct are described in three categories: Principles of Ethics, Ethical Proscriptions, Matters of Professional Propriety.

1. *Principles of Ethics.* Six Principles serve as a basis for the ethical evaluation of professional conduct and form the underlying moral basis for the Code of Ethics. Individuals[1] subscribing to this code shall observe these principles as affirmative obligations under all conditions of professional activity.
2. *Ethical Proscriptions.* Ethical Proscriptions are formal statements of prohibitions that are derived from the Principles of Ethics.
3. *Matters of Professional Propriety.* Mat-

ters of Professional Propriety represent guidelines of conduct designed to promote the public interest and thereby better inform the public and particularly the persons in need of speech-language pathology and audiology services as to the availability and the rules regarding the delivery of those services.

PRINCIPLE OF ETHICS I

Individuals shall hold paramount the welfare of persons served professionally.

A. Individuals shall use every resource available, including referral to other specialists as needed, to provide the best service possible.
B. Individuals shall fully inform persons served of the nature and possible effects of the services.
C. Individuals shall fully inform subjects participating in research or teaching activities of the nature and possible effects of these activities.
D. Individuals' fees shall be commensurate with services rendered.
E. Individuals shall provide appropriate access to records of persons served professionally.
F. Individuals shall take all reasonable precautions to avoid injuring persons in the delivery of professional services.
G. Individuals shall evaluate services rendered to determine effectiveness.

Ethical Proscriptions

1. Individuals must not exploit persons in the delivery of professional services, including accepting persons for treatment when benefit cannot reasonably be expected or continuing treatment unnecessarily.
2. Individuals must not guarantee the results of any therapeutic procedures, di-

rectly or by implication. A reasonable statement of prognosis may be made, but caution must be exercised not to mislead persons served professionally to expect results that cannot be predicted from sound evidence.

3. Individuals must not use persons for teaching or research in a manner that constitutes invasion of privacy or fails to afford informed free choice to participate.

4. Individuals must not evaluate or treat speech, language or hearing disorders except in a professional relationship. They must not evaluate or treat solely by correspondence. This does not preclude follow-up correspondence with persons previously seen, nor providing them with general information of an educational nature.

5. Individuals must not reveal to unauthorized persons any professional or personal information obtained from the person served professionally, unless required by law or unless necessary to protect the welfare of the person or the community.

6. Individuals must not discriminate in the delivery of professional services on any basis that is unjustifiable or irrelevant to the need for and potential benefit from such services, such as race, sex or religion.

7. Individuals must not charge for services not rendered.

PRINCIPLE OF ETHICS II

Individuals shall maintain high standards of professional competence.

A. Individuals engaging in clinical practice shall possess appropriate qualifications which are provided by the Association's program for certification of clinical competence.

B. Individuals shall continue their professional development throughout their careers.

C. Individuals shall identify competent, dependable referral sources for persons served professionally.

D. Individuals shall maintain adequate records of professional services rendered.

Ethical Proscriptions

1. Individuals must neither provide services nor supervision of services for which they have not been properly prepared, nor permit services to be provided by any of their staff who are not properly prepared.

2. Individuals must not provide clinical services by prescription of anyone who does not hold the Certificate of Clinical Competence.

3. Individuals must not delegate any service requiring the professional competence of a certified clinician to anyone unqualified.

4. Individuals must not offer clinical services by supportive personnel for whom they do not provide appropriate supervision and assume full responsibility.

5. Individuals must not require anyone under their supervision to engage in any practice that is a violation of the Code of Ethics.

PRINCIPLE OF ETHICS III

Individual's statements to persons served professionally and to the public shall provide accurate information about the nature and management of communicative disor-

---

[1]"Individuals" refers to all Members of the American Speech-Language-Hearing Association and nonmembers who hold Certificates of Clinical Competence from this Association.

ders, and about the profession and services rendered by its practitioners.

Ethical Proscriptions

1. Individuals must not misrepresent their training or competence.
2. Individuals' public statements providing information about professional services and products must not contain representations or claims that are false, deceptive or misleading.
3. Individuals must not use professional or commercial affiliations in any way that would mislead or limit services to persons served professionally.

Matters of Professional Propriety

1. Individuals should announce services in a manner consistent with highest professional standards in the community.

PRINCIPLE OF ETHICS IV

Individuals shall maintain objectivity in all matters concerning the welfare of persons served professionally.

A. Individuals who dispense products to persons served professionally shall observe the following standards:
   (1) Products associated with professional practice must be dispensed to the person served as a part of a program of comprehensive habilitative care.
   (2) Fees established for professional services must be independent of whether a product is dispensed.
   (3) Persons served must be provided freedom of choice for the source of services and products.
   (4) Price information about professional services rendered and products dispensed must be disclosed by providing to or posting for persons served a complete schedule of fees and charges in advance of rendering services, which schedule differentiates between fees for professional services and charges for products dispensed.
   (5) Products dispensed to the person served must be evaluated to determine effectiveness.

Ethical Proscriptions

1. Individuals must not participate in activities that constitute a conflict of professional interest.

might be served by a referral to a more experienced practitioner. Such a decision might work "against" the agency and the speech-language pathologist who made the referral, but in the long run, the best interests of the patient would have been met. Understanding communication and its disorders implies that practitioners know who can and cannot be helped by their direct intervention. Sometimes another audiologist, speech-language pathologist, a professional from an allied profession, or several professionals working together (such as a cleft-palate or orofacial-disorders team) can manage the problem best.

The ethical management of the patient with a communication disorder is the primary concern of ASHA's Code of Ethics. It is reprinted here from the ASHA *Application Booklet* (1983).

Matters of Professional Propriety

1. Individuals should not accept compensation for supervision or sponsorship from the clinician being supervised or sponsored.
2. Individuals should present products they have developed to their colleagues in a manner consonant with highest professional standards.

PRINCIPLE OF ETHICS V

Individuals shall honor their responsibilities to the public, their profession, and their relationships with colleagues and members of allied professions.

Matters of Professional Propriety

1. Individuals should seek to provide and expand services to persons with speech, language and hearing handicaps as well as to assist in establishing high professional standards for such programs.
2. Individuals should educate the public about speech, language and hearing processes, speech, language and hearing problems, and matters related to professional competence.

3. Individuals should strive to increase knowledge within the profession and share research with colleagues.
4. Individuals should establish harmonious relations with colleagues and members of other professions, and endeavor to inform members of related professions, of services provided by speech-language pathologists and audiologists, as well as seek information from them.
5. Individuals should assign credit to those who have contributed to a publication in proportion to their contribution.

PRINCIPLE OF ETHICS VI

Individuals shall uphold the dignity of the profession and freely accept the profession's self-imposed standards.

A. Individuals shall inform the Ethical Practice Board of violations of this Code of Ethics.
B. Individuals shall cooperate fully with the Ethical Practices Board inquiries into matters of professional conduct related to this Code of Ethics.

The profession of audiology and speech-language pathology continues to grow to meet the increasing demands of those with communicative disorders. The future clinical thrust of ASHA appears to be strong in the area of preschool intervention, with an emphasis on prevention. The report of the ASHA Committee on Prevention of Speech-Language and Hearing Problems (1984) felt that, with increased prevention, the following results could be expected:

Reduction of the incidence of communicative disorder.
A decrease in the prevalence of communicative disorders.
Reduction in the overall costs of services to the communicatively handicapped.

Expansion in the role of speech-language pathologists, audiologists, and special educators in the area of health promotion or communicative "wellness."

Reduction of the loss of human potential and human suffering that result from communicative disorders (p. 37).

Many adult communication problems have long been neglected, often because of a lack of financial commitment to doing something about a particular problem. Consequently, adult problems related to voice, stuttering, and speech and language changes as symptoms of neurogenic disorders are all areas in which an increase in clinical practice will probably be seen in the future.

As we increasingly utilize computer technology and mechanization, specific communication is vital. Computer application demands absolute specificity and sequence. We must know and perform the demands of machines without error if we are to function effectively with machines. We might speculate that we are spawning a new generation of communicatively handicapped people, those who have difficulty communicating (such as giving or receiving instructions) with the exactness that computers may require. The freedom of gesture, the sound of the voice, expression, melody, and prosody must all be taken out of the communicative message when we use a computer. Perhaps to counteract this exactitude, individuals may seek communicative situations that retain more spontaneity and lack a predictable outcome. The pragmatics of discipline required for communicating with the machine may give way to increasing our vocalization and verbalization of emotions, with a whole new pragmatic system developed for the spontaneous interaction of human beings. However, we will still employ the basic communicative modes of hearing, voice, articulation, language, and fluency. Deviations in communicative performance may always contribute to a lessening of communicative effectiveness.

As we learn more about human communication and improve its effectiveness by using various electronic aids, such as the computer or increasingly sophisticated telephones, communicative disorders seem less accepted. As our society has become more complex and machine-oriented unfortunately, we have become less tolerant of communicative ineffectiveness. Probably at no time in our history has there been greater interest in learning more about human communication and its disorders. As a consequence of this new interest, career opportunities are unlimited for the audiologists, speech-language pathologists, and other allied professionals.

REVIEW QUESTIONS

In this chapter, we have looked at some of the professionals who work with people with communication disorders. We gave special consideration to the profession of audiology and speech-language pathology, and looked at its professional organization, the American Speech-Language-Hearing Association. Let us now review our study with some questions.

1. Why must many kinds of professionals work together to manage and treat some communication disorders?

2. Can you think of other specialists who should be added to Table 13-1? List and discuss them.

3. What medical specialists might work together in the treatment of a child with cleft palate? For a teenager with a voice problem? For an older person who has had a stroke?

4. How do audiologists and speech-language pathologists differ? How are they similar?

5. Why do you think that audiology and speech-language pathology are considered to be one profession? Do you agree or disagree with this view? Why?

6. Of what value do you feel the American Speech-Language-Hearing Association is to the profession?

7. Are you interested in a career working with the communicatively handicapped? If so, what specialty interests you the most? Why?

REFERENCES

ASHA (1982). Ad hoc committee on a single profession and its credentialing report. *ASHA, 24:* 407–409.

ASHA (1983). *Application Booklet* (Revised, 1983). Rockville, Md.: American Speech-Language-Hearing Association.

Boone, D. R. (1977). Our profession: where are we? *ASHA, 19:* 3–6.

Committee on Prevention of Speech-Language-Hearing Problems (1984). Prevention: a challenge for the profession. *ASHA, 26:* 35–37.

Flower, R. M. (1984). *Delivery of Speech-Language Pathology and Audiology Services.* Baltimore: Williams and Wilkins.

Goldstein, R. (1970). The unity of communicology. *ASHA, 12:* 543–550.

Legislative Council, (1970). Resolution LC 19-69, the single profession. *Proceedings of 1969 Legislative Council.* ASHA, Bethesda, Md.: American Speech and Hearing Association.

Legislative Council (1979). Resolution 50-78, referred one profession resolution to ASHA Association Advisory Committee. *Proceedings of 1978 Legislative Council.* ASHA, Rockville,

Md.: American Speech-Language-Hearing Association.

Marge, M., Johnston, T., and Boone, D. (1985). The epidemiology and prevention of voice disorders. *Short Course, ASHA Annual Convention,* Washington, D.C.

Matthews, J. (1982). Bases of human communication, in *Human Communication Disorders: An Introduction,* ed. G. Shames and E. Wiig. Columbus, Ohio: Charles E. Merrill.

National Conference on Undergraduate, Graduate, and Continuing Education (1984). *ASHA, 25:* 49–60.

Paden, E. (1970). *A History of the American Speech and Hearing Association, 1925-1958.* Bethesda, Md.: American Speech and Hearing Association.

Rees, N. S., and Snope, T. L., eds. (1983). *Proceedings of the 1983 National Conference on Undergraduate, Graduate, and Continuing Education. ASHA Reports #13.* Rockville, Md.: American Speech-Language-Hearing Association.

Glossary

adaptation effect: In stuttering therapy, the increase of fluency caused by successive speaking or reading of the same passage.

addition error: A type of speech articulation error characterized by the client adding a sound to the target phoneme or word; for example for the word *bed,* a child pronounces it *beda.*

affricate: A consonant that begins with a plosive phoneme and ends with a fricative, such as /tʃ/.

air-conduction audiometry: Testing hearing by introducing the tone into the ear canal with the sound waves then traveling to the drum membrane at the end of the canal (as opposed to bone conduction).

allophone: One of the variant forms of a phomene that is still recognized by the listener as the target phoneme.

Alzheimer's disease: The most common form of dementing illness (confusion for time and place, loss of memory), particularly in the older population.

anarthria: A severe form of motor speech disorder (paralysis and weakness of muscles required for speech) characterized by a complete lack of speech.

anomia: An inability to name objects, often part of an aphasia related to brain damage, particularly of the left hemisphere.

aphasia: A loss or a reduction of language function (understanding what is said, reading, speaking, and writing) as a result of acquired brain damage to the left cerebral hemisphere.

apraxia of speech: Inability to say voluntarily a word that one could say automatically (as a result of brain damage). For example, patient could not repeat *dam* but could say *damn* as an automatic profane utterance.

arytenoid cartilages: The paired, pyramid-shaped cartilages that sit on the signet portion of the cricoid; aid in abduction-adduction of vocal folds.

assimilation: The sounds that precede or follow a particular sound will influence the production of that sound, a process called *assimilation.*

ataxia: A motor disorder characterized by marked loss of coordination, often associated with cerebellar disease.

athetosis: A form of cerebral palsy characterized by twisting and flailing of the extremities, neck, and trunk.

audiogram: A graphic measure of tested auditory sensitivity depicting hearing intensity thresholds at various frequencies.

audiology: The study of normal and disordered hearing. Professionals in audiology are known as audiologists.

audiometer: An electronic instrument used by the audiologist or the otolaryngologist for the measurement of hearing sensitivity.

auditory stimulation: Hearing emphasis given in training of hearing-impaired child or adult.

aural language: Spoken language. We listen to aural language (language that has been spoken).

auricle: The external ear, also known as pinna.

autism: A severe affective disorder in children, often classified as child schizophrenia. A childhood psychosis.

axon: The effector nerve fiber leading from a neuron. For example, a long motor axon could leave the cerebral cortex and travel down uninterrupted to its final spinal nucleus.

behavioral approach: A learning approach to acquiring a new behavior. Training procedures are initiated with stimulus-response behavior shaped by reinforcement procedures.

bone-conduction audiometry: In hearing testing, the sound waves are introduced directly into the cochlea via the bones of the skull.

brain stem: The brain structures at the base of the brain excluding the hemispheres above, the cerebellum, and the spinal cord below.

carcinoma: A cancer or malignancy.

central auditory problem: Difficulty in the auditory processing and understanding of both nonverbal and verbal stimuli.

central nervous system: The brain and spinal cord, exclusive of the cranial and peripheral nerves.

cerebellum: This structure which sits under the hemispheres and above the pons plays an important role in muscular coordination.

cerebral localization: A theory of brain function that specifies particular functions and behaviors to particular sites of the brain.

cerebral palsy: A developmental motor disorder related to brain injury; the most common forms are seen in spasticity, athetosis, and ataxia.

cleft lip and palate: A congenital fissure or absence of tissue of the lip, premaxilla, hard palate, and/or velum.

cluttering: A disorder of fluency often characterized by rapid speech, breaks in fluency, and faulty articulation.

coarticulation: The simultaneous production of two or more consonants and vowels in normal speech production of a word, such as in the word *tram*. The first three consonants (/t/–/r/–/æ/) might be said overlapping in time.

cochlea: The snail-shaped auditory part of the inner ear containing the sensory organs of hearing.

cognate: A pair of sounds, such as /p/ and /b/, produced similarly with the exception that one /p/ is unvoiced and one /b/ is voiced.

cognitive approach: An approach to learning language in which children must first experience percepts and concepts specific to their environment as a prerequisite to language development.

communication: An interaction or exchange of one's feelings, ideas, thoughts, and wants among two or more people by such modes as speech, writing, expression, gesture, or touch.

conductive hearing loss: A loss of hearing related to obstruction or disease in the middle ear with sound transmission failing to reach the cochlea in the inner ear.

consistency effect: An observation among stutterers that certain words are more likely to be stuttered on.

continuant: A speech sound that can be continued or prolonged, such as /m/ or /s/.

cortex: The outer layer of the cerebrum of the brain containing the cortical neurons.

cranial nerves: Twelve-paired peripheral nerves that exit from or come into the cranial cavity, such as cranial nerves I, olfactory, or II, optic.

cricoid cartilage: The ring of cartilage that forms the base of the larynx.

cricothyroid muscles: The paired laryngeal muscles that have much to do with changing the pitch of the voice.

decibel: A logarithmic unit of measurement of sound intensity.

deep articulation testing: A systematic way of testing articulation errors to determine the influence of adjacent sounds on the production of a target sound.

denasality: Insufficient nasal resonance; hyponasality.

dendrites: The receptors attached to each neuron in the central nervous system.

diacritics: Markings that modify phonetic symbols, indicating slight change in the sound of the phoneme.

diadochokinesis: The rapid, alternating movements of a body part, such as in the lips and tongue rapidly saying *pataka*.

diagnosogenic theory of stuttering: Normal disfluencies are labeled as stuttering.

diaphragm: The muscular-tendonous partition that separates the thorax from the abdomen, serving as the primary muscle of respiration.

dichotic listening: Simultaneous presentation of two different signals separately to each ear, often used as a measure of "ear effect" and cerebral dominance.

diphthong: A blending together of two vowels in the same syllable, such as heard as /aI/ in the word *right*.

disfluency: A breakdown in the prosodic flow or fluency of speech.

distinctive features: Particular elements that are characteristic of a phoneme, such as its duration and voicing elements.

distortion error: The production of a target phoneme utilizes a sound that is not in the language, such as in a lateral lisp.

dyadic communication: Two people communicating with one another.

dysarthria: A motor speech disorder as a result of brain damage that may affect respiration, articulation, voice, and fluency.

dyslexia: A problem in reading comprehension believed to be the result of brain damage or dysfunction.

dysphemia: Poor timing control for speech related to some kind of brain dysfunction, possibly leading to cluttering or stuttering.

dysphonia: A disorder of voice, such as hoarseness, breathiness, or harshness.

ear canal: The external opening into the ear.

eustachian tube: The air tube that connects the middle ear with the nasopharynx.

expressive aphasia: A loss of or reduction in the ability to speak, write, or sign because of brain damage.

expressive language: A coded system of communication that uses the modalities of speaking, writing, and signing.

extrapyramidal tract: A motor tract within the brain that lies outside the pyramidal system, making many connections between cortical-subcortical-brainstem nuclei.

flaccid dysarthria: A motor speech disorder produced by muscles lacking tonicity and contraction; the opposite of spastic dysarthria.

frequency: The number of cycles per second of a sound wave; the physical measurement of pitch.

fricative: A speech sound produced by the airstream passing between or through a constricted opening, such as /f/ and /v/.

frontal lobe: The anterior part of each cerebral hemisphere, anterior to the Rolandic fissure.

functional dysphonia: A voice problem that has no physical or structural cause.

geriatrician: A physician specializing in normal aging and the diseases of aging.

glossectomy: The surgical removal of the tongue.

glottis: The opening between the vocal folds.

granuloma: Hard, granulated tissue, sometimes found along the glottal rim in the larynx; sometimes seen following intubation during surgery or from continuous esophageal reflux.

habitual pitch: The modal or most frequently occurring voice pitch.

hemianopsia: A visual field defect in which half of the vision of each eye is lost.

hemiplegia: A unilateral weakness or paralysis of one side of the body.

hypernasality: Excessive nasal resonance.

impedance audiometry: Air pressure and air volume differences are measured within the external and middle ear as a method of detecting conductive hearing loss.

intensity: A measure of the magnitude or pressure of a sound wave; the measurement of loudness.

interaction theory of stuttering: Stuttering can be the result of negative interaction between children who are disfluent and their critical listeners.

intercostals: The muscles (internal and external) between the ribs.

internist: A physician specializing in internal medicine.

involuntary repetitions: A form of stuttering characterized by unexpected syllable or word repetitions.

jitter: Variations (perturbations) in vocal frequency heard in dysphonic voices.

laryngeal trauma: A direct, external blow to the larynx.

laryngeal web: A membraneous growth across the laryngeal glottis, usually in an anterior to posterior direction.

laryngectomy: Surgical removal of the larynx (usually because of cancer).

laryngoscopy: Viewing the internal structure of the larynx by mirror (indirect) or at the actual site (direct).

learning disability: Educational difficulties in reading, writing, listening, speaking, and/or in arithmetic, believed to be related to some kind of central brain dysfunction.

lexicon: The terms and words of one's vocabulary.

linguist: A scientist who studies the origin, structure, and use of language.

mandible: The lower jaw.

manometer: An instrument for measuring oral and nasal air pressures.

maxilla: The upper jaw.

medial geniculates: The small nuclei (left and right) on the posterior thalamus from which the auditory pathways ascend to the primary auditory cortex.

medulla: The upper bulb of the spinal cord which lies directly below the pons, containing a number of motor and sensory nuclei.

mental retardation: Reduced cognitive abilities, confirmed by measured intelligence quotients of 70 or below.

middle ear: The tympanic cavity containing the three small middle ear bones: incus, malleus, and stapes.

minimal brain dysfunction: Believed to be one of the causes of specific learning disability as defined by federal regulations.

misarticulations: Speech articulation errors of omission, addition, or substitution.

mixed hearing loss: A hearing loss caused by both conductive and sensorineural problems.

morpheme: Words or the smallest unit of a word that has meaning. For example, the word *cat* is a morpheme; in the plural form *cats,* the *s* is an added morpheme.

morphology: The study of words and word-forms; the study of morphemes.

multi-infarct dementia: A form of dementia related to the patient having had many small strokes (or infarcts).

myofunctional therapy: Muscle training of the tongue to reduce tongue pressures on dentition, i.e., therapy for reverse swallow and tongue thrust.

nasoendoscopy: By inserting a flexible viewing scope through the nose and positioning it in the pharynx, the nasopharynx can be viewed above and the hypopharynx and larynx can be viewed below.

naturalistic approach: Sometimes called the maturation or innateness theory of language acquisition, the normal child acquires language by being around people who speak and communicate with the child in everyday, natural settings.

neologisms: New or made-up words, such as what are often spoken by patients with jargon aphasia.

neonate: Newborn.

neurologist: A physician who specializes in the diagnosis and treatment of neurological diseases.

nucleus: The central core of a neuron or the neural centers of lower brain structures, such as in the basal ganglia or the thalamus.

obturator: An acryllic or metal appliance used to cover a gap or opening, such as to cover an unrepaired cleft in the hard palate.

occipital lobe: The posterior part of each cerebral hemisphere.

occlusion: The fitting together of the lower molars with those of the upper jaw; the bite determined by the relationship of lower-upper dentition.

occupational therapist: A rehabilitation specialist who works with patients on fine motor control and on acquiring skills needed for daily living activities, such as dressing and feeding.

omission errors: One of the four types of articulatory errors, where the sound is totally omitted.

ophthalmologist: A medical specialist specializing in the diagnosis of disorders of the eye and their treatment.

optometrist: A non-medical specialist who treats disorders of the eye by exercise and corrective lenses.

oral language: Language that is spoken.

oral stereognosis: Recognition of various forms by placing them in the mouth for tactual recognition.

orbicularis oris: The circular, sphincteric muscles that circle the lips.

orthodontist: A dentist who specializes in the straightening of teeth and correcting of dental malocclusion.

orthopedist: A physician who specializes in the diagnosis of physical and motor deformities and their treatment by exercise and surgery.

ossicles: The three small bones (incus, malleus, stapes) that form the ossicular chain in the middle ear.

otitis media: Inflammation of the middle ear.

otolaryngologist: Sometimes called an *otorhinolaryngologist,* a physician who specializes in the diagnosis and treatment of diseases of the ear, nose, and throat.

otosclerosis: The formation of spongy bone in the middle ear, particularly around the footplate of the stapes where it articulates with the oval window.

oval window: The footplate of the stapes is inserted in the oval window wall in the vestibule of the cochlea. Vibration of the stapes footplate sets the oval window in vibration.

palatal lift: A dental appliance designed to raise a paralyzed or weakened velum to the pharyngeal wall to produce closure of the velopharyngeal port.

palate: The roof of the mouth; anteriorly, the hard palate is bone, covered with a membrane; posteriorly, the soft palate (velum) is muscle covered with a membrane. The palate separates the oral and nasal cavities.

papilloma: A wart-like tumor that can grow in the airway and larynx of primarily young children, possibly causing airway obstruction and severe dysphonia.

parietal lobe: One of the four lobes of the cerebral hemisphere, extending posteriorly from the Rolandic fissure to the occipital lobe.

pediatrician: A physician specializing in the normal development of children and in the diagnosis and treatment of childhood diseases.

pedodontist: A dentist specializing in the dental care of children.

peripheral nervous system: The nervous system that extends beyond the brain and the spinal column; peripheral sensory nerves feed affector impulses into the central nervous system while motor nerves carry effector impulses to peripheral structures.

phone: A speech sound.

phoneme: The smallest sound unit of speech represented by a symbol of the International Phonetic Alphabet.

phonetics: The study of the perception and the production of speech sounds.

phonetic placement: A method of teaching articulation production by emphasizing the motor features-movement-placement of the articulators.

phonologic process: The systematic simplification by children of the production of adult-model articulation, such as by deleting the final consonant of words or deleting a syllable within a word.

phonology: The study of the sounds of spoken language, including the rules of phoneme use, phonemes, phonetic production, and voicing characteristics of prosody and suprasegmentals.

phoniatrist: A specialist in the treatment of speech-language-voice disorders; the phoniatrist is found primarily in European and South American cultures (similar in the United States to *speech-language pathologist*).

physiatrist: A physician specializing in physical medicine and rehabilitation.

plastic surgeon: A physician who specializes in the surgical repair or restoration of absent, injured, or deformed parts of the body.

pragmatic approach: An approach to learning language that focuses on how the child interacts with others in the environment.

plosive: A speech sound produced by impounding air behind an articulator and suddenly releasing it, as in /p/ or /b/.

presbycusis: The higher-frequency hearing loss associated with old age.

progressive approximation: Moving slowly by increments in articulation therapy from the best production of the target sound to the correct production of the target sound.

prolongation: A form of dysfluency often observed in stuttering, when a speech sound or syllable is prolonged in duration.

prosody: The melody-flow and rhythm of a spoken language; melodic changes in syllable stress, pitch, loudness, and duration.

prosthesis: An appliance designed to compensate for a missing body part or a part that does not function properly, such as an artificial eye for an absent eye or a hearing aid for a hearing loss.

prosthodontist: A dentist who specializes in making dental prostheses.

protoword: In the infant's emerging spoken language, occasional sounds are produced that sound almost like a meaningful or target word; the early spoken production (usually with the correct vowel and faulty consonants) of a target word.

psychiatrist: A physician specializing in the diagnosis and treatment of mental disorders.

psychologist: A specialist in the diagnosis and treatment of mental disorders.

pure tone: A periodic sound wave of a particular frequency that is generated in the audiometric testing of hearing.

pyramidal tract: A descending bundle of neural motor fibers within the central nervous system that descend uninterrupted to a final nucleus in the brain stem or spinal cord.

round window: A round opening under the oval window on the cochlea, permitting the displacement or movement of fluid within the cochlea.

schizophrenia: A form of psychosis, popularly described as found in a split-personality.

segment: A linguistic term for a word.

seizures: The convulsions of an epileptic attack; epilepsy.

semantics: The study of the history and the meaning of words.

sensorineural hearing loss: A hearing loss caused by disease of the inner ear and/or eighth cranial nerve.

shimmer: A perturbation or variation in vocal intensity found in dysphonia.

social worker: A professional who works with patients and families in making fiscal, social, and psychological adjustment to physical and mental problems.

spasticity: A paralysis characterized by extreme tension and hypercontraction of muscles with hyperactive tendon reflexes.

special educator: A special education teacher or adaptive educator who works with exceptional and handicapped children.

specific language impairment: A diagnosis of a school-age child who demonstrates impairment in understanding spoken language, speaking, reading, and writing with no other demonstrable impairment.

speech discrimination: The ability to hear and recognize acoustic differences among the phonemes of word segments.

speech-language pathology: A profession that specializes in the diagnosis and treatment of communication disorders related to problems of hearing, articulation, language, voice, and fluency.

speech reception threshold: The amplification level or threshold where the subject is able to repeat correctly after the examiner 50 percent of the words presented on a spondee-list.

spinal cord: The lower portion of the central nervous system, originating at the medulla and extending down within the spinal vertebra.

stimulability testing: In testing articulation, to determine how well the client can produce the target sound when the sound has been repeatedly presented (visually and auditorially).

stroke: A cerebrovascular accident (CVA), usually one of three types: thrombosis, embolus, or hemorrhage.

structural approach: An approach in learning language in which the child acquires systematically and in predictable sequence the rules and structure of language.

stuttering: The involuntary repetitions and prolongations of speech sounds and syllables which the individual struggles to end.

subglottal pressure: The air pressure within the airway below the vocal folds; outgoing air moves between the vocal folds when pressure below the folds is greater than air pressure above them.

substitution error: A type of articulation error characterized by an incorrect phoneme used in place of a target phoneme, such as a /w/ said for a /r/.

successive approximation: A technique used in articulation therapy where the client experiences step-by-step success moving from the errored sound to production of the target phoneme.

syntax: The grammatical structure and word order of a language.

tachyphemia: Extremely rapid speech.

target sound: The correct model; the phoneme selected for articulation therapy.

temporal lobe: One of the four lobes of a cerebral hemisphere, lying below the Sylvius fissure.

tension-athetoid: A mixed form of cerebral palsy characterized by both spasticity and flailing-athetosis.

thalamus: A large gray mass of sensory nuclei deep within the hemisphere, bordering the third ventricle.

thyroarytenoid muscles: The paired vocal folds in the larynx.

thyroid cartilage: The shield-shaped outer cartilage protecting the larynx; popularly called the Adam's apple.

tidal volume: The amount of air expired in a normal at-rest breathing cycle.

tinnitus: A ringing or noise in the ears, often associated with a hearing loss.

tongue thrust: Abnormal tongue positioning, particularly during swallowing, which may have an adverse effect on the anterior dental bite.

transduction: The converting of a soundwave in the external ear and its vibratory patterns in the middle ear into neural impulses in the inner ear.

traumatic laryngitis: A dysphonia related to excessive abuse and misuse of the larynx, such as the hoarseness experienced after prolonged yelling.

velopharyngeal port: The closing site where the elevated velum makes contact with the pharyngeal wall, separating the oral and nasal cavities; a depressed velum connects the two cavities at the site of the port.

velum: The soft palate.

vital capacity: The total volume of air one is able to expire after a maximum inhalation; a maximum expiration.

vocal nodules: Benign growths on the vocal folds, usually bilateral, which are usually the result of laryngeal abuse and voice misuse.

vocalization: Voicing or phonation.

Subject Index

Author Index